THE EMERGING INTERNATIONAL
ECONOMIC ORDER

ADVANCES IN POLITICAL SCIENCE
An International Series
Published in cooperation with the International
Political Science Association

Series Editor
Richard L. Merritt
University of Illinois

Editorial Board

Helio Jaguaribe de Mattos, *Conjunto Universitário*
Cândido Mendes
Hans Klingemann, *Freie Universität Berlin*
Jean Laponce, *University of British Columbia*
Arend Lijphart, *University of California, San Diego*
John Meisel, *Queen's University, Kingston*
Marcel Merle, *Université de Paris I (Sorbonne)*
Elinor Ostrom, *Indiana University*
Vadim S. Semenov, *Institute of Philosophy, Moscow*
Michitoshi Takabatake, *Rikkyo University*

Volumes published in this series:

Edited by
Harold K. Jacobson
and
Dusan Sidjanski

THE EMERGING INTERNATIONAL ECONOMIC ORDER

Dynamic Processes, Constraints, and Opportunities

*Published in cooperation with the
International Political Science Association*

SAGE PUBLICATIONS
Beverly Hills / London / New Delhi

For information address:

SAGE Publications, Inc.
275 South Beverly Drive
Beverly Hills, California 90212

SAGE Publications India Pvt. Ltd.
C-236 Defence Colony
New Delhi 110 024, India

SAGE Publications Ltd
28 Banner Street
London EC1Y 8QE, England

Printed in the United States of America

Library of Congress Cataloging in Publication Data

The emerging international economic order.

(Advances in political science; 1)
1. International economic relations—Addresses,
essays, lectures. I. Jacobson, Harold Karan.
II. Sidjanski, Dusan. III. International
Political Science Association. IV. Series.
HF1411.E429   337′.09′048   82-3357
ISBN 0-8039-1833-X   AACR2

FIRST PRINTING

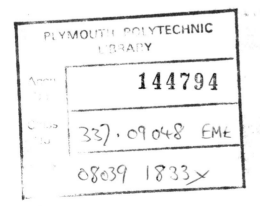

CONTENTS

FROM THE SERIES EDITOR

Advances in Political Science: An International Series reflects the aims and intellectual traditions of the International Political Science Association: the generation and dissemination of rigorous political inquiry free of any subdisciplinary or other orthodoxy. Along with its quarterly companion publication, the *International Political Science Review,* this series seeks to present the best work being done today (1) on the central and critical controversial themes of politics and/or (2) in new areas of inquiry where political scientists, alone or in conjunction with other scholars, are shaping innovative concepts and methodologies of political analysis.

Political science as an intellectual discipline has burgeoned in recent decades. With the enormous growth in the number of publications and papers, and their increasing sophistication, however, has also come a tendency toward parochialism along national, subdisciplinary, and other lines. It was to counteract these tendencies that political scientists from a handful of countries created IPSA in 1949. Through roundtables organized by its research committees and study groups, at its triennial world congresses (the latest of which takes place in August 1982 in Rio de Janeiro), and through its organizational work, IPSA has sought to encourage the creation of both an international-minded science of politics and a body of scholars from many nations (now from more than 40 regional associations), who approach their research and interactions with other scholars from an international perspective.

With the publication of *The Emerging International Economic Order: Dynamic Processes, Constraints, and Opportunities,* edited by Harold Jacobson and Dusan Sidjanski, the editorial board is pleased to initiate *Advances in Political Science: An International Series.* This volume represents well the intent of IPSA when it created the series: It comprises original papers which focus in an integrated manner on a single important topic; and its authors, from various countries and social systems, take differing approaches to the central theme. Like most other volumes in the series, it taps the vast intellectual resource of political scientists linked to the International Political Science Association.

Urbana, Illinois   *—Richard L. Merritt*

PREFACE

This book is the product of the activities of the International Political Science Association's Research Committee on the Emerging International Economic Order. The editors chair this committee and all of the authors are members. Earlier versions of several of the chapters were presented in the panels convened by the research committee at IPSA's Eleventh World Congress which met in Moscow in August 1979. These chapters and the book have been enriched as a result of the discussions that took place in the panels.

Professor Richard Merritt of the University of Illinois, who served as program chairman for IPSA's Eleventh Congress, and Sara Miller McCune, publisher of Sage Publications, originally suggested that several of the papers of the research committee should be brought together and published as a book, and both have been vital sources of encouragement and advice throughout our efforts to realize this suggestion. They have also sought—though not always successfully—to keep us to our schedule. We appreciate all that they have done, even their scolding. The book exists because of them, and it is a far better book than it would have been had we not had their counsel.

We also appreciate the penetrating comments of an anonymous reader appointed by IPSA to review the manuscripts. We are grateful for these comments, and we have attempted to be responsive to them.

Harold Jacobson gratefully acknowledges the opportunity to work as co-editor of the volume that being a Resident Scholar at the Rockefeller Foundation's Bellagio Study and Conference Center provided him.

Barbara Opal of the Center for Political Studies at the University of Michigan put the final manuscript in shape, almost miraculously deciphering bad handwriting in two languages. Betsy Schmidt of Sage Publications carefully oversaw the transformation of the manuscript into a finished book. They both have our deep gratitude.

—Harold K. Jacobson
Ann Arbor, Michigan

—Dusan Sidjanski
Geneva, Switzerland

January 1982

ABBREVIATIONS

ACABQ—Advisory Committee on Administrative and Budgetary Questions
ACP—African-Caribbean-Pacific Countries—Pays des l'Afrique-Caraibes-Pacifique. The group of less developed countries associated with the European Economic Community through the Lomé agreements.
AGREF—Association des Grandes Entreprises faisant appel à l'épagne, France—Association of Large Enterprises appealing for saving
AIAT—Association Internationale pour le Développement Economique et l'Aide Technique—International Association for Economic Development and Technical Assistance
AISI—American Iron and Steel Institute
ANASE—Association des nations de l'Aisie du Sud-Est *(see ASEAN)*
APD—Assistance publique au développement *(see ODA)*
ASEAN—Association of Southeast Asian Nations *(see ANASE)*
BIRD—Banque internationale pour la reconstruction et le développement *(see IBRD)*
CAD—Comité d'aide au développement *(see DAC)*, OCDE
CAEM—Counseil d'assistance économique mutuelle—*(see CMEA)*
CAP—Common Agricultural Policy
CE—Communautés européennes *(see EC)*
CEE—Communautés économique européene *(see EEC)*
CEPD—Coopération économique entre pays en développement *(see ECDC)*
CES—Conseil Economique et Social *(see ECOSOC)*, Nations Unies
CFDT—Compagnie Française pour le Développement des Fibres Textiles—French Company for the Development of Textile Fibers
CGT—Confederation Général du Travail, France—General Confederation of Labor
CIASI—Comité interministeriel pour l'amenagement des structures industrielles—Interministerial Committee for the Adjustment of Industrial Structures
CIEC—Conference on International Economic Cooperation
CIRIT—Centre inter-professional de renovation des structures industrielles et commerciales de l'industrie textile, France—Interprofessional Center for the Renewal of Industrial and Commercial Structures of the Textile Industry
CMEA—Council for Mutual Economic Assistance *(see CAEM)*
CNPF—Confédération Nationale du Patronat Français—National Confederation of French Employers
CNUCED—Conférence des Nations Unies pour le commerce et le développement *(see UNCTAD)*
DAC—Development Assistance Committee *(see CAD)*, OECD
DTS—driots de tirage spéciaux *(see SDR)*, Fonds monétaire international
EC—European Communities *(see CE)*

9

ECDC—Economic Cooperation Among Developing Countries *(see CEPD)*
ECOSOC—Economic and Social Council *(see CES)*, United Nations
EDA—Economic Development Administration, USA
EEC—European Economic Community *(see CEE)*
EIU—Economist Intelligence Unit
EPA—Environmental Protection Agency, USA
FDES—Fond de développement économiques et social, France
FMI—Fonds monétaire international *(see IMF)*
GATT—General Agreement on Tariffs and Trade—Accord général sur les tariffs douaniers et le commerce
GNP—Gross National Product *(see PNB)*
IBA—International Bauxite Association
IBRD—International Bank for Reconstruction and Development *(see BIRD)*
IDA—International Development Association
IDI—Institute de Développement Industriel—Institute for Industrial Development
ILO—International Labor Organization
IMF—International Monetary Fund *(see FMI)*
LDC—less developed country *(see PVD)*
MFA—Multi Fiber Agreement, GATT
MTN—Multilateral Trade Negotiations, Tokyo Round Negotiations, GATT
MSA—most seriously affected country
NIEO—New International Economic Order *(see NOEI)*
NOEI—Nouvel ordre économique international *(see NEIO)*
NU—Nations Unies *(see UN)*
OAU—Organization of African Unity *(see OUA)*
OCDE—Organisation de coopération et de développement économique *(see OECD)*
ODA—Official Development Assistance *(see APD)*
OECD—Organization for Economic Cooperation and Development *(see OCDE)*
ONUDI—Organisation des Nations Unies pour le développement industriel *(see UNIDO)*
OPEC—Organization of Petroleum Exporting Countries *(see OPEP)*
OPEP—Organisation des pays exportateurs de pétrole *(see OPEC)*
OUA—Organisation de l'unité africaine *(see OAU)*
PMA—pays moins avance—least developed country
PME—petits et moyens enterprises—small- and middle-sized enterprises
PNB—Produit national brut *(see GNP)*
PNUD—Programme des Nations Unies pour le développement *(see UNDP)*
PVD—pays en voie de développement *(see LDC)*
SDR—Special Drawing Rights *(see DTS)*, International Monetary Fund
SELA—Système économique latino-américain—Latin American Economic System
SGICF—Syndicat de l'industrie cotonnière Française, France—Association of the French Cotton Industry
STN—société transnationale *(see TNC)*
TAB—Trade and Development Board, UNCTAD
TNC—Transnational Corporation *(see STN)*
TPM—Trigger Price Mechanism, USA
UIT—Union de l'industrie textile, France—French Industry Textile Union
UN—United Nations *(see NU)*
UNCTAD—United Nations Conference on Trade and Development *(see CNUCED)*
UNDP—United Nations Development Program *(see PNUD)*
UNGASS—United Nations General Assembly, Special Session
UNIDO—United Nations Industrial Development Organization *(see ONUDI)*
WIPO—World Intellectual Property Organization

PART I

La Mise en Scène

CHAPTER 1

THE CONTINUING EVOLUTION OF THE GLOBAL POLITICAL ECONOMY

HAROLD K. JACOBSON
DUSAN SIDJANSKI

From the end of World War II through the early 1970s, the global economy grew at an unprecedented rate. Throughout the world, material welfare could be and generally was sharply improved. The ultimate foundation of the economic growth that occurred in the quarter century following World War II was the application of technology to the processes of production, but national and international institutions and policies were also essential ingredients. Even during the period of rapid growth, however, there were criticisms of some of these institutions and policies, generally on the ground that the benefits of economic growth were not distributed broadly enough throughout the world. In the 1970s, these criticisms came to be voiced more frequently and stridently, and new criticisms were raised that underscored the costs of continued rapid economic growth. Even supporters of the existing global political economy became troubled in the 1970s as institutions and policies that had previously worked well began to flounder and global economic growth slowed. Efforts were mounted to adjust institutions and policies so that they would function effectively again, but by the end of the 1970s the outcome was far from clear.

What was clear was that economic issues will be prominent in world politics in the closing two decades of the twentieth century. Populations everywhere have come to expect rising standards of living, and they increasingly hold their governments accountable for fulfilling this expectation. Aware that their tenure in office is at stake and aware that the performance of their countries' economies is inextricably linked with that of the global economy, governments must be concerned with the global economy. They shape their foreign policies so as to enhance their countries' economic prospects. Thanks to the interaction of states' foreign policies, the functioning and the nature of the global political economy are high on the agenda of world politics.

This book is about the global political economy. Its focus is on some of the more important national and international institutions and policies that shape this economy. It is primarily concerned with the global economy's continuing evolution. It analyzes national and international forces for change in the late twentieth century and constraints on the processes of change, and it assesses the consequences of some of the efforts at adjustment in institutions and policies that were made in the 1970s. By analyzing the recent past, it seeks to clarify the possible direction, nature, and extent of change in the near future in the institutions and policies that guide the global political economy.

The Structure of the Global Political Economy

As a point of departure, it is important to delineate the structure of the global political economy. States have different political-economic systems, and they have widely divergent levels of economic development. Although all states and territories have some foreign trade, the extent and nature of their ties with the global political economy vary tremendously. These structural features in themselves simultaneously create pressures for change in the global political economy and set limits on what is possible.

In broad terms, the global political economy can be divided into three major components: the market economies that have achieved a high level of industrialization, the centrally planned economies, and the developing economies of the Third World.

The first category includes the several states of Western Europe, the United States and Canada, and Japan, Australia, and New Zealand. It roughly coincides with the membership of the Organization for Economic Cooperation and Development (OECD).[1] Although the extent of governmental intervention in the economies of these states varies greatly, all of the states rely substantially on the market forces of supply and demand to determine what shall be produced and how it shall be distributed, and all allow considerable private ownership of the means of production. OECD states are basically capitalist in orientation. This is the group of states that are typically referred to as "the West." Although this group of states accounted for less than 20 percent of the world's population in the late 1970s, more than 60 percent of the world product accrued to them (IBRD, 1980: 110-111). Their average annual per capita gross national product (GNP) was more than $7000. This group of states was collectively the richest in the world, and it was the source of more than 60 percent of the exports in world trade. The second category includes the states that rely on central planning rather than market forces to determine what shall be produced and how it shall be distributed and that have government ownership of the principal means of production. It includes the Soviet Union and the states in Eastern Europe with communist governments, all of which have achieved a relatively high level of industrialization, and the People's Republic of China and states in Asia and the Caribbean with communist governments, which are in the process of industrialization.[2] In the late 1970s, states with centrally planned economies accounted for almost 32 percent of the world's population and gained about 19 percent of the world's product. Their average per capita GNP was about $1200. China's per capita GNP of about $230 was the lowest of the group; all of the other states had per capita GNPs of more than $700. Without China, the other states of the group comprised less than 10 percent of the world's population, but gained more than 16 percent of the world's product. The average per capita GNP of this subset of states was close to $3500. China, with more than 22 percent of the world's population, gained less than 3 percent of the world's product. Ten percent of the world's exports came from countries with centrally planned economies.

The third category, the developing states of the Third World, included more than half of the world's population in the late 1970s and received about 18 percent of the world product. Although this group of states is collectively often referred to as the less developed countries (LDCs), or developing countries, it contains a wide variety of states.[3] Their per capita GNPs vary from less than $100 per year to more than $3000. It even includes the capital surplus oil-exporting countries such as Saudi Arabia that have per capita GNPs comparable to or above those of western states. Although there is considerable governmental intervention in the economies of several of the LDCs, none of the states included in this category as it is used here has complete central planning. LDCs as a group were the source of less than 30 percent of the world's exports.

These figures give some dimensions of the structure of the global political economy; trade statistics give others. Table 1.1 shows the direction of international trade in 1977. It shows the percentage of exports from each category of states going to each of the three categories. The first feature to be noted about Table 1.1 is the extent to which western states trade with each other. Because of this concentration of their trade and the fact that western exports constituted more than 60 percent of global exports, more than 40 percent of world trade was West-to-West trade. The second salient feature is that LDC exports were even more heavily concentrated on western states than those of the western states. More than two-thirds of the exports of

LDCs, countries that are generally located in the South, go to western states. The third important characteristic that Table 1.1 shows is the concentration of the trade of countries with centrally planned economies with other countries with the same type of economic systems. When this feature is seen in conjunction with the fact that centrally planned economies are the source of only 10 percent of world exports, the limited role of these states in the global economy is obvious. States with centrally planned economies tend to have a lower level of exports and imports than do countries of comparable levels of economic development that rely on market forces, and they tend to trade primarily with other countries with similar economic systems. It should also be noted that states with centrally planned economies trade more with western states than they do with less developed countries.

These structural dimensions highlight the crucial role that the western states occupy in the global political economy. They also provide some indication of the extent of global interdependence. Western states have more wealth, production, and trade than any other group of states. The economies of the western states are closely linked together by extensive international trade. Changes in economic conditions in major western countries are rapidly felt in the other western states. What happens in the economies of the western states will in addition have significant effects on the economies of the LDCs because of the extensive trade between the South and West. It will also have significant effects in the states with centrally planned economies even though these effects will be muted because of the relative isolation of this group of states from the others. Given the dominant position of the western states in the global economy, economic conditions in these states must be of concern to everyone. There is a dynamic interaction between economic developments in the West and economic developments throughout the world. What the general trade statistics do not show is the extent to which the western states are dependent upon importing raw materials from the

TABLE 1.1   Direction of Merchandise Trade, 1977 (composition in percentages)

| | DESTINATION | | | |
Origin	Western States	Less Developed Countries	Centrally Planned Economies	Unallocated
Western States	65.7	28.7	5.2	.5
Less Developed Countries	67.0	28.0	4.4	.6
Centrally Planned Economies	27.2	14.9	54.5	3.4

SOURCE: International Bank for Reconstruction and Development, *World Development Report, 1980* (Washington, DC: IBRD, 1980), p. 100.

other groups of states. This dependence is a crucial ingredient of global interdependence, and it is a vital component in the dynamic interaction between the West and the rest of the world.

The disparities in levels of material welfare that the structural dimensions show constitute another dynamic force in the global political economy. Because their populations expect rising standards of living, governments of all states are impelled to seek economic growth. Governments of LDCs, however, are under particular pressure to achieve rapid economic development, among other reasons because of the enormous gap between the levels of material welfare in their countries and that that has been achieved in the industrialized countries. The drive to promote the economic development of the less developed countries has been a major feature of the post-World War II global political economy. Given the strength of their economic ties with the western states, the LDCs cannot pursue their drive for economic development without concern for these links.

This book concentrates on certain important aspects of economic relationships among western states and between western states and less developed countries. Trade among these two categories of states accounts for more than 85 percent of the world total. Relations among these states will exercise a determining effect on the evolution of the global political economy in the immediate future. This book deals with the national and international institutions and policies that shape relationships among western states and between western states and LDCs.

Relationships between the states with centrally planned economies and the West and the LDCs could give rise to another dynamic force within the global political economy. From all sides there are pressures to amplify the ties that now exist. The centrally planned economies offer western states potential markets of vast dimensions and also can serve as sources of important raw materials. The western states in turn have technology and food that the centrally planned economies could use. With their relative wealth, the states with centrally planned economies that have achieved high levels of industrialization could assist substantially in the economic development of LDCs. As they do for the West, the LDCs offer the centrally planned economies valuable raw materials and markets. There is little sign, however, that the relative position in the global political economy of the states with centrally planned economies will change dramatically in the near future. During the 1970s the proportion of world trade going to or coming from these countries remained virtually constant, even declining slightly. Even if their trade with other states were to expand sharply, given its extremely low level at present, it would be some time before the states with centrally planned economies became a major force in the global political economy. Relationships between these states and those in other categories will eventually pose important issues, but they need not be subject to intensive analyses for an assessment of major trends in the near-term evolution of the global political economy.

The Post-World War II International Economic Order

The global political economy consists not only of the national economies that give it its basic structure, but also of the international institutions and policies that shape relations among these economies. These institutions and policies constitute regimes in particular substantive areas such as trade, shipping, and monetary relationships. They provide rules and procedures for transacting day-to-day business and thereby facilitate cooperation and help to avoid disputes. Regimes can also offer ways of settling disputes should they arise. In short, regimes contribute to making relationships in particular substantive areas predictable. Collectively, regimes comprise the international order. Regimes and the international order that they comprise structure relationships and thereby simultaneously facilitate and limit change. Because economic relationships in particular substantive areas can seldom if ever be totally isolated from economic relationships in other substantive areas, there is strong pressure for regimes to follow compatible broad principles. The international order therefore tends to have a certain philosophical consistency. Regimes and the overall international order can be weakly or strongly supported. International orders can collapse, as they tend to during wars, and patterns of relationships can disintegrate. Regimes and the overall international order can also be modified in ways that command broad consent thereby accelerating change and minimizing disruptions.

The events of the 1970s posed a challenge to the post-World War II international economic order. The growing criticisms, the failure of the institutions and policies to perform as they had and as it was thought that they should, and the slowing of growth in the world economy, placed the future of this order in question. Efforts have been made to preserve the international economic order through modification of some of its features. These efforts could succeed, or the order could collapse or be significantly altered. What ultimately happens will be the result of national and international forces and of individual and collective decisions.

Before these basic forces can be analyzed, and the nature of possible decisions examined, the essential features of the existing international economic order need to be described. The existing international economic order was largely shaped by the major western countries. When the key international institutions were created at the end of World War II, the majority of less developed countries were still under colonial rule, and most of the countries that then had centrally planned economies chose not to participate in several of the nascent institutions. The western countries created an international economic order that followed modern neoliberal prescriptions. Its purpose was to facilitate international trade and hence international specialization in production among countries.

The mixed character of the economies of the industrialized states made facilitating international trade an intellectually and politically challenging task. Had the governments of these countries been willing to allow market forces to operate in a totally unfettered manner, the issue of facilitating international trade would simply have been that of applying the classical liberal solution of removing whatever obstacles to international trade existed. But the governments of the western countries were determined to intervene in their economies to achieve various social goals, particularly to prevent a recurrence of the high levels of unemployment of the 1930s. Had the western countries moved to total governmental ownership of the means of production and to complete central planning, the issue would simply have been that of coordinating national plans. But they did not follow the example of the USSR and there continued to be limits on the role of government in their economies.

Because of the mixed character of their economies, facilitating international trade among the western states would inevitably involve simultaneously lowering obstacles to trade and coordinating—at least to some extent—their macroeconomic policies. Many of the obstacles to trade were the result of governments wishing to isolate their countries' economies so that external forces would not hamper their efforts to achieve social goals. A state's efforts to create employment could be frustrated by a flood of inexpensive imports, or its efforts to counter inflation could be negated by a surge in demand for its exports or a sudden influx of foreign investment. The western states had no intention of giving up their economic sovereignty, or their ability to set their own economic goals within the context of their particular economic situations, but if they were to gain the benefits of increased trade they would have to find ways to avoid pursuing mutually contradictory macroeconomic policies.

One of the most important among the international institutions that were created at the end of World War II, the International Monetary Fund (IMF), was given functions with respect to both reducing obstacles to trade and coordinating macroeconomic policy. In the 1930s, the governments of many western countries adopted strict controls over the exchange of their currencies, and these controls persisted into the 1950s. Designed so that the governments could regulate all foreign purchases of goods and services, these controls constituted a formidable barrier to the expansion of trade. One of the functions assigned to the IMF was to facilitate governments removing these exchange controls and making their currencies freely convertible. When member states accept the obligations of Article VIII of the IMF's Articles of Agreement, they agree to make their currencies freely convertible. Since 1958, all major western states have accepted the obligations of Article VIII. The IMF assists member states to maintain the value of their currencies by loaning them funds that they can use for open market operations in support of their currencies. Loans for limited amounts are given automatically, but larger amounts require the fund's approval, and by specifying conditions for the approval of a loan, the IMF exercises surveillance and leverage over a borrower's macroeconomic policies. The funds that IMF loans come from a pool to which the member states contribute in proportion to their share in world trade. Voting power in IMF is weighted according to contributions; consequently the states that play the largest role in world trade—the western states—have the greatest voting power. Since there is such a strong mutual interest in maintaining the convertibility and relative stability of member states' currencies, and since compatible macroeconomic policies are so crucial to these goals, the national officials who participate in the IMF and the members of the IMF secretariat are inevitably drawn into discussions of macroeconomic policies. Binding decisions are certainly not an issue, but at a minimum relevant information is exchanged.

The General Agreement on Tariffs and Trade (GATT) is a second major international institution in the contemporary global economy. During the 1930s, the western states increased their tariffs to prohibitively high levels and also enacted quantitative restrictions limiting trade. For several of the states, this development represented a culmination of a trend that had begun in the late nineteenth century with the collapse of the liberal international economic order that had been established under British hegemony. Combined with currency controls, these tariffs and quantitative restrictions sharply restricted the possibilities for international trade. By the late 1930s, the value of international trade had fallen from what it had been in the 1920s by almost 30 percent. Whether the intent of these measures was merely a protectionist desire to isolate national economies so that domestic goals could be pursued without interference or a mercantilist desire to increase the power of the state, their effect was equally harmful for international trade. After World War II, the governments of the major western states were determined to revive and stimulate international trade. They were convinced that the growth of their own economies depended upon it. The creation of the IMF was one step. The creation of GATT was another. GATT provided a framework for reducing tariffs and other obstacles to trade. GATT sponsors negotiations in which member states bargain and reach agreements about mutually reducing tariffs and other obstacles to trade. The provisions of these agreements are then extended to all GATT member states because the basic rule of GATT is nondiscrimination: The contracting parties to GATT commit themselves to extend most-favored-nation (MFN) treatment to each other. Through these procedures substantial progress has been made in reducing obstacles to trade. When GATT's Tokyo round of multinational trade negotiations was completed, the tariffs of the major western countries averaged less than 10 percent of the value of the imported goods. There was relatively free trade in manufactured goods among the western states. Each member state has one vote in GATT, but votes are seldom taken. What counts in inducing a state to reduce the level of its tariffs is what reductions a trading partner can offer in return. Bargaining power in GATT thus closely accords with shares of international trade, and as in the IMF, the states with the greatest influence in GATT are those that play the largest role in world trade—the western states.

The Organization for Economic Cooperation and Development (OECD) is a third major international institution promoting the creation and functioning of the neoliberal international economic order. Unlike the International Monetary Fund and the General Agreement on Tariffs and Trade, that are potentially open to all states, the OECD's membership is confined to western states. The OECD is the principal forum for the voluntary harmonization of their macroeconomic policies. Each year, the OECD's member states mutually review the performance of their economies and their economic forecasts and plans. Member states are encouraged to take each other's problems and interests into account in formulating their own policies. OECD member states have a vital stake in the health of each other's economies: A recession or depression in one member state would lessen its demand for exports from the others thereby weakening their economies, and inflation in one could spread to the others through an excessive demand for their exports. The member states of the OECD have also negotiated and adopted codes of conduct covering several issues. The one dealing with capital transactions is among the more important of these codes. Thanks to this code, it is relatively easy for citizens and corporations of one western country to invest in another.

With the currencies of the major western countries freely convertible, their tariffs reduced to relatively insignificant levels, minimal restrictions among them on direct foreign investment, and a forum for the voluntary harmonization of their macroeconomic policies, the essential ingredients of the neoliberal international economic order were in place. Other states were brought into this order in varying degrees.

International trade flourished under the neoliberal international economic order. In the quarter century between 1948 and 1973, the value of world exports increased by almost six times (UN, 1976: I,96). This growth in international trade provided a powerful stimulus to global economic growth. Although states in all three categories shared in the growth in international trade, the value of the exports of the western states grew more rapidly than those of states with centrally planned economies or less developed countries.

The international economic order was also propitious for the growth of transnational corporations (TNCs), almost all of which had their headquarters in western states. With few barriers to trade and freely convertible currencies, managers of TNCs could internationalize production processes: producing goods in one country for sale in others and even producing components in several countries, assembling the components in still another country, and selling the finished product in others. Direct foreign investment from the western countries expanded at an even more rapid rate than that of their exports.

Although all of the western states prospered in the post-World War II neoliberal international economic order, some fared better than others. Japan's exports grew more rapidly than those of any other western country, and those of the six original members of the European Economic Community (EEC)—Belgium, France, the Federal Republic of Germany, Italy, Luxembourg, and the Netherlands—grew more rapidly than those of several other western countries including the United States. The gross national products of Japan and the original members of EEC also grew more rapidly than the U.S. GNP.

This differential performance was in part attributable to Japan's and Europe's recovering from the devastation that they suffered during World War II. Another important factor, however, was that for political and security reasons the United States was interested in these two areas having strong economies, and it was willing to accept a measure of economic discrimination against itself to promote their prosperity. The United States sponsored Japan's entry into GATT and its obtaining most-favored-nation treatment, while tolerating some protectionist Japanese trading and investment practices. The United States strongly supported the creation and development of the European Economic Community even though the creation of a common market in Europe completely eliminating barriers to trade among the member states would mean that U.S. exports to these states would be treated less favorably than those of EEC members. The EEC's Common Agricultural Policy (CAP), with its system of variable levies on imported agricultural products, involved even more serious discrimination against U.S. exports. The U.S. government accepted these discriminations because it believed that if Western Europe and Japan were economically strong, they would be better bulwarks against the spread of communism.

Because of their economic links with the western states, the less developed countries had little choice but to participate in the neoliberal international economic order. In the years immediately after World War II, more than 70 percent of their exports went to the western states. They were economically heavily dependent upon the western states. The developing countries were brought into the International Monetary Fund and the General Agreement on Tariffs and Trade. By 1979, the membership of these two institutions had grown to 138 and 84 respectively. A major explanation of why so many more states have joined the IMF than GATT is that it is necessary to be a member of the fund to join the World Bank or, more formally, the International Bank for Reconstruction and Development (IBRD). The World Bank (which had 135 members) is a major source of financial assistance for its member states. Even though neither the IMF nor GATT requires its LDC member states immediately to comply fully with its regulations concerning currency and commercial practices, membership in the two institutions does imply a commitment ultimately to adhere to their neoliberal rules and procedures.

As evidenced by their disproportionately low share of world exports, the states with centrally planned economies played only a marginal role in the global polital economy. International trade has historically been less important to the USSR and the People's Republic of China (PRC) than it has been to smaller states. Each country is richly endowed with natural resources, and because of their large populations and territories, each contains ample opportunities for specialization and the realization of the advantages of the economies of scale. In addition, central planning has a propensity toward autarky. Planners are reluctant to rely on economic imputs that are not under their administrative control. As practiced in the USSR and the PRC, central planning is accompanied by a state monopoly of foreign trade and total state. control of currency conversions. Countries with centrally planned economies generally have proportionately less foreign trade than countries with market economies of comparable size and levels of economic development. Finally, as part of its security policy, the United States controlled and limited its exports to countries with communist regimes and refused to grant them most-favored-nation treatment. Other members of the North Atlantic Treaty Organization (NATO) also adopted restrictions on trade with countries with communist regimes. What international trade states with centrally planned economies had was predominantly among themselves, just as western states traded primarily with themselves. Until 1980, when China joined IMF and the World Bank, neither the USSR nor the PRC belonged to the major international institutions of the neoliberal international economic order. Some smaller states with centrally planned economies, however, have for some time been members of the IMF, IBRD, and GATT.

Trade cooperation among the USSR, the Eastern European countries, and various other small states with communist regimes came to be handled in the Council for Mutual Economic Assistance (CMEA).[4] Specialization agreements and joint projects are negotiated within the CMEA, and an effort is also made to coordinate the member states' economic plans.

Whatever the ultimate consequences of their minimal connections with the global political economy, the states with centrally planned economies achieved annual rates of economic growth through the mid-1970s that were on the average above those of the western countries.

The post-World War II global political economy also included several international institutions, mainly connected with the United Nations system, that have virtually universal membership and that performed functions for the entire world economy. The statistical services of the United Nations and several of the specialized agencies developed standardized concepts and methodologies for national data collection efforts and then compiled and aggregated the national data. Thanks to these efforts, since about 1960, data that are reasonably adequate to monitor basic economic and social trends have been available for most areas of the world. This monitoring flagged the population explosion that occurred in the post-World War II period and the growing gap between the per capita GNPs of the western countries and those of the LDCs.

These same organizations provide a forum for general discussions of the functioning of the world economy and a framework for the adoption of normative pronouncements. These normative pronouncements tend to reflect the views of the less developed countries which predominate in the membership of these institutions. Decisions in these institutions are taken on the basis of each member state having one vote and LDCs easily comprise the simple or two-thirds majority that is required. The less developed countries created a caucus to coordinate their views and to insure as much solidarity as possible among them. Because 77 states participated in the first meeting of this group, it came to be known as the Group of 77. By 1980, however, it had more than 120 members.[5]

Spurred by the Group of 77, the General Assembly of the United Nations, the United Nations Conference on Trade and Development (UNCTAD), the United Nations Industrial Development Organization (UNIDO), and other UN agencies, have each adopted a number of resolutions favoring LDC causes. They have set targets for the economic growth of LDCs and for the transfer of resources to these countries.

UN agencies have also become purveyors of technical assistance to the less developed countries, and the World Bank and various regional development banks have supplied financial assistance. Over the years the flow of resources to the less developed countries has increased substantially so that by the mid-1970s the net flow of capital was more than $40 billion per year (OECD, 1977: 188). However, the flow of resources has remained very much under western control. Western countries supplied more than 90 percent of the funds that were transferred to LDCs, and more than 60 percent of these funds were supplied through ordinary commercial transactions. Of the funds that were transferred as Official Development Assistance (ODA), the greatest part was transferred on a government-to-government bilateral basis; thus the choice of the recipients and of the purposes for which the funds could be utilized was subject to the discretion of the western donor governments. Less than 30 percent of ODA funds was channeled through international institutions, and the western countries exercised preponderant influence in the institutions that received the bulk of these funds. More than 80 percent of the funds that the western countries channeled through international institutions went to the World Bank and regional development banks where there were weighted voting systems. The largest share of the funds that the UN and the specialized agencies used for technical assistance came from the United Nations Development Program (UNDP), which depended for its income on annual voluntary contributions. While the voluntary character of the UNDP financing put the program at the mercy of unilateral decisions of the western countries, these states generally regularly increased their contributions. For a short period in the mid-1970s, however, the United States, which was the largest single contributor to UNDP, reduced the size of its contribution. This heightened LDC sensitivity to the vulnerability of the program.

The states with centrally planned economies supplied less than 1 percent of the funds that were transfered to less developed countries. Except in a few instances, therefore, they did not constitute a realistic alternative to the western countries as a source for assistance for the less developed countries. About 8 percent of the funds transfered to LDCs were provided by oil exporting countries, which in this analysis are themselves classified as LDCs. There were, however, limits to which oil exporting countries could expand their assistance. Their aid was a useful supplement to that of the western countries, but it could not be a substitute.

The post-World War II international economic order can be characterized as neoliberal and western-dominated for several reasons. Because of their relative size, the economies of the western states had a predominant weight in the global economy, and western states had predominant influence in the international institutions that controlled the most substantial resources and set the rules that governed basic economic relationships. These rules had a neoliberal orientation: they tried to adapt the classical liberal principles of free trade to economic conditions of the mid-twentieth century, especially the prevalence of welfare economies. There were, however, also other tendencies within the global political economy. The states with centrally planned economies constituted a separate sphere that operated according to different principles and that was only loosely connected with other states. While the influence of less developed countries was limited in the IMF and GATT, they could control the proceedings in the institutions of the UN system. LDCs used this capacity to voice their disappointment with and objections to the existing international economic order.

The Crisis of the Neoliberal International Economic Order

LDC criticisms of the neoliberal international economic order that had been created in the wake of World War II gained sufficient strength in the

1970s to pose a challenge to this order. But there were also other challenges, and their combined effect put the future of the neoliberal order in question.

One problem was the changed position of the United States. The post-World War II international economic order had come to depend heavily upon the United States playing a special role and bearing important burdens. The United States was the dominant force in the world economy and in the key international economic institutions.

Until the European Economic Community's common external tariff came into place in 1968, the United States was the world economy's largest market under a single jurisdiction. Because of this and the necessity of U.S. administrations having congressional authority to reduce U.S. tariffs, the rhythm of tariff-cutting in GATT depended upon U.S. legislation.

The United States contributed more funds for development assistance than any other country. In recognition of this, the president of the World Bank and the administrator of the UNDP were always U.S. citizens.

As the international monetary regime had developed under the International Monetary Fund, it had come to be a U.S. dollar-based system. The currencies of the major trading countries were denominated in terms of the U.S. dollar, and after 1958, they could be freely converted into dollars or other currencies. The U.S. dollar was convertible into gold at a fixed rate. With this system, currencies had relatively stable values, but the U.S. dollar played an overwhelming role. This gave the United States special privileges, but it also restricted U.S. actions.

Because governments, corporations, and individuals were willing to hold U.S. dollars as reserve assets, the United States could sustain deficits in its balance of payments without formally having to borrow. Consequently, the United States did not face the same fiscal discipline that other countries did. It was virtually immune from the IMF's system of surveillance. On the other hand, the United States faced greater difficulties than other countries in adjusting the value of its currency. If the U.S. dollar were overvalued, weakening the competitiveness of U.S. exports, getting an adjustment was almost impossible. Devaluation of the U.S. dollar would have enormous repercussions for reserve assets throughout the world. Moreover, the countries about which the United States was specifically concerned—those with which its exports competed—could respond by devaluing their own currencies. In effect, the United States had to rely on other countries to increase voluntarily the value of their currencies. Since this would make their exports less competitive, governments were extremely reluctant to do this.

When the U.S. gross national product was more than a third of the total world product, the special U.S. role was acceptable to other countries—or they regarded it as inevitable—but when the U.S. GNP slipped to about a quarter of the world total, as it had by 1970, such a preponderant U.S. role became less acceptable. Similarly, the United States became less willing and less able than it had been to bear the special burdens that the system imposed upon it.

As the United States ran persistent and substantial deficits in its balance of payments in the late 1960s and early 1970s, and as the number of dollars held abroad grew to vastly exceed the supply of U.S. gold reserves, the health of the international monetary system increasingly came into question. Those countries and individuals that disagreed with the U.S. pursuit of the war in Vietnam and were concerned about the expansion of U.S.-based transnational corporations, both of which caused heavy foreign expenditures, were particularly disturbed that the United States did not face the same fiscal discipline as other countries. Because of the difficulty that it faced in adjusting the value of its currency, the United States felt that it was denied policy instruments of macroeconomic management that other countries could use and that it needed to use in efforts to limit unemployment.

Beyond the changed position of the United States, there were also other difficulties that were at least as serious in the operation of the neoliberal international economic order. The very openness of the world economy began to bring problems as well as benefits. As obstacles to trade fell, buyers could shift to foreign suppliers more readily, and in many instances they did, leaving domestic suppliers without purchasers. New tasks had to be found for now unemployed resources and persons. These structural adjustment problems occurred within the western countries as trade among them increased. They also occurred as less developed countries began to industrialize. As wages within western states increased with the elaboration of welfare state principles, incentives increased for shifting labor-intensive industries, for instance the manufacture of textiles and shoes, to the less developed countries to take advantage of the low cost of labor there. As structural adjustment problems increased in severity, the governments of western countries increasingly turned to protectionist barriers to trade, especially quantitative restrictions on imports that were more or less voluntarily accepted by foreign exporters.

Another problem was the explosive expansion in the 1960s of transnational corporations, which roused unease among both western and less developed countries. In the western countries there was fear that as the TNCs invested abroad, jobs would move from the home country to the host countries. The less developed countries feared that because of their massive economic assets, the TNCs could gain undue and unacceptable influence in their economies.

The freedom that the neoliberal international economic order allowed TNCs was only one of the LDCs' concerns. Because of the dominant position of western countries and their dependence on them, the LDCs directed their complaints largely at the West. LDCs' representatives argued that the international economic order was insufficiently responsive to their interests and that it unduly favored those of the western countries. They cited as conclusive evidence the growing gap between their per capita GNPs and those of the western countries. They maintained that development assistance was insufficient to meet their broadly acknowledged needs. They were disturbed by the debt burden that they were assuming. They bridled under the conditions that were imposed on them when they sought to obtain financial assistance, arguing that the fiscal restraint that the IMF and other institutions frequently required of them often involved unacceptable social costs. They maintained that although tariffs had been reduced on items of interest to the western countries, they remained sufficiently high on raw material that had undergone basic processing to discourage the establishment of processing facilities in their countries. In addition, they argued that since they were latecomers to the industrialization process, their exports ought to receive preferential treatment in the markets of the richer countries, that is, in the West. They alleged that the prices of the raw materials that they exported were kept artificially low because of the oligopolistic position of the western countries' buyers. They argued that the fluctuations in the prices that they received for the commodities that they exported placed impossible and unjust burdens on their economies.

While the western states and the less developed countries became increasingly troubled by the functioning of the neoliberal international economic order in the late 1960s and early 1970s, those with centrally planned economies increasingly began to seek greater economic contacts with other countries. The governments of countries with centrally planned economies concluded that greater contacts with other countries would be helpful in their efforts to continue to increase the per capita GNPs of their countries.

As the 1970s developed, the global political economy faced a series of challenges: adapting to relatively diminished U.S. economic strength and an appropriately more modest U.S. role; facilitating the structural adjustments that would be required within western states because of increased international competition and the growing industrialization in the less developed countries; assuring that the beneficial potential of transnational corporations would be maximized and that their harmful potential would be minimized; dealing with the complaints of the less developed countries; and, accommodating the increased interactions between the states with centrally planned economies and other states. Efforts to meet these challenges would inevitably involve changes in the international economic order.

In the early 1970s, the undercurrents of problems with the functioning of the neoliberal international economic order and of criticisms of it burst to the surface. A series of shocks provoked and propelled negotiations concerning the evolution of the international economic order.

In August 1971, President Richard M. Nixon decreed that the U.S. dollar would no longer be convertible into gold, precipitating a search for a monetary system that would not be based so exclusively on the dollar and that would also ease the process of adjusting the value of the dollar.

During the course of 1973, the so-called Multi-Fiber Agreement was negotiated within GATT. This agreement legitimized states (particularly western states, though the issue was phrased in general terms) adopting quantitative restrictions against textile imports (particularly from developing countries, though again the issue was phrased generally). The agreement committed countries that took restrictive action to expand regularly the quantities that could be imported, and it established a mechanism for surveillance of the quantitative restrictions to insure that they complied with stated guidelines. This agreement, which was of limited duration and had to be renegotiated periodically, put the broad issue of structural adjustment on the agenda of international institutions. This issue gained increased salience two years later when the conference of the United Nations Industrial Development Organization, meeting in Lima, called for increasing the share of industrial production in the less developed countries from 7 percent of the world total, where it stood then, to 25 percent by the end of the twentieth century.

At their meeting in Algiers in September 1973, the heads of government of the nonaligned countries launched a call for the creation of a new international economic order (NIEO). At its Sixth Special Session in April 1974, the UN General Assembly endorsed this call by adopting a Declaration and a Programme of Action on the Establishment of a New International Economic Order (UN, 1974).

In the meantime, during the Fall of 1973, the member states of the Organization of Petroleum Exporting Countries (OPEC) decided to quadruple the price that they charged for crude oil, an increase that would affect all oil-importing states regardless of their level of economic development. This action marked the emergence of OPEC as a major force in the world political economy. In addition, in the imbroglio resulting from the resumption of military conflict between the Arab states and Israel, the Arab members of OPEC embargoed petroleum destined for those western states that supported Israel.

Jarred by the jump in the price of petroleum and the embargo, the western states became deeply concerned about the security of their access to the raw materials that were essential to the functioning of their economies and seriously alarmed by the prospect of further price hikes for petroleum and other commodities. The incentives for their being responsive to LDC criticisms of the international economic order suddenly sharply increased. Negotiations between the western states and less developed countries on changes in the international economic order started in the mid-1970s and dragged on throughout the decade. They will surely continue in the 1980s.

The petroleum crisis also raised the spectre of growing shortage of raw materials. The supply of some materials that are crucial to current production processes is undoubtedly ultimately finite. The issue is whether or not new technologies and materials will be discovered to replace those that are running out in sufficient time to prevent economic slowdowns or collapse. In a more general sense, concern arose about the capacity of the earth to support continued economic growth at the rates that had been achieved in the 1950s and 1960s. Some argue that this would lead to unacceptable environmental degradation. The effect of all of this was to throw into question the very goal of continued economic growth.

Starting in the early 1970s, the states with centrally planned economies greatly expanded their trade with the western countries. For instance, between 1970 and 1975 the USSR's imports from western states grew by more than four times. The exports of states with centrally planned economies, however, did not expand as rapidly, and the further expansion of imports from western countries and possibly even their maintenance at the levels that had been achieved came to be dependent on the West extending credit. To improve their access to credit and to western markets, some of the smaller countries with centrally planned economies moved to join or resume membership in the International Monetary Fund and the General Agreement on Tariffs and Trade, and in 1980, the People's Republic of China joined both the IMF and IBRD. The search for modalities for improving the linkages between the states with centrally planned economies and other states was underway by the end of the 1970s. It was evident, however, that progress would be slow and that results would be achieved only gradually. In addition, increasing economic relations between communist and western states would substantially depend on the level of political conflict between them being relatively low.

Of all of the negotiations that were launched in the 1970s, the greatest progress was made in matters that affected western states more than any other category and that involved only slight modifications of the post-World War II international economic order. After various fruitless attempts to reach agreement on a system that would provide for fixed exchange rates among their currencies, the western countries agreed to settle for a system of managed floating or flexible exchange rates, and the IMF's amended Articles of Agreement took effect in 1979. The new system, however, was severely tested by the varying rates of inflation in the major western countries. Another set of tariff cuts were negotiated in GATT's Tokyo round, which started in 1973 and was completed in 1979. Most importantly, the Tokyo round also succeeded in reaching agreement on efforts to reduce several nontariff barriers to international trade. These agreements were embodied in codes of conduct on such matters as export subsidies and countervailing duties, discrimination against foreign suppliers in foreign procurements, import licensing procedures, customs valuation systems, and health and environmental regulations. Starting in 1974, to facilitate the coordination of their macroeconomic policies, the heads of government of the seven economically most important western states—Canada, the Federal Republic of Germany, France, Italy, Japan, the United Kingdom, and the United States (the GNPs of which account for more than 85 percent of those of the western states) began to hold annual summit conferences. Economic issues were often the exclusive topic for discussion and they always dominated the agenda.

With respect to the complaints of the LDCs, the western states broadly agreed to increase the volume of their aid. The European Economic Community, Japan, and the United States all adopted generalized systems of preferences for imports from LDCs. The western countries agreed to limited measures to stabilize the prices of some commodities. Some western countries were willing to go further to aid LDCs. Some governments of Western European countries wrote off the debts that the poorest LDCs owed to them. The member states of the European Economic Community agreed to a comprehensive system to stabilize the earnings for the commodity exports of those African, Pacific, and Caribbean countries associated with the EEC through the Lomé Agreements. Oil-exporting LDCs were given a greater voice in international institutions, as befitted their increased economic strength.

None of these measures radically altered the character of the neoliberal international economic order. This order continued to be a system basically designed to facilitate the growth of international trade among states with welfare economies. Some of the measures were designed to take account of changed circumstances—the decline of the relative strength of the U.S. economy and the increased volatility of structural changes in a world in which there were few obstacles to trade—while others were designed to facilitate the growth of developing countries and thereby work toward a more egalitarian distribution of the benefits of global economic growth.

Even with these measures, the future of the neoliberal international economic order remained in doubt. Further modifications might be required to preserve it. Or, if the major western states shifted from relatively liberal to more protectionist policies, the system could collapse. It is also conceivable, though unlikely, that the neoliberal international order could be replaced by a completely managed international economic order such as exists among states with centrally planned economies. Growing links with states with centrally planned economies could push the system in this direction, but from the perspective of the early 1980s this seems at best only a distant prospect. There are stronger and more immediate pressures. Furthermore, a number of the states with centrally planned economies appeared to be moving toward more flexible types of economic planning. Increased links with the world political economy could pull them further in this direction. This too, however, is a distant rather than a near-term prospect.

The difficulties and pain of structural adjustment in the western states give rise to one significant pressure driving western states toward the adoption of protectionist measures. Should they move too far in this direction, it could destroy the monetary and trade regimes established under the IMF and GATT. The continuing dissatisfaction of the LDCs with their role in the international economic order and with the benefits that they receive from it are another source of significant pressure against the neoliberal order. Should the reforms that have been and may be adopted fall too far short of meeting LDC expectations, this group of states could ultimately reject the neoliberal international economic order and search for something different. This book is mainly concerned with these two pressures. They are the immediate challenges to the neoliberal international order. Responses to them will determine the future of the order.

The remainder of the book is divided into four sections. Part II, the next section, deals with broad domestic and international forces propelling change in the global political economy. Part III focuses on issues concerning structural adjustment in western industrialized states. Part IV deals with aspects of the external economic relationships of two major groups of less developed countries, oil-importing states and African states. The final section of the book, Part V, analyzes changes that have occurred in international institutions and regimes and assesses prospects for further changes. The four sections do not predict the future evolution of the international economic order. They do illuminate several of the factors that will be crucially important in shaping its evolution.

NOTES

1. The twenty-four member states of the OECD are: Australia, Austria, Belgium, Canada, Denmark, Federal Republic of Germany, Finland, France, Greece, Iceland, Ireland, Italy, Japan, Luxembourg, Netherlands, New Zealand, Norway, Portugal, Sweden, Spain, Switzerland, Turkey, United Kingdom, and United States. Any classification scheme is somewhat arbitrary. Those used here are based on those used by the International Bank for Reconstruction and Development. The IBRD does not, however, include four members of the OECD—Greece, Portugal, Spain, and Turkey—in its category of "industrialized countries," because of their relatively low per capita GNPs.

2. The IBRD places Albania, Bulgaria, Cuba, Czechoslovakia, German Democratic Republic, Hungary, Korea, Mongolia, Poland, Romania, and the USSR in this category.

3. This category includes what the IBRD classifies as low-income countries, middle-income countries, and capital-surplus oil exporters.

4. The members of the CMEA are: Bulgaria, Cuba, Czechoslovakia, German Democratic Republic, Hungary, Mongolia, Mozambique, Poland, Romania, the USSR, and Vietnam.

5. In 1980, the members of the Group of 77 were: Afghanistan, Algeria, Angola, Argentina, Bahamas, Bahrain, Bangladesh, Barbados, Benin, Bhutan, Bolivia, Botswana, Brazil, Burma, Burundi, Capa Verde, Central African Republic, Chad, Chile, Colombia, Comoros, Congo, Costa Rica, Cuba, Cyprus, Democratic Kampuchea, Democratic People's Republic of Korea, Democratic Yemen, Djibouti, Dominica, Dominican Republic, Ecuador, Egypt, El Salvador, Equatorial Guinea, Ethiopia, Fiji, Gabon, Gambia, Ghana, Grenada, Guatemala, Guinea, Guinea-Bissau, Guyana, Haiti, Honduras, India, Indonesia, Iran, Iraq, Ivory Coast, Jamaica, Jordan, Kenya, Kuwait, Lao People's Democratic Republic, Lebanon, Lesotho, Liberia, Libyan Arab Jamahirya, Madagascar, Malawi, Malaysia, Maldives, Mali, Malta, Mauritania, Mauritius, Mexico, Morocco, Mozambique, Nepal, Nicaragua, Niger, Nigeria, Oman, Pakistan, Palestine Liberation Organization, Panama, Papua New Guinea, Paraguay, Peru, Philippines, Qatar, Republic of Korea, Romania, Rwanda, Saint Lucia, Samoa, Sao Tome and Principe, Saudi Arabia, Senegal, Seychelles, Sierra Leone, Singapore, Solomon Islands, Somalia, Sri Lanka, St. Vincent and the Grenadines, Sudan, Suriname, Swaziland, Syrian Arab Republic, Thailand, Togo, Tonga, Trinidad and Tobago, Tunisia, Uganda, United Arab Emirates, United Republic of Cameroon, United Republic of Tanzania, Upper Volta, Uruguay, Venezuela, Viet Nam, Yemen, Yugoslavia, Zaire, Zambia, and Zimbabwe.

REFERENCES

International Bank for Reconstruction and Development [IBRD] (1980) World Development Report, 1980. New York: Oxford University Press.

Organization for Economic Cooperation and Development [OECD] (1977) Development Cooperation: Efforts and Policies of the Development Assistance Committee, 1977 Review. Paris: OECD.

United Nations General Assembly (1974) Resolution 3202 (S-VI) Programme of Action on the Establishment of a New International Economic Order. New York: United Nations.

United Nations Secretariat, Department of Economic and Social Affairs, Statistical Office (1976) 1976 Statistical Yearbook. New York: United Nations.

PART II

Forces for Change in the Global Political Economy

Several of the forces propelling change in the global political economy have been identified in chapter 1. The three chapters that follow analyze some of these forces in greater detail.

As was pointed out in chapter 1, the international order that was established at the conclusion of World War II made it possible to take steps toward the internationalization of production. The process of internationalizing production has had profound implications both within and among states.

In chapter 2, Robert W. Cox sets forth a framework for analyzing the mechanisms, consequences, and implications of the dynamic process of the internationalization of production. He is particularly concerned with power relations, and he uses the power relationships involved in production processes as a starting point for analyzing the global political economy. Professor Cox applies the concept of hegemony, as developed by Antonio Gramsci in his analyses of the Italian political economy, to the global political economy. Used in this manner, hegemony is not simply dominance achieved by physical strength, but rather involves broad acceptance of an order. This acceptance is induced by concessions to those who are not in a privileged position in the order and legitimated by an ideology that rationalizes the existing relationships. Professor Cox argues that the international political-economic order created after World War II was a hegemony founded by the United States and that the crises of the 1970s signaled the collapse of this order. He delineates different possibilities for the reestablishment of an international political-economic order.

The perspective that Professor Cox introduces is a distinctive way of viewing the global political economy. More conventional analyses by western officials and scholars give a more benign assessment of the consequences of the neoliberal international economic order and a more optimistic outlook for its future. The special merit of Professor Cox's approach is that it calls attention to power relationships in the structure and functioning of the global political economy and to the underlying social structures and dynamic processes that are involved.

Chapters 3 and 4, by Robert S. Jordan and Alice Hougassian-Rudovich, respectively, approach the issue of change in the global political economy from a different perspective and through a different type of analysis. Among the three categories of states that comprise the global political economy, the less developed countries have been by far the most vocal in criticizing the neoliberal international economic order. Their representatives have voiced these criticisms in a variety of forums, but especially in the United Nations and in the universal membership agencies of the UN system. They have also used these bodies to develop and articulate a program to alter aspects of the neoliberal international economic order in ways that they argue would result in greater advantages for their countries. Chapters 3 and 4 deal with the criticisms and demands made by representatives of less developed countries and with the international political processes that have been crucial to these efforts.

In chapter 3, Robert S. Jordan traces the several steps that were involved in the UN's calling for the creation of a new international economic order. He also outlines and analyzes the specific changes that the LDCs seek in the neoliberal international economic order to realize their vision of a NIEO. The reformist character of the demands for a NIEO becomes clear when the vision that the LDCs espouse in the agencies of the UN system is contrasted with the more radical possibilities outlined by Professor Cox in the concluding section of chapter 2.

In articulating their call for the creation of a NIEO, LDCs have taken advantage of the opportunities that international institutions offer to amplify their voice in the global political system. Although in terms of military and economic power they are individually and collectively relatively weak compared with the United States or the Soviet Union or other large industrialized states, because of their numbers they constitute a formidable force in international institutions and can dominate those that give each state one vote and require only a simple or a two-thirds majority to take a decision. To take advantage of the opportunities afforded by international institutions, however, LDCs must act cohesively. Alice Hougassian-Rudovich in chapter 4 deals with the problems that two groupings of LDCs—the African-Caribbean-Pacific (ACP) countries that are associated with the European communities through the Lomé conventions, and the Group of 77, the broad LDC caucus in the UN—face in maintaining their unity. She concentrates particularly on the consequences for cohesion of having formal institutional structures and especially a secretariat. The ACP countries have had such structures; the Group of 77 has not.

While chapter 2 deals with underlying forces that both propel and limit change, chapters 3 and 4 deal with some of the more visible manifestations of these forces. And while chapter 2 has a philosophical and normative perspective, chapters 3 and 4 are much more empirical in orientation. The chapters complement one another in these ways and show the many-faceted character of the pressures for change in the global political economy.

PRODUCTION AND HEGEMONY
Toward a Political Economy of World Order

ROBERT W. COX

Any attempt at theorizing about the order of societies or of the world will be assessed from two quite different perspectives. One perspective considers thought as an autonomous activity and tends to express itself in universal terms. The other perspective sees thought as related to a particular standpoint in time and place, to a particular set of preoccupations. The first perspective is useful critically in ensuring logical rigor and the internal coherence of theories. The second is necessary to avoid the hubris of leaping from a more or less adequate understanding of a particular historical conjuncture—adequate, that is, as a guide to action—into the proclamation of laws deemed to be true for all time.

The study of politics, in particular, is falsified when abstracted from the structures of power within which it takes place. To take one example relevant to the theme of this chapter: Anglo-Saxon thought since the late nineteenth century has tended to make a separation between economics and politics. In the first of the perspectives on theorizing just mentioned, this separation could appear as flowing from an internal logic of theoretical development, dividing up the whole social universe in order to be able to elaborate more fully the characteristics of its separated spheres. In the other perspective, however, which sees thought as taking place in a social and political context, the separation could be perceived as facilitated and encouraged by the prevailing structure of world power. The dominance first of Britain and then later of the United States took the form of economic expansion and penetration into all parts of the world. This appeared to take place according to nonpolitical economic laws but was made possible by the existence of a world economy which was in fact guaranteed by political and military power.

Power, as Karl Polanyi (1957) pointed out, is necessary to create a market and to guarantee the continuing observance of the rules of market behavior. Once that continuing position of power is achieved, however, behavior in the market can be studied in abstraction from the force that guarantees observance of market practices. Indeed, use of force to maintain the market becomes less necessary to the extent that people come to regard its rules as part of the natural order. This is the meaning of hegemony: the temporary universalization in thought of a particular power structure, conceived not as domination but as the necessary order of nature.

The intellectual separation of political power from economics was most easy to assume for persons near the top of the power structure in the dominant states. The role of these states was essentially to maintain the necessary conditions in the world economy for private economic activity to move forward. Private interests were sufficiently developed and powerful on their own under these conditions to expand on a world scale. The inference that this was happening according to universal natural laws of economics masked the power relationships underlying their opportunity.

Lower down in the hierarchy of power, in France or Germany or Japan for example, such a separation was more likely to appear artificial and unreal; the state played a more evidently necessary role in economic activity through protectionism and state mobilization of capital and direction of investment, and thus could not so easily be set aside in theory. Two contrary intellectual processes were at work here: in one, influenced by a consciousness of relative power position, political economy never gave way before a purely economic analysis; in the other, influenced by the prestige attaching to the theoretical perspective emanating from the top of the power structure, it did. Economics under the latter influence developed through marginalist analysis shorn of an earlier concern by classical political economists with the power of states and with the conflicting social power of classes formed through production.

This chapter is an attempt to sketch out an approach toward a political economy or world order which would be helpful in understanding the power relations of the present world and also the conditions for their transformation. It adopts a standpoint closer to the bottom than to the top of the power hierarchy. Accordingly, it takes a critical though not necessarily negative view of attempts to reconstruct world economy and is disposed to assess prospects more in terms of power potentials than in terms of the theoretical elegance of proposed orders. It is written in the conviction that awareness nearer the top of a relative decline in power and of greater uncertainty in power relations opens the prospect of a more realistic dialogue on the themes of future world order. Indeed, the recent revival of interest in political economy among political scientists in the United States is, no doubt, related to a perception of a relative weakening of U.S. world power (see for example Gilpin, 1975; Krasner, 1978).

This approach begins with the production process. It does not presuppose that everything is reducible to production but recognizes that production generates the material basis of civil society and the state. Production in this sense creates a primary accumulation of power that subsequently is transformed into other forms than that of wealth produced, forms such as social prestige, military strength, political organization, even (as just suggested by the discussion of economics and politics) ideology. One can recognize a material basis in production for all of these other forms of human activity without falling into the trap of maintaining that production (and those who own or control the means of production) directly determines all of them. Culture, politics, and ideology, all of which require a certain material basis, also react upon that basis and develop it in different directions. Ultimately, all forms of power—political or ideological, for example—depend upon control over production (i.e., they depend upon maintaining their material basis), but this control may as well emerge out of political struggle and revolution as come directly from a long-established class of owners of the means of production. The point is not that power emerges inexorably out of the production process, but that power and production are to be seen in necessary relationship one to the other. In short, production is a matrix of political economy, an activity through which politics and economics become transformed into one another.

Three forms of power must first be distinguished: control over the production process, social power or the relationship among classes, and political power or control over the state. These three forms of power are, at certain historical conjunctures, separable and can be used one against the others, though at other conjunctures they tend toward a symbiotic compatibility. There is always a correspondence among the three forms, though their relationships are not fixed from one historical period to another. The important thing is not to lose sight of any of the three.

A political science that focuses exclusively on "political actors" tends to abstract political power from social power and to relegate social power to the realm of the unconscious. Political actors take social power into account without articulating its presence. Social power defines the realm of "nondecision" or the actors' feeling for the limits of the possible (Bachrach and Baratz, 1962). This is not to say anything so crude as that politics becomes the mere unconscious expression of social power (or that the state is unwittingly the creature of economic interests). It is to say rather that social power determines the framework of political action; and when one's concern is with possibilities of structural transformation, the framework is the necessary starting point. What has been unconscious must first be raised to the level of consciousness.

Gramsci, in his concept of hegemony, addressed the problem of how forms of consciousness are connected with relationships of material forces. Hegemony, in his sense, describes a consciousness in which other social classes or the population as a whole accept an order in which one social class is dominant. It is thus a particular condition, not a universal characteristic, of consciousness. The utility of the concept lies in directing enquiry to the processes of establishing and maintaining, and also of challenging and overthrowing the hegemonies of particular social classes. Such an enquiry begins with the exploration of consciousness and proceeds toward an understanding of the reciprocal relations between forms of consciousness and material forces (see Gramsci, 1975; Hoare and Smith, 1971).

In the production process, these two reciprocally related aspects are (1) the physical organization of production (relations of forces embodied in particular technologies); and (2) the social relations of production (which become persistent patterns to the extent that people involved in the production process share a common mental picture of the process and of their mutual relationships). It may seem arbitrary which aspect is taken up first. A conviction of material determinism seems to argue for starting with the physical organization of production. Yet if one's concern is social action, there is good reason for starting with the social relations of production, for these provide the most direct manifestation of domination in the production process by raising the questions: Who controls? Who is directed? To what extent is control accepted (as inevitable if not as just) or challenged (as both unjust and removable)? Whichever aspect is taken up first, it is important, in the interests of acquiring knowledge that will be useful in the ongoing historical process, not to lose sight of the other.

The approach toward a political economy of world order suggested here involves three stages.[1]

First is a task of classification of the modes of social relations of production that reflect prevailing patterns of production organization. Such modes are structural models of persistent patterns of power relations in production. They are based upon observations of a very wide range of real situations in all parts of the contemporary world which are then reduced to a set of internally coherent patterns each of which defines the dominant and subordinate groups in the production process and the characteristic mechanisms of domination and of response by the dominated. Models of this kind have the form of ideal types, or, in the words of Reinhard Bendix, they are contrast concepts of limited historical applicability.[2]

Second, actual patterns of social relations of production corresponding more or less to these different modes are seen to exist in different combinations which together define concrete historical structures at the levels of social formations and world orders. I use the term "historical structure" here in the sense of a model of the essential features of an inclusive sociopolitical entity—inclusive in the sense both that it is to an extent self-contained and that general problems of authority arise within it, i.e., the problems of the state and of world order. Within such historical structures, modes of social relations of production are articulated to one another in specific ways:[3] A particular configuration of social classes derives from the particular combination of modes, and institutions of regulation and coercion exist for the maintenance of a particular order. Regulation and coercion in the social formation is a function of the state, and in the structure of world order, it is a function of interstate relations.

A *third* step is to identify (a) the contradictions and points of conflict that arise in typical form within the different modes of social relations of production and in a concrete form within social formations and world orders; and (b) the relationships of forces involved, which together would indicate the chances for stabilization or transformation. At the social formation level, there is a dialectic between the tendency of institutionalization to perpetuate existing social power relations, and the emergence of new social forces that tend to alter these relations, out of which come crises in the nature of the state. At the level of world order, there is a dialectic between a tendency toward a global class division derived from the internationalizing of production, and a countertendency toward interstate conflicts among social formations which separately aggregate internal class interests.[4]

This approach, by stressing the need to devise appropriate conceptual tools from observation of current conditions of production, strikes a note of caution against taking over definitions of modes of production and of social classes derived from nineteenth-century conditions and applying them uncritically to the social realities of the late twentieth century. Capitalism, for example, while a convenient concept to designate a whole epoch, has been used so variously as to have lost a good deal of analytic utility. In one sense, capitalism describes a world system of exchange and accumulation that includes forms of production that can only very questionably be called capitalist—e.g., crops produced by various forms of coerced labor (see Wallerstein, 1974a, 1974b; Frank, 1967). In another sense, capitalism designates a labor process in which workers are progressively divested of skills and of control over the pace and intensity of work, in which respect there are similarities between advanced capitalist and socialist countries (see Braverman, 1974). Such usages are confusing as a basis for categorizing production relations. The most valid use of the term would apply to production by workers who do not control the means of production and have only their labor power to sell; but today this definition would apply to a variety of forms of social relations of production with important differences. Similarly, the notion of a single homogeneous working class, which appeared to be obvious from Engels' survey of the British working class of 1846, takes no account of the social consequences of the more complex mix of modes of social relations of production that has emerged through intervening history (Engels, 1969).

Hegemony

The problem of hegemony arises at the three levels of (1) the social relations of production, (2) the social formation, and (3) the structure of world order. Hegemonic and nonhegemonic forms can exist at each of these levels, hegemony being the critical factor in stabilizing power relations and legitimizing authority.

HEGEMONY IN THE SOCIAL RELATIONS OF PRODUCTION

Hegemony in production relations in modern industry is akin to what Ralf Dahrendorf (1965) calls the institutionalization of conflict, but the concept applies also to preindustrial production relations. Where peasants tacitly accept the authority of the lord, whether as of divine right or as flowing from reciprocal obligations (production in return for protection), the hegemony of lords is established; just as participation by trade unionists in collective bargaining and grievance handling procedures implies acquiescence in an industrial hegemony.

The first of these forms of hegemony is now in decay in virtually every place where peasant-lord production relations still exist. The rates of extraction from the peasantry characteristic of such production relations are no longer accepted anywhere by peasants either as justified by the performance of some function or as just inevitable—as the prevalence of violence on the part of both landlords and peasants testifies.

Industrial hegemony emerged in northern Europe and North America from the late nineteenth century with the growth of a strong employer class and of strong trade unions of established workers, which together shaped a broadly accepted authority structure in industry. In southern Europe, by contrast, the same evolution did not occur: late industrialization, a relatively weak employer class, and a nonestablished labor force only recently and partially removed from its rural background, generated a more explosive challenge to employer authority, which characteristically took the form of syndicalism—ultimately a demand for worker control rather than participation in a more consensual labor-management relationship. Trade unionism is indicative of hegemonic industrial production relations, and syndicalism of nonhegemonic ones.

Claus Offe, in his demystification of the achievement principle, exposed the ideological mechanisms of hegemony in production. The achievement principle supposes that individual status and rewards are related to objectively measurable individual merit and contribution to the production process. The physical organization of modern industrial work has, however, progressively eliminated the possibility of measuring an individual's substantive contribution to the technical fulfillment of tasks; in effect, task fulfillment is more attributable to organizations than to individuals. The achievement principle is applied in practice, however, in recruitment and promotion so as to reward not so much technical performance as demonstrated acceptance by the individual of the organization's power relations. As ideology, therefore, it performs the functions of reinforcing the existing authority structure and eliminating any attraction to alternative social orders.[5]

HEGEMONY IN THE SOCIAL FORMATION

The locus of hegemony at the level of the social formation lies in the relationship of state to civil society. Two conditions for hegemony at this level may be stated as: (1) a broad coalition of classes under the leadership of one class that is able to make concessions adequate to maintain support or acquiescence from subordinate classes in the coalition, and (2) a state that acts to consolidate this class coalition and to promote the mode of social relations of production consistent with the continuing dominance of the leading class.

Historically known hegemonies have been led by industrial capitalist classes that have made concessions incrementally to secure the acquiescence of established workers, tending toward social democracy. The concept also includes (as historical speculation) the possibility, implicit in Gramsci's thought, of a hegemonic industrial working class leading a broader consensual social grouping including petty bourgeoisie and peasantry, i.e., an alternative to the dictatorship of the proletariat. It also can include a form (some historical instances of which are already apparent) of leadership by a "state class."[6] The hegemonic coalition does not need to extend to all social classes (or quasi-classes, i.e., social groups that have a distinctive relationship to production but lack a full consciousness of their position), but only to those capable of disturbing the social equilibrium. For example, certain marginalized groups of poor people have been excluded from the coalition by the separation of their interests from those of subordinate classes in the coalition, e.g., established workers. Furthermore, the state is not necessarily the emanation or agency of the hegemonic coalition, but its action must be functional to the maintenance of the system in which these groups are dominant. In hegemony, political action tacitly accepts social power as its limit.

In the hegemonic state, there is such a high degree of interpenetration of state and civil society that the distinction between the two ceases to reflect a distinction among real entities even though it may retain some analytical usefulness. The interpenetration of state and civil society can take a variety of forms: in Scandinavian countries, employer and trade union organizations manage the labor market and its institutions; in Switzerland, senior civil servants represent major interest groups within government administration; in France, the planning commissariat brings industry and some union representatives into a policy-making and policy-implementing relationship with state officials, and so on.

Forms such as these in which civil society becomes the framework for state behavior contrast with nonhegemonic attempts to mold and control civil society through the instrumentality of the state. These latter attempts arise in a context of fragmentation and conflict within civil society, e.g., where none of the coexisting modes of social relations of production have become dominant in relation to the others, or where the controlling group of a dominant mode remains too weak to build an effective coalition with other controlling groups (e.g., industrial employers with landowners), or where such a coalition has been unable to secure the acquiescence of subordinate classes (e.g., of established industrial workers and petty bourgeois elements, or peasants). In such conditions, controlling groups tend to look to the state to impose the order they have been unable to secure by virtue of their social power. Marx's analysis of the Bonapartist regime in *The Thirteenth Brumaire of Louis Bonaparte* is the classic portrayal of a nonhegemonic social formation. The coming of fascist rule in the wake of the labor upheavals in the north of Italy in the 1920s was a forerunner of a type of nonhegemonic social formation prevalent in the contemporary world most notably among military-bureaucratic regimes in late industrializing countries.

Since hegemony is rule by consent, it is achieved principally in the cultural and ideological realm through the spread of ways of thinking about work and authority, and patterns of behavior that conform to and strengthen the structure of social power. The coercive power of the state remains latent, since consensus renders its use very largely unnecessary.

HEGEMONY IN THE WORLD ORDER

Hegemony at the world order level is more complex in that it encompasses both of the other levels, i.e., social classes formed in the production process and states. There is, of course, a current meaning of the term "hegemony" in world affairs that refers exclusively to states and means the dominance of a powerful state over other states. This usage has little in common with the meaning of "hegemony" presented here and, in the context of this discussion, more conveniently replaced by the term "dominance." A state that maintained and extended its power through aggressive military and economic policies clearly exploitative of weaker states would not be hegemonic in the sense used here, though it might be or become dominant.

To be hegemonic, a state would have to found and protect a world order that was universal in conception, i.e., not an order directly expressing the interest of one state but an order that most other states could find compatible with their interests given their different levels of power and lesser abilities to change the order. The less powerful states could live with the order even if they could not change it. Such an order could hardly be conceived in interstate terms alone, for this would emphasize oppositions of state interests, but would most likely give prominence to opportunities for the forces of civil society to operate on the world scale. The hegemonic concept of world order is founded not only upon the regulation of interstate conflict, but also upon a globally conceived civil society, i.e., a mode of production of a global extent which brings about links among the social classes of different countries. The global structuring of social forces shapes the different forms of state, while states in turn influence the evolution of the regulatory pattern of the global hegemony. States appear in this perspective as mediating forces between local configurations of social forces and the global hegemony which itself influences the evolution of these social forces.

The conditions for hegemony in world order thus include (1) a globally dominant mode of production; (2) a dominant state (or conceivably dominant group of states acting in concert) which maintains and facilitates the expansion of that mode of production; and (3) a normative and institutional component which lays down general rules of behavior for states and the forces of civil society that act across state boundaries—rules which are also supportive of the dominant mode of production.

During the twentieth century, this last condition has been expressed through international organization, i.e., through the rules and procedures institutionalized by agreement among states which provide a framework for the actions both of states and of private agencies such as multinational corporations. The international organization of economic relations—the Bretton Woods system of the post-World War II period and whatever may be contrived to replace it—is of central importance.

Hegemony prevailed in world order under British leadership at mid-nineteenth century and under U.S. leadership at mid-twentieth. In both periods, a world economy embodying a dominant and expansive mode of production was organized with a dominant state as guarantor. The role of formal international institutions was more prominent in the second of these periods, whereas in the first the regulatory functions in the world economy were carried out mainly by the financial management of the City of London. The forms of control exercised by the dominant class changed as between the two hegemonies: the finance capital of the first period was, in the second, supplemented by managerial controls through the internationalizing of production.

The mid-nineteenth-century hegemony was followed by a nonhegemonic period of great power conflict and mercantilist fragmentation of the world economy as rising national economies challenged British supremacy. National states closely associated with national capitalist classes and national labor aristocracies confronted one another in the rivalry of imperialist expansion and ultimately in world war. The substance of a global civil society was severely shaken if not entirely demolished. A serious question is now again posed as to whether an analogous transformation of world order is to be anticipated in a phase of lesser U.S. world power.

During the 1970s, a new crisis of world order has seemed to open. The full nature of the crisis has been understood in very different ways with very different implications, though most agree that it is a crisis of world economy. At one extreme, it is perceived as reducible to an energy crisis and to making the adjustments consequent upon it—in effect, to an *accident de parcours*—a major disturbance but not a fundamental shift of direction. At the other, it is seen as the crisis point of world capitalism, presaging a secular decline and struggle of growing intensity over the world product.

Estimating probabilities as to what new structures of world order will emerge out of the crisis depends upon one's assessment of the nature and gravity of the crisis. Very broadly, three tendencies of structural development are each supported by different constellations of forces. One possibility is that the crisis could lead to a reconstruction of world hegemony, whether through a renascent U.S. power or, as envisaged by the Trilateral Commission, through collective management of the world economy by an inner group composed of the United States, the Federal Republic of Germany, and Japan with the support of other industrialized countries and the cooptation of some oil-rich and emerging industrial powers. Another is that the crisis could lead to a nonhegemonic situation of conflicting big powers and their spheres of influence. The debate over the New International Economic Order (capitalized in United Nations usage as an aspiration rather than a reality) is another manifestation of the crisis foreshadowing a third and more remote possibility. With the revival of more overtly conflicting interests among core countries, the peripheral countries have been able to muster a certain coherence and articulate a common set of demands (see Cox, 1979).

We have considered the problem of hegemony at three levels—production relations, social formation, and world order. These levels are, of course, interrelated, and current literature indicates that there are important differences of opinion as to which level should be regarded as determining. At one extreme is Wallerstein's world systems approach, the weakness of which lies in an unwitting structural-functional homeostasis that may underestimate the potential for transformation arising out of both the contradictions inherent in the articulation of different modes of production and the conflicts among social formations.[7] Another approach argues that foreign economic policies of the major capitalist states are the critical factors which determine the nature of the world economic order. Other states are confronted with the choice either of adapting to this order or, if they can, withdrawing from it (see Katzenstein, 1978). While not ruling out the efficacy of social and economic forces in civil society, the latter approach has tended to see these forces as a merely negative factor, a constraint on state policies which might introduce a certain incoherence into state behavior; it has not recognized the domain of production as an arena of power relations affecting both state behavior and world order.

The Internationalization of Production

Taking production as a point of departure can lead directly to some hypotheses both about the nature of the world economy as a whole and about the forms and behavior of states.

The dominant tendency at the world economy level has been the internationalizing of production, i.e., the organization of production on a world scale through industrial systems that transcend national boundaries (a computer industry, auto industry, or agribusiness structured on a world scale). This began well before the onset of the world crisis of the 1970s, during the expansive hegemony of the post-World War II period, and has continued through the period of crisis.

The internationalization of production should not be simply equated with the expansion of multinational corporations. Direct investment and hierarchical management structures have been very important mechanisms in the process, but its continuation is not necessarily dependent upon these same mechanisms. Technological dependency, for example, and the phenomenon of "truncated" national industries dependent upon critical inputs from abroad, can take other forms. Indeed, the multinationals may have passed the peak of their power during the late 1960s although the internationalization of production was not for that reason reversed.

International production has globalized a specific pattern of social relations of production that can be represented by a core-periphery model in both geographical and occupational terms. In geographical terms, the controlling functions of overall planning, investment decisions, research and development, and the determination of what is to be produced and how it is to be marketed are concentrated at the home-base core, while physical production is increasingly dispersed in peripheral locations including Third World countries. In occupational terms, core and peripheral status depends upon how closely the job is integrated and stabilized within the international productive system, so that there are some core workers in peripheral locations and some peripheral workers with core country operations. There is a core of skilled and very highly skilled workers and managers, whose personal interests are closely tied with those of the international industry through forms of enterprise corporatism. This occupational core is articulated with semiskilled production workers and smaller enterprise subcontracting and support suppliers and services, all engaged in a more precarious employment dependent upon fluctuations in economic activity.

The impact of the internationalizing of production on less developed countries has also had the effect of accelerating the marginalization of some traditional and mainly agricultural activities, contributing to the rural exodus of those displaced by agricultural "modernization." The internationalizing of production has thus been a potent force strengthening existing tendencies toward a triple-level labor force: an inner core of labor aristocrats, a middle layer of precariously employed semiskilled, and a bottom layer of the marginalized who are either unemployed or who scrounge a meagre survival from occasional and often parasitical activities.

The internationalizing process has produced political responses in both core and periphery countries, responses stimulated by the social consequences of the restructuring of the labor force and by the power implications of control over the industrialization process. In the core countries, the principal concern has been with loss of jobs, and this has led to demands for protectionism, for some control over exports of capital and technology, and for "reindustrialization" policies. Political conflict in these countries has tended to align forces, including both capital and labor, tied respectively to internationally oriented and locally based activities. In periphery countries, political elites have tried both to control the consequences of social restructuring (in particular, to organize the new industrial workers and prevent trouble among the marginals) and to gain more influence over production processes while at the same time encouraging the transfer of capital and technology. They have focused particularly on the way production in their countries articulates with the internationalization process through methods including nationalizations, state corporatism, and autocentric planning.

The internationalization of production has so far best been analyzed in terms of the material organization of production. Raymond Vernon's (1971, 1966) product life-cycle theory explains something of the international circulation of capital and technology: the concentration of innovation and control of the production process in core areas and the movement of standardized production and mature technology to the peripheries. Christian Palloix, acknowledging the usefulness of Vernon's picture of the process, describes it in terms of a hierarchy of producer goods, intermediate goods, and consumer goods sectors. Peripheral social formations are dependent on core formations for their producer goods, and an increasing number of countries (from France to Mexico) fall into an intermediate category, being dependent upon external sources for the most sophisticated technologies, while at the same time supplying technology to more peripheral countries (see Palloix, 1978, 1975). Bernadette Madeuf and Charles-Albert Michalet (1978) also focus on technological dependence, pointing to the inadequacy of neoclassical economics which tries to treat technology either as a factor of production or as a commodity, whereas they argue that technology must be understood as a form of control or of power. They propose that a study of the production and circulation of technology be made the basis for analysis of the emerging world economic system, for understanding, as they put it, "the logic of capital," (Madeuf and Michalet, 1978: 279).

These several approaches all serve to define the production process as a global power system expressed in technological terms. Madeuf and Michalet, by defining technology as a social process—"the social process whereby knowledge is integrated in production"—most explicitly avoid the trap of technological determinism and open the way toward exploring how social relations shape the development and choice of technology.

The social relations approach to the production process is as valid as that through the material or technological organization of production. The development of industrial production in Europe, North America, and Japan took place in the context of a division of the labor force into two categories: one of established workers who acquired a more stable status in employment, higher skills, and greater expectations of career development than the other category of nonestablished workers. Trade unionism and collective bargaining strengthened the position of the first and became an element in their established status, but had far less impact on the nonestablished workers. These latter were in general outside the scope of trade union activity, and their protection was directly dependent upon the state through the minimum wage, social welfare, and the like.[8] Following World War II, the social relations of production of established workers took several forms: a union-management bipartite bargaining relationship in North America, tripartism in which government played a greater role in Western Europe, enterprise corporatism in Japan with individual managements organizing a tutelary corporate welfare for employees while working closely with government in managing the economy.

For a long time, the nonestablished worker appeared as a historical residue of the smaller-scale industrialism of the nineteenth century, the enterprise labor market where workers offered their roughly equivalent labor powers to employers and benefited from no significant institutional protection whether by unions or the state. The production process developed through capital deepening, where employers continually substituted capital for labor as the relative cost of established labor increased.

Another complementary process has become observable particularly in the decades following World War II. Technology has been continually adapted to the existence of a supply of nonestablished labor so as to make possible the employment of an increasing proportion of the semiskilled. By fragmenting tasks into the simplest operations and combining them in sophisticated technical systems, such technology removed the vestiges of control over the pace and intensity of work from workers and concentrated control with management. Management has increased its power over established workers by extending enterprise corporatist practices among them, and also over the growing proportion of nonestablished workers who lack effective union protection in particular and social power in general. In this respect, the social relations of production have been as much a determinant of technology as technology of the social relations of production.

The supply of nonestablished labor is greatest in peripheral social formations. In Western Europe, the initial tapping of this pool took the form of importing migrant labor from the Mediterranean rim. Japan rejected immigration from the outset and began to transfer labor-intensive components of its industrial systems to its periphery (South Korea, Taiwan, the Philippines, and elsewhere). U.S.-based industries similarly shifted into export manufacturing enclaves in poorer countries. The transfer of industry rather than the transfer of population has become the principal method of utilizing this labor supply.

The supply meanwhile has continually increased as a result of the impact of the internationalization process on agriculture in poor countries which takes broadly two forms: the appropriation of extensive landholdings by multinational agribusiness for the growing of export crops; and the introduction of new technologies (the Green Revolution) which have also encouraged concentration of holdings on a smaller scale and production for distant markets. The former is a case of multinational management control, and the latter of independent owners who become dependent upon inputs of fertilizers and fuel for irrigation pumps, both outputs of internationalized industries (petroleum and fertilizer industries which are linked with each other). These changes in agricultural production reduce the manpower employed on the land and undermine further the traditional peasant-lord and subsistence modes of production, driving the excess population into the primitive labor market. This in turn acts as a disciplinary pressure on the nonestablished workers employed in the new peripheral manufacturing industries. At the same time, many poor and essentially agricultural countries and their non-established workers in particular, have become dependent upon imported food.

Social and Political Responses

The internationalization of production generates conflicting forces, some advancing its movement, others reacting against it, still others seeking to use it but to turn it to their own purposes. Since these diverse forces, all of which are traceable to a single matrix, are currently developing through time, it is not possible to pronounce definitively upon them. They may be considered as vectors, identified for heuristic purposes as elements for the analysis of specific national or sectoral problems. They are presented here as such, some arising at the level of world order, some within core social formations, and some in peripheral formations. In view of the necessarily summary manner in which these forces are identified, it is convenient to treat them as a series of numbered propositions.

GLOBAL LEVEL FORCES

1. The driving social force in the internationalizing of production is a transnational managerial class. The term class should not be used lightly. In this context it implies a dominant role (as a *managerial* class) in an internationalized production process, a consciousness of a commonality of purpose among its members even though their specific and immediate corporate interests may diverge, mechanisms for reproduction of the class, and a common ideological perspective accompanied by organs for common action. All of these elements are in fact present, although in different degrees of strength. The transnational managerial class exists, even though in some places and at some times it may be less influential than national capitalisms. Its personnel includes not only the top executives of multinational corporations but also national government and international organization personnel involved in creating the environment propitious for the expansion of international production. It may also include some coopted local business people who have found a symbiotic relationship with international production. The transnational class is predominantly, though not exclusively, centered in the United States, and is the carrier and transmitter of cultural values of unmistakably U.S. origin, yet it has a clear sense of its international role and clearly distinguishes its goals from those of purely national capital. Business schools with international and often itinerant programs recruit and socialize new class members. Informal networks of professional idealogues (some

economists, organization theorists, psychologists, and political scientists) have become the organic intellectuals of this class. More formal organizations like the Trilateral Commission, the Bilderburg conferences, and the Club of Rome develop policies and channels of influence into national government and business milieux.

2. The leading members of this transnational managerial class act to encourage a political alignment of core states—the United States, the Federal Republic of Germany, and Japan in the lead—in support of reconstituting an open world economy. The specific policies advocated vary with the circumstances. The major thrust has been monetarism which gives priority to stabilizing the value of major currencies and their mutual relationships as essential to a predictable environment for international investment and exchange. However, as monetarism engenders levels of unemployment which threaten political stability in some core countries (Britain, for instance) it is likely that economic policy will shift in favor of some stimulative measures for economic recovery. It is not so much the specific content of policy at any one time as the coordination of policy (and particularly the international coordination among major core countries) with the goal of an open world economy in mind which is the key factor.

3. Insofar as this class succeeds, its global hegemony is institutionalized through international organizations which reflect the predominant influence of the guarantor states, i.e., the Trilateral group of countries. The major international economic institutions have reflected this pattern of influence—the IMF, IBRD, and GATT. To become hegemonic, however, this dominant influence must be exerted in a form acceptable to other states and in a universal form. Thus some wider opening in the formal participation processes of these institutions is taking place, and the policies consistent with hegemony are likely to be packaged in symbolically universal form as a "new" or "reconstructed" international economic order.

4. The institutions of this world order in the process of reconstruction also take steps to counteract the threat to this emergent world order from the marginalizing of population and from dependency on imported foods in poor countries. This takes the form of promoting a "self-reliance" sector in which the poor outside of the internationalized production sector are encouraged to grow enough food to feed themselves as well as to practice birth limitation so as to keep their numbers down. The institutions of the world economy thereby recognize a division of the world system into integrated and marginalized sectors and take steps to control and limit the growth of the latter while promoting the development of the former. This proves, however, to be a labor of Sisyphus, since the very process of expansion of international production generates more marginality.

5. The more consensual welfare aspects of hegemonic policy are enacted through and are legitimated by international institutions. The more directly

regressive measures which become necessary when welfare measures are insufficient to dampen revolt are carried out by the dominant state or states through military and counterinsurgency aid. A capacity for riot control underpins global welfare policy.

6. A variety of disparate social forces which perceive relative disadvantage in the continuing internationalizing of production seek to oppose this tendency. Since this opposition is fragmented it cannot act effectively at the global level where transnational managerial class policy is formulated. It may, however, be able to wield greater influence upon the policies of particular states. Where such social forces achieve some cohesion at the national level, their basis of cooperation is neomercantilism. Were these opposition forces to outweigh the transnational managerial class, then the structure of world order would move in a nonhegemonic direction toward the formation of economic blocs or spheres of influence each striving toward a relative autarky.

CORE SOCIAL FORMATIONS

7. In the thinking of the transnational managerial class, the function of states is to adapt the internal economies of countries to the development of the world economy so as to maintain conditions in the world economy favorable to continuing capital accumulation. This involves what has been called the "internationalizing of the state" (see Palloix, 1975: 81-82) which gives preeminence within the state to those organs administering the key linkages between world and domestic economies. These are principally the ministries of finance as well as offices of heads of state and of government. These organs participate in the international organization consensus about policies appropriate for the world economy and apply that consensus in the development of national economic policy.

8. Internally, the critical policy relationship is between these state organs and the managements of the major corporations which account for a large proportion of total production and income. Established employees of these corporations and of the state are linked in a dependent relationship to this policy axis through enterprise corporatism. Nonestablished workers, small businesses, the self-employed, and the unemployed are in more vulnerable positions. The core state acts toward them in much the same way as the world structure acts toward the marginals in the periphery, with a combination of welfare and riot control, placing the accent by preference on the former while being ready to use the latter.

9. A critical contradiction arises when the requirements of adaptation to the world economy (e.g., "stabilization" measures to reduce inflationary pressures by controlling government expenditures and wage levels) worsen the relative position of workers and in particular, of some state employees,

and undermine state services that make the prevailing hegemony tolerable to nonestablished workers and marginals (educational services that hold forth the possibility of access to established status and various transfer payments). Priority to the accumulation function of the state undermines its legitimation function and thus weakens hegemony (see O'Connor, 1973).

10. An attempt to reconstruct a new hegemony within the core formation could take the form of a corporative state. Tripartism would then likely become the dominant mode of social relations of production, and would bring organized business and established labor interests into close relationship with the state—indeed, would resolve them into an enlarged view of the state—for the purpose of managing the national economy. This would entail rallying the support of social forces opposed to the transnational managerial class hegemony, and would give domestic interests priority over world economy requisites by means of neomercantilist policies.

PERIPHERAL SOCIAL FORMATIONS

11. The first impact of international production in peripheral formations took the form of creating externally oriented enclaves of production into which were transplanted modes of social relations of production prevalent in core areas. Unorganized and unskilled labor was employed on a turnover basis as required (the enterprise labor market mode). Enterprise corporatism which grants a more stable and relatively privileged status to some employees (usually those who have been given more training) was also introduced. The impact of internationalized production, especially on agriculture, then often put pressure upon surviving peasant-lord and subsistence modes of social relations of production and drove an increasing proportion of the population into the precariously marginalized existence of the primitive labor market (typically, casual services and unemployment among shanty-town dwellers). The internationalizing of production thus accelerated a restructuring of the labor force and social disorganization.

12. Civil society in peripheral formations is typically fractured and nonhegemonic: formerly dominant classes, e.g., landowners, have lost their hegemony and newer ones are often culturally alien and recently established. The state, lacking a basis of social consensus, is relatively more coercive, a propensity enhanced by the rising social tensions consequential upon the internationalizing of production. At the initial stage of this process, the state sometimes acted as a police force on behalf of foreign investors (the "banana republic" model), but the very exercise of coercive functions gave those groups which identified with the state (the military and the state bureaucracy) a sense of their own autonomy and power in relation to civil society and of their potential for wresting control over production. One can speak of a state class in such peripheral formations where groups, most often

of petty bourgeois origin, coalesce and through their control of the state acquire either direct control over production (through nationalization) or indirect control (through their leverage with foreign investors over the terms and conditions for investment and production).

13. State corporatism is the mode through which the new state class establishes its control: regulating employers and gaining bargaining strength vis-à-vis foreign investors, displacing the enterprise corporatism of the enclave industries with government-controlled worker organizations, and applying the coercive apparatus of the state against the burgeoning threat of disorder from the marginal population.

14. There is, of course, considerable structural variety among peripheral formations so that all cannot be reduced to a single model or a single predictable evolution. The nonhegemonic condition of civil society is, however, fairly general, and the prospect of the emergence of a hegemony a crucial question. The key factors affecting this prospect are the relative social powers of the state class, of the newly mobilized industrial workers, and of the marginals; the forms of consciousness that develop in each of these social groups; and the relationships or class alliances possible among them.

15. Three distinct strategies are possible for the state class: (a) Use state corporatism as a means of organizing the links between the peripheral formation and the world economy. State corporatism gives the local political leaders more control over local manufacturing and extractive industries and enables them to bargain more effectively with the foreign control points of the international industries into which they link. It is accompanied by an institutionalizing of coercion (police, paramilitary organizations, counterinsurgency forces, and unofficial "death squads") which represses marginals and others disaffected by the social consequences of internationalized production. This coercive apparatus is the national complement to international program of support for the "self-reliance" sector; (b) Opt out of the world economy and sever links with internationalized production and pursue autocentric development. This choice would require mobilization of broad popular support through a communal mode of social relations of production on the Maoist model. It would also imply the existence of conditions of territorial and population size, abundance of developable natural resources, and, above all, effective mass political organization not present in most peripheral countries; (c) Adopt a "dialectic of dependency" (the term is that of André Tiano [1977]) in which dependency relations with core formations are managed so as to acquire inputs to the peripheral economy which help serve endogenously determined development goals. This strategy involves a fine balance between tolerance of inequalities inherent in dependency, e.g., regional, sectoral, and occupational income disparities, and progress toward eliminating marginality and toward involving the whole population more

equitably in the development effort which would be essential to maintaining internal political support for the strategy.

16. The choice among these strategies will be determined by the pressures upon the state class from the other critical social groups and not solely by the consciousness of the state class (see Elsenhans, n.d.; Cox, 1979). Insofar as the state corporatist framework encourages a corporatist form of consciousness among newly mobilized industrial workers which limits their perspectives to a concern with their own status and welfare, the fractured, nonhegemonic condition of civil society is likely to remain. However, if these workers were to develop a broader class consciousness with, in addition, a sense of solidarity with the marginals of the primitive labor market (from which they themselves came) and of alliance with the rural population, then a prospect would open up for the formation of a new hegemonic coalition. While a worker-led coalition is conceivable, it seems more likely, given the recent origins of the working classes in most peripheral formations, that the coalition would be led by radical elements of the state class. This leadership would be constantly susceptible to the temptation to revert to the state corporatist form of linkage with the world economy, to compromise the locally determined development goals, and to encourage a degree of demobilization of popular pressure. All this would make the task of governing easier and the rewards of office greater. The state class could be kept on the "dialectic of dependency" course only by continuing political mobilization which would maintain pressure from workers' and peasants' milieux. The immature character of class consciousness and organization among the new working classes of peripheral formations renders them susceptible to populist and religious enthusiasms. This opens an opportunity for political opportunists to manipulate workers and marginals. It may also divert revolutionary energies into obscurantism and anachronistic resurrections which have no coherent connection with the organization of production and create obstacles for the consistent conduct of any development strategy. In the long run, therefore, the most critical factor influencing the future course of the peripheral formations may be whether or when a rational political consciousness emerges among the new working classes. Experience suggests that this is most likely with the growth of effective political organization through prolonged struggle.

NOTES

1. This article derives from a study being pursued jointly with Jeffrey Harrod. Earlier publications which give a sequence of views on our work include Cox (1977b, 1973, 1971) and Cox and Harrod et al. (1972).

2. Bendix's use of contrast concepts of limited historical applicability is in his article "The comparative analysis of historical change," in Argyle et al. (1967). Bendix has summarized

Max Weber's method in the following terms which apply to the notion of modes of social relations of production suggested here: "Such [hypotheses concerning causal relationships] are functional, in that they make assertions about what types of responses go with what conditions of human existence. They are also structural, in that they relate responses to the social and political environment of large numbers of men rather than impute them to their attitudes or motivations. Finally, these explanations involve comparisons in that they examine the same type of human experience . . . in divergent historical settings and hence lead to systematic contrasts of the relations between these settings and the responses men have made to them" (Bendix, 1962: 271).

3. On the notion of "articulation" see especially Foster-Carter (1978).

4. Brucan (1977) discusses the simultaneous validity of both lines of cleavage: classes and states. Skocpol (1979) also deals with this theme.

5. Offe (1976) does not expressly refer to the concept of hegemony.

6. Hartmut Elsenhans has used the notion of the "state class" in an unpublished manuscript (n.d.). On the application of this concept, see Cox (1979).

7. See in particular the sympathetic critique of Wallerstein's *Modern World System* by Theda Skocpol, "Wallerstein's world capitalist system: a theoretical and historical critique." *American Journal of Sociology* 82, 5: 1075-1090.

8. Some American labor economists have distinguished essentially the same cleavage in terms of primary and secondary labor markets. I have discussed this elsewhere (Cox, 1978, 1977a).

REFERENCES

ARGYLE, M. et al. (1967) Social Theory and Economic Change. London: Tavistock.

BACHRACH, P. and M. BARATZ (1962) "The two faces of power." American Political Science Review 56 (December).

BENDIX, R. (1962) Max Weber. An Intellectual Portrait. New York: Doubleday.

BRAVERMAN, H. (1974) Labor and Monopoly Capital. New York: Monthly Review.

BRUCAN, S. (1977) "Power and conflict." International Social Science Journal 29, 1.

COX, R. W. (1979) "Ideologies and the New International Economic Order: reflections on some recent literature." International Organization 33, 2.

———— (1978) "Labor and employment in the late twentieth century," in R. St. J. MacDonald et al. The International Law and Policy of Human Welfare. Alphen aan den Rign: Sijthoff & Noordhoff.

———— (1977a) "Labor and hegemony." International Organization 31, 3.

———— (1977b) "Pour une étude prospective des relations de production." Sociologie du Travail, No. 2.

———— (1973) "World systems of labor and production." Presented to the IXth World Congress of the International Political Science Association, Montreal.

———— (1971) "Approaches to a futurology of industrial relations." Bulletin of the International Institute for Labour Studies (Geneva), No. 8.

———— and J. HARROD et al. (1972) Future Industrial Relations. An Interim Report. Geneva: I.I.L.S.

DAHRENDORF, R. (1965) Class and Class Conflict Industrial Society. Stanford, CA: Stanford University Press.

ELSEHANS, H. (n.d.) "The state class in the Third World: for a new conceptualization of aspects of periphery modes of production." (unpublished manuscript)

ENGELS, F. (1969) The Condition of the Working Class in England. London: Granada.

FOSTER-CARTER, A. (1978) "The modes of production controversy." New Left Review 107 (Jan.-Feb.).

FRANK, A.G. (1967) Capitalism and Underdevelopment in Latin America. New York: Monthly Review.

GILPIN, R. (1975) U.S. Power and the Multinational Corporation. New York: Basic Books.

GRAMSCI, A. (1975) Quaderni del carcere. Turin: Istituto Gramsci.

HOARE, Q. and G. N. SMITH [eds.] (1971) Selections from the Prison Notebooks. New York: International Publishers.

KATZENSTEIN, P. [ed.] (1978) Between Power and Plenty. Foreign Economic Policies of Advanced Industrial States. Madison: University of Wisconsin Press.

KRASNER, S. (1978) Defending the National Interest. Raw Materials Investments and U.S. Foreign Policy. Princeton, NJ: Princeton University Press.

MADEUF, B. and C.-A. MICHALET (1978) "A new approach to international economics." International Social Science Journal 30, 2.

O'CONNOR, J. (1973) The Fiscal Crisis of the State. New York: St. Martin's.

OFFE, C. (1976) Industry and Inequality, trans. J.Wickham. London: Edward Arnold.

PALLOIX, C. (1978) Travail et production. Paris: Maspero.

——— (1975) L'internationalisation du capital. Paris: Maspero.

POLANYI, K. (1957) [1944] The Great Transformation: The Political And Economic Origins of Our Time. Boston: Beacon Press.

SKOCPOL, T. (1979) States and Social Revolutions. Cambridge: Cambridge University Press.

TIANO, A. (1977) La dialectique de la dépendence.Analyse des relations économiques et financières internationales. Paris: Presses universitaires de France.

VERNON, R. (1971) Sovereignty at Bay. New York: Basic Books.

——— (1966) "International investment and international trade in the product cycle." Quarterly Journal of Economics 80.

WALLERSTEIN, I. (1974a) "The rise and future demise of the world capitalist system: concepts for comparative analysis." Comparative Studies in Society and History 16, 4.

——— (1974b) The Modern World System. Capitalist Agriculture and the Origins of the World-Economy in the Sixteenth Century. New York: Academic.

CHAPTER 3

WHY A NIEO?
The View from the Third World

ROBERT S. JORDAN

The New International Economic Order (NIEO) has been a source of considerable international discussion and not a small bit of concern. Some governments view the NIEO as the embodiment of economic justice, while others dismiss it as "demands for everything from those who have nothing." For example, within the United Nations, many programs and activities are now, *pro forma,* linked to and justified by their connection to the NIEO. Even though the developing states have at times hailed the NIEO as being essential to the creation of a global economy based on equity, in the West and particularly in the United States, the NIEO has aroused a suspicion that it attacks the foundations upon which the economic wealth and social achievements of the West are based. The truth doubtless lies somewhere in between.

The purpose of this chapter is to explore and to analyze the nature of the NIEO, particularly as it is viewed by the Third World.[1] Such an inquiry raises a number of fundamental questions concerning the NIEO and its implications for international economic relations in the 1980s. First, who stands to benefit from the NIEO? Will it, as the Third World contends, benefit the global community as a whole by providing stability and prosper-

AUTHOR'S NOTE: I am indebted to Parley Newman, a former graduate student at Columbia University and a research assistant at the United Nations Institute for Training and Research (UNITAR) and to Judith Wilkinson, a research assistant at the University of New Orleans, for assistance in preparing this manuscript for publication. Research on this subject was initially carried out while the author was a professional staff member of UNITAR. The opportunity to do so was made possible through the encouragement and support of the executive director, Dr. Davidson Nicol, for which the author is grateful. Neither UNITAR nor any other United Nations body is responsible for the contents of this chapter.

ity through the introduction of a new set of equitable economic relationships? Or will it, as many of the industrial states fear, benefit the developing states at the formers' expense? Another important question is: Will the NIEO benefit *all* developing states, or only those that are producers of commodities and raw materials? What about the "most seriously affected" (MSA) developing states that are deprived either of the manufacturing capacity or the raw materials that they need to generate the foreign currency to pay for their imports, especially oil?[2]

One central aspect of development lies in meeting basic human needs, but it is far from evident that the NIEO is actually geared to the needs of the poorest segment of the population. One might argue that, as the rich states have gotten richer and the poor states have gotten relatively poorer, within the poorer states the rich elites have gotten richer and the poor people have become even more impoverished. And thus one must ask whether or not the poorest individuals can in fact be reached: Will the NIEO benefit these disadvantaged individuals or rather only states as collective institutions ruled by privileged elites (Mathieson, 1981)?

A second set of questions has to do with the goals and values to be pursued at the global level. Will the NIEO operate as a genuine means of economic and social development, or will it become a global welfare system? Upon retiring as president of the World Bank in 1981, Robert McNamara stated that changing economic relations offered "a plus-sum game as part of which [the developed states] can move to assist the developing countries to achieve economic and social advance with benefits to both the developing and industrial countries" (Silk, 1981: 16). Also, will the NIEO operate on the basis of relatively free or nonrestrictive trade practices, or on some other basis? This is an important question not only in terms of productivity, return on investments, and techniques of management, but also in terms of fundamental economic values. A related problem is the uncertain impact the NIEO will have on traditional societies; in some cases, difficult choices may emerge between the values of modernization and traditionalism. And finally, there is the problem of human rights (both political and economic), of whether or not they can and should be promoted through the NIEO.

A third set of questions has to do with the appropriateness of various means to adjust or resolve economic or trade problems. Are interstate negotiation and dialogue the only tools? If not, what other innovative means are available and how may they be applied? If so, which forums are most suitable for their effective use? Or perhaps these categories themselves are too broad and need further refinement. Does the United Nations, through the General Assembly and the Economic and Social Council, have the major role to play in this regard, or should alternative avenues be pursued as well? For example, although developing countries are members of such UN-related bodies as the General Agreement on Tariffs and Trade (GATT) and the International Monetary Fund (IMF), they feel relatively powerless in their ability to influence the policies of these bodies.

As the Director-General of the OPEC Fund for International Development put it in an article in *South:*

> There also exists a need for international public institutions such as the IMF to review the conditional nature of their loans, so that tens of billions of available dollars may be tapped for the benefit of the developing countries. The access to greater resources on more flexible terms through existing institutions should take priority over the continuous demands for the creation of new agencies. At the same time, the developing countries could themselves create collective mechanisms for guaranteeing their foreign debts, such as joint loan corporations or institutionalised swap arrangements [1980: 17].

In fact, at the Tokyo round of GATT negotiations, the participating Third World countries refused to agree with the results because they felt that the benefits to them did not justify "legitimizing" the outcome in this way (World Bank, 1980: 19-21).

Is there in fact a difference between dialogue and negotiation? If so, what are the results to be expected of each in terms of progress and commitment, and which should therefore be followed? And finally, is it necessary to deal with the NIEO package as a whole or would it be more profitable to deal with specific issues? The problem here is to determine whether or not separate negotiations would threaten to unravel the package and render it worthless. The Eleventh Special Session of the General Assembly (UNGASS), held in 1980, which considered the New International Development Strategy for the Third Development Decade, was yet another attempt at the "package" approach, with disappointing results.

These questions are difficult and not readily answered. The purpose here is to explore the NIEO from the Third World's perspective in order to gain an insight into these issues. In doing so, four basic themes emerge:

(1) Why have the developing states called for the creation of a NIEO?
(2) How have these states pressed their demands?
(3) What are these states' demands?
(4) What are the reactions of the western industrialized states to the Third World demands?

Why the Call for A NIEO?

The first and most fundamental point to be made here is that the international system has always had an economic order, planned or de facto. One definition of the present "order," and thus the one of most interest here, dates from the efforts to restructure the shattered international economy in the early period after World War II. The main instruments of the system are quite familiar, and include the GATT and the IMF.

As it has operated, the present system—the "Old International Economic Order"—has displayed two primary characteristics. First, it has been exclusive in that effective participation in the system has been limited to a small group of predominantly western states, epitomized by the Group of Ten. Only recently has a significant volume of trade emerged between the Socialist bloc and the West, and with the combination of global economic recession and a cooling-off of East-West relations, this may be short-lived. Other states, for the most part those that have received their independence since World War II, have had to participate on what has amounted to a second-class basis. Denied access to the "club" and unable to change the rules, these developing states have had to make arrangements as best as they could, either alone or in association with a major industrial country.

Second, until the early 1970s the system had been dominated by the United States. The volume of U.S. foreign trade, coupled with the use of the dollar as an international reserve currency, had placed the United States in a preferential position within the international economic system.

However, this system was not long-lived; two factors emerged which, over a period of several years, served to undermine its basic structure. The first of these factors was the emergence of the European Communities and Japan as sources of economic strength that rivaled the United States. The second of these factors has been the changes in the global political order. Since the end of World War II, colonialism has virtually disappeared under a rising flood of new states which have taken their places as members of the international political community. This political independence generated a sense of hope and enthusiasm among the new states. They saw, in the postcolonial period, the possibility of obtaining genuine assistance for their development from the industrial states (which to them included the Soviet Union) and felt confident that their entry into the global political arena would enable them to acquire the means and substance necessary for their rapid economic development. But as the years passed without significant economic and social improvement, the famous "revolution of rising expectations" soured into a "revolution of rising frustrations."

The challenges of economic growth and social development have proved to be more complex and intractable than either donors or recipients had anticipated; as a result, the developing states have frequently accused the industrial states of responding inadequately to their needs. In doing so, they not only made the obvious criticism that aid had been insufficient, but also, they raised a somewhat more subtle and certainly more pervasive charge:

that while colonialism may be gone, the colonial economic institutions that maintained economic inequality remain. The developing states have argued that the global economic system represents an order which is irrelevant to or insufficiently suited to their developmental needs. Therefore, they have demanded that the old global order of inequality be abolished and that it be replaced by a new global structure that is based on their notions of international equality and justice. And thus the NIEO takes on its familiar form: It is a set of demands and proposals from the Third World for a restructured world economy designed more nearly to fit their needs as they perceive them.[3]

It also should be stressed that the NIEO represents not only a call for equity, but an attempt to come to grips with the fundamental problems of human needs as well. Thus the new order is seen as a means to alleviate suffering and poverty and to provide for genuine human and social development. It is often difficult for individuals in the industrial states to comprehend the dimensions of human needs that exist in the developing countries. But an attempt must be made, otherwise much of the discussion surrounding the NIEO and development appears meaningless or blatantly self-serving.

The poverty of the developing world translates indirectly into social consequences. Almost 800 million people in developing countries live in absolute poverty; they cannot afford to purchase enough food to meet their minimum nutritional needs. The resulting malnutrition particularly affects children, many of whom suffer retardation and physical impairment for want of sufficient protein. Life expectancy in the developing world averages 50 years, which is one-third lower than that enjoyed by individuals in the western states (72 years). Infant mortality occurs at an average rate of almost 200 per 1000 in the poorest states compared to 16 in the West. The average adult illiteracy rate exceeds 60 percent in the developing states, which means that nearly 750 million people lack the basic educational tools to improve their social conditions. In contrast, less than 1 percent of the population of the industrial states lacks these abilities (World Bank, 1980: 33-34).[4]

Thus it is not difficult to understand why so many countries look forward anxiously to a new order which holds the possibility, if not the promise, of bringing a measure of prosperity to these impoverished people.

How the Developing Countries Have Pressed Their Demands

To many, the NIEO appeared at the outset of the 1970s, to have burst with dramatic suddenness onto the international agenda. In a sense this is true, but the explosion of the 1970s was ignited by a slow fuse which had been burning for many years.

The developing states have consistently sought to use the United Nations as a means for the promotion of their economic and social development. In doing so, they have taken the cue from the industrial states and have stressed the importance of economic factors in promoting political stability. This is captured in the phrase "development is a new name for peace." The UN regional economic commissions stand as good examples of the developing states' efforts to gain a greater measure of control over UN development programs and funds.[5]

As pointed out earlier, concerned with their own problems, the industrial states have not always been sympathetic to the pleas from the developing states. In fact, they were frequently accused of being callously insensitive to the Third World's needs. For their part, the developing states lacked the economic and political "clout" to press their case effectively against the industrial states: thus, for two decades there was little alteration in the North-South power relationship in international institutions. Even so, the decade between 1964 and 1974 witnessed two signal developments which were to transform significantly this unequal balance.

The first of these developments was the organization of a caucus among the developing states. In 1964, having become sufficiently numerous to take advantage of their collective voting strength, the developing states secured the establishment of the United Nations Conference on Trade and Development (UNCTAD). Sometimes called the poor man's GATT, UNCTAD was designed to serve as a forum wherein the newly independent former colonies could press the industrial states for more preferential terms of trade. But equally important, UNCTAD was intended to provide a framework wherein the developing states could come together in a single caucus to formulate and express a unified Third World position on matters of importance to them. Commonly known as the Group of 77, this caucusing mechanism has become an important element in securing and maintaining the cohesion among the developing states that is necessary for them to deal effectively with the economically more powerful industrial states.

The second significant development was the remarkable success of OPEC throughout the 1970s. The oil embargo of 1973 demonstrated that for the first time some developing states possessed an economic weapon that they could wield with telling effect against the industrial states. As Minic (1981: 35) put it:

> The change of power relations in the world became evident in 1974. The action of the OPEC countries was a shock to the tradition of international relations and reflected a crisis in the world economy.

No longer, therefore, would they have to bargain as unequals; instead, they found themselves in a position of surprising strength which, if not conferring equality of status, certainly demanded attention and hopefully, respect.

Heady with their new strength and success, the developing world "took on" the so-called First World in 1974, in the Sixth Special Session of the UN General Assembly. Though technically limited to the topics of trade and commodities, countries used their voting strength to pass, with the support of the Socialist bloc and over the objections of some of the industrial states, the package of resolutions known as the New International Economic Order.[6]

The adoption of these resolutions, however, did not lead to the immediate establishment of a new order. On the one hand, the resolutions are not a concrete plan of action; they are, rather, a collection of general statements of principle which must be translated into actual national policies and international legal instruments before becoming operational. And on the other, the industrial states, whose cooperation is vital for the effective rearrangement of international economic relationships, are at best reluctant partners. While they recognize the need, in some instances, for new relationships, they are opposed to many of the specifics of the NIEO which they see as contrary to their own interests and possibly counterproductive to the developing states' interests as well.

It should also be pointed out that the character of the Sixth Special Session itself served as an impediment to forward motion. The purpose of the session was to deal with the issues of raw materials and development, which had become acute problems due to the energy and monetary crises of the early 1970s. At the session, the developing states seized on these themes to press on the industrial states their demands for a redistribution of wealth. In doing so, the developing states adopted a stridently militant tone, and this, coupled with the seemingly radical nature of their demands, generated considerable resistance among the industrial states, particularly the United States. An additional complicating element was the fact that the Sixth Special Session coincided with the height of the Watergate crisis—President Nixon resigned three months later—which had brought U.S. policy initiatives to a virtual standstill. The United States, therefore, was largely unprepared for the Third World onslaught, and its representatives were forced into narrowly defensive positions.

In contrast to the confrontation and hostility of the Sixth Special Session, the Seventh Special Session of 1975 was a time of conciliation. By the opening of the session, the Ford administration had studied the lessons of 1974 and realized the importance of dealing cooperatively with the Third World in facing the vital issues on the global agenda. The developing states also seemed to have grasped the somewhat pyrrhic nature of their "victory" at the Sixth Session, and delegates from the rich and poor states stressed the importance of cooperation in meeting fundamental human needs. As Renninger (1981: 28) summarized it:

The resolutions of the 6th and 7th Special Sessions of the General Assembly and others such as the Charter of Economic Rights and Duties of States, emanated from the General Assembly. Economic issues were moving to the realm of high politics, although . . . perhaps not to the extent some observers believe.

The general conferences of UNCTAD and the United Nations Industrial Development Organization (UNIDO), have provided alternative forums for the debate of NIEO issues. In 1975, UNIDO II was held in Lima, Peru, and the Lima Plan of Action was adopted. This called for an increase to 25 percent in the less developed countries' (LDC) share of world industrial output by the year 2000. The LDCs' share of the world industrial output had barely reached 9 percent by 1979 (UN Chronicle, 1980: 26-27).

At UNIDO III, held in New Delhi in January and February of 1980, a declaration was adopted which called for the establishment of a North-South global fund. This fund, designed to promote the industrialization of developing countries, is to reach $300 billion by the year 2000, with, hopefully, the industrial countries providing much of the resources. A UNIDO conference was to be convened in 1981 to work out arrangements for the fund (UN Chronicle, 1980: 26-27).[7]

In 1976, UNCTAD IV, was convened in Nairobi, and out of this conference came the Integrated Program for Commodities. One of its primary objectives is to achieve commodity price stabilization through the use of International Commodity Agreements; this has become one of the central elements of the NIEO. Also at UNCTAD IV, intensive work was launched on the formulation of a set of principles and rules to regulate restrictive business practices. This came to fruition in April 1980 with the "Set of Principles and Rules" and a "Business Code of Behavior" that were adopted at the Thirty-Fifth Session of the General Assembly (CTC Reporter, 1980). Finally, in June 1979, UNCTAD V, held in Manila, proposed a comprehensive "Action Programme" designed to make the LDCs more self-sustaining. In response, the Thirty-Fifth General Assembly resolved to convene a conference on LDCs (called the Global Round) early in 1981 in order to adopt this program.

NIEO issues have also been discussed in several UN ad hoc global conferences. The World Food Conference, held in Rome in 1974, helped to encourage this trend (Weiss and Jordan, 1976). The International Labor Organization (ILO) sponsored the World Employment Conference that met in Geneva in 1976, where it approved the basic needs approach to development, and steps were taken to integrate this concept into the preparations for the Third Development Decade (ILO Report, 1977). In 1977, the United States withdrew its membership from the ILO, a serious step with, in the short run, demoralizing consequences.[9] Also linked to the basic needs approach was the United Nations Conference on Human Settlements (HABI-

TAT) which met in 1976 in Vancouver, British Columbia. As pointed out earlier, "basic human needs" as an operational concept has not met with universal approbation. The developing countries view it as signifying interference in their right to determine their own domestic priorities and to decide on what trade and aid projects, whether multilateral or bilateral, should be implemented.

In New York and Geneva, the Law of the Sea Conference continued throughout the 1970s to grapple with North-South issues relating to the exploitation of the resources of the seabed. Nonetheless, in 1981, the Law of the Sea Conference remained stalemated; although having narrowed the areas of disagreement, its efforts could well take another decade. Only gradually are the range of issues surrounding the means and conditions for exploiting the resources of the seabed being worked out so that the control and access demanded by the developing states can be reconciled with access to the technology and capital possessed by the industrial states—which in effect means primarily, the United States.

Another development of note at the United Nations in relation to the NIEO was the appointment of Ambassador Kenneth Dadzie of Ghana as director-general for development and international economic cooperation, a new post established in 1977 as part of the restructuring of the economic and social sectors. The post has been termed as ranking second only to the secretary-general in the UN system and is meant to facilitate the process of making the UN more responsive to the needs and goals of the developing member states.

In the meantime, Secretary-General Kurt Waldheim and Robert McNamara, president of the World Bank, sought to give some impetus to these efforts by proposing the establishment of a commission of personalities from both industrial and developing states, to find solutions to problems of development cooperation. On September 29, 1978, it was announced that such a commission had been established under the chairmanship of Willy Brandt of West Germany. The 17-member "Independent Commission on International Development Issues" submitted its report in December 1979 and it became one of the major documents for discussion at the 1980 Special Session.

Another NIEO forum was attempted outside of the UN system, with the convening of the Conference on International Economic Cooperation (CIEC) in 1977. In Paris, eight industrial and nineteen developing countries gathered under the general auspices of the United Nations to discuss a broad range of issues, without much hope of success—the CIEC ended inconclusively. In some quarters it was branded a failure for not having resolved any of the major issues before it. Other quarters, however, stressed the importance of the conference in clarifying issues and in maintaining the dialogue between North and South. There is some justification for both positions, but perhaps the most important aspect of the CIEC was its use as a barometer of international relations: If on the one hand it did not climb to new heights, neither did it revert to the tempestuous past.

Thus, major contributions of the conference appear to stand somewhat apart from substantive agreements, or the lack thereof. Unfortunately, the most important substantive proposal put forward by the industrial states—to create a Special Action Program of $1 billion in aid for the neediest countries—has not been implemented. Nonetheless, the conference served to provide all parties with a clearer understanding of each other's positions. The conference reflected the intensity with which each side adheres to its positions, thereby providing a better understanding of the kinds of steps which have to be taken to make real progress. As Mortimer (1980: 109) put it: "Perhaps CIEC's greatest merit was to clarify, if need be, that the problem was not one of communication but of conflicting interests." Third, and perhaps most important, the conference gave little indication of a movement of abandoning the North-South dialogue. Indeed, there appeared to be a genuine commitment on both sides to make real progress in resolving the issues which separated them. Such a commitment does not in itself ensure success, but it is unquestionably the *sine qua non* of progress.

Following the conclusions of the Paris Conference, the major work and discussions on the NIEO returned to the General Assembly in September 1977, with the resumption of the Thirty-First Session. The General Assembly had been suspended rather than adjourned in December 1976, in order to await the outcome of the Paris Conference.

Despite the contributions of CIEC noted above, the discontent of the developing states over the slowness of the pace and dearth of substantive agreements was soon evident at the resumed session. After considering a statement and reports on the CIEC by the secretary-general, including the full report of the conference, and statements by the co-chairmen of CIEC, a draft resolution was submitted on behalf of the Group of 77 (UN General Assembly, 1977b, 1977c, 1977d, 1977e, 1977f). Criticizing the lack of progress at Paris and in creating a NIEO generally, the resolution called for renewed efforts, the establishment of guidelines for future negotiations, and a special session of the General Assembly at the ministerial level by early 1980. Unfortunately, consensus could not be reached on the resolution, as the industrial states objected to the charges that no important progress had been made. Although the Group of 77 clearly had enough votes to pass the resolution in some form, after considerable discussion and informal negotiations had demonstrated the fruitlessness in gaining agreement between the industrial and developing states, it was withdrawn.

The president of the General Assembly, the late Mr. Hamilton Shirley Amerasinghe closed the resumed session with the following statement:

We must one and all realize that attitudes must change if we are to have a new order. Paradoxical though it may sound, there is only one thing that is constant in life and that is change. In no field of human relationships is this more true than in the international economic sphere. When you next consider this question, I would urge you to remember this. I do not ask you to be conservative or radical. I ask you representatives of the developed and the developing countries, to be just and fair to one another in your own interest [UN, 1977a].

The Thirty-Third Ordinary Session of the General Assembly opened in the Fall of 1978 with the intent of taking up these challenges, and there was some apparent interest on all sides to avoid letting the failure of the resumed session inhibit future undertakings. Frequently expressed was the view that real progress must be based on agreement obtained within the universal membership framework of the General Assembly. The Thirty-Third Session concluded with a carefully negotiated compromise between the Group of 77 and the industrial states on future negotiations. A resolution adopted by the General Assembly decided to convene another special session of the General Assembly in 1980 to assess progress on the NIEO and to take further action which would include a new International Development Strategy for the 1980s.

In addition, a Committee of the Whole (termed "the Committee Established under General Assembly Resolution 32/174") was created to monitor progress, to provide a forum for negotiation, and to recommend the procedures, time-frame, and a detailed agenda for subsequent global negotiations. The committee met for a substantive session in May of 1979, but little progress was achieved. Indeed, the session was suspended until early September 1979, when the committee agreed to report its inability to make progress to the General Assembly. Nonetheless, it continued its work through 1979 and submitted a report to the 1980 Eleventh Special Session.

The Eleventh Special Session (UNGASS) was convened on August 25, 1980 in order to work out the agenda and the procedural rules for a new round of global negotiations on the NIEO. After three weeks, the session failed when the United States, the Federal Republic of Germany, and Britain refused to accept a compromise proposal on how the negotiations should be conducted.

The Group of 77 initially wanted a general conference, which could be a modified Committee of the Whole, of all UN member states to have sovereign authority in NIEO global negotiations. "The council [conference] would define the objectives, refer the items of the agenda to the relevant specialized agencies of the UN such as the IMF, the World Bank, and GATT for their study and recommendations, and when these came back accept them or refer them back for modifications" (Peiris, 1980: 5). In addition, a one state/one vote system was advocated so that the proposals would be accepted or rejected by majority rather than consensus.

The industrial states maintained that the Global Round of negotiations should be decentralized, and take place in the specialized agencies or non-UN international institutions. The findings of these agencies would be final so that, in effect, the general council would merely be a referring body that would determine general objectives, through consensus rather than majority voting. This procedure would tend to work in favor of the western industrial states since they are able to control more effectively the work of these institutions.

A compromise proposal was finally agreed upon. The details of specific agenda items, such as energy, would be negotiated in the specialized or other agencies of the UN system, and the conference would receive the results "with a view to reaching a package agreement." However, it was not clear whether the findings of the specialized or other agencies could be renegotiated by the conference. Then, creating great frustration, Britain, the Federal Republic of Germany, and the United States refused again to accept a compromise. Their main concern was that the integrity of the specialized agencies might be jeopardized. Having failed to reach a compromise, the Special Session decided to leave to the Thirty-Fifth Session of the General Assembly the task of finding a way out of the impasse.

What These Demands Are

Many of the issues grouped collectively under the NIEO consist of highly complex and technical problems which cannot be explored fully in this chapter. For present purposes, however, demands of the NIEO may be analyzed in four major categories. The discussion in this section will present each of these categories—economic sovereignty, trade, aid, and participation—along with an explanation of the components as viewed by both North and South.[10]

ECONOMIC SOVEREIGNTY

Freedom From Intervention. Perhaps first and foremost on the developing states' agenda is the demand for complete sovereignty over the nature of their economic systems and their operation. They argue, and not unreasonably, that every state has the right to resist or to be free from outside economic intervention or, stated conversely, that no state has the right to interfere in the economic activities of another. The thrust of this contention is, quite obviously, against colonial and "neo-colonial" relationships under which a dominant state virtually controls the economic activities of its client state.

The difficulty with this contention from the western perspective is not so much in the ideal—they, too, do not wish intervention in their economies—but with the problems involved in defining the concept of intervention itself. They fear a situation wherein their national acts may be branded as intervention because of their impact on third parties, and thus they stress the idea of "interdependence," which emphasizes the interaction of legitimate choices in economic policy. But this approach is not well received by the developing states, who fear that interdependence may simply be another word for the old, unequal relationship. The result of this divergence has been an official recognition of both independence and interdependence, but without any substantive agreement as to what each means in terms of international policies and structures.

Control of Natural Resources. To eliminate practices wherein foreign consortia controlled the exploitation of Third World resources without adequate recompense to the host state, the developing countries have asserted the right to "full permanent sovereignty" over the disposition of their natural resources. The industrial states do not deny this right as such, but they express concern over what they see as potential abuses. On the one hand, they stress that national control of natural resources must not be exercised in violation of existing treaty obligations. And on the other, they are worried about the organization of natural resource cartels along the lines of OPEC, which may then be used as a weapon against them.[11] In other words, they are anxious to avoid situations where seemingly capricious acts may jeopardize existing economic relationships, to the possible detriment of both parties. At present, there is no accepted framework to govern the development and exploitation of natural resources. This issue is linked to ongoing trade discussions, which will be discussed later in this chapter.

Regulation of Transnational Corporations. Developing states view transnational corporations with a good deal of ambivalence. On the one hand, they are seen as foreign intruders that seek personal profits without due consideration for the social and economic needs of the host country, that repatriate earnings and thereby siphon off money that is sorely needed for local reinvestment, and that, as publicized by the Lockheed scandal, may become involved in the internal political affairs of the host country. But on the other hand, they also serve as sources of technology, employment, training, and entrepreneurial skills that are simply not available elsewhere.

In order to derive maximum benefits with a minimum of risk from transnationals, the developing states have asserted the right "to regulate and supervise" transnational corporations in accordance with their own domestic laws and policies. This assertion alarms the industrial states, and particularly the United States (the home of most transnationals), because it may open the door for capricious and politically motivated actions directed against foreign holdings. The industrial states admit to some abuses by the transnationals, but they do not feel that nonsystematic and potentially heavy-handed regulation by national governments is the answer, particularly as many Third World governments lack the expertise necessary to regulate sophisticated corporations in a productive manner. The United States has argued in favor of a system of self-regulation by the transnationals, but this is rejected by the developing countries, fearing that self-regulation means self-serving or no regulation.

A potentially acceptable compromise between these two positions would be the regulation of transnationals under a set of international standards. Within the United Nations, work has begun in this area. In 1974, the General Assembly created a 48-member Commission on Transnational Corporations and a Centre to serve as its secretariat. Among other things, the commission was charged with preparing an international code of conduct, which it completed in 1981. In addition, the commission had a major resolution adopted by the Economic and Social Council which concerned "the right of States to regulate and, accordingly, to monitor the activities of transnational corporations" (CTC Reporter, 1980: 4).[12]

Right of Nationalization. The assertion by the developing states of a right to nationalize or to expropriate foreign holdings is not in and of itself objectionable to the industrial states, for nationalization has long been a legitimate state action under international law. The difficulty, rather, emerges on the issue of compensation. The older, mostly western states insist that full and adequate compensation be made for any expropriated property. The developing countries, however, argue that they are not bound by the provisions of a law which they did not help to create and to which, in any case, there have been many exceptions in practice. They do not deny that compensation should be made; rather, they stress that it is the decision of the nationalizing state. This, however, is wholly unacceptable to the industrial states; they see this practice as a means of avoiding all but token payments, and they continue to insist that compensation must be agreed to by both parties. This issue is far from settled, and it is likely to remain a particularly sensitive area of international relations for some time to come.

TRADE

Raw Material and Commodity Markets. Raw materials and commodities have always been of great importance to the Third World. In many instances, the sales of these goods constitute the major source of revenue on which developing states depend to finance their national development projects. The problem faced by the developing states, however, is that these products are particularly vulnerable to cyclical price fluctuations.

Until recently, efforts to improve the world commodity market have largely consisted of ad hoc agreements reached bilaterally or between various groups of states. The resulting lack of systemic and systematic work in this area left the world economy, as a 1976 UNCTAD report noted, "essentially unprotected against the consequences of sudden substantial shifts in the balance of supply and demand in major commodity markets" (UNCTAD, 1976). This vulnerability was sharply emphasized in the early 1970s. In 1972 and 1973, primary commodities underwent a substantial boom as investors turned to commodities as a hedge against inflation. But in 1974, this boom was followed by a sharp contraction, due in part to the world economic recession. And in 1975, the volume of world trade actually declined, thereby creating serious market uncertainties for commodity exports.

To redress this situation, the developing countries have sought to create an international means for the realization of commodity markets. At the Sixth Special Session and particularly at UNCTAD IV, they put forward proposals for the establishment of international regulatory machinery. These new institutions would comprise four principal functions: (1) international stockpiles of commodities which would be used to maintain supplies and support prices; (2) a multilateral system of long- and medium-term contracts to protect supplies, markets, and prices; (3) compensatory financing for most seriously affected nations; and (4) an international fund to finance these arrangements.

The industrial states have generally agreed to the need for the stabilization of commodity markets and export earnings, but they have been dubious about the developing states' package of proposals in its entirety. The United States, in particular, has opposed the kind of large-scale market intervention these would entail, and prefers a minimum of interference in the natural operation of market forces. For example, late in 1976, then-Secretary of the Treasury William Simon stated that:

> We do not regard indirect resource transfer schemes—such as generalized debt rescheduling, price indexing, and commodity funds—as the best means to provide resources to the developing world. To the contrary, such proposals are likely to lead to inefficiencies and distortions which will make most, if not all, worse off.[13]

Initially, both the Ford and Carter administrations had opposed the integrated scheme proposed by the Group of 77 through UNCTAD, and preferred to proceed with negotiations on a commodity-by-commodity basis. In particular, they opposed the Common Fund, which had been described by government officials as arbitrary and likely to have a negative impact on the market system. Instead, the United States favored an increase in direct development assistance as the best means to effect a transfer of wealth.[14] The Carter administration, however, later showed a greater willingness to compromise. At the CIEC in Paris, it accepted the principle of a Common Fund, and in 1980, the United States was one of twenty-four countries to sign the agreement establishing the fund.[15] Unfortunately the donor countries have not yet actually paid in their contributions to the fund.

Access to Markets. The developing states have noted the need to increase exports, not only of raw materials and commodities, but also of manufactures and semimanufactures, in order to strengthen their domestic economies. To achieve this goal, they have insisted that the industrial states grant them access to markets by removing all tariff and nontariff barriers to Third World products on a nonreciprocal and preferential basis. Additionally, they have asked that the present Generalized Scheme of Preferences (GSP) be incorporated permanently into the world trading system and have asserted the right to employ export incentives to make their manufactured products more competitive without countervailing duties and levies being applied by the industrial states.

In response, the industrial states have agreed to extend the GSP into the 1980s but are dubious about its utility as a permanent arrangement. In the long run, the GSP could create problems for a number of industrial states, particularly with regard to semiprocessed and processed goods, which do not face tariff barriers when they are exported. Ironically, at least in regard to the export of high-technology goods, this has the appearance of placing the industrial states in a quasi-colonial relationship with some of the former colonial territories that had claimed to have been objects of exploitation.

The industrial states have also balked at the idea of eliminating trade barriers in a nonreciprocal and preferential manner. Instead, they have proposed that all such questions should be dealt with in the context of multilateral trade negotiations within the GATT framework. The developing countries, however, prefer to use UNCTAD, where the strength of the 77 is most concentrated. Thus, there is disagreement not only on the issues, but also on the proper forum to be utilized for their resolution. This difference has existed for some time, and it does not appear that any immediate solution is likely.

Another aspect of this issue, which introduces further complications, is the insistence by the United States that the question of access to markets be linked to reciprocal commitments, such as guaranteeing to the industrial states access to supplies of commodities and raw materials from the Third World. The United States does not feel that the developing states should be in a position where, on the one hand, they obtain a guaranteed preferential access to the markets of the industrial states, and on the other, retain to themselves the right to restrict or cut off the flow of raw materials vital to the economies of the industrial states. This issue, too, is being pursued in both UNCTAD and the GATT, but because of the sensitivity and complexity of the entire package, it is difficult to envision rapid progress. However, the Tokyo round of multilateral trade negotiations, completed in 1979, did make valuable contributions to breaking this stalemate. The industrial states agreed to reduce tariffs by 38 percent in eight years, and to impose stiffer regulations on nontariff barriers (World Bank, 1980).

AID

Targets, Flows, and Terms of Assistance. As part of the NIEO, the developing states have recommended that the industrial states increase the level of assistance given to the Third World and to improve the conditions and terms of this assistance. Central to this process are the Official Development Assistance (ODA) targets established by the UN General Assembly in 1970. In conformity with these targets, the industrial states are to earmark 0.7 percent of their GNP for development.[16] The targets have not been met by most of the industrial states.

The United States even opposes the fixing of such targets, asserting that setting targets is not only unlikely to achieve their purpose, but may, in fact, be counterproductive. Until recently, the United States has placed far greater emphasis on capital derived from other sources, especially from the International Development Association (IDA) of the World Bank group and from private investment. Today, Congressional support for replenishing IDA funds is far from certain, and in any event the Reagan administration plans to contribute only $550 million to the IDA in 1982, which, to the consternation of the IDA, is only half the amount stipulated for the United States by IDA rules. Thus, the issue of target implementation remains an unresolved item on the international agenda.[17]

More progress has been made in the area of multilateral aid as the resources of international financial institutions were increased in the 1970s. This does not wholly satisfy the developing states, however, as funds from these sources are, generally, available on market and not on concessional terms. The developing states have continued to press for greater concessional aid flows, which they feel is essential to ease their own balance-of-payments problems. They also are anxious to untie aid contributions from conditions attached by donor states. To some extent this has been achieved by the multilateral disbursement of funds through such institutions as UNDP. Even so, donor states retain considerable influence over the spending of aid monies. For example, in 1981, outgoing World Bank President Robert McNamara wanted the Bank to establish an energy affiliate to foster research on energy in the developing states. However, the Reagan administration has opposed the idea.[18]

Debt Rescheduling. An issue closely related to that of concessional aid involves the rescheduling of the external debts of developing states. In the early 1970s, the rapid escalation of oil prices and a rampant global inflation placed severe strains on many developing states, especially the most seriously affected (MSA) states who were already experiencing severe balance-of-payment problems. On one hand, their combined external debts have reached a level exceeding $100 billion, while on the other their currencies have been badly undermined. As one declaration put it:

> What is of cardinal importance is to ensure that the state of affairs witnessed in the last few years in which "developing countries remained largely 'off-stage' as the world liquidity problem emerged, successive crises affected the currencies of the major industrial nations, urgent international consultations were conducted and a variety of instruments were introduced to patch up the existing international monetary system without their interests being taken into account during this period," is not allowed to continue.[19]

Because of the IMF's strict rules governing loans and repayments, some developing states have not been able to obtain sufficient access to its funds to support their currencies and still manage their debts. To improve what was rapidly becoming a critical situation, the most seriously affected countries have been pressing for some form of debt rescheduling or even debt forgiveness. During the Seventh Special Session, they proposed that the United Nations convene a conference of major creditor and debtor states to review the problem of external debt and to explore possible means of mitigating the burden. The idea of such a conference was strongly opposed by most industrial states.

The UN Committee of the Whole specifically recommended that disbursements from the IMF Trust Fund to the most seriously affected countries should be accelerated, and UNCTAD, as the lead agency in the United Nations, scheduled a Conference on the Least Developed Countries, to be held in Paris in September 1981. The Conference was intended to launch a "Substantial New Programme of Action."

Initially, the creditor and donor states, led by the United States, held that it might be possible to make specific arrangements on a case-by-case basis, but that it was not possible to prepare a universal plan. The United States has emphasized the need for maintaining credit-worthiness, and is particularly concerned with the implications of rescheduling for large-scale private loans (many of which originated in the United States). A concern that rescheduling efforts might be used as a means to reduce temporary balance-of-payments difficulties—a tactic which the United States felt to be highly unsuitable—also has been expressed. Consequently, even though the problem of rescheduling was taken up at UNCTAD IV, no substantial progress was made. The only action taken by the conference in this regard was the adoption of a resolution (94 [IV]) which requested further international examination of the problem and further review by the UNCTAD Trade and Development Board (TAB).

Prior to the TAB session of March 1978, some creditor nations, Canada and Sweden among them, announced unilaterally that some of the debts for ODA, but not for commercial transactions, would be cancelled. The TAB session which followed was marked by some optimism. However, the other donor countries agreed only to seek measures either for an adjustment of the terms of past ODA debts or for other equivalent measures. In favor of the most seriously affected countries, the Brandt Commission, formed later in 1978, underscored this need.

> As an immediate step, we recommend that the various international institutions begin immediately to study and articulate the range of likely debts and debt servicing problems as they emerge, particularly in the various categories of developing countries, and the likelihood of existing private and public institutions being able to meet these needs [Independent Commission on International Development Issues, 1980: 239].

Hopefully, the UNCTAD Conference on the Least Developed Countries, mentioned above, will have some measure of success, for there is growing concern that, for example, those 87 non-oil-producing countries most plagued by high oil prices will stop making payments on their debts, estimated by the IMF to be $418 billion. This could cause a "run" by depositors on those large international banks involved, and this could have very serious global consequences.[20]

Science and Technology. This has been one of the major items on the international agenda, and one in which substantial progress is likely to be made. There is widespread agreement on the need to improve the scientific and technological capabilities of the developing states; the primary difficulties have centered on the rate and the means. The developing states have sought rapid and open access to industrial technology, particularly that possessed by transnational corporations. The industrial states, however, have pointed to the fact that the developing states lack the capacity to absorb and sustain advanced industrial technology; hence, they have tended to emphasize the importance of creating local manpower, manufacturing, and marketing infrastructures prior to the actual acquisition of such technology.

Another problem frequently stressed by the United States is the fact that much of current American technology is held by nonpublic corporations and protected by patents; therefore, it is neither readily available nor subject to governmental control. Thus, some form of international arrangements needs to be devised before access to such information can be given. This problem was one of the subjects of the United Nations Conference on Science and

Technology for Development, held in Vienna in 1979. It also is the responsibility of one of the United Nations' newest specialized agencies, the World Intellectual Property Organization (WIPO).

PARTICIPATION

Perhaps this issue, more than any other, lies at the heart of the developing states' demands for a new international economic order. Not only do these states want to share the material benefits presently found in the industrial states, but they also want to participate on an equal footing with the industrial states in making decisions which determine the direction of the international economic system. That they do not enjoy their current status and that they perceive themselves as not enjoying fuller participation in the foreseeable future is clearly reflected in this assertion:

> All states are juridically equal and, as equal members of the international community, have the right to participate fully and effectively in the international decision-making process in the solution of world economic, financial and monetary problems, *inter alia,* through the appropriate international organizations in accordance with their existing and evolving rules, and to share equitably in the benefits resulting therefrom.[21]

Quite obviously, the developing states have been dominating the UN General Assembly and are attempting to dominate many of the United Nations' specialized agencies and subsidiary bodies. But effective membership and participation in the real centers of economic and financial decision making—the IMF, the World Bank, GATT—continues to elude them.[22] Many proposals have been put forward to remodel these institutions in order to align them more closely with the needs of the developing states. But greater access does not necessarily imply effective participation. For, as Fred Hirsch (1976: 525) aptly pointed out: "The old members can always do the real business of the club elsewhere, as in its formal proceedings the institution becomes more of a talking shop."[23] The real issue, then, is whether the industrial states will continue to attempt to preserve their prerogatives outside of those international institutions in which they lost voting control, or whether they will open the way for a truly new order based not on inequality of wealth but on equality of need and participation. This is a very difficult issue, and the goal will not be achieved without major concessions on both sides.

The Reaction of the Industrial States to the Third World's Demands

The failure of the United Nations Eleventh Special Session seems to have brought at least a temporary halt to the North-South dialogue. Yet it also seems to have fostered some contemplation about the NIEO itself. What are the proper forums for discussion of global economic issues? Can UN institutions, either centralized or decentralized, provide these forums? Should economic assistance to the Third World proceed along multilateral or bilateral routes? How should the industrial states react to the Third World's demands?

Both industrial and developing states seem to have, at least temporarily, become disenchanted with using the United Nations to carry on North-South negotiations (Peiris, 1980: 5-9; and 1981). In May 1981, the Reagan administration said that it "wants to put off until the fall any talk of transferring resources from rich to poor nations" (Nossiter, 1981). Also in May 1981, the industrial western states used NATO as a forum for discussing the problem of economic stability in the Third World. At the Rome Conference, the NATO member-states, particularly West Germany, called for increased economic aid for development (Pond, 1981). The West German Foreign Minister, Hans-Dietrich Genscher, argued that, "the West should capitalize on what it has to offer the underdeveloped countries in the way of economic aid." The United States concurred in this strategy, which may indicate that the Reagan administration's posture toward the Third World is not entirely unsympathetic.

However, the Reagan administration has also indicated its preference for bilateral rather than multilateral economic assistance. Speaking before the Senate Foreign Relations Committee in March 1981, Secretary of State Alexander Haig (1981: 2049) stated that:

> Over the past two decades, a growing percentage of U.S. official aid has gone to support multilateral development banks. We intend to meet our existing obligations to these institutions as we move, in an evolutionary way, toward a greater emphasis on bilateral rather than multilateral assistance.

The West's current interest in bilateral assistance and the use of forums other than the General Assembly, can be coupled with the West's negative reaction to the developing states' demand for greater influence in the governance of such trade and financial institutions as the IMF, GATT, and the World Bank. Understandably, the industrial states, particularly the United States, Britain, and West Germany do not want to relinquish their influence in these institutions; yet, an equitable global economic system requires a greater distribution of decision-making authority over multilateral economic and financial agencies.

But the North-South dialogue is not totally abandoned. At Cancun, Mexico, in October 1981, the leaders of fourteen developing states and seven industrialized states, met to see if they could arrive at a compromise basis for resuming global negotiations. Initially, the Reagan administration had treated the prospect of such a conference with skepticism. The conference had been proposed by the Brandt Commission to focus attention at the highest level of governmental authority on North-South relations. The major subjects discussed were trade, energy, external finance, food and population, and international institutions. President Reagan's emphasis on "the magic of the marketplace," rather than foreign aid supplied by governments, remained intact, although apparently a greater common appreciation emerged of the desirability of a mix of private/public sector development, according to the circumstances of each developing state.

The outcome of the conference was that the United States agreed to further talks, but not in the form of "global negotiations" at the United Nations that would give the edge—according to the one state/one vote formula—to the majority Third World. Rather, the United States preferred to see the follow-up take the form of meetings of specialists within existing international economic and financial organizations, where the United States could protect its own interests more effectively. Also, regional groups and bilateral discussions were still viewed as reasonable alternative negotiating situations.

Whether or not such negotiations begin, or even whether agreement can be reached on the appropriate forum(s), may well become beside the point because the rate of change going on all over the world simply will not await human events. As Jean-Jacques Servan-Schreiber (1981: 45) put it:

> Development is now linked to a universe that is totally different from a world of scarcity. It is associated with expansion and creativity. We are passing from an industrial society, which consumes natural resources, to a computerized society, which creates material goods and develops human faculties; from commercial wars over limited markets to a worldwide system of production and communication; from one historical era to another.

> The Third World is asking to be transformed in order to live and create. Triggering a new dynamic among the nations of the West, OPEC, and the Third World is matter of common recognition of a new world economy, of the information society, of a shared future.

> This recognition is not negotiable. It either will or will not occur. It is up to everyone to look, to reflect, to decide. This awareness alone will determine the chances for our future.

NOTES

1. The industrialized socialist countries also view the NIEO with suspicion, although to a lesser extent than do most western states. In particular, members of the socialist bloc are wary of participating in western-dominated institutions such as the International Monetary Fund (IMF) and the World Bank. This chapter will focus primarily on the views of western states and the Third World since the restructuring of economic relations between the West and Third World is at the core of the call for a new international economic order.

2. It is important to note that not all Third World economies are alike; obviously, some developing states are "more seriously affected" by the present economic order than others. There are several methods for grouping Third World states. For example, if one uses GNP as an economic gauge, then these states can be divided into "low-income" countries whose per capita GNPs are $300 or less, and "middle-income" countries, whose per capita GNPs are $300 or more.

3. For a complete review of key issues in the world economy in the context of NIEO, see Laszlo (1978).

4. Another description of the scale and consequences of global poverty can be found in the report of the Independent Commission on International Development Issues (1980).

5. These include the Economic and Social Commission for Asia and the Pacific (ECAFE, 1947, now ESCAP); the Economic Commission for Latin America (ECLA, 1948); the Economic Commission for Africa (ECA, 1958); and the Economic Commission for West Asia (ECWA, 1973). See also Gregg (1972).

6. The Sixth Special Session adopted two resolutions, the "Declaration on the Establishment of a New International Economic Order," (Res. 3201, S-VI) and "Programme of Action on the Establishment of a New International Economic Order," (Res. 3202, S-VI). These were later supplemented by the "Charter of Economic Rights and Duties of States" (Res. 3201, XXIX) and the "Lima Declaration and Plan of Action on Industrial Development and Cooperation," adopted by the UNIDO Conference, March 1975. For a description of the origins of UNCTAD, see Hagras (1965).

7. Other than agreement on the fund, the conference ended in an impasse.

8. But as one observer pointed out in the World Press Review (1981: 36): "The Business Code of Behavior and the transport agreement are nothing more than codifications of existing rules and standards. They are in no way an indication of progress toward a new world economic order. . . . The Common Fund is certainly a step toward a new economic order, and the accord reached in 1980 was the product of previous agreements. But if this fund is to be effective, it must be accompanied by other provisions concerning trade in raw materials."

9. The United States returned to the International Labor Organization in 1980 (Commission to Study the Organization of Peace, 1979). Ironically, it is the Soviet Union that has recently come under fire in the ILO. Charges have been made that Soviet trade unions are not as effective as independent agents as they should be (see Francis, 1981).

10. For a useful parallel account, see Gosovic and Ruggie (1976: 328-341).

11. For the moment, however, this does not appear to be a likely prospect, even though developing countries themselves have raised the possibility (see Smith, 1977: 1-28).

12. More recently, relations between the host countries and the multinationals have been improving, as each has come to understand the other better.

13. World Bank (1976) Annual Meetings of the Board of Governors: Summary Proceedings. Washington, DC: World Bank, p. 188.

14. See the address of Assistant Secretary of the Treasury for International Affairs, C. Fred Bergsten, as reported in the New York *Times,* February 11, 1977.

15. These countries were Bangladesh, Canada, China, Denmark, Ecuador, Finland, France, Haiti, Indonesia, Italy, Japan, Luxembourg, Malaysia, Mexico, Morocco, Netherlands, Norway, Portugal, Sri Lanka, Sweden, United Kingdom, United States, Venezuela, and Zambia.

16. These states are those which are included in the Joint Development Committee of the International Monetary Fund and the International Bank for Reconstruction and Development (World Bank).

17. For a useful discussion of targets, see World Bank, Global Targets for Development Cooperation (1977). Also, the definition of ODA was narrowed as regards the donors' contributions in order to maximize actual resource transfers. See "Report of the Committee of the

Whole Established Under General Assembly Resolution 32/74" (UN General Assembly, 1980).

18. See "McNamara's band loses its music." (1981) *The Economist* (March 14).

19. As quoted in Laszlo (1978: 112).

20. "Bankers fear default by oil-poor countries." (1981) New Orleans *Times-Picayune* (July 13).

21. Charter of Economic Rights and Duties of States, ch. II, art. 10.

22. It should be noted that when the Interim Committee of the IMF met in Japan in January 1976, the voting quotas of the Third World countries were enlarged, especially those of Arab states, thus providing for a somewhat greater participation.

23. See also the special issue of *Scientific American,* "Economic Development," September 1980, for a discussion of the variety of approaches to economic development.

REFERENCES

Commission on Transnational Corporations (1980) The CTC Reporter (Winter).

Commission to Study the Organization of Peace (1979) The United States and the ILO (December).

FRANCIS, D. (1981) "Moscow faces double embarrassment at ILO meeting in Geneva." Christian Science Monitor (June 5).

GOSOVIC, B. and J. G. RUGGIE (1976) "On the creation of a New International Economic Order: issue linkage and the seventh special session of the UN General Assembly." International Organization 30 (Spring).

GREGG, R. W. (1972) "The U.N. regional economic commissions and multinational cooperation," in R. S. Jordan (ed.) Multinational Cooperation: Economic, Social and Scientific Development. New York and London: Oxford University Press.

HAGRAS, K. M. (1965) United Nations Conference on Trade and Development: A Case Study in U.N. Diplomacy. New York: Praeger.

HAIG, A. (1981) "Statement before Senate Foreign Relations Committee, March 19, 1981. Department of State Bulletin 81 (April).

HIRSCH, F. (1976) "Is there a New International Economic Order?" International Organization 30 (Summer).

Independent Commission on International Development Issues (1980) North-South: A Program for Survival. Cambridge, MA: MIT Press. (This is also called the Brandt Commission Report.)

International Labor Organization (1977) Employment, Growth and Basic Needs: A One-World Problem.

LASZLO, E., R. BAKER, Jr., E. EISENBERG, and V. RAMAN (1978) The Objectives of the New International Economic Order. New York: Pergamon.

MATHIESON, J. A. (1981) Basic Needs and the New International Economic Order: An Opening for North-South Collaboration in the 1980s. Overseas Development Council, Working Paper No. 4. Washington, DC: Overseas Development Council.

MINIC, L. (1981) "Third world challenge." World Press Review (March).

MORTIMER, R. A. (1980) The Third World Coalition in World Politics. New York: Praeger.

NOSSITER, B. (1981) "U.S. policy at U.N.: a superficial shift." New York Times (May 18).

PEIRIS, D. (1981) "South-South collaboration." World Press Review (March).

———— (1980) "Punching holes in the smoke." South (October).

POND, E. (1981) "NATO pledges to zero in on third-world crisis." The Christian Science Monitor (May 6)

RENNINGER, J. (1981) The 11th Special Session and the Future of Global Negotiations. New York: UNITAR Policy Study.

SERVAN-SCHREIBER, J.-J. (1981) "The world challenge." World Press Review (July).

SILK, L. (1981) "McNamara warns U.S. of perils in reducing aid to world's poor." New York Times (June 21)

SMITH, T. (1977) "Changing configurations of power in North-South relations since 1945." International Organization 31 (Winter).

South (1980) "OPEC: facts and myths." (October).

United Nations Chronicle (1980) April.

United Nations Conference on Trade and Development (1976) U.N. Document TD/184.

United Nations General Assembly (1980) U.N. Document 34(A)/34/34.

_____ (1977a) U.N. Document A/31/PV.109 (September 19).

_____ (1977b) U.N. Document A/31/108 (September 13).

_____ (1977c) U.N. Document A/31/PV.108 (September 13).

_____ (1977d) U.N. Document A/31/48 (September 9).

_____ (1977e) U.N. Document A/31/478/Add.1 (August 9).

_____ (1977f) U.N. Document A/31/78 (June 24).

WEISS, T. G. and R. S. JORDAN (1976) The World Food Conference and Global Problem Solving. New York: Praeger.

World Bank (1980) World Development Report. Washington, DC: International Bank for Reconstruction and Development.

World Press Review (1981) Various issues.

CHAPTER 4

COHESION ET DISPERSION AU SEIN DU NOEI

ALICE HOUGASSIAN-RUDOVICH

L'émergence des pays du Tiers Monde au rang d'acteurs internationaux constitue un des traits dominants des relations internationales au cours des vingt dernières années. Les pays en voie de développement (PVD) se sont rendus compte de l'efficacité politique d'une approche collective dans des négociations internationales où les États individuels ont peu de poids. Les PVD ont appuyé leurs demandes sur des structures qui leur ont permis d'articuler leurs intérêts parmi lesquels l'organisation des pays exportateurs de pétrole (OPEP) pour les pays producteurs de pétrole, le groupe de 77, regroupant 122 pays, le groupe des états ACP (États de l'Afrique, du Pacifique, et des Caraïbes), au nombre de 60, pour les pays associés à la Communauté européenne et le Mouvement des Non-alignés. Ces coalitions dont le succès a été très variable ont marqué l'existence dans les instances internationales d'un pouvoir collectif du Tiers Monde. Par leur intermédiaire, les PVD ont exprimé des revendications de plus en plus spécifiques.

L'unité et la solidarité sont devenues pour l'ensemble des PVD des normes contraignantes dans la mesure où elles ne sont que rarement transgressées. Mais, une question se pose, comment cette solidarité et cette unité peuvent-elles résister à l'extrême diversité des PVD et aux tensions qui les opposent? Les réponses apportées par les PVD pour préserver leur unité ont été diverses. Le groupe des États ACP a préservé son unité et a cherché à légitimer son existence en institutionnalisant le groupe dès sa création en 1973. Par contre le groupe des 77 ne s'est doté d'un cadre institutionnel que fort tardivement. Aussi peut-on se demander si cette institutionnalisation assure ou non des avantages accrus pour les PVD et un maintien de leur unité? D'autre part, la solidarité entre les PVD dépend des revendications que défendent âprement ces pays. Il faut concevoir les diverses coalitions comme des relais par lesquels passent les revendications du Tiers Monde. Le groupe des 77 reprend certains thèmes chers au mouvement des Non-alignés et l'essentiel des revendications des 77 est repris par les ACP.

L'analyse du groupe des États ACP et du groupe des 77 qui défendent des intérêts similaires, mais, l'un dans un contexte ponctuel et l'autre dans un cadre plus général de réflexion est l'objet de cette étude. Le groupe des États ACP dispose de structures institutionnelles, diplomatiques et politiques qui doivent lui permettre d'agir comme un catalyseur pour les PVD et de concrétiser l'ensemble de ses revendications. Mais, malgré ses structures, le groupe ne reste uni que dans le cadre de ses négociations avec la Communauté européenne (CE). Il ne peut défendre la même unité au sein du groupe des 77. Les ACP ne constitueraient-ils pas une représentation réduite des contradictions qui agitent les PVD: condamnés à agir collectivement tout en ayant à assumer, de manière permanente, leurs divisions internes?

Structure, demandes et strategie du groupe des Etats ACP

Les ACP ne constituent pas à l'origine un groupe homogène. Lorsque les négociations de Lomé débutent en 1973, les ACP regroupent des Associés francophones liés à la CE par les Conventions de Yaoundé I et Yaoundé II et des Associables anglophones.

Dans une première phase, les Associés (EAMA) parviennent à négocier collectivement par la mise en place d'un mécanisme de coordination qui agit, en quelque sorte, extérieurement au groupe. En effet, l'Union africaine et malgache, dont la création en 1961 est appuyée par la France, coordonne les positions des Associés et développe leur action autour de trois axes: (1) garanties pour un développement et une industrialisation rapides; (2) maintien d'un tarif préférentiel; et (3) conditions avantageuses d'accès pour les produits tropicaux.

Sur le plan interne, lorsque les institutions paritaires de la Convention de Yaoundé se mettent en place, les EAMA aménagent des structures de coordination. Le Comité des ambassadeurs siège au niveau des ambassadeurs et le Conseil de coordination des EAMA, au niveau des ministres. Un secrétariat embryonnaire est chargé de la préparation des réunions et de l'élaboration des positions communes.

L'entrée des pays anglophones, opposés à des relations avec la CE qu'ils jugent néo-colonialistes, pose un problème en terme de pouvoir collectif de négociation. Le mécanisme de coordination organisé au niveau des pays associés ne peut suffire puisqu'il n'est constitué que de pays francophones et que le centre de décision se déplace vers les pays anglophones comme le Nigéria qui est particulièrement actif dans ces négociations. L'Organisation de l'Unité africaine (OUA) prend le relais de l'UAM. C'est à la conférence de Lagos, en 1973, que les dix-huit associés à la CE, la vingtaine de pays associables et trois pays des Caraïbes—qui participent en tant qu'observateurs—confient à l'OUA la tâche d'organiser un secrétariat unique pour les négociations avec la CE. Le rapprochement entre pays anglophones et pays francophones ne se fait pas sans difficulté. Mais, cette fois, le groupe manifeste la volonté d'agir collectivement. Le choix de Wenike Briggs (Nigéria) comme porte-parole des ACP aux négociations, symbolise cette détente entre futurs partenaires de la CE.

Fort de leur cohésion, trois mois après la signature de la Convention de Lomé, les quarante-six pays ACP se réunissent à Georgetown (Guyane) et y adoptent un accord par lequel les ACP se constituent officiellement en groupe d'états ACP.

STRUCTURE

Sur le plan institutionnel, les ACP reprennent le modèle d'organisation des négociations. Chaque organe conjoint ACP/CE,[1] à l'exception de l'Assemblée consultative, se double d'un organe spécifiquement ACP: le Conseil des ministres ACP et le Comité des ambassadeurs, assisté de quatorze sous-comités composés d'ambassadeurs ACP qui couvrent tous les domaines de la coopération. Dans les négociations de Lomé, les sous-comités qui se révèlent de précieux organes de discussions techniques, n'étaient qu'au nombre de sept.[2]

Les bureaux du Comité des ambassadeurs et du Conseil des ministres sont composés de six états ACP représentant chaque zone régionale de l'Afrique (Afrique de l'Ouest, du Sud, de l'Est, Afrique centrale), le Pacifique, et les Caraïbes. Un État ACP occupe, pour une durée de six mois, la présidence de ces bureaux. Depuis 1974, cependant, quelques pays comme la Guyane, la Jamaïque, le Sénégal, la Zambie, et le Rwanda ont occupé plus d'une fois ce poste.

Enfin, l'ensemble de ces organes est coiffé par le Secrétariat dont les tâches sont précisées. Il devient un organe permanent d'exécution non seulement dans les domaines internes à la vie de la Convention mais également en ce qui concerne les relations entre la CE et les ACP. Une vingtaine d'experts couvrent chacun des domaines de la Convention de Lomé. Mais, la structure interne du secrétariat se modifie en fonction des orientations définies lors des Conseils des ministres ACP.

Ainsi, dès avril 1977, le Conseil des ministres désire renforcer le secrétariat en ajoutant une division chargée de la coopération régionale, la division est effectivement créée non sans quelques difficultés. La Tanzanie et le Swaziland s'opposent à la création de cette nouvelle division et se prononcent pour la création d'un poste de vice-président chargé de la coopération régionale. En 1980, lors de la réunion de Montego Bay (Jamaïque) consacrée au développement et à la promotion des échanges commerciaux, les ministres ACP recommandent la création au sein du secrétariat d'une section chargée précisément du développement des exportations.

Les ACP ne sont en mesure de défendre une politique commune et opératoire qu'en adoptant une contrepartie institutionnelle à chaque nouveau domaine de la coopération. On peut expliquer cette position par l'hypothèse de l'externalisation, conçue par Philippe Schmitter (1969) à partir de l'exemple européen mais qui se vérifie davantage dans le cadre de l'action menée par les ACP à partir de 1973.

Dans le cas de la CE il y a bien une politique commune et opératoire à l'égard des ACP mais, des conflits de compétence entre le Conseil et la Commission et des divergences très profondes entre les états membres ont affaibli sa capacité d'externalisation.

L'institutionnalisation prônée par les ACP s'explique par le fait, comme le souligne le premier ministre de la Jamaïque, lors de la réunion de Montego Bay en 1980, "que la seule raison d'être des ACP ne peut provenir de la nécessité de négocier tous les cinq ans avec l'Europe. Un ensemble aussi vaste que le groupe des Etats ACP a besoin d'un ciment autre que les liens économiques avec l'Europe."

Les ACP poursuivent une stratégie très précise. Ils cherchent à assurer leur légitimité et à préserver leur unité en intégrant chaque politique dans une structure appropriée et en affirmant leur solidarité avec les pays en voie de développement.

STRATÉGIE

Les ACP constituent un groupe hétérogène. Au sein du groupe, les tensions entre les zones régionales ne sont pas rares. Les rapports entre États francophones et États anglophones ne sont équilibrés ni au sein du secrétariat ni au sein du groupe. Le secrétaire général et le secrétaire général adjoint, respectivement Okelo-Odongo—qui remplace, en 1981, Téoulé Konate— et Edward Carrington sont anglophones et le recrutement des fonctionnaires du secrétariat privilégie les anglophones dans une proportion de trois anglophones pour un francophone.

On ne peut sous-estimer le poids de certains pays comme le Nigéria qui comprend près d'un tiers de la population globale ACP. Lors des négociations de Lomé I, le Nigéria qui détenait la présidence de plusieurs groupes de travail dont le comité industriel pouvait utiliser ces diverses postes pour promouvoir ses intérêts.

Si certaines positions sont communes aux ACP,[3] comme le souligne Cosgrove-Twitchett (1979) d'autres points de négociation concernant notamment les matières premières font l'objet de revendications spécifiques à chaque état ACP. Sous Lomé I, le protocole sucre est négocié séparément entre la CE et les Caraïbes. Il n'est pas renégocié sous Lomé II et les Caraïbes peuvent se montrer plus exigeantes envers la CE que le reste des ACP qui doit défendre individuellement l'accès de certaines matières premières aux marchés européens.

D'une manière générale, les clivages entre les États ACP apparaissent davantage dans les négociations de Lomé II que de Lomé I: pays enclavés ou pays côtiers, pays possédant ou non des richesses minières, pétrolières ou agricoles, pays à options idéologiques différentes, pays aux capacités administratives et diplomatiques plus ou moins étendues. Ces divergences sont encore accrues par le fait que les décisions au sein du groupe des États ACP ne sont pas adoptées sur la base du vote mais par consensus. En cas de conflit, les États ACP doivent s'appuyer sur une structure de conciliation extérieure au groupe,[4] notamment l'OUA.

Condamnés à négocier sur une base commune face à la CE, le groupe des états ACP doit préserver sa cohésion en dehors des seules périodes de négociations. Le moyen utilisé par le groupe est l'affirmation de sa solidarité avec les PVD. Le groupe des États ACP prévoit dès le préambule de la déclaration de Georgetown l'entrée immédiate de tout État au sein des organes institutionnels ACP dès son accès à la Convention.

DEMANDES

Un an avant que ne débutent les négociations de Lomé II, le Conseil des ministres ACP, réuni à Fidji, adopte un programme d'action—la Déclaration de Suva—pour l'amélioration de la coopération régionale entre États ACP mais, qui constitue avant tout une plate-forme de négociations pour les ACP. La totalité des aspects abordés dans ce programme sera reprise au moment des négociations. Six secteurs concentrent l'attention des ACP: les transports et communications, la coopération commerciale, la création d'entreprises intra-ACP, le financement du développement, le transfert de techniques et enfin, la coopération scientifique et culturelle.

Jusqu'à présent seuls les deux premiers secteurs ont fait l'objet de réunions dans lesquelles sont reprises les principales revendications défendues également par le groupe des 77. La conférence de Bangui, organisée en 1977, recommande la ratification par les états ACP du Code de conduite des conférences maritimes, établi par la Conference des Nations Unies pour le commerce et le développement (CNUCED) et la création des Conseils nationaux et régionaux de chargeurs, d'organismes d'assurance à l'échelle de trois zones ACP, de centre régionaux d'études et de documentation sur les transports maritimes et d'écoles régionales de formation de cadres maritimes et aériens.

La conférence de Nairobi recommande, quant à elle, la création et le renforcement d'unions régionales de chambres de commerce et d'industrie, la mise en place de systèmes de crédit et d'assurance-crédit à l'exportation, un système d'informations commerciales entre états ACP et des organisations multilatérales de commercialisation.

Cependant la portée de ces programmes est considérablement réduite car ces revendications ne concernent que le groupe. Elles visent essentiellement à renforcer la cohésion du groupe, en dehors des seules périodes de négociation par l'approfondissement de liens régionaux. Or, la coopération régionale entre les États ACP est appuyée par la CE, mais celle-ci fixe des limites à la coopération intrafricaine. Dans l'esprit de la CE, la coopération intrafricaine qui repose sur une composante spécifiquement africaine à plus ou moins long terme doit être compatible avec la coopération euro-africaine qui défend quant à elle les intérêts économiques de l'Europe. A cet égard, les Conventions de Lomé I et Lomé II préservent l'ordre économique international fondé sur l'exportation par les PVD de matières premières contre l'importation par les pays industrialisés de produits finis et de biens d'équipement, comme le soulignent plusieurs auteurs (Shaw, 1979; Dolan, 1978; Myttelka, 1977).

D'un autre côté, certaines revendications ne font pas l'unanimité parmi le groupe des États ACP. Ainsi en est-il de la banque d'investissement ACP, proposée, dès décembre 1975, par le Conseil des ministres ACP réuni au Malawi. Le projet est confié à un groupe d'experts internationaux qui remettent leurs conclusions en février 1979.[5] Cette banque doit permettre de financer les échanges intra-ACP, de promouvoir et de réaliser quelques orientations de la coopération intra-ACP qui est au centre des revendications des ACP. La banque disposerait de pouvoirs étendus. Le rapport soumis au Conseil des ministres ACP, examine la structure des participations au capital et fixe les souscriptions selon un classement des États ACP, établi en fonction de leur part dans une échelle combinée du PNB et des exportations. Selon cette échelle, des pays comme le Nigéria, la Côte d'Ivoire, le Ghana, le Zaïre, la Zambie, Trinité et Tobago apporteraient une contribution plus importante au fonctionnement de la banque.

La Conseil des ministres de Montégo-Bay, en 1980, renvoie le rapport pour examen complémentaire. Les raisons invoquées sont révélatrices: la banque n'intègre pas suffisamment les structures bancaires existantes, le système de participation au capital doit être libéralisé et la concertation élargie avec les opérateurs bancaires ACP.

Le groupe des États ACP est donc le produit de contradictions. Extérieurement, il tente de présenter un front uni face à la CE, mais, intérieurement, il n'en présente pas moins des problèmes de cohésion. Face aux pays développés, le groupe des États ACP appartient au Tiers Monde ce qui lui confère une importance stratégique. La CE utilise, dans les divers forums internationaux, ses relations préférentielles avec les ACP comme témoin de sa bonne volonté. Face aux pays en voie de développement, les ACP occupent une position particulière puisqu'entretenant des relations privilégiées avec la CE. Les ACP se considèrent comme solidaires du Tiers Monde sans pour autant songer à abandonner leurs relations avec la CE.

De paradoxale, cette situation devient délicate: lors de la réunion de Fidji, début 1979, étape préliminaire dans le renouvellement de la Convention de Lomé, la CE recommande aux ACP d'exercer un rôle modérateur au sein du groupe des 77 et insiste sur le fait que les négociations de Lomé entrent dans leur phase finale avant l'ouverture de CNUCED V à Manille, en mai 1979. De leur côté, les ACP ne veulent pas reconduire la Convention avant la conclusion des travaux de CNUCED V.

La position des ACP est d'autant plus paradoxale qu'appartenant à titre individuel au groupe des 77, les pays ACP sont représentés collectivement à la CNUCED où ils ont été admis depuis 1978 comme organisation inter-gouvernementale. Les ACP essaient de concilier ces diverses positions. Face à la CE, ils appuient les demandes des PVD en faisant de leurs relations avec la CE un test pour les revendications du Tiers Monde. Face aux PVD, les ACP reprennent l'essentiel des revendications du groupe des 77 et tentent de leur donner une application concrète.

Structure, demandes et stratégies du groupe des 77

Au sein du groupe des 77, le problème de l'unité du mouvement se pose différemment. Par rapport aux ACP, le groupe des 77 est dépourvu de cadre institutionnel formel comme le notent plusieurs auteurs (Mortimer, 1980; Rothstein, 1979). Cette faiblesse institutionnelle tient, d'une part, à la diversité d'un groupe qui compte 122 membres et, d'autre part à son étroite symbiose avec l'organisation dans le cadre de laquelle le groupe agit: la CNUCED. Le personel de la CNUCED remplit le rôle de secrétariat du groupe des 77.

STRUCTURE

Le groupe des 77 fonctionne à l'aide d'une structure très simplifiée. Les différentes positions avant d'être harmonisées au niveau global font l'objet de négociations régionales entre le groupe africain, latino-américain, et asiatique.

Le groupe africain a d'ailleurs adopté un modèle décisionnel proche de celui des ACP. Les membres du bureau de la Commission de travail du groupe africain sont élus proportionnellement suivant la division régionale retenue par l'OUA.[6] L'élection au niveau du groupe et au niveau de sa commission se fait par pays. Le pays qui détient la présidence du groupe africain occupe également le poste de porte-parole de la Commission.

Les groupes asiatique et latino-américain nomment chacun un président. Au niveau global, le groupe élit un président choisi par rotation parmi les trois groupes régionaux. Les quatre chairmen constituent en quelque sorte le bureau des 77.

On retrouve dans le cas du groupe des 77, les liens fonctionnels entre revendications et formation de cadres institutionnels appropriés. Les 77 ont créé onze groupe subsidiaires s'occupant des différents domaines de négociation[7] et parmi lesquels figurent des pays représentant les trois groupes régionaux.

Depuis 1976, certains PVD parmi lesquels le Mexique et le Pakistan ont proposé l'augmentation de la capacité opérationnelle du groupe des 77 par la création d'un secrétariat, d'un comité d'experts permanent et par la réunion régulière de "sommets" des 77. Seule cette dernière proposition a été retenue, lors de la conférence de Mexico, en 1976. Le groupe africain et les pays non alignés ont estimé qu'un secrétariat accentuerait la duplication coûteuse et inutile d'organismes. Il ne faut pas sous-estimer également les considérations politiques. Un secrétariat permanent constituerait une contrainte limitant la capacité de pression de certains pays au sein des 77. Quant à la création d'un comité de cinq à six experts, la conférence de Caracas, en 1981, a réexaminé cette proposition sans toutefois l'adopter.

En fait, il existe un consensus au sein des 77 pour que le groupe conserve une structure essentiellement informelle. Aucun pays ne semble manifester la moindre intention de briser la compartimentalisation qui caractérise les regroupements de PVD. En effet, chaque regroupement se cantonne dans sa propre sphère d'activité sans interférer, de quelque manière, dans d'autres domaines.

Néanmoins l'unité du groupe des 77 n'a été entamé ni par sa faiblesse institutionnelle ni par les multiples clivages qui divisent le groupe. Branislav Gosovic (1972) distingue trois grands groupes de clivages dans le groupe des 77: politiques et idéologiques selon le régime adopté par les états, économiques entre pays plus ou moins avancés et, enfin, les pays qui entretiennent ou non des liens spéciaux avec les pays développés. Ces clivages ne sont pas figés et évoluent en fonction de l'environnement international.

Les clivages économiques se sont considérablement accentués par la division entre pays du Tiers Monde, producteurs et non producteurs de pétrole. Le problème de l'énergie n'a pas seulement ébranlé les pays industrialisés mais, a provoqué un véritable reclassement des forces au sein du Tiers Monde. La proposition de Costa-Rica d'inscrire une discussion sur les problèmes de l'énergie lors de CNUCED V à Manille, en mai 1979, a bloqué les négociations pendant quelques jours, au détriment d'autres points importants de discussion et, a failli entraîner une rupture au sein des 77.

En février 1980, Costa-Rica, appuyé par tous les états membres du Marché commun de l'Amérique centrale (MCAC)[8] a effectué une démarche auprès du Vénézuela et du Mexique—producteurs et exportateurs de pétrole—afin d'obtenir un traitement préférentiel pour l'approvisionnement énergétique du groupement. Cependant, l'action de pays tels que le Vénézuela, le Brésil, le Mexique qui exercent une surenchère dans tous les forums internationaux, a fait passer le clivage des liens discriminatoires avec les pays industrialisés au second plan des préoccupations du Tiers Monde. Ces décalages entre niveaux économiques de développement sont renforcés par des divergences politiques entre pays d'Amérique latine dont l'indépendance remonte au XIXème siècle et pays d'Afrique dont les problèmes de construction nationale ne sont pas encore résolus.

Néanmoins, ces divisions peuvent permettre de mener des négociations approfondies et d'arriver, paradoxalement, à un compromis entre les différents points de vue. Le système des préférences généralisées, introduit par un accord de la CNUCED en 1970, fournit un exemple de cette démarche.[9] Il faut toutefois préciser que comme au sein du groupe des Etats ACP, les décisions du groupe des 77 sont adoptées par consensus.

STRATÉGIE ET DEMANDES

Parmi les revendications du groupe des 77, le fonds commun pour les matières premières a fait l'objet de plusieurs études (Rothstein, 1979; Mortimer, 1980). Nous reprendrons ici un des thèmes qui est commun au groupe des États ACP et au groupe des 77, la coopération économique entre pays en développement (CEPD).[10]

La CEPD représente un exemple de la transformation du style des revendications des PVD. Les thèmes ne sont certes pas nouveaux—ils sont au centre des travaux de la CNUCED depuis 1964—mais, ils ont été intégrés dans un programme d'action précis et cohérent envisageant des mesures aussi bien techniques qu'économiques.

L'établissement d'un système mondial de préférence constitue l'armature de la CEPD mais ce système s'accompagne d'une série de mesures qui lui sont indissociables et qui sont revendiquées de la même manière par les ACP: système de crédits à l'exportation et de garanties de crédits, arrangements mutuels d'assurance, entreprises multinationales de commercialisation et de production, coopération entre organismes de commerce d'état, coopération en matière de transfert de technologie.

Ces différents secteurs exigent un cadre commun dans lequel la coopération puisse être menée simultanément sur tous les fronts. Les systèmes

régionaux et sous régionaux fournissent les rouages et les structures nécessaires à l'application de ces diverses structures.

Bien que les initiatives régionales existent dans les divers domaines
d'action de la coopération économique entre pays en développement—
préférences commerciales, système de promotion des entreprises multinationales[11]—elles restent circonscrites géographiquement. L'Association des
Nations de l'Asie du Sud-Est (ANASE) étant sur ce plan le groupement le
plus dynamique.[12] Plusieurs organisations sont affiliées à la chambre de
commerce de l'ANASE: association de producteurs de bois de construction
de l'Asie du Sud-Est, fédération automobile, fédération des fabricants de
ciment et de verre, fédération des industries alimentaires, club des industries
chimiques.

L'accent est mis au sein du groupe des 77 sur les groupements de producteurs. Jusqu'à présent, ces groupements ont été limités au continent latino-
américain ou africain. On trouve peu d'accords intercontinentaux malgré la
production commune de matières premières. Sur ce plan, le groupe des 77
peut permettre de réaliser les rapprochements nécessaires.

Ces groupements poursuivent un double objectif: assurer aux exportations de matières premières des prix justes et rémunérateurs et construire des
cellules à partir desquelles les pays producteurs adoptent des positions communes qu'ils défendront dans les négociations internationales. La seconde
préoccupation est au moins aussi prometteuse que la première dans la mesure où les mécanismes qui commandent les marchés mondiaux de matières
premières se trouvent concentrés dans les pays industrialisés.

Sous-jacente à ces alliances, comme à l'ensemble des secteurs de la
coopération économique entre pays en développement, "l'autonomie collective" est érigée en symbole et en but ultime par les PVD et demeure, par
conséquent, très peu explicitée par les textes. Toutefois, elle signifie que les
PVD désirent assumer la responsabilité de leur développement dans
l'aménagement des structures économiques.

Mais l'autonomie collective repose sur une contradiction. Les PVD
veulent établir des relations plus équilibrées avec les pays développés et
participer à l'élaboration d'une nouvelle organisation économique, mais ils
n'envisagent pas la remise en cause des fondements de l'ordre économique,
la division internationale du travail. En fait, l'autonomie collective telle
qu'elle est conçue par les PVD n'implique aucunement la modification des
relations d'interdépendance entre pays développés et pays en développement
puisque cette interdépendance demeure un élément essentiel de l'autonomie
collective.

Un rapide bilan de la CEPD fait apparaître des perspectives très inégales
selon les domaines. Les limites de la CEPD sur le plan de son efficacité
réelle tiennent à la faiblesse institutionnelle du groupe des 77.

Le groupe des 77 avait prévu à Mexico un cadre intergouvernemental adéquat destiné à assurer la mise en oeuvre effective des mesures de la CEPD. La réunion ministérielle du groupe des 77 ne pouvant fournir ce cadre. Cependant, si le groupe des 77 était d'accord sur la nécessité de ce mécanisme institutionnel, il n'arrivait pas à définir sa véritable nature. Le groupe des 77 hésitait entre diverses formules allant d'une unité d'appui technique à la création d'un secrétariat, organe de coordination et de réflexion.

Dans ce domaine, ce sont les recommandations du groupe de travail de la CNUCED sur la coopération régionale entre pays en développement qui ont été approuvées, sans qu'elles aient été appliquées pour autant. Ces recommandations minimisent la portée des conclusions du groupe des 77. Deux structures ont été retenues, l'une d'entre elles repose sur un organe intergouvernemental, subsidiaire au groupe des 77, qui délègue ses pouvoirs à des comités intergouvernementaux permanents. L'autre structure reprend l'idée d'un secrétariat, mais sous la forme d'un groupe consultatif intersecrétariat. Encore faut-il ajouter que ce groupe est mis en place à titre provisoire et officieux.

D'autre part, le secrétaire-général de la CNUCED n'a pas nié la nécessité d'un secrétariat mais soumet son existence à la restructuration du système des Nations Unies et de la CNUCED qui est loin d'être réalisée et qui remettrait en question les relations étroites qui existent entre la CNUCED et le groupe des 77.

Conclusion

Le groupe des 77 et le groupe des États ACP bien que vivant des situations diamétralement opposées, semblent encore dénués de la volonté politique de parvenir à la concrétisation de leurs revendications.

Des situations diamétralement opposées car dans le cas du groupe des 77, les revendications précises de la CEPD butent sur la faiblesse institutionnelle du groupe qui est précisément dûe à la seule volonté des pays membres du groupe des 77. Par contre, dans le cas des ACP, on constate un "surpouvoir." Les revendications des ACP ne sont pas limitées par des structures inadéquates. Mais elles sont paradoxalement vidées de leur sens par l'existence de la Convention de Lomé.

Prenons par exemple le fonds régional. Un groupe d'experts, réuni en 1973, soulignait la nécessité d'une planification intégrée exigeant une collaboration entre PVD sans littoral et pays voisins de transit et une assistance internationale accrue.[13] Or, les États ACP et les groupements régionaux disposent dans Lomé I de 10 pourcent de l'aide communautaire totale prévue pour les ACP et de 15 pourcent dans Lomé II. Ce fonds régional a financé des projets portant sur des entreprises de production et de commercialisation de matières premières (projet du Conseil africain de l'arachide), des projets d'infrastructures visant à désenclaver des régions isolées et des projets présentés par des organisations sousrégionales et régionales pour la mise en valeur de bassins fluviaux et l'aménagement de zones agricoles (Comité interétats pour la lutte contre la sécheresse des pays du Sahel, organisation de mise en valeur du fleuve Sénégal, Comité du fleuve Niger). Dans l'ensemble, les solutions apportées par le fonds régional, aux problèmes de transit ou de coopération régionale restent modestes. Essentiellement, parce que le nombre de projets véritablement régionaux[14] appuyés par des structures régionales sont en nombre fort limité. Pourtant, un des thèmes défendus par le groupe des États ACP concerne précisément l'amélioration et le renforcement de la coopération régionale entre États ACP. Reste encore le problème de la compatibilité entre un système de relations liant des économies inégalement développées et un système de relations horizontales entre les États ACP. Il est certain que la CE a une conception précise de la coopération régionale entre États ACP qui n'est pas forcément partagée par les ACP. Mais on ne peut nier l'existence d'une convention qui privilégie des relations verticales entre, d'une part la CE et, d'autre part les États ACP, même si ceux-ci veulent devenir un groupe autonome défendant un nouvel ordre économique international.

Si l'institutionnalisation des coalitions de PVD, tels les groupes des États ACP ou les groupes des 77, ne constitue pas un critère déterminant pour assurer l'unité du Tiers Monde, il n'en demeure pas moins que la convergence de leurs revendications, permet au Tiers Monde d'augmenter sa pression sur les pays industrialisés.

Mais la concrétisation de ces revendications dépend en dernier ressort de la stratégie développée par les pays industrialisés. La Convention de Lomé en constitue un exemple. Les coalitions sont l'expression de relations d'interdépendance, non seulement économiques mais également politiques, existantes entre les pays en développement et les pays développés.

NOTES

1. Les organes sont le Conseil des ministres, le Comité des ambassadeurs, et l'assemblée consultative, mais les organes spécifiquement ACP ne couvrent que les deux premiers.

2. Ce sont les comités de la coopération douanière, industrielle, commerciale, stabilisation des recettes d'exploitation, sucre, bananes, coopération financière et technique.

3. Stabilisation des recettes d'exportation et extension du Stabex aux produits miniers, sous Lomé II, augmentation du montant du FED alloué aux projets nationaux et régionaux, amélioration des mécanismes de sélection des projets et participation des états ACP dans les organes décisionnels.

4. Un conflit a opposé le Soudan et le Togo après la sélection, au niveau régional, des pays qui accueilleraient les signataires de la Convention de Lomé II. Le conflit n'a pu être résolu au

sein du groupe et c'est l'OUA, qui dispose d'un bureau exécutif à Bruxelles, qui a tranché en faveur du Togo.

5. Ce groupe comprend sept experts dont des représentants du secteur bancaire, des membres d'organisations internationales et des fonctionnaires internationaux. Un certain nombre de hauts fonctionnaires ont assisté aux quatre réunions de ce comité d'experts.

6. Pour l'Afrique de l'Ouest, le Nigéria, le Niger et la Gambie; pour l'Afrique centrale, le Zaïre, et le Rwanda; pour l'Afrique de l'Est, le Kenya, le Malawi et la Tanzanie et, enfin, pour l'Afrique du Nord, le Soudan et le Maroc. Cette division ne correspond pas à la division retenue par les ACP. Puisque le groupe africain des 77 englobe des pays ne participant pas à la Convention de Lomé.

7. Groupe des quinze sur les produits manufacturés, sur les pratiques commerciales restrictives, sur les problèmes monétaires et financiers, sur la rationalisation, la stratégie internationale du développement et le transfert de technologie; groupe des trente-trois sur le fonds commun, groupe des trente sur la coopération économique entre pays en développement; Comité de coordination sur les négociations commerciales multilatérales.

8. Le MCAC comprend Costa-Rica, El Salvador, Guatemala, Honduras, et Nicaragua.

9. Les ACP étaient opposés à un système qui aurait érodé leur accès commercial privilégié à la CE. De nombreux pays, dont les états latino-américains, désiraient l'introduction du SPG et considéraient Lomé comme discriminatoire pour eux. Finalement, un accord a été conclu: l'introduction du SPG en échange de mesures en faveur des pays les moins développés.

10. Depuis 1976, plusieurs réunions ont permis de préciser et d'établir un programme d'ensemble de la coopération économique entre pays en développement: réunion ministérielle du groupe des 77, en 1976; réunion du mouvement des Nonalignés à Colombo en 1976; réunion du groupe des 77 à Arusha en 1979.

11. Le groupe Andin, le CARICOM, l'union douanière et économique de l'Afrique centrale (Cameroun, Gabon, RCA, et Congo) ont mis en place des systèmes de promotion des entreprises multinationales. Plus de 50 pays membres de groupements régionaux participent à des accords de préférences commerciaux.

12. L'ANASE comprend la Malaisie, l'Indonésie, les Philippines, la Thaïlande, et Singapour.

13. La Commission pour la CEPD, quant à elle, recommandait que dans le cadre de plans régionaux de coopération entre PVD, des dispositions soient prises en vue d'exploiter conjointement les bassins fluviaux communs ou les autres ressources potentielles en prévoyant un appui spécial pour les pays moins avancés, d'exécuter des programmes de formation régionaux et sous régionaux et, enfin, d'améliore les réseaux de communication interétats.

14. En effet, la plupart des institutions financières internationales ont retenu le critère de multinationalité. La CE elle-même considère que les "projets régionaux sont ceux qui contribuent directement à la solution d'un problème de développement commun à deux ou plusieurs pays par la réalisation d'actions communes ou d'actions nationels coordonées." Or, le critère de la multinationalité ne semble pas déterminant. Les projets d'infrastructure illustrent cette ambiguïté. Ils peuvent intéresser plusieurs états et être réalisés dans un cadre national; UNCTAD (1975) le rôle des institutions financières multinationales dans la promotion de l'intégration économique entre PVD (Nations Unies, 1978).

RÉFÉRENCES

BERHANYKUN, A. (1979) Regionalism and the U.N. Oceana publications. Sijhtoff and Nordhoff.

COSGROVE-TWITCHETT, C. (1978) Towards London. London: Royal Commonwealth Society.

_____ (1978) A Framework for Development: The EEC and the ACP. London: Allen & Unwin.

GOSOVIC, B. (1972) UNCTAD and Compromise. Leiden: Sijhtoff & Nordoff.

Groupe des Etats d'Afrique, des Caraïbes, et du Pacifique (1980) Compte-rendu de la 25ème session du Conseil des ministres ACP, Montego-Bay. Bruxelles: ACP.

_____ (1980) Compte-rendu de la conférence ACP-CEE sur le developpement de la promotion des échanges commerciaux ACP, Nairobi. Bruxelles: ACP.

_____ (1978) Rapport de la conférence sur la coopération intra-ACP dans le domaine des transports et des communications, Bangui. Bruxelles: ACP.

_____ (1979) Accord de Georgetown relatif à l'organisme des Etats d'Afrique, des Caraïbes et du Pacifique. Bruxelles: ACP.

HAAS, E. and E. ROWE (1969) "Is there externalization?" International Studies Quarterly 17 (March): 340-370.

MORTIMER, R. (1980) Third World in International Politics. New York: Praeger.

Nations Unies, Conseil économique et social (1978) Stratégie globale pour la mise en oeuvre du programme de la décennie des Nations Unies pour les transports et les communications en Afrique. New York: Nations Unies.

ROTHSTEIN, R. (1979) Global Bargaining: UNCTAD and the Quest for a NIEO. Princeton, NJ: Princeton University Press.

SCHMITTER, P. (1969) "Three neo-functionnal hypotheses about international integration." International Organization 23 (Winter): 161-165.

UNCTAD (1979a) Coopération économique entre pays en dévelopement: domaines d'actions prioritaires. New York: Nations Unies.

_____ (1979b) Evaluation des progrès réalisés sur la voie du Nouvel ordre économique international. Genève: Nations Unies.

_____ (1978) Quelques aspects relatifs à la création d'entreprises multinationales de commercialisation en Afrique. Genève: Nations Unies.

_____ (1977) Rapport de la Commission de la CEPD. New York: Nations Unies.

UNCTAD/UNDP (1979) Rapport sur les réunions du groupe d'experts de la coopération entre pays en développement. Genève: Nations Unies.

_____ (1978) Secteurs favorables à la création d'entreprises multinationales. Genève: Nations Unies.

PART III

Changes in the Global Political Economy and Western Industrialized States

Change in the global political economy both depends upon and will force changes within the political economies of states since they are the components of the global system. Because of the predominant position of the western states in the global political economy, they inevitably will be seriously affected by global change and their capacity and willingness to accept domestic change will be a major force in determining the pace of global change. Thus it is appropriate to begin an analysis of changes in the global political economy by examining how this affects western states.

Employment is a key issue. The relatively open neoliberal international economic order fosters international competition. As the competitive advantage in the production of particular products shifts from one area to another, those enterprises that are no longer competitive will lose their share of markets. If they cannot regain their competitiveness or shift to other product lines where they have a competitive advantage, the firms will face bankruptcy and their workers will face unemployment. Adjustments to meet competition, whether they involve revitalizing existing enterprises or creating new industries, can be difficult and painful.

Since all western countries are committed to maintaining high levels of employment, their governments are under considerable pressure to take actions to ease adjustments. Creating a protected market can appear attractive because it has relatively modest short-term costs. Moreover, enterprises can blame the loss of their market share on unfair competition rather than on a loss of competitiveness, and given the complexity of modern economies, it is not always easy to determine whether the regulations of different governments and the pricing policies of enterprises in different jurisdictions do result in enterprises in one state having unfair competitive advantages over those in another. This makes taking protectionist measures even easier. They can be justified—or rationalized—as being necessary to prevent unfair competition.

Preserving employment is not the only reason why states resort to protectionist measures. Governments may choose to protect certain domestic industries even though by global standards they are not competitive. They may feel—rightly or wrongly—that these industries are essential to preserving the national way of life or are vital to national military efforts.

For whatever reason they may be adopted, protectionist measures can slow the impact of change on global patterns of production. Further, if the major western states moved substantially in the direction of protectionism, this could threaten and destroy the neoliberal international economic order.

The two chapters that comprise this part of the book are case studies of how two western states, the United States and France, respectively, have responded when enterprises in particular industrial sectors have faced increasing international competition. Chapter 5, by Robert S. Walters, is an analysis of U.S. policy with respect to the steel industry during the late 1970s. There was a surge of steel imports into the United States in 1977 that seriously threatened the U.S. steel industry. The U.S. reaction to this situation is of particular interest because of the role that the United States has played in the creation and operation of the neoliberal international economic order. The fact that having a domestic steel industry has traditionally been seen as being crucial to a state's military power elevated the stakes and the significance of the issues involved. Professor Walters shows how the steel industry and government officials developed quite different theories about the cause of the crisis, and he shows how the government attempted to develop policies for dealing with the crisis that would at the same time preserve the U.S. steel industry and the neoliberal international economic order. His lack of optimism about the long-run viability of the solution highlights some difficulties that the United States and other western states will face in the closing decades of the twentieth century.

The sixth chapter, by Lynn Krieger Mytelka, examines French policy concerning the textile industry in the period since the end of World War II. Textile industries have typically been created during early stages of industrialization, and they have traditionally been seen as low-productivity industries in which regions and states that have a large supply of low-wage labor would have a competitive advantage. Textile industries in all of the industrialized capitalist states have faced difficulties in the post-World War II period, so the problem that France faced is not atypical. On the other hand, in contrast to most other western states, France has long had a tradition of strong intervention by the government in the economy. A strong inclination toward protectionism has been part of this tradition. Professor Mytelka traces the several actions that French governments have taken with respect to the French textile industry, analyzes why these particular actions were taken, and assesses their consequences. By the end of the 1970s, even though employment in the French textile industry had dropped substantially and production had been concentrated in larger enterprises, the industry remained in a troubled state and the government was subject to renewed protectionist pressures.

Neither the U.S. steel nor the French textile case study reveals a formula by which western states could easily manage the domestic aspects of change in the global political economy. On the contrary, each reveals how difficult this task is. By showing the many factors that are involved and how policies must take into account national traditions and local conditions, however, each contributes to a better understanding of this task and perhaps thereby to making the task somewhat easier.

CHAPTER 5

THE U.S. STEEL INDUSTRY
National Policies and International Trade

ROBERT S. WALTERS

The prosperity of western states (advanced market economies) and growth prospects for less developed countries are widely perceived to have been advanced by an open international trade order since World War II. This trade order is being severely tested by massive structural shifts[1] in international production and trade for a rapidly expanding list of major industries such as steel, textiles, apparel, footwear, consumer electronic goods, shipbuilding, automobiles, petrochemicals, semiconductors, and computers. Structural shifts in international production and trade in key industries produce wrenching domestic economic, social, and political adjustment problems. They give rise to intense protectionist pressures from laborers, firms, and regions adversely affected by import penetration. Demands are made for bold national programs either to restore the beleaguered industry's competitiveness or to cushion the domestic impacts of its demise in response to the imperatives of the marketplace. Maintenance of a relatively open international trade order will require controlling traditional forms of protectionism as well as creating more effective multilateral mechanisms for managing the trade distorting effects of national adjustment policies.[2]

The United States has since 1945 provided leadership for the liberal international trade order. Stephen Krasner (1976), Robert Gilpin (1970), and many others have suggested that this role is likely to change as U.S. hegemony in the global political economy erodes. More particularly, the

AUTHOR'S NOTE: I wish to express my thanks to the University of Pittsburgh for the Research Expenses Grant that enabled me to conduct this research during the Summer of 1979.

American commitment to a liberal trade order in the years immediately ahead will depend upon its capacity for rapid domestic adaptation to basic changes in international competitiveness for a wide array of important industrial sectors within which the U.S. competitiveness has traditionally been very strong. If the challenge is not met successfully, the United States will turn to more protectionist policies and the international trade order will lose the engine that has for three decades provided its liberal thrust.

How is the United States to face the challenge of a declining competitiveness in a number of its major industries? What differences exist between industry analysts and key government analysts in their assessments of the challenge? How do these assessments determine the shape of policies adopted by the private sector and the federal government? To what extent do market forces and/or government policies account for shifts in competitiveness, and to what extent are each to be relied upon to direct the adjustment process? What is the character of the interplay between domestic policies that promote orderly adjustments in key industries threatened by imports and trade policies seeking to preserve an open international economy? A better understanding of these sorts of questions can yield important insights about America's prospects for economic adjustment in an atmosphere of rapidly developing changes in international production. The success or failure of the United States in meeting this challenge will have a significant impact on multilateral efforts at international economic peacekeeping among advanced market economies and between these countries and a more aggressive group of newly industrializing states in the Third World.

These sorts of problems typically confront industries and governments as political-economic shocks impacting in very pointed ways upon vulnerable segments of an economy. Our understanding of the political-economic dynamics surrounding domestic and international adjustment efforts requires sectoral analyses rather than (or in addition to) aggregate approaches. Accordingly, we will examine U.S. policy toward the steel industry during the late 1970s in terms of what it suggests about the country's capacity to confront the larger challenges of adjustment to structural shifts in international production and trade.[3]

The steel industry provides us with an excellent empirical referent for dealing with the larger questions being raised here. The steel industry in the United States, and in every industrialized state, provides the foundation for a wide range of economic activity and national security. It is virtually inconceivable that any country would stand idly by in the face of a serious threat to its indigenous steel-making capacity, thereby inviting increased foreign leverage over its economic stability and military capability. Steel making is the third largest industry in the United States behind petroleum and automobiles. Policy responses designed to meet threats from foreign competition to the viability of this significant an industry in the U.S. economy are bound to provide indications of policies vis à vis other industries facing similar challenges in the future.

The steel sector is also a good choice for our analysis because a global overcapacity in steel making has emerged in recent years. This means that the European Economic Community (EEC), Japan, and a number of newly emerging steel exporters (such as Spain, South Africa, Taiwan, South Korea, Mexico, Brazil, and Argentina) as well as the United States are facing policy choices about how to manage shifts in international steel production and trade. This industry permits observation of multilateral as well as domestic efforts to manage economic adjustments with obvious potential for generating international economic conflict.

The U.S. Steel Crisis of 1977

The focus of our analysis will be the U.S. responses to the surge of imports in steel mill products during 1977 and the implications suggested by that response for overall U.S. trade policy.[4] The steel import challenge in 1977 must be understood against the backdrop of a secular decline in the U.S. steel industry's position in international production and trade.

The decline in U.S. steel making is evident on a number of dimensions. The data in Table 5.1 provide a sense of change in the shares of the United States and other major steel producers since 1955, when the reconstruction in the steel industries of Europe and Japan was completed. Whereas world production of raw steel increased 153 percent between 1955 and 1976, U.S. production rose only 9 percent. By 1976, the United States produced only 17 percent of the world's raw steel, compared to its share of 39 percent in 1955. The decline has continued through 1980. During this period, the USSR became the world's largest steel producer; Japan is generally conceded to have become the world's most efficient steelmaker with output increases of over 1000 percent since 1955; and numerous new entrants into steel making have seriously eroded the dominant position that the United States and Europe traditionally occupied in international steel production. This lack of growth in steel output has been paralleled by a reduction of the labor force in the U.S. steel industry. Employment declined from approximately 500,000 in the mid-sixties to 385,000 in mid-1977 (U.S. Council on Wage and Price Stability, 1977: 17).

The position of the U.S. steel industry in foreign trade also reflects a significant alteration over the past 25 years. While the world's steel exports as a proportion of world steel production increased from 13 percent in 1955 to 23 percent in 1975, U.S. steel exports as a proportion of U.S. steel production decreased from 5 percent to 3 percent (U.S. Council on Wage and Price Stability, 1977: 111). Moreover, the United States, which used to

TABLE 5.1   World Raw Steel Production, 1955 and 1976
            (in millions of net tons and as percentage of world total)

	1955		1976	
United States	117	(39)	128	(17)
European Economic Community	80	(27)	148	(20)
Japan	10	(4)	118	(16)
Other noncommunist countries	21	(7)	105	(14)[a]
Communist countries	70	(23)	253	(34)[b]
TOTAL	398		752	

SOURCE: U.S. Council on Wage and Price Stability, 1977: 106-107.

a. The principal steel producers here in order of importance are: Canada, Spain, India, Brazil, Australia, South Africa, Mexico, Sweden, Austria, South Korea, Argentina, Turkey, Finland, and Taiwan.

b. The principal Steel producers here in order of importance are: USSR (162 million net tons), China, Poland, Czechoslovakia, Romania, East Germany, Hungary, North Korea, Yugoslavia, and Bulgaria.

be a net steel exporter, has become since 1959 a net importer of steel mill products. Imports as a proportion of U.S. steel consumption rose from an average level of 5 percent in the early 1960s to an average level of 14.5 percent over the 1970-1976 period (U.S. Council on Wage and Price Stability, 1977: 14). The significance of the United States in world steel trade now lies primarily in its position as the world's largest and most accessible market.

These trends in production, employment, and trade indicate an unmistakable decline in the U.S. steel industry for the past two decades. Superimposed on these long term trends were a series of shocks to the U.S. steel industry during 1977. Steel imports rose abruptly to 19.3 million tons—35 percent above the level of imports in 1976. Import penetration rose to 17.8 percent of total U.S. consumption of steel mill products in 1977, compared to 14.1 percent the previous year (see Table 5.2). During the last ten months of the year, steel plants with a combined raw steel capacity of 5.6 million tons were closed down. Over 20,000 steel workers were thrown out of jobs—most of them concentrated in traditional steel-making communities of New York, Pennsylvania, and Ohio (Hogan, 1977: 1-2). During the period from 1976 to mid-1977, the U.S. government certified 67,000 steelworkers eligible to receive trade adjustment assistance (U.S. House of Representatives, 1977c: 323). The U.S. industry as a whole was utilizing only 78 percent of its capacity to produce raw steel (American Iron and Steel Institute, 1978a: 58). Finally, the financial status of the industry was abysmal. "The U.S. steel industries ranked 37th among 40 domestic industries in net profits as a percentage of net worth in 1976. During the first half of 1977, Citibank cited iron and steel industry earnings declines as the highest in 22 industry categories" (U.S. House of Representatives, 1977c: 322).

The United States was not alone in having to confront a steel crisis. The steel industries of the EEC and Japan were operating at only 63 and 71 percent of capacity, respectively (European Economic Community, 1979: 1). These producers, too, were undertaking programs to eliminate excess production and tens of thousands of jobs (see U.S. House of Representatives, 1978: 107). There was a global overcapacity in raw steel production— a cyclical industry, undergoing profound structural change internationally, was in one of its worst downswings in the postwar period.

Industry Appraisals of the Sources of the Steel Challenge to the United States

As the dimensions of the steel challenge became evident in 1977, there was no shortage of assessments of the sources of the steel industry's problems and prescriptions for their solution (Putnam, Hayes, and Bartlett, Inc., 1977; Hogan, 1977; U.S. Committee on Wage and Price Stability, 1977; U.S. Federal Trade Commission, 1977; Business Week, 1977). Spokesmen on behalf of the industry view imports as the major source of the steel industry's malaise in the United States. They insist that in the U.S. market, domestic steel producers are competitive with foreign producers—including the Japanese. The average production costs of making steel in the United States are roughly equal to the average costs of producing and transporting steel to the U.S. market from Japan (the most efficient steelmaker). U.S. costs are less than average production and transportation costs in the case of European imports. Import penetration is viewed as a function of a series of unfair trade practices on the part of foreign producers, as well as a lack of political will on the part of the U.S. government to apply trade laws designed to cope with these unfair practices.

Among the practices cited as constituting unfair trade are export incentives, border tax rebates (such as the value-added tax rebates for EEC exports), subsidized loans for foreign steel producers, continued access of foreign steelmakers to loans for modernization and expansion of capacity notwithstanding market conditions and debt-to-equity ratios that would make further borrowing impossible for U.S. firms, cartelization practices, and agreements between the EEC and Japan that have diverted Japanese steel exports to the United States from Europe (U.S. House of Representatives, 1977c, 1978b: 171). However, spokesmen on behalf of the U.S. steel industry have concentrated on dumping as the most explicit form of unfair trade underlying import penetration of the U.S. steel market. They emphatically claim that steel imports in massive quantities are coming into the United States at prices below the average costs of production and delivery and/or below prices in the home market of foreign producers. Particularly when faced with an overcapacity in steel production, foreign producers are believed by the U.S. industry to engage in predatory pricing in the U.S. market as a countercyclical policy to sustain production and jobs, and to cover their high fixed costs (U.S. House of Representatives, 1977c: 190-191, 1977a: 241-244).

These import problems are compounded, in the industry's view, by the US government's unwillingness to administer, forcefully, existing trade laws designed to deal with dumping and subsidized imports. Among other things, industry spokesmen decry the Treasury Department's finding that giving rebates for the value-added tax for exports from the EEC is *not* an unfair trade subsidy providing grounds for the imposition of countervailing duties under U.S. law. Similarly, they object to the administration's determination that the steel industry failed to provide proof that the bilateral agreement limiting Japanese steel exports to the EEC had injured the U.S. industry through diversion of Japanese exports to the United States (U.S. House of Representatives, 1978b: 79-80). More importantly, the government's administration of antidumping legislation is criticized repeatedly for such things as the Treasury Department's reluctance to undertake investigations of dumping on its own initiative, the burdens of data-gathering and proof placed on firms in their efforts to convince the Treasury to undertake dumping investigations, the length of time the process takes to obtain a finding that dumping has occurred, and the lenience in penalties exacted on foreign firms found to have been engaged in dumping (U.S. House of Representatives, 1977b: 72ff, 1978b: 88-89). In short, the U.S. steel industry has felt itself to be "up against not only the importers, but also our own government (U.S. House of Representatives, 1977a: 243).

Continued import penetration at levels anything like those of 1977 is seen to undermine the vitality of the domestic industry. Not only do imports directly displace domestic production and workers, but they lower the U.S. industry's utilization of capacity. That in turn reduces productivity levels, earnings, and access to credit necessary to finance modernization programs enabling the industry to remain competitive, and to finance the installation of apparatus enabling firms to comply with environmental standards.

Excessive reliance on imports, it is pointed out, discourages new investment and reinforces the unique status of the United States as the only major industrialized state unable to supply its steel needs via domestic production. This not only raises national security questions, but will make the United States vulnerable to very high steel prices from foreign producers upon whom we are dependent, should steel shortages predicted for the mid-1980s materialize (U.S. House of Representatives, 1977c: 191; Stinson, 1979: 6-9).

In addition to these import-related problems, U.S. steelmakers feel a host of government policies have inhibited growth and efficiency in the industry.

Most prominent among these policies in recent years, of course, are mandated reductions in air and water pollution emissions. The steel industry since 1975 has been spending roughly $500 million per year for pollution control. This constitutes about 25 percent of the industry's total capital expenditures. It is anticipated that pollution abatement costs will comprise between 5 and 10 percent of the price of steel in the near future (U.S. House of Representatives, 1978: 28). While accepting the general goal of improving environmental standards, the steel industry views "nonproductive investment" for pollution abatement as an important restraint on "productive" investment enabling domestic steelmakers to improve their competitiveness. Beyond the costs, per se, industry spokesmen (and analysts outside the industry) are deeply concerned about incentives and uncertainties in the Environmental Protection Agency's (EPA) regulations which encourage retention of old facilities and discourage development of new ones (U.S. Council on Wage and Price Stability, 1977: 36-37). George Stinson of the National Steel Corporation characterized the industry's frustration with environmental regulations as follows:

> While I have expressed our concern with government regulation . . . I hasten to add that I didn't challenge the motives of our regulators. Most are concerned and highly dedicated people. But, unfortunately, many are like well-meaning, but inexperienced, story-book knights who rush out to slay dragons for God and country, only they are not quite sure what is a dragon and what is a cow. Right now, we're losing a lot of cows, and we wish they would be a bit more selective in pollution regulation and pay a great deal more heed to cost-benefit relationships [1979: 13].

Additional complaints of government policy inhibiting growth and efficiency in the steel industry are focused on the "jawboning" practice of numerous administrations since President Kennedy's celebrated confrontation with Roger Blough and U.S. Steel that rolled back price increases in 1962 (see McConnell, 1963). Defenders of the steel industry feel this protracted "jawboning" has kept steel earnings and investment below what they could have been—particularly during peak periods of the steel industry's performance when capital resources must be acquired to enable the cyclical industry to ride out the lean years.

Finally, industry spokesmen point to the conflict and confusion caused by an array of thousands of regulations pertaining to the iron and steel industry administered by over two dozen government agencies. "The Federal Energy Administration might want to turn out every other light to save electricity, then OSHA [Occupational Safety and Health Administration] turn them back on for safety reasons" (Steel Cities Coalition, 1977: 24). The regulatory inconsistencies and the lack of comprehension of their overall impact, inhibit the industry's efficiency. David Ignatius (1979: 8) supports this industry complaint about the awesome regulatory environment confronting U.S. steel producers:[5]

> In its dealings with the industry, the government has behaved like the worst sort of monopolist: remote, arbitrary, and inefficient. Even as steel's problems worsened, the various components of the federal establishment clung to their separate bureaucratic imperatives—unplanned and, for the most part, uncomprehending.
>
> By the 1970s, the federal government had a hand in virtually every aspect of the industry. . . . For the most part, the various bureaucracies were too busy tilling their own gardens to worry much about the overall health of the industry. That wasn't anybody's job really.

This overview of the sources of the problem confronting the U.S. steel industry is necessarily oversimplified; but, it can provide the basis upon which to understand the U.S. industry's general approach to coping with steel import challenges. The orientation clearly embodies no recognition of the need for U.S. steelmakers to accommodate a structural shift in international production and trade of steel. Growth in the share of the U.S. steel market accounted for by imports is not a sign of a loss in competitiveness by the U.S. steel industry. It is not a reflection of "real" market forces at work, to which domestic steelmakers should adjust:

> Theory . . . argues that the market works well to allocate resources only when prices reflect full costs of production, including an adequate return on equity. If some producers are able to maintain protected prices in their home market while using lower prices to displace competition in the export market, the resulting market shares are undesirable for the importing country [U.S. House of Representatives, 1977c: 188].

Beyond normal modernization efforts, the burdens of adjustment to import penetration threatening U.S. steelmakers should be borne principally in several places other than the U.S. steel industry. Foreign steel producers seeking access to the United States should have to face the discipline of the market. That is, the insulation they are provided from market forces by their home governments through a wide array of subsidies and export incentives should be dismantled. Their exports should be priced at levels which reflect full costs of production, transportation, and an adequate return on equity—i.e., they must not be allowed to dump steel in the U.S. market below fair value. Also, the U.S. government should adapt in two fundamental respects. First, trade laws designed to protect domestic producers from unfair trade should be administered promptly, effectively and "nonpolitically" by various executive agencies responsible for trade—unlike past practices which have been ineffective, lethargic, and excessively timid in the view of the industry. Second, the federal government should begin to acquire at least some sense of the comprehensive impact that the aggregate policies of over two dozen government agencies (often acting independently and at cross-purposes) are having on the steel industry as a whole (see U.S. House of Representatives, 1977c: 187). These policies must be rationalized if U.S. steel producers are to remain competitive.

Government Appraisals of the Sources of the Steel Challenge to the United States

Government analysts of the steel industry are sharply at odds with industry spokesmen on the basic sources of increased import competition facing U.S. steelmakers. Instances of dumping may occur, but dumping is felt to account for only a small portion of total steel imports. Subsidies provided to foreign steelmakers by European states and Japan are held to be generally too small to account for any significant import penetration of the U.S. market. A study by the Federal Trade Commission examined a wide variety of subsidies to steel producers in Japan, Germany, France, Italy, Belgium, and the United Kingdom. With the single exception of subsidies to the British Steel Corporation (amounting to $11 per metric ton), none of the subsidies granted by other governments were calculated to have amounted to as much as one percent of the selling price of steel in the United States (U.S. Federal Trade Commission, 1977: 368-369). Subsidies to the Japanese steel industry, for example, were found to amount to less than one-fifth of one percent of the average price of steel sold in the United States (U.S. Federal Trade Commission, 1977: 367). More generally on the issue of subsidies, government analysts and officials see U.S. trade law on provisions for imposing countervailing duties as applicable only to subsidies *clearly distorting international trade*—not to *any* benefits governments might provide industries within their jurisdictions that have no special impact on exports (U.S. House of Representatives, 1977c: 146).

Government analyses of the steel industry concede that the manner in which pollution abatement measures are being administered by the EPA creates some important disincentives for modernization of the steel industry. Moreover, there is no question that the costs of compliance with environmental standards are imposing significant demands on the U.S. steel industry's limited investment capital (U.S. Council on Wage and Price Stability, 1977: 35-37). On the other hand, these analyses also point out that foreign steel producers face strong demands by their governments for pollution abatement. In 1976, pollution control outlays by the steel industry in Japan, for example, exceeded those of the U.S. industry and constituted 20 percent of the Japanese steel producers' overall investment (U.S. Council on Wage and Price Stability, 1977: 37). Thus, as great a challenge as pollution abatement processes and expenses pose for U.S. steelmakers, the challenges are much the same for major foreign steel competitors. This would not appear to account significantly for differences in production costs, competitiveness, or import penetration.

Costs of production, price levels, inflexible price policies, and relatively high costs of modernization in the United States lie at the heart of the long- and short-term challenges confronting U.S. steel producers according to government analyses. Over the past twenty years, the combination of these factors has made U.S. steel producers increasingly vulnerable to competition from imports.

Coal, iron ore, and labor, together, account for approximately 60 percent of total steel production costs. In the case of each of these factor inputs, U.S. costs have risen dramatically in absolute terms and relative to those faced by the major competitor in the U.S. market, Japan.

Labor costs in the U.S. steel industry have also risen dramatically—much more rapidly than in the overall manufacturing sector of the U.S. economy. Labor agreements during the 1970s have pushed total hourly employment costs in the steel industry to over 60 percent above the corresponding costs for all manufacturing in the United States. This *margin* by which steelworkers hourly compensation in 1976 exceeded compensation in all manufacturing, has *doubled* since 1967 (U.S. Council on Wage and Price Stability, 1977: 31). While labor compensation levels in the U.S. steel industry have increased well above most of those elsewhere in the manufacturing sector, productivity increases have lagged far behind (U.S. Council on Wage and Price Stability, 1977: 34)[6]

These developments in factor costs from such major components of U.S. steel production have helped drive steel prices upward more rapidly than the national industrial average in the United States (U.S. Council on Wage and Price Stability, 1977: 19). Government analyses also note that steel prices have been the least flexible of industrial prices in the United States. During periods of over-capacity and general economic contraction, U.S. steel prices have remained comparatively stable in relation to the significant price discounts offered by foreign producers (U.S. Council on Wage and Price Stability, 1977: 20). Such was the case during 1976 and 1977, critics of the U.S. steel industry contend (U.S. House of Representatives, 1977c: 157). Both the level of prices and their inflexibility lie at the heart of import competition for U.S. steel producers in key government assessments of the industry (U.S. Council on Wage and Price Stability, 1977: 48).

The problem of eroding competitiveness is compounded by the very high costs of modernizing the U.S. steel industry, particularly in comparison with Japanese modernization costs. U.S. producers have, quite sensibly in the view of government analysts, chosen to modernize through "rounding out" existing facilities rather than developing totally new "greenfield" facilities—the latter being prohibitively costly in the United States. Yet in Japan, the costs of new sites appear to be lower than the costs of round-out investment in the United States (U.S. Council on Wage and Price Stability, 1977: 83). The long-term implications of such disparities in the realistic modernization choices facing U.S. and Japanese steelmakers are obvious—even if at present the U.S. industry remains competitive with the Japanese in the American market.

In summary, this combination of production costs, price performance, and modernizing strategies suggests to government analysts that developments intrinsic to the U.S. steel industry are the principal source of its major difficulties and account for both the long-term increases in foreign producers' penetration of the U.S. market since 1959, and steel import surges of the sort confronting the United States in 1977.

Contrary to the industry's position, government analysts tend to see a structural shift in the international production and trade of steel to the detriment of the U.S. industry. Most importantly, the structural shifts and cyclical import surges are, indeed, understood to be a consequence of "real" market forces for the most part. The implication is, clearly, that the U.S. steel industry should accommodate to the imperatives of the structural shifts dictated by, and reflected accurately in, the market.

Political Mobilization by the Steel Sector and the Solomon Plan[7]

Whatever disagreements existed over the root causes of the U.S. steel industry's difficulties, it was clear in late 1977 that some public policy response was required in the face of steel plant closings, huge layoffs, accelerated import penetration, low utilization of capacity, and dwindling cash flows within the steel industry. Pressures for urgent government action came from numerous quarters.

The steel industry, which viewed the import surge as a function of predatory pricing (dumping) by foreign producers, filed a host of antidumping complaints with the Treasury Department during the fall of 1977 covering the gamut of steel mill products from Europe and Japan. These complaints each required extensive product-by-product investigations by the Treasury Department to determine if the specified product from each foreign supplier was entering the U.S. market at less than fair value. Then the International Trade Commission (ITC) had to investigate whether or not, in each case, imports were causing injury to U.S. producers. This challenge to the government to administer antidumping provisions in U.S. trade laws was paralleled by a vigorous public information effort linking unfair trade practices and pollution abatement costs to the predicament confronting U.S. steel producers. The United Steelworkers of America joined the industry in demanding immediate action.

During the Fall of 1977, pressure was exerted on President Carter to address the mounting problems associated with the steel industry. In addition to industry and labor activity, this pressure came from a newly created Steel Communities Coalition comprised of public officials representing over two dozen communities in traditional steel-making areas (particularly in Ohio, Pennsylvania, and New York) whose social, political, and economic fabric depends upon the steel industry. A steel caucus was also created at the initiative of Representative Charles Carney from Youngstown, Ohio that came to include 160 members of the House of Representatives and 30 members of the Senate. It focused congressional attention on the steel crisis and developed legislative proposals to deal with it. Several congressional hearings[8] were held on the steel crisis (U.S. House of Representatives, 1977a, 1977b, 1977c) and administration studies were rapidly completed in the face of the steel industry's problems (U.S. Council on Wage and Price Stability, 1977; U.S. Federal Trade Commission, 1977).

These pressures culminated in a White House Conference on the steel industry held on October 13, 1977. Out of this conference emerged President Carter's creation of a high-level, emergency task force with instructions to develop a comprehensive program for the steel industry. The task force was directed by Anthony Solomon, under-secretary of the Treasury Department. Its membership included representatives of numerous government agencies dealing with various aspects of the steel industry—such as the Department of Labor, Department of Commerce, the Environmental Protection Agency, and others. The core agencies/offices defining the shape of the proposed program were, however, the Council of Economic Advisers, the Council on Wage and Price Stability, and the Treasury Department, which took the lead (Interviews, 1979). In developing its proposals, the task force consulted widely within the government as well as with industry, labor, and legislators (Interviews, 1979).

The Solomon Task Force produced a comprehensive program for the steel industry in January 1978.[9] The program was cast in a form requiring no new legislation, so it could be implemented immediately by administrative action. It consisted of several components designed to provide U.S. steel producers relief from unfair trade practices, to provide some additional incentives and capability for modernization, to encourage a rationalization of environmental policies and procedures, and to offer assistance to communities and workers affected by plant closings.

The heart of the program was a trigger price mechanism (TPM) designed to deal head-on with the industry's complaints that dumping, and the Treasury Department's passive posture with regard to dumping, were the primary sources of the 1977 steel import surge. At the same time, the TPM was designed to permit, unhampered, continued steel imports entering the U.S. market at or above fair value (i.e., prices that cover average production costs, transportation charges, and an adequate [8 percent] profit margin).

The Treasury Department established trigger prices for a large number of steel mill product groups (rods, slabs, billets, plate, wire, and so forth) by calculating estimated costs of producing and transporting steel products made in Japan to various regional markets in the United States. These trigger prices were adjusted quarterly. While calculated on Japanese production and transportation (the most efficient steel exporter), trigger prices were applied to all steel imports regardless of the country of origin (U.S. House of Representatives, 1978b: 17-18). Different trigger prices for the same steel product from different countries of origin were deemed too complex to calculate and inordinately difficult to administer. By basing trigger prices on Japanese costs, the administration's programs responded to the U.S. steel industry's assertion that it could compete effectively and recapture a larger share of the market if all steel imports were priced at levels above the costs of even the most efficient steel producer—Japan (U.S. House of Representatives, 1978b: 268-269).

The Treasury Department checked import prices of every steel shipment to the United States against the trigger prices. Any steel imports entering below them would trigger immediately a Treasury Department-initiated formal investigation of dumping. By undertaking dumping investigations on its own initiative, and committing itself to concluding them within 60 to 90 days, the Treasury Department was meeting the steel industry's major complaints about the government's unwillingness to enforce vigorously U.S. trade law. This being the case, the Treasury Department requested and secured from U.S. steel producers an agreement to withdraw and hold in abeyance the nineteen specific dumping complaints they had placed before the department in 1977 to reduce steel imports.[10]

Trigger prices, while primarily designed to permit a fast-track system for Treasury Department-initiated investigations of dumping, also established de facto price floors for steel imports.[11] Foreign producers, for the most part, were forced to terminate their aggressive price discounting in sales to the United States. Also, the trigger prices at which they sold in the U.S. market increased an average of about 17 percent during the first year of the TPM. The TPM reduced the gap between prices of imported and domestically produced steel, thus permitting U.S. steel producers to increase prices (during a period of global overcapacity in steel production) and at the same time confine imports to a smaller share of the U.S. market. These developments clearly contributed not only to an alleviation of the steel import challenge by 1979, but also to an improvement in the financial position of the U.S. steel industry. At the same time, steel price increases produced by the TPM has led to criticism of the Solomon program for its inflationary impact (see Adams and Dirlam, 1979: 103-106).

The TPM was the component of the Solomon Task Force's program designed to confront the short-term import threat facing the U.S. steel producers in the late 1970s. To be sure, prompt import relief from unfair trade practices was the centerpiece of the industry's appeal to the government and of the government's program. But the Solomon program was ostensibly a comprehensive approach to the industry's problems, so an appreciation of its remaining components is also important.

Modernization of the steel industry was to be encouraged through several devices. The task force recommended that the Treasury Department investigate the feasibility of reducing the guideline life for depreciation of new steel industry machinery and equipment from eighteen years to fifteen years to encourage investment and increase the industry's cash flow (U.S. House of Representatives, 1978b: 26). The Treasury Department accepted the recommendation, but not until the Fall of 1979. The Economic Development Administration (EDA) of the Department of Commerce was urged to appropriate more funds for loan guarantees to steel firms: (1) with serious financial problems and little or no access to capital markets, (2) seeking funds for modernization of plants located in areas of high and rising unemployment or threatened with massive layoffs, and (3) with viable modernization plans (U.S. House of Representatives, 1978b: 27).

The Economic Development Administration did set aside $100 million with which to guarantee up to $500 million in loans for steel firms to these ends. However, this is a pittance relative to the $4 billion per year capital needs of the U.S. steel industry cited by the Solomon Task Force (U.S. House of Representatives, 1978b: 25-26). Also, there has been no effort since the initial $100 million earmarking in 1978 to expand this source of financial support for future years.

The EDA loan guarantees went primarily to help marginal steel firms in traditional steel-making areas to comply with environmental standards, rather than to underwrite modernization, per se (Interviews, 1979). Those EDA loan guarantees intended for direct modernization that would increase production and/or permit the recipient firm to move into new product lines, prompted heated conflicts within the U.S. steel industry. The EDA loan guarantee to Phoenix Steel Corporation, for example, resulted in a lawsuit brought by a competing U.S. steel producer claiming, among other things, that the loans would permit an increase in production of plate where excess capacity already existed (Mallino, 1979: 13).[12] Similarly, a loan guarantee being considered by EDA for Wheeling Pittsburgh to diversify its output by moving into rail products, prompted strong opposition from other steel firms already marketing rails—Bethlehem Steel, U.S. Steel, and Colorado Fuel and Iron (U.S. Senate, 1979).

The industry is deeply divided over government subsidies for modernization through the EDA loan guarantees or other means for a number of reasons. The subsidies are by their nature bound to alter the relative competitive positions and market shares of domestic steel firms within specific product lines. Those firms not receiving subsidies are obviously going to be upset, particularly (1) when they have to assume all the risks and raise all the capital without government support to produce the same products, and (2) when in the absence of government support for modernization and product diversification, the subsidized firm might well go out of business and leave the market to others. Finally, except in the case of those firms that desperately need government subsidies to survive, industry spokesmen tend to be very concerned about even modest government subsidies leading to substantial government interference in the steel industry and its modernization decisions. Thus, the modernization component of the Solomon Task Force's comprehensive steel program remained small in its pretentions and its resources because of industry as well as government's reluctance to see it otherwise.

With regard to community adjustment assistance, the program called upon EDA to make available an additional $20 million for assistance to communities with adjustment strategies and worthwhile proposals for economic development that were threatened by, or had suffered, unemployment due to cutbacks in steel production. It also recommended the preparation of a study evaluating alternative uses for abandoned steel facilities (U.S. House of Representatives, 1978b: 32, 33). Very modest grants were made to state and local agencies in traditional steel-making areas (New York, Pennsylvania, and Ohio) to assist in their working out strategies of economic diversification and development (Mallino, 1979: 21-22). While the administration favored some changes in trade adjustment assistance for laborers whose jobs were threatened by imports, it was unwilling to support (on budgetary grounds) legislative reforms proposed to ease eligibility criteria, expand benefits, and institute certain innovations in retraining programs, for example. It is clear the Solomon program was not intended to provide much substance to come to grips with the burdens of adjustment that local communities and labor bear in the face of steel import competition.

The burdens confronting the steel industry as it attempts to comply with environmental and safety regulations were recognized in the comprehensive program as well. The task force recommended against relaxing basic environmental goals or offering differential (more lenient) treatment to the steel industry in enforcing these goals. But it did call upon the EPA to review its regulatory processes and standards in order to reduce rigidities and needless barriers to modernization (U.S. House of Representatives, 1978b: 28-31).

The comprehensive steel program probably helped to sustain and reinforce the EPA/steel industry dialogue over adjustments of and compliance with regulations governing environmental standards. It cannot be said that the Solomon Task Force's program produced concrete results in this area. On the other hand, it may have helped the long-standing EPA/steel industry confrontation by (1) nesting the pollution abatement dialogue more saliently in the larger import competition and modernization challenges that the industry must confront simultaneously and (2) encouraging a shift in the general tone of EPA/steel industry relations away from virtually unmitigated mutual hostility (Interviews, 1979).

Finally, the comprehensive steel program produced institutionalization of a Tripartite Committee that became an important forum in developing U.S. steel policy. The committee grew out of the extensive consultations the Solomon Task Force conducted across the industry, labor, and the government in late 1977 and early 1978 in the process of developing the comprehensive steel program. It was convened first in January 1978 as an informal group to help evaluate and implement more effectively the Solomon Task Force's program for the steel industry. It met as a formal, institutionalized body on June 25, 1979 to review the impact of the comprehensive steel program after one year of operation.[13] Its subsequent work program consisted of a series of small workgroups composed of industry, labor, and government officials charged with assessing the current status of the industry and the problems it faces, as well as recommending solutions in each of several key problem areas for the industry (trade, labor and community assistance, modernization and capital funds, environmental protection, and research and development of steel technology).

The significance of the Tripartite Committee lies less in its work program, however, than in its very existence and the intangible consequences that it is believed to produce. Without attempting to completely resolve profound differences among industry, labor, and government approaches to steel problems, the committee institutionalized a new commitment on all sides to replace a nearly unmanageable set of adversary relationships with a meaningful private/public sector dialogue on major challenges confronting the steel industry. This alone represents a radical departure in government/steel industry relations. The committee's review of and aggregated approach to the gamut of challenges confronting the steel industry helped sensitize individual government agencies to the impact of their policies on the industry, and to the impact of *other* agencies whose activities deal with other facets of U.S. steel production (Interviews, 1979). The basic definition of the Tripartite Committee's function and scope remain purposefully ambiguous. This reflects divisions within both the government and the industry on just how central a role the committee should occupy on developing steel policy.

In sum, the Solomon Task Force's comprehensive steel program was an innovative, ad hoc, response to strong protectionist pressure from the steel sector. It constitutes something more than traditional protectionism and considerably less than a systematic effort to administer adjustments in the U.S. steel industry sufficient to deal with the forces underlying its long-term decline in competitiveness.

The program goes beyond traditional protectionism, because careful limits were placed on the manner and extent to which steel imports would be inhibited. In particular, the TPM focuses primarily on "unfair" steel imports priced below cost; it does not establish limits on, or targets for, the level of steel imports. Moreover, its scope goes well beyond protection through a special steel import regime, to address related problems of modernization, capital formation, impacts of regulatory policies, and community and labor adjustment—unlike any earlier trade measures to assist the U.S. steel industry.[14]

On the other hand, the resources and instruments of the comprehensive steel program designed to deal with issues beyond unfair import competition are too modest and underdeveloped to respond effectively to structural shifts in international production and trade challenging U.S. steel producers. This is not surprising, since neither the government nor the U.S. steel industry, for different reasons, conceived of the comprehensive program as a device to deal with structural shifts.

A combination of strong demand for steel in the United States, international currency developments during 1978, and the implementation of the Trigger Price Mechanism after May 1978 produced a remarkable recovery in the U.S. steel industry by 1979 (see Table 5.2). In 1978, steel imports continued to rise, capturing over 19 percent of the U.S. market; but steel production in the United States also began to rise. Note especially the increase in the utilization of capacity of U.S. steel mills. In early 1979, steel imports dropped to approximately two-thirds of their early 1978 level. More importantly, US producers were operating their plants at over 90 percent of capacity. Along with this improvement in the import picture and domestic production, U.S. steelmakers enjoyed dramatic improvements in earnings, and employment in the industry increased.

The overall condition of the U.S. steel industry in mid-1979 reflected a remarkable recovery since 1977, but steel remains a highly cyclical business. The economic forecast for the United States and other advanced industrial states suggests the U.S. steel industry's mid-1979 position cannot en-

TABLE 5.2   Steel Imports and U.S. Utilization of Capacity, 1976-1979

| Year | IMPORTS | | UTILIZATION |
	(millions of net tons)[a]	(percentage of U.S. consumption)[b]	(percentage of capacity of U.S. mills)[c]
1976	14.3	14.1	80.9
1977	19.3	17.8	78.4
1978	21.1	19.3	86.8
1979	17.5[d]	15.2[d]	88.4[e]

a. American Iron and Steel Institute [AISI], Annual Statistical Report: 45 (Washington, DC, 1978).

b. AISI, Apparent Supply of Steel Mill Products (Washington, DC, 1976, 1977, 1978, 1979).

c. AISI, Annual Statistical Report: 58 (Washington, DC, 1978).

d. AISI, Steel Import News. Press Release (January 31, 1980).

e. AISI, Steel Import News. Press Release (January 4, 1980).

dure. Therefore, notwithstanding the Solomon program's success in helping to revitalize U.S. steel production since 1977, steel trade and production are likely to reemerge as highly contentious domestic and international political economic problems in the years ahead.

The Steel Challenge and the Multilateral Trade Negotiations

The steel import challenge and the U.S. response to it, of course, took place during the active stages of the Multilateral Trade Negotiations (MTNs). The administration had to make sure it dealt effectively with the U.S. steel industry's problems not only through the Solomon program, but also through the results of the MTN. Steel industry support was important for passage of the administration's legislation implementing the MTN agreements, yet too blatant a protectionist policy on behalf of U.S. steel producers would undermine progress toward a successful conclusion of the Tokyo round. The administration handled this challenge imaginatively and adroitly.

The trigger price mechanism proposed by the Solomon Task Force was conceived with the Multilateral Trade Negotiation very much in mind. The TPM's simplicity (for example, trigger prices based solely on estimated Japanese costs of production rather than different trigger prices for different countries of origin) was, in part, an effort to avoid erecting a complicated apparatus that would paralyze the progress of the Office of the Special Trade Representative in the Tokyo round (Interviews, 1979). Most importantly, the barrage of dumping complaints placed before the Treasury Department by U.S. steel producers during 1977 were targeted primarily against Europe. The antidumping investigations by the Treasury had emerged as a major barrier to the Europeans' willingness to engage in intensive discussions with the United States in the MTN. The Solomon Task Force's insistence that the steel industry withdraw its dumping complaints upon implementation of the TPM removed that barrier and was very important in permitting the MTN to move ahead at a very critical juncture (Interviews, 1979).

A comprehensive analysis of the role of the steel industry in the Multilateral Trade Negotiation is not permitted within the scope of this chapter. On the other hand, a brief explanation of some central aspects of the MTN relating to the U.S. steel industry is necessary to evaluate the prospects of steel trade policies in the future. The steel industry over the course of the Tokyo round remained particularly interested in sectoral trade negotiations for steel, in tariff structures on steel products, and in the development of effective codes on subsidies, safeguard mechanisms, and other nontariff barriers to trade.

The 1974 Trade Act included a provision establishing the objective of "negotiating by product sector on both tariff and nontariff trade agreements, to the extent consistent with maximum overall economic benefit" (Congressional Quarterly, 1974: 554). The Senate Finance Committee report on the bill identified steel as a product sector appropriate for negotiations. The U.S. steel industry was most interested in a sectoral trade agreement, along the lines of the Multi-Fiber Agreement in textiles, clearly delimiting import ceilings and market shares for foreign producers. U.S. trade negotiators were very cool to this approach. It was viewed as blatantly protectionist, and a sectoral trade agreement in steel would remove such an important industry from the overall trade negotiation that progress in the MTN might be threatened (Interviews, 1979). More generally, U.S. trade officials are philosophically opposed to the sectoral approach as a threat to international market mechanisms and to the liberal trade system envisioned in the General Agreement on Tariff and Trade. Nevertheless, the Office of the Special Trade Representative was instructed by President Ford in 1976 to pursue sectoral steel discussions within the MTN (Interviews, 1979). These efforts failed because of a combination of European and Japanese unwillingness to engage in such talks, and, one suspects, an equal measure of actual disinterest on the part of U.S. trade negotiators themselves.

As an alternative to a sectoral trade agreement within the MTN context, U.S. trade officials pushed for the creation of a Steel Committee in the Organization for Economic Cooperation and Development (OECD). The Steel Committee was formally established in October 1978 (see OECD, 1978). U.S. trade officials recognize the body falls far short of the sectoral agreement desired by U.S. steel producers, but they see it as significant in several respects: (1) It constitutes broad recognition among the advanced industrial states that governments are to an extraordinary degree intervening in steel production and trade as a matter of social policy. (2) It signifies mutual recognition that advanced industrial states require continual consultation on the manner of their interventions in steel production for social policy, because important trade distorting effects are becoming evident. (3) It provides a mechanism for international scrutiny and advice for government policies designed to cope with both cyclical problems and adjustments to structural shifts in steel production and trade. (4) It is a forum that can keep steel issues before the international trade community (Interviews, 1979).

The tariff agreements that emerged from the Tokyo round will not seriously affect the U.S. steel industry. Duties on steel products were reduced by 27 percent versus the 31 percent average tariff cut for all dutiable industrial goods in the MTN (Pittsburgh Post Gazette, 1979: 7). Tariff reductions on steel imports to the United States will be deferred for two years and gradually phased in over the eight years following. Thus, over a ten-year period, average trade-weighted steel tariffs will drop to approximately 4.5 percent from their previous level of 6.1 percent (Pittsburgh Post Gazette, 1979: 7). European and Japanese tariffs on steel were cut by a larger margin, but they will remain about 1 percent higher than the U.S. level. The phased reduction of steel tariffs by 1.5 percent and the similarity of tariff levels for steel in the advanced industrial states make it unlikely that new tariff structures will produce significant alternations in steel trade.

The subsidies code and implementing legislation governing U.S. administration of countervailing duty and antidumping petitions are particularly important aspects of the MTN to domestic steel producers (see U.S. House of Representatives, 1979: 1-45; U.S. Office of Special Trade Representative, 1979: 13-133). Industry representatives were consulted extensively by U.S. trade officials on these aspects of the Tokyo round and U.S. trade legislation. The subsidies code of the MTN provides an important new instrument at the disposal of U.S. producers to obtain countervailing duty relief in the face of imports determined to have been subsidized and causing injury to U.S. industries. The implementing legislation of the MTN clarifies, accelerates, and generally makes more effective protection against subsidized foreign production and dumping.[15] These provisions of the MTN are particularly important to U.S. steel producers who see unfair trade in the forms of subsidies and dumping as the major source of their import competition and modernization problems.

Overall, the outcome of the Tokyo round was acceptable to the U.S. steel industry, notwithstanding the absence of a sectoral steel agreement or a safeguards code which they sought. At the Tripartite Committee meeting of June 25, 1979, the industry formally announced its support for the Trade Act of 1979 which embodies the MTN agreement.

Likely Prospects in the Steel Industry and U.S. Trade Policy

The sources are present for a vigorous resurgence of protectionism in the U.S. steel industry and in the U.S. economy more generally. The economies of the United States and of most advanced industrial states are widely believed to be entering another period of recession, accompanied by strong inflation. This suggests a softening of U.S. and international steel markets in the face of a global overcapacity in steel production. The very high utilization of capacity in U.S. steel mills, reduced steel import penetration, high employment levels, and improved earnings enjoyed by the industry in mid-1979 are likely to give way to problems of the sort witnessed in 1977. Given the industry's concept of the source of its problems, we can expect it to mount a renewed offensive against unfair trade. The trigger price mechanism, the new subsidies code, and trade legislation that should permit greater dispatch in processing countervailing duty and antidumping petitions will provide the steel industry with potent instruments in their new offensive that were not available in 1977.

In the short term, at least, steel producers and other industries seeking an aggressive application of U.S. trade laws designed to protect against unfair trade practices are likely to find government agencies more responsive than they were in 1977. Congressional attention in the drafting of legislation implementing the MTN was directed not only at streamlining procedures for investigating subsidies and antidumping complaints, but also at strengthening the commitment of the administration to apply to the limit U.S. trade law offering protection against unfair trade practices. Indeed, legislation implementing the MTN called for reorganizing and restructuring executive agencies handling various U.S. trade functions (U.S. Office of the Special Trade Representative, 1979: 366-88). The Treasury Department's rigid adherence to liberal trade policies and, in particular, its reluctance to apply its antidumping and countervailing duty authority as vigorously as Congress intended made the department one of the primary targets of the trade reorganization (Interviews, 1979). These functions were ultimately stripped from the Treasury Department and handed to the Commerce Department in 1980. The Commerce Department will certainly remain mindful of the Congressional message underlying its enhanced position in administering U.S. trade policy.

Rising protectionist pressures in the United States could also face less resistance because of the absence of a major negotiating round in the GATT. This point should not be overstated, but the threat of undermining a major multilateral trade negotiation can provide limits on the adoption of protectionist trade policies. The trigger price mechanism to control steel imports was proposed to head off more blatantly protectionist alternatives (such as quotas or orderly marketing arrangements) that would have undermined the MTN. Opponents of increased trade protection will miss the presence of the Tokyo round.[16]

Conclusion

Developments in the steel industry since 1977 highlight several particularly important problems facing the United States in maintaining a liberal trade posture and adapting rapidly to structural shifts in international production. Foremost among these is a lack of confidence in both market mechanisms and sectorally focused public policy approaches to deal with declines in competitiveness for major industries like steel making. The result is an overemphasis on protectionist trade policies and an underemphasis on adjustment by the beleaguered U.S. industry.

American steelmakers attribute increased steel import penetration to unfair trade practices abroad rather than to fundamental shifts in comparative advantage and competitiveness based on real market forces. The market mechanism is, accordingly, providing false signals about the need for U.S. manufacturers to adjust to international shifts in steel production and trade in their view. The industry is adamantly opposed to the creation of government programs designed to promote rapid adjustment in steel making because (1) the burdens of adjustment should properly be borne by foreign firms engaged in unfair trade practices, not by U.S. steelmakers; (2) the government lacks the expertise to direct adjustments in steel making—only the industry possesses these skills; and (3) an active government role in promoting adjustments within the steel industry would lead eventually to government control over the industry. Protectionist trade policies by the United States offer an appropriate solution to the domestic industry's problem and are consistent with each of these basic tenets. Protectionism places the burdens of adjustment on foreign producers (and domestic consumers), keeps the government out of the steel industry, and minimizes changes necessary within the domestic industry as it stands.

Government and economic experts generally oppose protectionism. They must balance the particularistic interests of domestic industries losing their market share to imports against the larger national and international economic and political benefits to be derived from maintaining an open international trade system. Yet, in the case of steel as in so many other instances, trade protectionism (even if carefully constrained) emerges as the centerpiece of government action to deal with beleaguered industries. Government analysts may well see a domestic industry's loss of market share to imports as an accurate reflection of real market forces (as was the case in steel); but particularly if plant shutdowns and unemployment impacts are large and regionally concentrated, trade protectionism is likely to be adopted both as a political necessity and as a matter of social policy to alleviate regionally focused unemployment and fiscal chaos. Trade protection is viewed by government economic and trade experts as an undesirable, but necessary, policy to provide a breathing spell for a domestic industry. The industry is expected to use the brief period of temporary import relief to make rapid accommodations to market imperatives. In the case of steel, the United States faces a serious dilemma. The government sees trade protection as a temporary expedient enabling domestic producers to adjust to shifts in international production and trade. The industry sees trade protection as an appropriate means of forcing foreign producers to bear the adjustment burdens. The result of both government and private sector behavior is a greater emphasis on trade protectionism than an adaptation to structural shifts in international production, by domestic steel producers at least.

The U.S. government is able to play a very marginal role in promoting adaptation to structural shifts in international production and trade. There is little to distinguish most economic and trade experts in the U.S. government from industry spokesmen in their philosophical abhorrence of an activist, sectorally targeted role for the state in directing adjustments to changes in international competitiveness by U.S. industry (Interviews, 1979). Beyond a philosophical opposition for movement by the state in this direction, lack of expertise in government would likely condemn such efforts to failure in the view of public and industry officials. Government economic and trade experts are accordingly likely to emphasize accommodation to the imperatives of the international market. Such a policy permits them to champion liberal trade policies, to keep all investment and adaptation decisions within the private sector, and to keep government at the industry's edge.

The institutional structures and policy instruments available to deal with the challenge of structural shifts are confined basically (1) to adjustment assistance programs for firms, workers, and communities *after* import penetration has already closed domestic production and (2) to macroeconomic policies to assure growth, high employment levels, and price stability that enables structural shifts to take place in response to market forces relatively painlessly. Few would argue that either of these two instruments are working well. The heavy reliance on two blunt policy tools is entirely consistent with Peter Katzenstein's general characterization (1977: 881) of the United States as a political economy that follows "a liberal strategy in permitting market forces to operate and in giving policymakers few instruments to apply directly to particular sectors and firms."

The U.S. economy seems to be emphasizing protectionism rather than rapid industrial adaptation as a response to shifts in international production and trade—at least in mature manufacturing industries such as steel. Trade protection responds to strong political demands of industry, labor, and communities threatened by imports. It keeps government out of the affected industries—the strong desire of industry as well as most government economic and trade officials. Policy instruments other than trade protection that can bring targeted relief to or promote adaptation by threatened industries, labor, and communities are virtually nonexistent. A tremendous burden is being placed on trade policy by default. This is likely to remain the case until adjustment policies for industry, labor, and communities are promoted with the same political intensity as import relief for ailing industries.

This augers poorly for a constructive U.S. role in maintaining an open international trade system. U.S. industries are likely to be slow in adjusting to shifts in international production and trade. Particularly in the absence of targeted relief and adjustment policies in the United States, ailing industries will increasingly cite other states' policies along these lines as evidence of unfair trade—justifying greater protectionism. An open international trade order will require development of multilateral mechanisms for managing the trade distorting effects of national adjustment policies on a sectoral basis. The United States is unprepared to play an active role in this multilateral process, because present government/industry approaches prevent effective action at the domestic level.

NOTES

1. By structural shifts we mean permanent as opposed to cyclical or aberrant alterations in comparative advantage or competitiveness.

2. For an excellent analysis of the failure of international agreements to manage structural shifts and global surplus capacity in the textile, steel, and shipbuilding industries, see Strange (1979).

3. It would be preferable to conduct a more comprehensive analysis with a common set of domestic industries in several countries facing strong foreign competition. That would permit the development of generalized behavior patterns going well beyond the tentative conclusions obtainable from the study of policy towards one industry in one state. However, that requires time and resources which considerably exceed those available to me. The approach I have adopted embodies a healthy respect for profound differences in the institutions, processes, and political/economic cultures of various developed market economies that affect their capacities, political wills, and strategies in developing policy responses to these types of trade challenges. It also embodies a healthy respect for profound differences in policy likely to emerge with regard to different industries facing severe import competition within the same nation. Variations in regional concentrations of production, market structures, the sources of major foreign competition, importance to the overall national economy, entrepreneurial vitality, and financial posture, for example, are likely to produce very different policy responses by a government in dealing with different economic sectors confronting import surges. There are severe limitations to case study research. But, our empirical foundations must be expanded considerably and take on more precision before we are in a position to develop and explain behavior patterns appropriately characterizing government/industry relations cross-nationally in various economic sectors.

4. These are products other than specialty steels such as stainless and alloy tool steel products already protected by quotas introduced in 1976.

5. In this candid appraisal of the industry's problems, steel firms and the United Steelworkers are criticized as well as government policies.

6. Wage levels have increased even faster in Japan than in the United States, but they are still under one-half of those in the United States. Also, labor productivity has increased much faster in Japan, to the point where the lead the U.S. industry used to enjoy has been eliminated (U.S. Federal Trade Commission, 1977: 476-477).

7. Much of the descriptive material, data, and analysis in the remainder of this chapter rest upon interviews conducted during June 1979 with nineteen officials directly involved with trade issues relating to the steel industry. They include individuals in the Department of Labor, the Office of the Special Trade Representative, the Treasury Department, the State Department, the Department of Commerce, staff members of the Trade Subcommittee of the House Committee on Ways and Means, staff members of two congressmen active in legislation on trade and steel policy, the staff of the Steel Caucus, the United Steelworkers of America, the American Iron and Steel Institute, the Steel Communities Coalition, and officials of a major steel-importing company. Everyone interviewed was assured they would not be cited with specific attribution. When a citation to information from any of these sources is appropriate, it will be documented as: Interviews, 1979.

8. The subcommittees conducting these hearings were chaired by Charles A. Vanik of Youngstown, Ohio and William S. Moorehead of Pittsburgh, Pennsylvania—two congressmen whose constituencies have more than a casual interest in the health of the steel industry.

9. For the text of the report see U.S. House of Representatives (1978b: 1-35).

10. This was an unprecedented number of antidumping petitions for a single industry in such a short period of time (U.S. House of Representatives, 1978: 13). The industry continued to keep these and other dumping complaints updated and ready to resubmit as an incentive (or threat) to the Treasury Department to pursue investigations of dumping of steel products on its own initiative (Roderick, 1979: 4; Interviews, 1979).

11. The average trigger price for steel mill products entering the United States moved from $298 per net ton during the second quarter of 1978 to a high of $352 per net ton during the first two quarters of 1979. It was set at $348 per net ton for the third quarter of 1979 (see U.S. Treasury Department, 1979).

12. The EDA loan guarantee program has a statutory prohibition against increasing production in product lines where excess capacity exists.

13. The Tripartite Committee is composed of (1) eight industry representatives—the chief executive officers of U.S. Steel, Bethlehem Steel, National Steel, Armco Steel, Republic Steel, Cyclops, and Kaiser as well as the president of the American Iron and Steel Institute; (2) eight labor representatives—the president and two other leading national officers of the United Steelworkers, and five regional directors of the United Steelworkers, and (3) government representatives of the EPA, the Special Trade Representative, and the Treasury, co-chaired by the Secretaries of Labor and Commerce.

14. Such as the Voluntary Restraint Agreements of the late 1960s and early 1970s, as well as the Specialty Steel Quotas of 1976-1980.

15. Implementing legislation defines, for example, what shall constitute subsidies, dumping, and injury in U.S. trade law, as well as establishing the time-frame within which the administration must determine whether or not relief to petitioners is merited.

16. Developments since this article was written in mid-1979 have proven consistent with these assessments of the steel industry's likely condition and trade policy. Late 1979 and 1980 witnessed a dramatic downturn in steel shipments and utilization of American steel-making capacity. U.S. Steel closed fifteen plants affecting about 13,000 workers and announced what

at the time was the largest quarterly loss in corporate listing for the fourth quarter of 1979 (New York Times, 1980a: A1). The American Iron and Steel Institute launched an aggressive campaign calling for revitalization of the U.S. steel industry (AISI, 1980). The U.S. Steel Corporation, convinced that the trigger price levels were too low and that European steelmakers were dumping in the U.S. market, filed antidumping petition against firms in France, West Germany, Belgium, Luxemburg, Italy, Britain, and the Netherlands (New York Times, 1980b: A1). It was taking advantage of more expeditious and tougher procedures in administering antidumping complaints provided by implementing legislation of the Multilateral Trade Negotiations. The Carter administration, viewing the TPM as a fast-track substitute for processing industry initiated anti-dumping suits, suspended the trigger price mechanism in March 1980. During this period there was widespread concern that the steel industry's demands for protection would provoke the filing of petitions by the Europeans charging dumping and unfair subsidies by U.S. exporters of acrylic fibers (Business Week, 1979: 32). An element of stability in the trade picture was reintroduced by the Carter administration's reinstatement of an improved trigger price mechanism with higher trigger prices in the fall of 1980. In return, U.S. Steel once again withdrew its antidumping suits. Import penetration and the U.S. steel industry's preoccupation with unfair trade practices remain as prominent features of the U.S. trade policy environment. Clearly these features are capable of unleashing severe trade conflicts among the advanced industrial states in the protectionist atmosphere following the Tokyo round.

REFERENCES

ADAMS, W. and J. B. DIRLAM (1979) "Unfair competition in international trade," pp. 99-108 in Tariffs, Quotas and Trade: The Politics of Protectionism. San Francisco: Institute for Contemporary Studies.
American Iron and Steel Institute (1980a) Steel Production News. Press Release (January 4).
———— (1980b) Steel Imports News. Press Release (January 31).
———— (1980c) Steel Shipments News. Press Release (February 15).
———— (1980d) Steel at the Crossroads: The American Steel Industry in the 1980s. Washington, DC: AISI.
———— (1978a) Annual Statistical Report. Washington, DC: AISI.
———— (1978b) Apparent Supply of Steel Mill Products. Washington, DC: AISI.
Business Week (1979) "A spreading rash of dumping disputes." December 10.
———— (1977) "Steel's sea of troubles." September 9.
Congressional Quarterly (1975) 1974 Almanac, Vol. 30.
European Economic Community (1979) Memorandum of the European Community for the Steel Committee of OECD. Brussels: EEC.
GILPIN, R. (1970) "The Politics of Transnational Economic Relations," pp. 48-69 in R. Keohane and J. Nye (eds.) Transnational Relations in World Politics. Cambridge, MA: Harvard University Press.
HOGAN, W. T. (1977) Steel in Crisis. Niles, OH: Steel Communities Coalition.
IGNATIUS, D. (1979) "How steel industry's spirit of progress sputtered." Pittsburgh Post Gazette (April 2): 8.
KATZENSTEIN, P. J. (1979) "Conclusion: domestic structures and strategies of foreign economic policy." International Organization 31 (Autumn): 879-920.
KRASNER, S. (1976) "State power and the structure of international trade." World Politics 28 (April): 317-347.
KRAUSS, M. B. (1978) The New Protectionism. New York: New York University Press.

MALLINO, D. (1979) "Status report on the recommendations of the interagency steel task force." Steel Tripartite Committee, Washington, D.C. (mimeo)

McCONNELL, G. (1963) Steel and the Presidency, 1962. New York: Norton.

The New York Times (1980a) January 30.

———— (1980b) March 21.

Organization for Economic Cooperation and Development (1978) Press Release A (78) 43. Paris.

The Pittsburgh Post Gazette (1979) April 19.

PUTNAM, HAYES, and BARTLETT, Inc. (1977) Economics of International Steel Trade: Policy Implications for the United States. Washington, DC: American Iron and Steel Institute.

RODERICK, P. (1979) Press Release. New York: American Iron and Steel Institute.

Steel Cities Coalition (1977) The Future of American Steel Cities: Problems, Options, Actions. Niles, OH: Steel Communities Coalition.

Steelweek (1979) 2, 26 (June 25): 2.

STINSON, G. A. (1979) Press Briefing. New York: American Iron and Steel Institute.

STRANGE, S. (1979) "The management of surplus capacity: or how does theory stand up to protectionism 1970s' style?" International Organization 33 (Summer): 303-334.

U.S. Council on Wage and Price Stability (1977) Report to the President on Prices and Costs in the United States Steel Industry. Washington, DC: Government Printing Office.

U.S. Federal Trade Commission (1977) The United States Steel Industry and its International Rivals: Trends and Factors Determining International Competitiveness. Washington, DC: Government Printing Office.

———— U.S. House of Representatives (1979) Multilateral Trade Negotiations: International Codes Agreed to in Geneva, Switzerland. Committee on Ways and Means, 95th Cong., 1st Sess. Washington, DC: Government Printing Office.

———— (1978a) "Actions taken by the congressional steel caucus." Washington, D.C. (mimeo)

———— (1978b) Administration's Comprehensive Program for the Steel Industry. Committee on Ways and Means, Subcommittee on Trade, 95th Cong., 2nd Sess. Washington, DC: Government Printing Office.

———— (1977a) The Council on Wage and Price Stability's Steel Industry Report. Committee on Banking, Finance, and Urban Affairs, Subcommittee on Economic Stabilization, 95th Cong., 1st Sess. Washington, DC: Government Printing Office.

———— (1977b) Oversight of the Anti-Dumping Act of 1921. Committee on Ways and Means, Subcommittee on Trade, 95 Cong., 1st Sess. Washington, DC: Government Printing Office.

———— (1977c) World Steel Trade: Current Trends and Structural Problems. Committee on Ways and Means, Subcommittee on Trade, 95th Cong., 1st Sess. Washington, DC: Government Printing Office.

U.S. Office of the Special Trade Representative (1979) "Draft proposal of the trade agreements act of 1979." Washington, D.C. (mimeo)

U.S. Senate (1979) Hearings on the Economic Development Administration's Steel Loan Program and Supplemental Appropriations for FY 78-79. Committee on Appropriations, Subcommittee on State, Justice, Commerce and Judiciary, 96th Cong., 1st Sess. Washington, DC: Government Printing Office.

U.S. Treasury Department (1979) "Steel trigger price mechanism: a one year review for the steel tripartite committee." Washington, D.C. (mimeo)

CHAPTER 6

THE FRENCH TEXTILE INDUSTRY
Crisis and Adjustment

L Y N N   K R I E G E R   M Y T E L K A

At the close of World War II, French industry, for the most part, was both economically and technically inefficient (Shonfield, 1965; Sheahan, 1963). *Patrons,* planners and politicians agreed that as a result of change in the international division of labor,[1] French industry would face increasingly stiff international competition both at home, notwithstanding a traditional policy of protectionism, and in foreign markets. Restructuring was clearly necessary but the direction a process of industrial adjustment[2] would take was not self-evident.

The chapter explores the social dynamics underlying the process of industrial adjustment in France focusing, in particular, upon the textile industry as it moved through successive crises—marked by noncompetitiveness, manifest or disguised unemployment, and bankruptcies—in each of the three postwar decades. The analysis highlights the role of the state in promoting industrial concentration, the rise and consolidation of big capital in the French political economy, and the marginalization of organized labor from the process of industrial planning by industry and the state. It is within this social context that the implementation of contradictory policies to promote concentration yet preserve labor-intensive, small-scale, family-owned firms in traditional industries during the 1950s and 1960s is situated. Four factors help to explain why the state, which in other industries, directly

AUTHOR'S NOTE: The author wishes to thank Suzanne Laurent and Monique Angers for their research assistance and Jane Jenson, Steven Langdon, Jeanne Kirk Laux, and Rianne Mahon for their helpful comments on an earlier draft of this chapter. The support of the German Marshall Fund and the Social Sciences and Humanities Research Council of Canada is gratefully acknowledged.

intervened to promote industrial concentration, did not pursue similar policies in the textile industry. These are: (1) the vast number of small, family-owned firms in this industry; (2) the centrality of these firms in the center-right political coalitions which dominated France from 1958 to 1981; (3) the absence of large firms to serve as viable interlocutors for the state in the kind of state/big capital process of "concertation" through which industrial restructuring was effected in this period; and (4) the large, substantially unorganized labor force employed in textiles and potentially vulnerable to the labor militancy that had characterized organized labor in France since the 1930s.

State immigration and employment policies, the subsidization of labor costs to the employer through payments for *chômage partiel,* and high levels of protection for the domestic market were all policies whose thrust was to preserve the traditional nature of the textile industry. While such policies may have been politically expedient, they tended to discourage new investment in the textile industry and thus rendered this industry extremely vulnerable to changes in the international environment. During the 1960s and early 1970s, therefore, the unmodernized and hence economically inefficient textile firms were repeatedly plunged into crisis. Internationalization of production to the former French colonies, while it had briefly benefited a few of the larger firms which emerged in this period, did not provide an overall solution to the problems of this industry.

Not until the late 1960s did large firms emerge in the textile industry. At first they struggled to gain control of the main textile professional association, the Union des Industries Textiles, and working with the state, set up the Centre Inter-Professionel de Renovation des Structures Industrielles et Commerciales de l'Industrie Textile (CIRIT) to restructure the textile industry. When this strategy failed, the textile professional association was bypassed. Through the Comité interministeriel pour l'aménagement des structures industrielles (CIASI) and other state agencies created in the 1970s, the model of state-capital concertation pursued in other industries was extended to textiles. So, too, was the growing awareness that concentration must be accompanied by rationalization and modernization of production if French industry was to become internationally competitive. Applied to the textile industry this meant a set of industrial, labor, and commercial policies which by promoting modernization undercut small capital and displaced labor. Such a major policy change, it is argued in the conclusion, was only possible in the changed political context of the late 1970s.

The Choice of an Industrial Strategy

Although there is a long tradition of state intervention in the French economy, in the immediate postwar years the role of the state was particularly central in the process of capital accumulation. Partly this was a result of the elaborate system of direct controls on building, borrowing, and importing, and on the allocation of scarce materials imposed by the state in the circumstances of war and reconstruction (Cohen, 1969: 21). But even as these controls were relaxed, the low level of self-financing in French industry, less than 30 percent in the late 1940s (Cohen, 1969: 22) and the inadequacies of the French banking system (Morin, 1974) made it practically impossible in this period to finance a major industrial investment without state support. The state limited its support to those investments that conformed to the guidelines set out in the national plans. As self-financing increased to nearly 50 percent of investment costs toward the end of the First Plan (1947-1952) and remained at this level during the Second Plan (1953-1957), the planning commission lost what was tantamount to a veto over investment decisions but retained its ability "to *promote* selected investment projects" (Cohen, 1969: 23). This was particularly true in industrial sectors singled out for special attention in the plan. The plan and the financial and fiscal instruments of the state to which it was linked were thus powerful agencies orienting the process of industrial change during the 1950s.

The First Plan—the Monnet Plan—was designed by the vanguard of a new group of French technocrats who were motivated by a desire for change and, in particular, for expansion over stability. The Monnet Plan concentrated on six basic sectors—coal, electricity, steel, cement, agricultural machinery, and transportation—in order to eliminate what were perceived to be bottlenecks to economic growth and thereby bring production levels above those in 1939 by 1950. Although the First Plan spoke little of industrial concentration and more of reconstruction, by the Second Plan there was no doubt that the French state had embarked upon a conscious process of support for industrial concentration and from the First through the Seventh Plan (1976-1980) the thrust of state policy remained the promotion of industrial concentration.

Two assumptions underlay the adoption of an industrial strategy based on fostering concentration: One concerned the relationship of firm size to technological innovation and international competitiveness; the other concerned the impact of concentration on the attainment of other social and economic goals. According to the first, international competitiveness is predicated upon technological innovation. As there are assumed to be widespread economies of scale in production and in research and development (R&D), the ability to innovate would increase with firm size and so, too, would the possibilities of specialization in technologically advanced products. In the Gaullist era, the logic of international competition as contained in this assumption would lead the state to stress specialization in designated technologically sophisticated sectors and later to promote the internationalization of production by French industry.

The second assumption posited that very large firms, even in industries characterized by oligopolistic market structures, would not behave in ways prejudicial to the realization of other economic and social goals such as full employment, geographical decentralization of industry, or a more equal distribution of income. This assumption follows from a long French tradition, evidenced again in the Executive Decree of 1953, which differentiates "good" cartels, that is, those which do not raise costs or prices but permit specialization, from "bad" cartels.[3]

Cartelization, with its absence of price competition, and protectionism in domestic and colonial markets are distinguishing features of French capitalism and both were responses to the underlying weakness of the French industrial bourgeoisie within the grand class alliance formed in the 1870s. The disincentive to invest which these practices and policies induced is reflected in the post-World War II size of the French "traditional sector," that is, the class of small, independent property owners engaged in small-scale, relatively labor-intensive production under family ownership and personalistic management, many of whom are concentrated in industries associated with the first industrial revolution, such as the textile industry. The reproduction of the traditional sector, however, must also be seen to flow from a policy which can be called "political" protectionism. Thus subsidies, legislative restrictions on competition, or special treatment such as the state's apparent willingness to overlook violations of legislation on social security, minimum wages, and working conditions are all part of the process of reproducing the traditional sector (Berger and Piore, 1980: 92). Although tariffs and quotas progressively were reduced in the context of the European Economic Community (EEC), cartelization left its legacy in the legitimacy accorded the process of industrial concentration. Protectionism, too, would persist, albeit in other forms, as the state pursued an active role in managing the adjustment process. The seeming paradox of promoting concentration yet preserving *les petites et moyennes entreprises* (PME) which these diverse policies suggest, is easily resolved if we situate the traditional sector within the French economy in terms of its function in permitting the expansion of the modern sector and in maintaining political stability. Thus Suzanne Berger argues that, as a low-wage, labor-absorbing sector, the traditional sector permits large firms to reduce costs and increase flexibility by subcontracting as the economic conjuncture requires (Berger and Piore, 1980: 106). Traditional firms, moreover, put obstacles in the path to radical mobilization of the working class

> by placing it in a setting in which organization and mobilization of labor are extremely difficult. The dispersion of the workforce in small productive units, the personalized relations between worker and employer in these small units, and the characteristics of the workforce all reduce the chances for mass action in traditional firms [Berger and Piore, 1980: 110].

Finally, in France, Professor Berger argues that "the traditional middle classes . . . are important elements in the political consensus underpinning the regime" and "groups with an economic and social base in the traditional economy are pivotal in the political alliances on which the governing parties . . . depend" (Berger and Piore, 1980: 109).[4]

The Marginalization of Labor and the Emergence of an
"Economie Concertée"

The absence of stiff worker opposition to an industrial strategy which emphasizes concentration can only be understood in the context of changing state/capital/labor relations in the postwar period. The starting point for such an analysis lies in the modernization commissions set up under the First Plan and rapidly transformed into the loci of economic concertation between big capital and the state (Cohen, 1969; Ehrmann, 1957; Seibel, 1975; Sulieman, 1974; Zysman, 1977). By drawing together labor, capital, and the state in the planning process, the modernization commissions reflected a move toward a corporatist postwar settlement and away from the dramatic confrontations between capital and organized labor which produced the Matignon Agreements of 1936 and led to a split between big capital, public and private, and *les petites et moyennes entreprises*.[5] Effective collaboration between capital, labor, and the state, however, was over almost before it had begun. With the onset of the Cold War in 1947, communist ministers were eliminated from the French government and the Confédération Générale du Travail (CGT), France's largest trade union, was weakened by a politically inspired breakaway of *Force Ouvrière* and *FEN*. Then in 1950, Jean Monnet was replaced at the head of the planning commission by Etienne Hirsch, a former director of Kuhlmann Chemical Corporation. The CGT now charged that the technocrats of the plan were an instrument of big capital (Cohen, 1969: 123). A vivid debate over strategy within the CGT ensued. Ultimately a position of unconditional opposition to participation in the planning process prevailed (Cohen, 1969: 209; Reynaud, 1966: 92-95; interview with J. L. Moynot, CGT, January 1979; Ross, forthcoming).

Membership in the modernization commissions was by invitation of the Commissariat Général du Plan. The CGT's adoption of a confrontational strategy thus facilitated its exclusion from the preparation of the second (1953-1957) and third plans (1957-1961). Of the 612 persons who participated in the preparation of the Third Plan, only 9.3 percent were trade union representatives while 33.7 percent were businessmen and 22.2 percent were civil servants (Cohen, 1969: 193). Even more importantly, the effective influence of the state over the preparation of the plan was enhanced by the leading role played by technocrats in all commissions and working groups as either chairmen or vice-chairmen and rapporteurs (Shonfield, 1965: 159).

> One of the senior officials of the Commissariat du Plan once described the
> actual process of planning during the 1950s as "a rather clandestine affair." It
> relied essentially on the close contacts established between a number of like-
> minded men in the civil service and in big business. Organized labour, small
> business . . . were largely passed by [Shonfield, 1969: p. 131].

With the marginalization of organized labor from the planning process,
the close collaboration between the state and big capital which characterized
the *économie concertée* became manifest. The plan itself was restructured to
serve the interests of large firms in technologically sophisticated industries
and responded, in particular, to their need for macroeconomic data and for
financing. Thus under the Second Plan econometric modeling techniques
involving final demand project were introduced. Under the Third Plan
(1957-1961), this form of "indicative" planning became the dominant motif
and the plan took on the characteristics of a general market survey. In the
context of "indicative planning," a number of industrial sectors, notable for
their technological intensity, were selected for special attention. Within
these sectors the state worked closely with owners and managers of the most
important firms to promote concentration, modernization, and expansion of
their enterprises (Cohen, 1969: 129-131). A number of instruments were set
up for this purpose. Of these the principal vehicle for state financing of
industry was the Fonds du Développement Economique et Social (FDES)
created in 1955. Comité No. 1 Quinquies of the FDES council, chaired by
the Commissaire Général du Plan, was mandated from the outset to grant tax
relief to firms engaged in takeovers and mergers or overseas investment.
Comité No. 1 bis handled loans to the designated firms (France, 1977). In the
Eighth Plan, the sectoral focus which characterized the first through the
seventh plans was abandoned but the close collaboration between the state
and selected firms was maintained through instruments set up in 1979 and
legitimized in the Eighth Plan.

It is important to note that although this notion of an *économie concertée*
applied only to the large corporations in nontraditional industries; the instruments designed to promote concentration, specialization, and internationalization of production in these industries were available to large firms in more
traditional industries as well. Only a very small number of textile firms,
responding to the opportunities created by the French planning process and
the pressures emanating from the international environment, however, did
transform themselves into large, internationalized companies. As a whole,
the textile industry well into the 1970s remained predominantly an industry
of small, family-owned firms. Uneven modernization and the war in Indochina which led not to a drive toward international competitiveness but to a
reorientation of exports away from Asia and toward the *protected* markets of
France's African colonies, destined the French textile industry to undergo

successive crises in the 1960s and 1970s. It is to this period of the 1950s, then, that we can trace the emergence of a dualistic structure in the French textile industry and find the seeds of future crises.

The Crisis of the 1950s and the Preservation of Traditional Firms

The French textile industry was notably inefficient in the immediate postwar years (Capronnier, 1959; Sheahan, 1963). In the late 1940s, modernization in the spinning branch of the textile industry slowly began, especially among textile firms with integrated spinning and weaving operations. "The five largest companies in the spinning branch owned 38 plants in 1946 and 31 by 1950, with 10 percent more spindles per plant in the latter year" (Sheahan, 1963: 134). But in weaving, vintage looms could be made to function under almost any condition and a substantial number of firms did precisely this.

The French textile industry depended heavily upon sales in protected colonial markets during the 1950s. Fully 40 percent of total French textile exports went to countries within the franc zone, all of which were then colonies. "For cotton yarns, the share of export sales going to the franc zone increased from 9 percent in 1929 to 60 percent in 1951. For cotton cloth, the proportion rose from 50 to 90 percent" (Capronnier, 1959: 282). Within the franc zone, moreover, Indochina was the single largest market.

By 1951, as the cotton textile industry came under severe pressure from international competition and from the closing of the Indochina market, conflicts within the industry became acute as a result of textile "dumping" by marginal firms (Reynaud, 1966: 178). Having taken the decision to refrain from further capital investment, marginal firms, by maintaining production with old, amortized machinery and making use of relatively cheaper female and immigrant labor, were able to undersell their rivals. As self-financing was the dominant form of investment financing among textile firms (Guibert, 1975: 119), this behavior reduced the incentive to modernize for competing firms and indeed made it more difficult for these firms to accumulate capital and to invest despite the need to do so engendered by the crisis. In 1953, although "nonautomatic looms had practically disappeared from the American industry . . . they still totaled three-fourths of all the looms in use by nonintegrated firms in France, and 42 percent of those in use by the integrated companies (Sheahan, 1963: 134).[6]

As some firms began to fail and others proved unable to adjust without assistance, in 1953 the Syndicat Général de l'Industrie Cotonnière Française (SGICF), then dominated by small, family-owned firms (Ehrmann, 1957: 39) created a *service de réconversion* to survey firms which had shut down and to search for a means whereby these plants might be reconverted to new activities or sold. The *service de réconversion* was also mandated to explore possibilities for cooperative action with the banking sector and establish a liaison with agencies of the state involved in industrial adjustment, as to this point the state had paid scant attention to traditional industries.

In June 1954, the SGICF established the Association d'Etudes pour la Réconversion de l'Industrie Cotonnière with the participation of the Société Générale, the Banque de Paris et des Pays-Bas, and the Union Française des Banques. At the same time, in cooperation with the Ministry of Industry and the Planning Commission, the SGICF prepared a five-year program for the reconversion of the cotton textile industry (SGICF, 1956). In this program, the SGICF recommended the establishment of a fund to encourage the elimination of marginal firms *(assainissement)* and the modernization of others by the purchase and scrapping of older machinery *(riblonnage);* it did not, however, give in to pressures from the state for a major drive toward "restructuring"—which in the French lexicon means concentration. This fund, the Caisse de Riblonnage, whose revenues came from the receipts of a tax on textile sales, was thus designed to purchase and scrap old textile machinery thereby making funds for modernization available to hard-pressed firms especially in the weaving branch. Although the funds came from a state-administered tax, the Caisse de Riblonnage was managed exclusively by the Syndicat Général de l'Industrie Cotonnière Française which used these funds to preserve the small-scale nature of the textile industry (Capronnier, 1959: 232).

In 1954, 14.6 percent of the labor force employed in manufacturing were in the textile industry and textile firms represented 4.7 percent of all industrial firms in France (UN, 1963: 276). From a political perspective, the textile industry was thus of considerable importance. French labor militancy, although attenuated in the textile industry by limited unionization and by the existence of a partial collective agreement,[7] heightened the salience of labor in this crisis. Strikes in all industries, which during the years 1947-1950 had resulted in an annual average of 13 million working days lost, diminished in the early 1950s when the number of working days lost through strikes declined to 1.7 million in 1952 but then rose dramatically to 9.7 million in 1953 (INSEE Yearbook, 1966, Table 13). As the textile crisis deepened in the mid-1950s and the number of workers laid off or on short hours increased, the textile industry seized upon the prospect of social unrest to demand a number of concessions from the state.

These included protection against foreign competition within metropolitan France and in the colonies. Regarding the latter, the government restricted the use of non-franc currencies for purchases of textile products and increased the import duties on textile products originating outside the franc area [Berrier, 1978: 21-22].

The industry's appeal was well received by those in the Treasury then concerned about deficits in the French commercial balance. In 1949, in order to secure cheap supplies of cotton for the domestic textile industry the Compagnie Française Pour le Developpement des Fibres Textiles (CFDT) was established by the French state and granted a monopoly on the distribution of seed and credit to peasant farmers, the purchase of their cotton, and all ginning operations in France's thirteen sub-Saharan colonies. Nevertheless, in the period 1950-1953, the French textile trade deficit accounted for over 25 percent of the total French external trade deficit (Campbell, 1975: 41-42). A neomercantalist policy which not only secured the supply of cheap raw materials from the colonies but guaranteed colonial markets to exports of manufactures from the metropole was, thus, quite appealing. Such a policy, moreover, had a number of important supporters among the large French commercial firms—La Compagnie Optorg, La Compagnie française de l'Afrique occidentale (CFAO), la Société commerciale de l'ouest africain (SCOA), and La Compagnie du Niger française (CNF)—which by this time dominated the francophone African import-export trade and had an extensive network of commercial outlets throughout the thirteen sub-Saharan colonies and in North Africa (Hay, 1976). In the post-World War II period, these commercial companies entered into close relationships with a number of large French textile firms, organizing their sales in Africa.[8]

With a secure market in the French colonies, production in textile plants in the Vosges and Alsace, hardest hit by the loss of the Indochina market, were reoriented away from that market with the encouragement of the state toward sales in Africa. As the textiles sold in the Indochina market were narrower than those demanded by African consumers, this necessitated a complete conversion of looms (interviews with the P-D.G. of Ets. Jules Marachal and Ets. Perrin and the Director of Schaeffer Impression, December 1978). Following the creation of the Fonds de Développement Economique et Sociale (FDES), therefore, its funds were used in conjunction with the Caisse de Riblonnage to modernize and reconvert the textile industry. By 1955, 172 factories had closed (30 in spinning and 142 in weaving) and 15 had been reconverted, 8 through the use of funds from FDES (SGICF, 1956).

Three years later, at the completion of the five-year plan developed by the SGICF in collaboration with the Ministry of Industry and the Planning Commission, the number of looms had been "reduced one-fifth and the proportion of automatic looms raised from 45 to 60 percent" (Sheahan, 1963: 136). Some improvements in productivity had thus been made, but they were unevenly distributed between the larger, integrated firms and the smaller firms. Although a total of 240 plants had been withdrawn from production, of which 150 (25 in spinning and 125 in weaving) were in the East (Chardonnet, 1958: 249) this "still left a goodly crowd: nearly 2000 plants, including only 255 with more than 200 employees" (Sheahan, 1963: 136). Not only did a large number of small, relatively more labor-intensive firms weather the textile crisis of the 1950s, but employment in the textile industry remained high. Some 542,000 persons were still employed in the French textile industry in 1961 (Berrier, 1978: 2, Table VI-1). The bulk of the decline in textile employment, which fell to 294,483 in 1949, does not occur until the 1970s[9] (Ministère de l'Industrie, 1979). In comparison with other major European textile-producing countries, such as the Netherlands or the United Kingdom, the decline in employment in France was far less pronounced.[10]

The Subsidization of Labor and the Disincentive to Invest

In what follows I shall argue that the preservation of a large number of small firms and the maintenance of a sizable labor force in the textile industry in France were due to two principal factors: first, the industry's ability, given state immigration and employment policies,[11] to segment its workforce into core male workers, rendered less militant by the collective "agreement" signed in June 1953 (Reynaud, 1966: 178-180) and female and immigrant workers who served as buffers in the business cycle; and second, the state's decision to maintain an industry-initiated system of payments for *chômage partiel* (reduced hours). In the case of the northern textile area of Roubaix-Tourcoing, where some 33 percent of the cotton textile industry and 73 percent of the thread production were located in the 1950s, when the crisis became severe, "only 7.7 percent of the local workers lost their jobs . . . while 40 percent of the frontaliers [immigrant workers from Belgium] and Pas-de-Calais workers [mostly working wives of miners and farmers] lost theirs" (Berrier, 1978: 16).[12]

As in the East, where a 32-hour work week in the textile industry had become common (Chardonnet, 1958: 249) and nearly half the workforce was on short hours, in the North "the average number of hours worked during the crisis was 38" (Berrier, 1978: 16). There, when workers were placed on short hours, that is, when they worked a week of less than 40 hours, they were compensated at the rate of half their normal wage from a general fund supported by a levy on all workers' salaries and a contribution by employers from 65 of the major textile firms in the region (Berrier, 1978: 16-18). Workers who were laid off or permanently released were given "severance pay" equal to the amount they had paid into the general fund but the employer's contribution remained in the fund and was used to compensate local workers on reduced hours. Frontaliers, women workers from the Pas-de-Calais, and other foreign workers thus subsidized the core workers whose jobs were preserved through these payments.

As unemployment and bankruptcies threatened in traditional industries during the French economic boom of the 1960s, a generalized system of payments to workers on reduced hours was instituted by the state. On December 18, 1963 the Fonds national pour l'emploi was created and was used to support a policy of payments for *chômage partiel* which helped underwrite labor costs in the textile industry. The textile industry was a major beneficiary of state support from this fund. In 1965, at the height of the textile crisis of the 1960s, of the equivalent of 295,300 days of reduced hour payments, 168,300, or 57 percent, went to 40,500 textile workers on reduced hours (INSEE Yearbook, 1970-1971: 73). Again in 1967, of the equivalent of 211,100 days of reduced hour payments, 48.5 percent went to 24,700 workers in the textile industry. In 1974, when the generalized crisis in the capitalist world[13] began to affect French industry, the number of equivalent days of reduced hour payments made by the state rose to 325,700. Of this amount, 21.3 percent went to 15,100 workers in the textile industry and 41 percent went to 48,600 workers in the steel industry (INSEE Yearbook, 1976: 79).

Not only did payments for *chômage partiel* persist into the 1970s, but segmentation of the labor market, which rendered all but the core, locally resident male labor force vulnerable to layoffs, became a permanent feature of the textile industry as well. The Roubaix-Tourcoing region is a case in point. Whereas in 1952, of the 124,000 persons employed in the textile industry in the North, 90,000 (72.6 percent) lived in the Roubaix-Tourcoing local area (Berrier, 1978: 15), 25 years later, of 46,521 persons employed in the textile industry in the North, only 60.8 percent lived in the Roubaix-Tourcoing local area and among workers *(ouvriers)* this figure drops to only 51.3 percent (Syndicat Patronal, 1978). Africans in 1977 now numbered 10 percent of the workforce in textiles and 13.5 percent of those classified as workers. Foreign Europeans resident in France (primarily from mediterranean countries) constituted 11.9 percent of the workforce (15.5 percent of the workers), and frontaliers numbered 7.7 percent of the workforce (7.6 percent of the workers). Women in all national and residential categories totaled 39.2 percent of the workforce, but 42.3 percent of the workers (Syndicat Patronal, 1978).

Although employment in textiles fell some 62 percent in the Roubaix-Tourcoing area from 1952 to 1977, the bulk of the firms in the textile industry remained small, and a dualistic structure was very much in evidence in the latter years. Thus, of the 303 firms which were members of the Syndicat Patronal Textile de Roubaix-Tourcoing and participated in its industrial survey in 1977, 68 percent had under 100 employees and an additional 13.9 percent of the firms had between 101 and 200 employees. Of the medium-sized firms, 10.9 percent had between 201 and 500 employees, and

4.6 percent had between 501 and 1000 employees. Only eight firms (2.6 percent) had over 1000 employees (Syndicat Patronal, 1978).

The presence of cheaper immigrant and female labor and the partial compensation paid to core workers on reduced hours helped to maintain the size of the labor force in textiles, to keep wages below what they might otherwise have been, and to reduce labor costs relative to those in other industries. Thus in 1977, the average salary in the textile and clothing industries in France was only 70 percent of the average salary in the top three branches of French industry—arms, aerodynamics, and naval construction; mechanical and electrical industries; and automobiles (Commissariat, 1978: 25).

The implicit subsidization of labor costs which this implied made possible the survival of many small, family-owned firms well into the 1970s. But obliging the labor force to bear the brunt of adjustment for slumps in the business cycle and cheapening labor as a factor of production through lower wages and subsidized wages (*chômage partiel* payments) also reduced the incentive for these small, family-owned firms to modernize. Short working hours, moreover, meant that there was an excess capacity and this, too, discouraged new investment in the smaller firms as we shall later see. As the process of concentration proceeded during the 1960s, the very existence of a large number of less modernized small firms, their ability to "dump" textiles onto the domestic market, and the mounting pressure from international competition brought a downward pressure upon profits. Under these conditions the high penchant for self-financing in the textile industry made modernization in the larger firms more difficult as well (de Bandt, 1978: 36).

At the close of the 1950s, the textile industry was characterized by a dualistic structure within which a process of uneven modernization had emerged. Disincentives to invest for both small and large firms, pressures for concentration, and inducements for the preservation of small firms all coexisted and rendered the textile industry vulnerable to changes in the international environment in the 1960s.

The Conflict Between Big and Little Capital

The constant competition during the 1960s *within* the Union de l'Industrie Textile over the use to which funds for adjustment should be put is evidence of the difficulty the large firms encountered in consolidating their dominance over the textile industry—a difficulty which resulted from the downward pressure on profits due to international competition, the disincentive to invest flowing from the continued existence of numerous small, unmodernized firms, and the process of concentration with limited—rationalization which these firms began in this period. The contradictions inherent in such a situation were heightened by the loss of export markets in Africa as these newly independent countries sought to industrialize behind high tariff walls which only the larger textile firms could leap and by the need to compete within the newly created European Economic Community (EEC).

Within the EEC, French textile firms were considerably smaller than those of other European countries. Whereas the average number of employees per textile firm in France was 24 in 1962, it was 46 in Germany and 111 in the Netherlands (Morvan, 1972: 283-288). Even within France the textile industry differed in its structure from those industries which had been the object of considerable restructuring by the state and big capital. Only 1.8 percent of the firms in the textile industry, for example, had over 500 employees, whereas 15.6 percent of the aeronautical firms, 14 percent of the firms in the steel industry, and 20 percent of the chemical firms had over 500 employees. (Morvan, 1972: 161-162). The weight of these large textile firms in terms of their share of total textile industry turnover (46 percent), value added in the textile industry (54 percent), and textile investments (57 percent) was considerable (Morvan, 1972: 161-162). Within the main employers associations, the Syndicat Général de l'Industrie Cotonnière Française (SGICF) and the Union de l'Industrie Textile (UIT), however, these firms were in a tiny minority. The largest firms were thus more inclined to approach the state directly than to work through these employers associations (interviews with French textile firms Dollfus Mieg, Schaeffer, Agache-Willot, Prouvost). From the state's perspective, such an approach was highly complementary because those in the plan and the Ministry of Industry regarded only the largest firms as viable interlocuters.

Exposure of French industry to European competition following implementation of the Rome Treaty sparked renewed interest in the process of industrial concentration. Indeed, the objective of pursuing a policy of concentration became explicit in the Fourth Plan (1961-1965) which called for the vigorous pursuit of concentration policies by firms and their support by the state. The Fifth Plan (1966-1970) emphasized that France needed "un petit nombre d'entreprises ou de groupes de taille internationale capable d'affronter les groupes étranger" and it acknowledged that "dans la plupart des grandes secteurs de l'industrie . . . le nombre de ces groupes devrait être limité souvent même à un ou deux" (Journal Officiel, 1965: 68-69). Additional credits were thus made available through the FDES for "restructuring" in 1965 and again in 1967 and tax laws were modified on July 12, 1965 to permit firms which merged to enjoy considerable advantages. Depreciation rules also biased opportunities in favor of larger firms.

The Fifth Plan also stressed the role of small, traditional firms in relation to these large "groups." In particular it noted that the development of small firms "specialisées dans des productions de qualité ou dans des activites de complément, par example, de sous-traitance" might be encouraged (Journal Officiel, 1965: 69). Nonetheless, the major beneficiaries of funds from FDES were not the PME but the larger firms who used these funds to further the process of concentration (interviews with M. Poitrine, representant du tresor au Comité No. 1 Quinquies, FDES, June 1979; M. Klein, FDES, Ministère de l'Economie, February 1979).

These new incentives stimulated the ongoing process of concentration among large firms in the chemical, electrical, and electronics industries where rapid growth was based on technological innovation. They also appear to have provided opportunities for firms in more traditional industries, such as textiles, to pursue merger and takeover strategies. Thus the total number of recorded mergers and takeovers rose from 625 in 1950-1960 to 1188 in 1961-1970. On a yearly basis the number of mergers rose from an annual average of 63 in the 1950s to 113 in 1961-1965 and 124 in 1966-1970 (Guilbert, 1975: 98).

In the textile industry there had been only one preeminant firm in the 1950s—the family-owned firm of Boussac, with some 25,000 employees. Its largest French competitor, Gillet, was only half its size. In 1961, Dollfus Mieg and Cie. (DMC) was created through a merger of the two largest spinning companies in France—Dollfus Mieg and Cie. based in Mulhouse (Alsace) and Ets. Thierrez et Cartier Bresson with plants in the North, the Vosges, and in the Paris region. DMC moved ahead of Boussac during the 1960s but was overtaken in turn by Agache Willot, the product of a fusion of Ets. Agache and Société M. J. Willot in 1967 and the firm which would ultimately take over the Boussac empire when it collapsed in 1978-1979. Other firms, St. Frère, later absorbed by Agache Willot; La Lainière de Roubaix (Prouvost); Motte-Bossut, and Ets. Schaeffer (SAIC-Velcorex) were also beginning to expand in this period, but compared to the more technologically sophisticated sectors, the process of concentration in the textile industry was advancing far more slowly.

Faced with renewed crisis in the textile industry as international competition stiffened and independent African states erected tariffs in an attempt to spur their own industrialization process, technocrats in the Ministry of Industry argued that the inefficiency of the textile industry was due to the slow pace of concentration and this in turn was a result of the dominance of small firms in the industry. These firms, in control of the SGICF and its resources, undertook their limited modernization by eliminating old machinery without expanding the scale of their operations. New inducements to concentrate would, thus, have to be developed and above all they would have to bypass the established channels of the patronal associations. One possible vehicle was an old tax imposed on domestic textile turnover in 1945 as a means of subsidizing production of cotton in the colonies. The proceeds from this parafiscal tax, the Ministry of Industry proposed, could be used to encourage concentration in the textile industry. By retaining control of these funds, moreover, the Ministry of Industry sought to increase its direct intervention in the textile adjustment process. Thus the state, which had hitherto played a major, if indirect, role in preserving the small-scale nature of the textile industry by sheltering it from international competition in domestic and African markets and by subsidizing labor costs through payments for *chômage partiel,* now sought to play a role more in line with its activities in nontraditional industries by promoting concentration in the textile industry.

The Union de l'Industrie Textile (UIT), a federation of local patronal associations in different branches of the textile industry, however, preferred to see the proceeds of a parafiscal tax used for modernization and to subsidize the Institut Textile de France, the sector's research institute. The UIT also demanded control over these funds much as the SGICF had managed the Caisse de Riblonnage in the 1950s. Not only did the *petite et moyenne entreprises* which dominated the UIT fear that the autonomy of their association would be reduced by direct state involvement in textile restructuring, but they anticipated the likely concertation between the state and big capital which would result.

Such fears were not unwarranted. Big capital in the textile industry did not hide its antagonism toward the PME as the textile crisis of the 1960s worsened. In fact, many of the larger firms accused small, marginal companies of exacerbating the effects of international pressures. Thus the Dollfus-Mieg Administrative Council in its report to the General Assembly argued that the difficulties DMC encountered in 1965 were only partly due to a

> fall in domestic textile consumption . . . a small drop in exports and a notable increase in textile imports . . . independently of these general causes, these difficulties resulted from . . . the irrational and abnormal competition . . . of marginal firms which use outdated, largely amortized machinery in their effort to survive [Dollfus-Mieg and Cie., 1968: 5-6].

Dollfus-Mieg, Agache Willot, and Schaeffer, moreover, were then in the process of jumping the protective tariff barriers erected by French-speaking African countries and locating import-substituting finishing operations within these overseas markets. As the larger French firms internationalized production to the former French colonies, these African markets were effectively closed to exports of calico and Guinea cloth from the smaller Vosges and Alsacian cotton textile firms. Once again these firms were plunged into crisis as the conflict between big and little capital in France was played out in African markets.

Many of the small- and medium-size firms in the Vosges, in order to increase sales within France to compensate for lost African markets, now demanded protection of the domestic market and in some cases ran down existing equipment while attempting to diversify once again (interview, ets. Jules Marchal, December 1978). Ultimately the small- and medium-size firms which weathered this crisis did so through the modernization of plant and equipment and the specialization in high quality or design-intensive products for the domestic and EEC markets (interviews with Ets. Perrin, Schaeffer Impression). As they modernized however, they also grew—expanding both the scale of their operations and taking over smaller firms. Table 6.1 reveals that the number of firms in the cotton textile sector fell by 26 percent from 1963 to 1969 while the top four firms' share of total turnover in cotton textiles rose from 15.8 percent in 1963 to 22.6 percent in 1969.

At the height of the textile crisis, in 1965, it was the opposition of large- and medium-size, dynamic firms to the small, marginal firms which found echoes in a report on the textile industry tabled by M. Jean Precheur in the Conseil Economique et Social.[14] The Precheur Report begins its recommendations by noting that a competitive textile industry requires "an acceleration of regroupments, of inter-firm agreements, of mergers or of concentration." Moreover, in certain sectors, the report points out "the existence of outdated machinery and excess capacity, thwart efforts at the necessary elimination of marginal firms [*assainissement*]" (Precheur, 1964: 790-791). As the "rhythm of concentration remains too slow," the report advocates the creation of a textile fund, to be fed by the receipts of the new parafiscal tax proposed by the state, and whose function would be to accelerate the process of concentration in this industry (Precheur, 1965: 791).

In 1966, the patronat and the state joined hands to create this textile fund—the Centre Inter-Professionel de Renovation des Structures Industrielles et Commerciales de l'Industrie Textile (CIRIT).[15] Assignment of

TABLE 6.1   Concentration in the Textile Industry, 1963-1969

	Top Four Firms (percentage share in total turnover of the sector)		Number of Firms in the Sector		Turnover of the Sector (in millions of francs)	
	1963	*1969*	*1963*	*1969*	*1963*	*1969*
All Textiles	15.0	12.5	7439	4763	20349	21495
Cotton Textiles	15.8	22.6	1025	755	6067.4	6915.6
Synthetic and Artificial Fibers	94.5	100.0	7	4	7.2	85.9

SOURCE: Jenny and Weber, 1974: 78-79.

nominal control over this fund to the Union de l'Industrie Textile was quite unexpected considering the bias for concentration expressed in the Precheur Report. Bureaucratic politics, notably the long-standing efforts of the Ministry of Industry to secure a measure of discretionary autonomy from Treasury surveillance, played a large role in assuring this outcome. The CIRIT Conseil de Direction composed of one representative each from the nationalized banking sector—the Crédit National and the Caisse Nationale des Marchés de l'Etat—one representative each from the Ministry of Finance and the Ministry of Industry, plus six members from the UIT appointed by the Ministry of Industry, could not act without the consent of Finance.

Within the UIT, conflict over the purpose to which these funds should be put pitted the larger firms, which supported concentration, against the smaller firms, which sought modernization through the purchase of old machinery and the reconversion of marginal plants (*riblonnage* rather than *assainissement*). As both ministries favored using CIRIT funds to promote concentration (which inevitably implied *assainissement*), and as the Ministry of Industry studies all requests for funds and exercises considerable influence over the choice of UIT representatives, there was little doubt that control over this fund would actually remain in the hands of the state and the larger firms within the industry despite UIT nominal control.[16] Nevertheless, the Treasury initially chose to reduce the rate of taxation and hence limited CIRIT funds in its first years of operation to barely 40 million francs (Friedberg, 1976: 187). Efforts to increase the funds available persisted.

In 1968, new negotiations with the state raised the amount available for restructuring assistance through CIRIT to 100 million francs (OECD, 1974: 95). By 1978 and 1979, the fund totaled 122 million francs and 136 million francs, respectively (Senat, 1978: 56). CIRIT funds, controlled by the state and the larger firms in the textile industry, thus come to nearly one-third of all funds invested in the cotton spinning and weaving branches of the textile industry during the decade after its creation.

Although the 1968 negotiations also stipulated that CIRIT funds might be used for modernization, such funds could only be allocated if modernization were accompanied by restructuring, that is, by mergers or takeovers (Friedberg, 1976: 187). CIRIT has, thus, above all furthered the interests of the larger firms in the industry. In the cotton textile branch, for example, it facilitated the restructuring efforts of many of the largest firms—Agache Willot, Dollfus-Mieg, Ets. Schaeffer, Motte-Bossut, Ets. Marchal, and Ets. Perrin (interviews with these firms in 1978-1979). As CIRIT fostered the takeover of small firms by larger textile companies, the equilibrium between big and little capital in the textile industry ruptured. Only the support of large firms for continued protection of the domestic market helped maintain the appearance of unity in the textile industry.

The largest textile firms, however, also sought state assistance in their

overseas expansion. Large firms in the textile and other traditional industries, in commerce, banking, mining, insurance and transportation, all of
which had interests in francophone Africa, formed the Association Internationale pour le Développement Economique et l'Aide Technique (AIAT) in
1959 and campaigned for continued tariff preferences in the former French
colonies (SGICF, 1969: 19-20). In particular, in the late 1960s they spear-
headed the movement for a renewal of the Yaoundé Convention which bound
these colonies to the EEC and thus to France in a system of reverse tariff
preferences. Subsequently AIAT campaigned vigorously for the preservation of privileged trade and investment ties to France's former colonies
through the Lomé Convention which succeeded the Yaoundé Accords in
1975. Lobbying directly in Brussels and working through a special commission on Franco-African relations within the peak patronal association, the
Confederation Nationale du Patronat Français (CNPF), AIAT became a
major force influencing French foreign economic policy during the 1960s
and early 1970s and it proved tremendously successful in securing continued
privileged access for French industry in African markets during this period
(Dolan and Mytelka, 1980).

Despite an alliance between large and small firms in the textile industry in
order to protect the domestic market, in the wider context of the French
society the conflict between big and little capital was growing as the process
of concentration brought large firms to the fore in most industrial branches
and as these firms attempted to further solidify their position of privileged
access to the state.[17] Debates in the Conseil Economique et Social (CES)
during the late 1960s and 1970s revealed the persistent opposition of small
capital delegates[18] to further efforts at industrial concentration. In 1967, for
example, the PMEs opposed drafts of the Lagrandré Report, a study of the
problems posed by the process of concentration, because it concluded in
favor of further industrial concentration. "Mergers," the PMEs declared,
"must not be considered to be the sole solution to the problems of size in a
modern economy" (CES, 1967: 263). A few phrases to the effect that some
small, specialized firms had a role to play in the French economy were
inserted into the final draft, but this rhetorical appeasement neither reduced
the efforts by big capital to consolidate its position within the industrial
sector nor did it still the PME's opposition. In May 1971, the PME's discontent was again in evidence in the CES debate over the Sixth Plan (1971-
1975). This time an open schism within the business delegation resulted
when all PME delegates abstained while all big firms voted for the proposed
plan which underscored the "consolidation of large industrial 'groups' and
the enlargement of their development base" (Journal Officiel, 1971: 51).

As the crisis of capitalism deepened in the mid-1970s and "stagflation"
combined with international competition to force a decline in textile profits,
a rise in textile unemployment, and an increase in textile bankruptcies, large

firms in this industry faced a new set of choices. On the one hand, they could maintain their alliance with small, family-owned firms and thereby preserve the "traditional" nature of the French textile industry by lobbying for protection of the domestic market, subsidization of labor costs (payments for *chômage partiel*) and privileged ties to Africa. The consequence for larger firms, however, would be a disincentive to modernize and specialize production at home, a fall in profits levels, and hence a growing need to relocate productive activities to the protected markets of Africa with a view to the global rationalization of production. Reimports of cotton yarn and cloth as required under this option, however, would ultimately lead larger firms to advocate selective, as opposed to across-the-board, protection, and this, in turn, would result in renewed conflicts with the PME.

On the other hand, large textile firms could join with the dynamic firms in nontraditional industries as they consolidated their dominance within the French political economy. In so doing, these firms would be obliged to modernize plant and equipment with a view to specialization in technologically sophisticated or design-intensive products and/or to pursue policies of diversification—moving into new product lines, new industrial branches, or new sectors. They would have to stress exports, as well as the internationalization of production. If the latter option were chosen, a diminished role for traditional industries and a new role for small, specialized firms could be anticipated. The textile industry thus reached a major turning point in the 1970s.

The Changing International Division of Labor and the French Textile Industry in the 1970s

By the 1970s the process of change begun in the 1950s had produced a textile industry marked by industrial concentration at the top and the preservation of a vast number of small, family-owned firms at the base. Among the largest textile firms, those with over 2000 employees, concentration further accelerated in the 1970s. In 1969, for example, 19 firms had over 2000 employees and they accounted for 20.4 percent of total textile turnover; by 1975, only 14 firms fell into this category but they alone now accounted for 20 percent of textile turnover (Ministère de l'Industrie, 1969, 1975). Many of these firms, moreover, belonged to one of the six large textile groups— Agache Willot, Dollfus-Mieg, Rhône Poulenc (Textile), Prouvost, Devanley and Recoing, or Boussac. By 1980, even fewer top firms remained as independent companies once Agache Willot absorbed Boussac. Disaggregated by branch, the four-firm concentration ratio reveals that by 1976, the top four firms in cotton spinning accounted for 22.6 percent of total sales in their branch and the top four firms in cotton weaving accounted for 34.9 percent of total sales in that branch (Ministère de l'Industrie, 1979).

Within the cotton textile industry this dualism resulted in a pattern of uneven modernization which is apparent from investment figures provided in Table 6.2. There it can be seen that the smallest firms, those with under 100 employees, continued to dominate numerically within the cotton textile industry well into the 1970s. Although they constituted 62 percent of all firms in this industry in the period 1970-1976,[19] they accounted for only 14.2 percent of the investments, averaging 194,271 francs per year per firm. In contrast, the largest firms, those with over 1000 employees, constituted only 3.8 percent of all cotton textile firms in the 1970s but accounted for an average of 37.7 percent of the investments made or some 9.3 million francs per firm, per year.

Size was also related to the degree of vertical integration in the textile industry. Although only 16 percent of the 300 cotton textile firms were integrated in 1976, 26.5 percent of the firms with over 500 employees were integrated in that year (SGICF, 1977: 26, 27). Of the ten largest firms in the industry, nine had fully integrated spinning, weaving, and finishing operations. What is truly remarkable about these figures, however, is the low overall level of vertical integration in the cotton textile industry.

Unlike the small, cotton textile producers, the largest cotton textile firms, Dollfus Mieg (DMC), Agache Willot, Schaeffer, Motte Bossut, and Perrin, for example, had considerably diversified their activities (interviews with these companies). By the 1970s, all had moved into synthetics or wools, most were engaged in textile-related activities such as carpet manufacture, knitting, clothing or textile distribution, and some had entered completely unrelated industries or sectors.[20] Diversification was seen as a hedge against the boom and bust cycles which, in unsynchronized fashion, affected different branches of the textile industry (DMC, 1969: 8-10). Diversification, however, did not imply specialization or rationalization of production within these conglomerate structures.[21] Nor did it indicate a process of rapid modernization for which few incentives existed. To the contrary, only limited efforts to rationalize production were undertaken by the largest cotton textile companies as they took over smaller firms, many of which were experiencing severe difficulties (interviews with Agache Willot, November 1978; Dollfus-Mieg, January 1979). Although it pioneered among these large, family-owned, cotton textile firms in the adoption of modern management techniques, even Dollfus-Mieg only elaborated its first group-wide three-year development plan in 1973 (DMC, 1972). In the aggregate, therefore, statistics on changes in the number of firms and plants in cotton spinning, weaving, and synthetics as presented in Table 6.3 reveal that, with the exception of the spinning branch, concentration, here operationalized as a reduction in the number of firms, proceeded more rapidly than rationalization, operationalized as a reduction in the number of plants.

With limited rationalization and modernization, production and export of

TABLE 6.2 Differential Levels of Investment Among Large and Small Cotton Textile Firms, 1970-1976

	1970	1971	1972	1973	1974	1975	1976
LARGE FIRMS[a]							
N	15	17	17	16	16	14	11
Percentage of total cotton textile firms	3.5	3.8	4.0	3.6	4.4	3.9	2.9
Percentage of total investment by cotton textile firms	26.7	40.5	44.8	41.7	39.4	34.2	36.9
Average level of investment per firm[c]	5713.8	7405.7	9849.8	9610.8	10523.3	9578.7	12447.5
SMALL FIRMS[b]							
N	269	291	275	259	211	214	230
Percentage of total cotton textile firms	63.3	65.2	63.7	61.8	57.7	59.5	62.5
Percentage of total investment by cotton textile firms	36.0	18.1	9.4	9.6	8.0	7.7	10.6
Average level of investment per firm[c]	431.9	194.5	127.3	137.2	161.8	140.1	167.1

SOURCE: Calculated from data supplied by the Ministry of Industry, STISI, 1970-1976.
a. Over 1000 employees.
b. Under 100 employees.
c. In thousands of francs.

TABLE 6.3   Concentration and Rationalization in Cotton Spinning, Weaving, and
            Synthetic Textile Production, 1969-1977

	1969		1977		Percentage Change (1969-1977)	
	number of firms	number of plants	number of firms	number of plants	number of firms	number of plants
Cotton Spinning	115	147	101	124	−12.2	−15.6
Weaving	314	371	238	294	−24.2	−20.8
Synthetics	7	20	4	17	−42.9	−15.0

SOURCE: UIT, Statistique Générale de l'Industrie Textile Française, 1969, 1977 (Paris: UIT).

cotton yarn and cloth remained high and throughout the 1960s the franc zone
continued to play an important role as a market for French textile exports
(Table 6.3). Production and export of synthetics rose even faster in this
period. Then in 1973, the Multi-Fiber Agreement[22] was signed and within
two years, a large rise in textile and clothing imports (especially knitwear)
occurred. Goods entered France at what was described as abnormally low
prices (CES, 1978: 137). Cotton tee shirts and underwear from Taiwan,
South Korea, and Hong Kong were selling at 20 percent of the French price
and acrylic fibers were being sold at 40 percent below French prices. Imports of cotton and linen cloth rose, as a percentage of total consumption,
from 38 percent in 1974 to 50 percent in 1977 (CES, 1978: 142).

The shock of increased international competition was amplified when the
French economy, along with the economies of other advanced, capitalist
societies, entered into a crisis of inflation, production cutback, and unemployment. The crisis, which began in France in 1974-1975, was also marked
by a declining rate of profits in French industry. Only the automobile industry was exempted from this general trend, while textiles and clothing were
particularly affected. The number of bankruptcies among French industrial
firms also rose from an annual average of 10,000 in the period 1968-1973 to
13,000 per year in 1974-1977. By 1978, the number of bankruptcies in
France totaled 15,598 (Maurus, 1979). As French industry concentrated and
moved toward greater capital-intensive production, unemployment rose and
the number of industrial conflicts also increased. From an average of 2.5
million working days lost per year in 1965-1969, the number of days lost to
strike action rose in 1970-1974 to 3.4 million and to 4.2 million in 1975-
1977 (ILO, 1974: Table 27, 1979: Table 24).

Under pressure from international competition and "laboring" under a
legacy of protectionism, of concentration with limited rationalization, and
of uneven modernization, the French textile industry underwent its third
major postwar crisis. As Table 6.5 reveals, the number of firms having less
than fifty employees dropped 45.2 percent in the period 1970-1976, as small

TABLE 6.4   Production and Export of Cotton and Synthetic Yarns and Cloths

	1965-1969	*1970-1974*	*1975-1977a*
Cotton Spinning			
Average annual production[b]	259.16	265.12	232.5
Percentage exported	5.5	7.5	7.2
Percentage exported to franc zone	29.0	13.4	12.0
Cotton Weaving			
Average annual production[b]	215.1	206.5	185.8
Percentage exported	15.9	19.0	23.1
Percentage exported to franc zone	40.5	14.5	10.3
Synthetics			
Average annual production[b]	244.08	360.9	321.2
Percentage exported	18.9	21.3	28.0
Percentage exported to franc zone	17.0	n.a.	n.a.

SOURCE: UIT (1969, 1972, 1977); SGICF (1977); OECD (1976).
a. 1975-1977 for production figures; 1975-1976 for export figures.
b. in thousands of tons.

firms collapsed or were absorbed. The larger firms, those with over 500 employees, were now forced into a major rationalization effort in order to survive, and the result was a marked decline of 30 percent in employment by these large firms over the years 1970-1976. Unemployment in the textile industry, which had averaged 15,347 persons per year in the period 1968-1974, rose to 27,813 in 1975, to 29,394 in 1976, and to 35,195 in 1977 (ILO, 1978: 305). A large number of textile workers were, in addition, receiving payments for reduced hours (discussed earlier in this chapter).

Pressure rose for renewed protection of the domestic market and in 1975, a Groupe de Travail interministériel administratif sur l'industrie cotonnière was constituted (interview, M. Sciallon, Direction des Relations économiques étrangères (DREE), Ministry of Finance). Along with the textile sector group which met to discuss preparations for the Seventh Plan (1975-1980), the interministerial committee called for greater involvement of CIRIT in restructuring the textile industry. In June, the EEC Commission invoked safeguard clauses under the Multi-Fiber Agreement (MFA) for shirts, tee shirts, and cotton yarn, and a more restrictive MFA was adopted in that year. Those in the state, however, were agreed that the next MFA, to go into affect in 1982, would be more favorable to textile exporters. The French textile industry thus had a five-year grace period in which to adjust. While new credits would be made available to assist the textile industry to modernize, to specialize in the more sophisticated product lines, or to diversify out of the textile industry, the prevailing sentiment among those occupying policy-making positions was that further efforts by the state to insulate the textile sector from pressures to adjust would not be forthcoming.[23]

That such sentiments had become widespread in the key organs of the

TABLE 6.5   The Changing Structure of the Textile Industry, 1970-1976

	1970		1976		Percentage Change (1970-1976)	
Number of Employees	Number of Firms	Number of Employees	Number of Firms	Number of Employees	Firms	Employees
0-49	2,440	49,244	1,342	35,402	−45.2	−28.1
50-99	502	35,850	408	29,350	−18.7	−18.1
100-199	367	51,870	320	45,847	−12.8	−11.6
200-499	245	74,476	216	67,305	−11.8	− 9.6
over 500	150	207,318	117	144,111	−22.0	−30.5
ALL FIRMS	3,704	418,758	2,403a	322,015a	−35.1	−23.1

SOURCE: Ministry of Industry, STISI, 1970: 46, Table 33, 1976: 86, Table 10.
a. 6312 employees and 159 firms could not be accounted for in this table.

state reflects two significant changes which had become notable by the late 1970s. First, the growth of nontraditional industries, encouraged by the state since the 1950s, culminated in the reduced importance of the textile industry as a whole in the French economy by the end of the 1970s. In 1977, textile firms represented only 1.8 percent of all industrial establishments and accounted for only 4.9 percent of those employed in industry (CGT, 1978: 21-22). Large firms, moreover, employed 45 percent of all textile employees.

Second, as a result of these changes in the structure of French industry, large and dynamic medium-size, export-oriented firms in nontraditional industries consolidated not only their access to the state, but their influence within the capitalist class. Changes in the composition of key commissions within the Confédération Nationale du Patronat Français (CNPF) are indicative of this.

In 1944, Léon Gingembre created the Confédération Générale des Petites et Moyennes Entreprises (CGPME) which, in the immediate postwar period, held a predominant position within the CNPF (Ehrmann, 1957: 121). As the process of concentration proceeded, large firms emerged in the dynamic sectors of the economy. In 1969, these firms established the Association des Grandes Entreprises faisant appel à l'épargne (AGREF) with a view to exercising greater influence over the policies of patronal associations such as the CNPF. A decade later, AGREF achieved its objective when in January 1979, with 11 representatives out of 36, its members came to dominate the key Commission de Politique Economique Générale within the CNPF. Allied with the dynamic, medium-size, technologically sophisticated firms oriented toward exports or investment abroad, AGREF led a move away from close ties to the slow-growth markets of francophone Africa and toward more buoyant markets in Latin America and Asia. A month after their victory within the CNPF, therefore, the special commission which had dealt with Franco-African relations and was dominated by the AIAT—the association of large firms in traditional industries and other large firms with trading and investment interests in francophone Africa—was abolished and all questions involving industrial strategies and their relationship to foreign economic policy were channeled through the Commission de Politique Economique Générale which the AGREF controlled. It was to the needs of large and medium-size dynamic firms in technology-intensive activities that state policy increasingly addressed itself in the 1970s. Indeed, in the preparation of the Eighth Plan (1980-1984), a single industrial commission to deal with questions of financing investments that increase productivity, innovation, and exports replaced the sectoral commissions of previous planning processes (interviews with Mme. Cap de boscq, M. Gonesse, and M. Gabet [Plan], June 1980).

The State and Industrial Adjustment in the 1970s

French industry in the 1970s not only suffered from international competition but from capital constraints resulting from the long-standing preference for self-financing in small, family-owned firms, and from the nature of the French banking system. In part to remedy these deficiencies, state assistance to industry in the form of subsidies, loans, and tax credits rose considerably in this period. As the general economic crisis deepened and bankruptcies in a number of traditional industries—textiles, clothing, steel, and shipbuilding—threatened, the state intervened directly in the restructuring process as a shareholder in selected enterprises, through the Institute de Développement Industriel (IDI) and by organizing takeovers and managing restructuring activities through the Comité interministeriel pour l'aménagement des structures industrielles (CIASI).

Previously established funds were now reoriented toward the promotion of concentration *and* modernization and new subsidies and credits were made available for specialization in high technology "niches." FDES became a mere shadow of its former self as additional policy instruments were developed to facilitate direct state intervention in the internationalization of production and in the promotion of exports.

In administering these funds there is no doubt that the state continued to favor the larger firms. As much as 80 percent of the export credits, for example, have helped only six to ten different firms (interview with M. Pagé, Ministry of Industry, January 1979). As to the sectoral aid, *il y a quelsques gros preneurs,* among them, naval construction, aeronautics, steel, and automobiles. Within these sectors, a small number of large private and state corporations have emerged and they are the principal recipients of state assistance (interview with M. Poitrine, FDES, January 1979). Even in those state agencies (such as IDI) set up to fund small and medium-size firms in preference to the *grands groupes,* the tendency has been to progressively concentrate on the larger firms.

In the mid-1970s, as the crisis of the small firms, especially those in traditional industries, intensified, and the Lip affair[24] presaged the imminent collapse of other small firms or their takeover by workers, the state created yet another interministerial agency to oversee funds designed expressly to aid smaller firms that were fundamentally sound but in financial difficulty.[25] The Comité interministeriel pour l'amenagement des structures industrielles (CIASI) began to function in late 1974.

CIASI became the principal state instrument influencing adjustment in the textile industry. Its aid to this industry reflects the increasingly more *direct* role of the state in the process of textile adjustment—a role which changed from one of marginal involvement in the cotton textile industry (the SGICF-administered Caisse de Riblonnage during the 1950s) to partnership with the textile industry (UIT) in CIRIT, the principal textile restructuring body in the 1960s, to direct involvement in restructuring exclusive of industry representation through CIASI in the 1970s. CIASI is chaired by the Ministry of Economy and Finance and its secretariat is located within this Ministry in the Treasury. Among the nine members of CIASI, the Ministry of Economy and Finance and the Prime Minister's office through the Délégué à l'aménagement du Territoire et à l'action régionale (DATAR) are said to exercise predominant influence.

Along with the Ministry of Industry and the Commissariat Général du Plan, the Ministry of Economy and Finance identifies sectors for funding and designates the size of the funding *enveloppes* for each of these sectors. CIASI dispensed 394.6 million francs in 1975, 210.1 million francs in 1976, and 108.5 million francs in 1977. In 1978, CIASI funds totaled 387 million and 300 million in 1979 (interview M. Jaclot, CIASI, June 1980).

Exclusion of industry representation from CIASI, however, should not be taken to imply an end to the *économie concertée* in the mid-1970s. To the contrary, CIASI brings together *industriels, banquiers, et administration* in order to resolve the financial difficulties of the firms whose dossiers are before it. But CIASI does not involve the trade unions in this concertation process. CIASI's *direct involvement* in textile adjustment, moreover, complements the state's move into equity participation as a vehicle for adjustment in other traditional industries.

In playing a more direct role in textile adjustment the state is clearly responding to the continuing crisis in this industry. But its diagnosis, at least at the outset, remained fundamentally the same—that the process of concentration, through which the textile industry can become internationally competitive, is proceeding too slowly. Thus, from November 1974 to October 1978, CIASI examined 818 dossiers of which 60 percent (504 dossiers) were the objective of CIASI assistance and 224 were rejected. Among those firms that received CIASI assistance in 1976, only 7 percent had turnovers of over 100 million francs, but they received 35 percent of the loans. Although only 21 percent of the firms had turnovers of over 100 million francs in 1977 and 1978, they were the beneficiaries of 63 percent and 95 percent of the funds respectively (France, various years). The type of assistance rendered by CIASI in this period thus favored larger firms and it was heavily weighted toward the promotion of industrial concentration. Fully one-third of the cases settled during the period November 1974 to April 1978 involved industrial takeovers. In the last few months of 1978, however, the proportions began to shift. Of 66 dossiers settled from April to October 1978, 50 involved assistance for modernization and rationalization of production and only 16 dossiers were settled by the takeover of the firm in difficulty by another firm. In February 1979, M. René Monory, minister of economy and finance, following upon the new policy of price liberalization just implemented, announced that CIASI's activities were to be decentralized, an action which would permit greater funding of small- and medium-size firms (*Le Monde:* February 23, 1979). The regional antennae of CIASI, the CO-DEFI, which made only three loans in 1977, were handling one-third of the loan applications in 1979.

Throughout the 1970s, however, larger firms remained the major beneficiaries of state industrial assistance through FDES, IDI, CIASI, sectoral programs, and other instruments. Continued concertation with big capital marginalized both labor and the PME from the process of planning industrial change in the 1970s. As many of the professional associations in traditional industries were dominated by small, family-owned firms, these associations tended increasingly to be bypassed in the industrial planning process. Thus M. Noblot, director of economic policy at the Union de l'Industrie textile, noted that the state negotiates directly with big capital in the textile industry over the head of the UIT and he cited the role CIASI played in engineering Agache-Willot's takeover of the moribund Boussac Empire[26] as a case in point (Interview, February 1979). M. Limouzy, a Gaullist deputy and a spokesman for the PME, in his report to the National Assembly in November 1977 similarly charged that the state failed to consult the professional and patronal associations (Assemblé National, 1977-1978). State-big capital concertation, while dating back to the 1950s, had certainly become the dominant feature of industrial planning in the 1970s.

Conclusion

By the late 1970s it had become apparent that concentration was neither a means to increase industrial research and development nor a benign transformation in industrial structures. Concentration led to sharp drops in employment, regional imbalances, and increases in profits which were used to reduce endebtedness rather than increase levels of investment (Morvan, 1972; Jenny and Weber, 1976; CGT, 1979; Mathieu, 1979). Flexible adjustment seemed more a facility of medium-size firms than of the conglomerates which had come to dominate traditional industries. But only when some of the largest firms—Boussac in textiles, Leroy in wood—were in danger of imminent collapse at the end of the decade did the fundamental assumptions of the post war industrial strategy come into question. International economic pressures and domestic social changes, moreover, made a new industrial strategy thinkable.

Even though 63 percent of all French textile firms in 1977 still had less than 100 employees, big capital was in the process of consolidating its dominance in the textile industry and had forged close links to the French state. The emergence of big capital in traditional industries, the rise of big capital and smaller, dynamic firms in nontraditional, technologically sophisticated industries, and the growing salience of these industries in the French economy have brought forward "new middle classes" (Carchedi, 1979) which provide a new set of partners for both left and centrist political coalitions in France.

Political struggles in the 1970s confirmed the availability of new options. In the aftermath of May 1968, left forces in France appeared to be on the rise. In 1972, a Union de la Gauche was forged when the Parti Socialiste (PS) and the Parti Communiste Française (PCF) agreed to contest future elections on the basis of a common program. The common program stipulated a number of significant industrial changes that would be implemented in the wake of an electoral victory, notably the nationalization of eleven major industrial firms and all remaining private banks. As labor militancy had made participation in a corporatist industrial planning process unfeasible, an eventual victory of the left with its common program appeared at that time to be the only possibility for labor participation in industrial change. Both major unions, thus, focused their energies in the period 1972-1978 at the national level and on the political arena of electoral competition.

Two consequences flowed from the rupture of the Union de la Gauche in 1978. First, the CGT and CFDT were forced to reconsider their strategy of relying upon electoral contests to bring about industrial change. Taking the lead, the CGT now published the first union-oriented study of an industry in crisis—the steel industry—and labor militancy once again rose as layoffs at Usinor, Sacilor, and Rhône Poulenc were announced.

Second, the break-up of the Union de la Gauche led to left losses in the French legislative elections of 1978 and seemed to confirm the disappearance of a left-threat to the center-right coalition then in power. Within the PS, moreover, conflict pitted those who advocated a center-left coalition against those who supported a Union de la Gauche thus weakening François

Mitterand's stature at an important electoral moment. Then in 1979, the European parliamentary elections marked a change within the ruling center-right coalition. The victory of Giscard's list, headed by Mme. Simone Veil, reduced the "credibility of Jacques Chirac, leader of the Gaullist RPR, as a presidential candidate for 1981" (Jenson, 1979: 32) and partially freed the Giscardiens from their dependence on the traditional social forces which have formed the base of Gaullist support since 1958.

This changing social basis of political alliances gave impetus to the post-1978 Giscardien presidency in its search for a new industrial strategy. As the near collapse of *large* firms in textiles, steel, automobiles, and wood testified to the failure of concentration as a stimulus to innovation and efficient production, such rethinking clearly became necessary. In the textile industry a new strategy was imperative.

Within a context of protected markets, high employment in the textile industry had been maintained by subsidizing labor costs (through payments for *chômage partiel*) and by segmenting the labor market. What this meant is that workers were put on short hours at reduced pay rather than into retraining programs for transfer to higher skilled jobs in other industries. This induced workers to remain in the textile industry when economic conditions would have facilitated mobility. The apparent sociopolitical gains, however, were achieved at the expense of modernization.

The downward pressure on profits resulting from mounting international competition, including rising competition from German and Italian producers,[27] combined with the continued existence of vast numbers of small, marginal firms selling at or below cost to discourage new investment in France. Internationalization of production to the former French colonies, while it had briefly benefited a few of the larger firms, did not provide an overall solution to the problems of this industry. Indeed, choice of sophisticated production technology by these foreign firms for their African subsidiaries raised import costs and inflated the wage bill because of the need to employ expatriate personnel. Heavy borrowing to meet this investment program, moreover, led to high interest payments. These factors contributed to the relatively higher costs of production in subsidiaries designed for export-oriented manufacturing and made global rationalization of production impossible even for the larger textile firms such as Dollfus-Mieg and Agache Willot (Mytelka, 1981). The textile industry thus remained under constant pressure from foreign competition leading to a kind of restructuring engineered by larger firms in conjunction with the state that frustrated worker participation and eliminated jobs while it kept wages lower than they might otherwise have been. In the crisis of the 1970s, small firms collapsed, unemployment and disguised unemployment rose, and some of the largest firms were on the brink of bankruptcy as they borrowed heavily for their takeovers but failed to rationalize production. It was from these large firms that there arose a demand for more liberal firing procedures as job security provision enacted since 1968 had made layoffs and firing extremely difficult.

These were the firms which now favored a reorientation of state aid to promote specialization and the internationalization of textile production—noting that France had less extensive foreign investment guarantees than some of its EEC partners (interviews with DMC, Agache Willot, Prouvost, Rhône Poulenc Textiles). Joining forces with the medium-size, export-oriented firms that had emerged in a number of dynamic industries, they raised anew their demand for the elimination of marginal firms in traditional industries or in product lines then under pressure from international competition. Theirs are the views articulated in the influential Berthelot Report which studied *L'Evolution du Tiers Monde et l'Appareil Productif Francaise* (Commissariat Général du Plan, 1978) and in the Peillon Report on *l'Avenir des Industries Francaises et la Nouvelle Répartition Internationale de la Production Industrielle* (CES, 1978).

Both of these reports advocate direct foreign investment as a spur to further exports. Each, moreover, recommends "a reorientation of financial and technical cooperation toward more dynamic zones of the third world, without compromising relations with Francophone Africa," (Commissariat Général du Plan, 1978: 41). Neither of these reports considers the possible employment effects of either the internationalization of production or the closure of small firms in traditional industries. Although business views were solicited, labor representation was systematically excluded from the working groups which prepared these key reports on French industrial adjustment. In neither case was the exclusion of labor an oversight. Rather, as interviews with the principals involved revealed, there was a marked reluctance to examine the effect of French direct foreign investment on domestic employment—a question of immediate concern to the unions (interviews with Berthelot [now at OECD], Peillon [CES], Hennekine [Foreign Affairs], Moynot [CGT], and Prévôt [CFDT], 1978-1979).

Each report, moreover, echoes the sentiments expressed in the Pisani report on *Les enjeux et les conditions des équilibres extérieur de la France* to the effect that France's future "is not tied to specific sectors of production or geographical zones but to flexibility, to adaptability, and to creativity" (Senat, 1978: 58). "Il faut organiser un repli ordonné des secteurs sans avenir," the report concludes (Senat, 1978: 138). As to the textile industry, what better authority to cite than the president, who in a televised interview with J-L. Servan-Schreiber, observed that

> what cannot be denied is that we cannot continue to make products with a low domestic value added, in sectors where we cannot pay workers and where there is no profit for the firm . . . I feel that France should . . . renounce the

manufacture of simple products which can be made elsewhere more cheaply [*Le Monde,* October 18, 1978: 13].

The new Giscardien industrial strategy thus started from the assumption that France would become increasingly more dependent upon raw material imports[28] and that industrial exports would have to pay the bill. This, André Giroud, minister of industry went on to point out, required that French industry become more competitive and export-oriented [*Le Monde;* September 1979: 13]. Instead of further concentration, the state would encourage *les moyennes enterprises performantes* capable of sustaining international competition for new export markets in sophisticated products (interviews with P. Mordacq [Plan]; P. Pagé [Industrie], January 1979, and Mme. Capdeboscq [Plan], June 1980). This view was reflected in recent planning documents which, looking to Japan and Germany as models, proposed that the state play a major role in adjustment policy since

> French and foreign experience show that the conversion of certain industries in difficulty cannot be done without an active effort of national solidarity. It falls to the State to organize, to this effect, all necessary public assistance, on condition that these funds do not serve to maintain situations without solutions, but contribute to those adaptations imposed by evolving world conditions. It is in this spirit that the Fonds spécial d'adaptation industrielle has been created [*La Documentation Francaise,* 1979: 58].

The Fonds spécial d'adaptation industrielle (FSAI) has three billion francs at its disposal. Half of these funds were to be used as subsidies and half as *prêts participatif,* that is, loans converted into equity capital in the recipient firm (interview with M. Lorentz [FSAI], January 1979). FSAI funds have thus far been used primarily to aid the automobile industry and to restructure the steel industry in its most recent crisis. By converting some of the industry's CIASI loans to the steel industry into equity participation, the state opened new opportunities to play a direct role in a restructuring process which envisages a loss of 20,000 jobs.

As M. Giraud pointed out, although the state did not nationalize the steel or other industries in difficulty and "does not intend to substitute for industry this does not imply, however, a policy of 'laissez faire-laisser passer'" (*Le Monde,* September 15, 1978: 32).

In addition to an increasingly more direct role for the state in industrial adjustment, now that concentration was a prominent feature of the French economy, the Giscardien industrial strategy was now intended to emphasize invention and innovation:

> No economy can maintain its dynamism without the continuous creation of new firms. This reanimates and stimulates competition. The growth of firms

is often the result of a new idea, of a new product. . . . Thus the government has recently taken significant measures to encourage the creation of enterprises, and more generally, the development of small and medium-sized firms [*La Documentation Francaise,* 1978: 61].

Seen from this perspective, the establishment of an Agence pour la création d'entreprises and the interest in promotion small and medium-sized industries in dynamic sectors, specialized in technology or design intensive product (*La Documentation Francaise,* 1979: 57-62) had little to do with the preservation of the traditional sector. To the contrary, the new strategy sought to preserve only those segments of traditional industries which through specialization find niches *(crénaux)* in which they can become internationally competitive (interviews with Bizec [Industry] and Boublil [Plan], January 1979). Giscard's new industrial strategy thus implied a reduced role for traditional industries in the economy of the future. That the new industrial strategy paid scant attention to the needs of labor was the logical outcome of three decades of social conflict in France marked by labor militancy and the marginalization of organized labor from industrial planning by firms and the state.

While the process of adjustment in the textile industry has been far slower in France than in many other advanced, industrial countries—notably the United Kingdom, Netherlands, and Japan, there is little doubt that a major juncture in the evolution of the French political economy has now been passed and with its passage, a changed role for the traditional sector can be anticipated in the future. In the state and among the more dynamic textile firms there is both increased recognition that protectionism has stunted the textile industry and a growing reluctance to subsidize inefficient production. Despite both the awareness of a need for a new industrial strategy and the changed social basis which makes implementation of such a strategy possible, however, some effort to spare the French market continues to be made as the economic crisis worsens. With one and a half million unemployed anticipated in 1981, voluntary restraints were imposed on textile-exporting countries from among the EEC's associated African, Caribbean, and Pacific States in 1980, and succumbing to pressure from traditional agricultural interests, President Giscard d'Estaing dashed Spain's hopes for an early entry into the European Common Market. In contrast to Germany or Holland, France thus remained a protected market. Protectionism, however, coupled with the rapid modernization which now began, did not save many jobs and dissatisfaction with the new industrial strategy was clearly evident in the results of the French presidential election of 1981. While François Mitterrand's victory cannot change the technological forces and competitive pressures which have led to a need to modernize the French textile industry, a number of proposals made by Mitterrand during the campaign, if adopted, would significantly alter the process of industrial policy making and open it to the search for alternative industrial policies.

NOTES

1. The International Division of Labor refers to the global distribution of specialization and exchange which first emerged with the expansion of European mercantile capitalism in the sixteenth century. A discussion of contemporary changes in the international division of labor can be found in Fröbel et al. (1978) and Balassa (1979). For our purposes, the characteristics of most relevance are the increased export of manufactures from less developed countries and the growing internationalization of production.

2. Industrial adjustment is the process whereby firms, in an industry under pressure from competitive imports or substitutable domestic production, initiate changes in response to these pressures. Industrial adjustment may be induced by state policies. In English, industrial adjustment and restructuring are usually synonomous. In the French lexicon, however, restructuring implies only a process of industrial concentration irrespective of any rationalization, specialization, or other change within the new structure.

3. As many observers have pointed out, however, there is little record of enforcement even against "bad" cartels (Sheahan, 1963: 45).

4. The traditional sector, however, can become a destabilizing force, Berger notes, to the extent that it turns against the state as did the CID-UNATI movement led by Gérard Nicoud in the 1970s. "Nicoud, like Poujade before him, laid the troubles of small independent property at the doorstep of the technocrats and big-business interests in government and declared that the only effective resistance was a frontal attack on the state" (Berger and Piore, 1980: 113). This led to numerous concessions to small capital some of which sacrificed the immediate interests of big capital. That these groups attack the state rather than the left, moreover, has led some elements of the French Socialist Party (PS) to see these forces as progressive and conceive of an alliance between the progressive elements of this *petit bourgeoisie* and the working class.

5. During 1936, one million French industrial workers staged a sit-down strike to demand higher wages, the right to bargain collectively, job security, and a shorter work week. At first refusing to negotiate, a delegation from the Confédération Générale de la Production Française, composed of representatives of the large Paris-based corporations in steel, metals, railroads, chemicals, and electricity finally met the Confédération Générale du Travail at the Matignon Palace under the auspices of Premier Leon Blum. The concessions granted to the CGT in the Matignon Agreements were deemed unacceptable to many firms which dominated traditional industries. The result was that one "of the best organized of the industrial federations, that of the textile industry, left the peak association immediately after Matignon in wrath over the agreements." (Ehrmann, 1957: 15). The Confédération Générale des Petites et Moyennes industries (CGPME) was founded by Léon Gingembre not long after.

6. In the 1950s, less than 14 percent of the cotton firms were integrated spinning and weaving operations and the percentage of integrated firms never rose higher than 17 percent throughout the 1970s (SGICF, 1977: 26, 27).

7. In February 1951, the textile industrialists and the major trade union federations signed one of the first collective agreements of the postwar period. In June 1953, a subsequent *déclaration commune, dite accord* was signed with the CFTC alone and the CFTC was subsequently criticized by the CGT for *collaboration de classe*. By the 1960s, the CFTC, then in the process of breaking with its Catholic roots and reforming as the socialist CFDT, came to agree

with the CGT that the joint technical commissions were a sham and the agreement was denounced. At the time, however, it rendered those core male workers who were unionized less militant than they might otherwise have been (Reynaud, 1966: 178-180). It is important to remember, however, that in France "la négociation collective . . . est faible et discontinue" and "la discussion sur les salaires réduite à la détermination des minima par branche profession-nelle" (Bunel and Saglio, 1976: 383). Moreover, unions have no legal recognition in the workplace as they do under the Wagner Act in the United States. Hence, only where the majority of members in any enterprise are unionized and the union actively pressed for a collective agreement at the level of the enterprise are workers able to affect their actual conditions of work and their salaries. Unionization of a majority of the workers, however, is uncommon in enterprises with less than 100 workers. The result, therefore, is that "il n'y a eu accord que dans 18 percent des établissements de moins de 100 salariés et que ce pourcentage s'éléve à 61% pour les établissements de plus de 1000 salariés" (Bunel and Saglio, 1976: 391). Given the low level of unionization in the small firms which predominate in the textile industry, collective agreements, such as the one referred to here, are likely to have had only a limited impact on the conditions of work or on salaries.

8. Boussac, the largest French textile firm in the early 1950s with over 25,000 employees, maintained through its subsidiary the Comptoir de l'Industrie Cotonnière, its own network of commercial outlets, and had extended its activities directly to the production of cotton in Africa (Campbell, 1975: 40-51).

9. From 1959 to 1971, employment declined in the textile industry and in the leather industry by an average of 2 percent per year, in clothing by -1.7 percent, and in wood by -0.5 percent. Over the same period, employment rose in nonelectrical machinery by 2.2 percent, in electrical machinery by 3.7 percent, in automobiles by 3.1 percent, and in chemicals by 2.3 percent (OECD, 1974: 20).

10. For the United Kingdom, an index of employment in spinning and weaving of cotton and man-made fibers shows a decline from 100 (1963) to 52 in 1974 (CEC, 1975: 21). The Netherlands shows a drop of 42 percent in textile and clothing industry in the period 1961-1974 alone (CIRFS, n.d.: 42).

11. In France from 1924 to 1945, recruitment of foreign labor was in the hands of a private company. In 1945, the state took over this function and created the Office Nationale de l'Immigration (Carchedi, 1979: 59).

12. The two major textile regions in France are the "North" centered on Lille, which accounted for 32 percent of textile production in 1979, and the "East" comprising the Vosges and Alsacian mills, which produced 24 percent of French textiles in that year (UIT, 1980).

13. Inflation began in 1973 just prior to the first OPEC oil price rise. Unemployment and reduced levels of production became evident in 1974 and were generalized to most of the advanced, industrial capitalist countries in the 1974-1975 period. Balance of payments prob-lems are also characteristic of the crisis. For details on the crisis in France see Mandel (1978) and Mathieu (1980).

14. The CES, a corporatist body of 200 representatives, was established by the state in 1958 to advise on social and economic policy. Its advice is contained in a series of reports undertaken at the initiative of the chairmen of the various CES working groups. No labor delegate has ever chaired the key economic or commercial committees within the CES. These key positions have gone to the representatives of the business sector, as in the case of M. Précheur. The distribution of representatives, moreover, has reinforced the position of the state within the postwar CES compared to its weight in the CES under the Fourth Republic (Merloz: 1976).

15. In the course of debate over the Précheur Report, labor delegates proposed that control over these funds be placed in the hands of *all* interested parties, stipulating in particular, *"pouvoirs publics, organisations patronales, organisations de salariés."* Although all dele-gates from the business sector voted against this motion, an amendment to this effect was

successfully inserted into the report. Union representatives, however, were less successful in altering the thrust of this document and thus the Précheur Report with its advocacy of concentration was adopted unmodified by the CES over the negative votes of the 14 CFDT and 12 CGT delegates (Précheur, 1965: 781). As labor was marginalized from the planning process and from the locus of political decision making dominated by a center-right Gaullist coalition, it is not surprising that union representatives were excluded when CIRIT was established. The discussion of CIRIT is informed by Friedberg 1976 and by interviews with an industry member of CIRIT and the Ministry of Industry representative to CIRIT in Paris: January 1979 and the Secretary General of CIRIT in June 1980.

16. The representative of the Ministry of Industry also retains the power of veto over CIRIT decisions although M. Prévôt argues that it is largely symbolic because it has never been used. Given the kind of concertation between the state and larger firms, it would appear to be unnecessary to exercise this veto in any case (interview, Ministry of Industry Representative to CIRIT, January 1979, and Secretary General of CIRIT, June 1980).

17. The CDI-UNATI movement led by Gérard Nicoud in the early 1970s was clearly a reaction to the intimate links between big capital and the State but their successes were largely confined to the commercial sector whose inefficiency could be tolerated more easily in the changing French economy.

18. CGT and CFDT delegates also consistently voted against reports and opinions which favored further concentration.

19. Small firms were particularly concentrated in the weaving branch of the textile industry where throughout the 1970s they comprised nearly 70 percent of the firms in this branch. This compares with the spinning branch where small firms constituted only 30 percent of all firms. The largest firms in the textile industry were also located in the weaving branch, although they were integrated vertically by the 1970s. This points again to the dualistic structure of the textile industry.

20. DMC for example, had moved from a position where 100 percent of its turnover in the early 1960s came from spinning to a situation in 1977 where only 23 percent of turnover came from spinning (DMC, various years).

21. Although for some of the medium-sized companies the reverse was true. Filauchy, for example, diversified away from cotton spinning (100 percent in 1972) to spinning polyester and cotton (16 percent of turnover in 1977) and specialized in threads for velours. Motte Bossut gave up cotton spinning altogether and specialized its weaving activities in velours (interviews, November 1978).

22. As comparative advantage in labor-intensive or technologically less sophisticated products shifted to the newly industrializing countries of the Third World, their exports to the advanced, industrial countries encountered high tariffs and low quotas. The MFA signed by GATT members sought to liberalize trade in textiles between "Third" World exporters and "first" world importers by providing for a gradual increase in import quotas.

23. Such a conclusion is warranted by the discussion of textiles in the *Berthelot Report* (Commissariat Général du Plan, 1978) and by evidence of this sentiment in interviews with M. Sciallon (Finance), M. Pagé (Industry), M. Boublil (Plan), and M. Hennekine (Foreign Affairs) in January 1979, and M. Crinetz (Economy) and Mme. Capdeboscq (Plan) in June 1980.

24. LIP was a watch manufacturing firm and the case involved an attempt by the workers to continue to manufacture LIP watches on their own despite the bankruptcy of the firm.

25. The following discussion of CIASI is based on interviews with Guitton (CIASI), February 1979; Klein (FDES), February 1979; Pagé (Industry) January 1979; and M. Jaclot (CIASI) in June 1980; and on a number of mimeos dealing with CIASI distributed by the Ministry of Economy and Finance.

26. Boussac, a family-owned and managed textile firm was the largest firm in the textile industry during the 1950s. The Boussac family had diversified its holdings to include a newspa-

per, racetrack, and various textile-related activities. In 1965 Boussac began to borrow. In 1975, as Boussac's debts and difficulties mounted, the Crédit Lyonnais and BNP, two nationalized banks, were encouraged to loan 80 million francs to the company while CIASI loaned it an additional 35 million. In 1976, the firm lost 60 million francs and in 1977, it lost 100 million francs, and owed approximately 400 million to the nationalized Banks. The firm was placed under *"reglement judiciare"* in May 1978 and negotiations with Agache-Willot and Dollfus-Mieg led eventually to the takeover of Boussac by Agache-Willot.

27. Italian wages were lower and a putting-out system in the clothing industry reduced costs considerably. German textile and clothing manufactures, on the other hand, rationalized production by outward processing, that is, delocalizing labor-intensive segments of the production process to Eastern Europe and Asia while they modernized those segments of the production process which remained in Germany. This produced tremendous cost savings and made German clothing competitive in France, thus cutting into the forward linking market for the French textile industry.

28. The interest in assuring cheaper supplies of raw materials is evident in the attention paid to a new minerals facility in the Lomé II convention concluded in 1979.

REFERENCES

Assemblée Nationale (1977) Rapport fait au nom de la Commission d'enquete parlementaire chargée d'examiner les conditions dans lesquelles ont lieu les importations sauvages de diverses categories de marchandises. M. Limouzy, rapporteur. Paris: Assemble Nationale 3230, 1ere Session Orgininaire.

BELASSA, B. (1979) The Changing International Division of Labor in Manufactured Goods. World Bank Staff Working Paper 329. Washington, DC: World Bank.

BERGER, S. and M. PIORE (1980) Dualism and Discontinuity in Industrial Societies. Cambridge: Cambridge University Press.

BERRIER, R. J. (1978) "Segmentation and differential marginality in the textile labor market." Unpublished manuscript, Department of Political Science, University of Pennsylvania.

BUNEL, J. and J. SAGLIO (1976) "La faiblesse de la négociation collective et le pouvoir patronal." Sociologie du Travail 19, 4: 383-401.

CAMPBELL, B. (1975) "Neocolonialism, economic dependence and political change: a case study of cotton and textiles production in the Ivory Coast, 1960 to 1970." Review of African Political Economy, No. 2: 36-53.

CAPRONNIER, F. (1959) La Crise de l'Industrie Cotonnière Française. (Paris: Ed. Genin).

CARCHEDI, G. (1979) "Authority and foreign labour: some notes on a late capitalist form of capital accumulation and state intervention." Studies in Political Economy: A Socialist Review, No. 2: 37-74.

CHARDONNET, J. (1958) L'Economie Française. Paris: Dalloz.

CIRFS (n.d.) L'Emploi Dans l'Industrie Textile et l'Industrie de l'Habillement dans le CFE (six) et le Royaume-Uni. Paris: Comité pour la Rayonne et les Fibres Synthetiques.

COHEN, S. (1969) Modern Capitalist Planning: The French model. Cambridge, MA: Harvard University Press.

Commissariat Général du Plan [CGP] (1978) Rapport du Groupe chargé d'etudier l'évolution des économies du tiers monde et l'appareil productif français (Berthelot Report). Paris: Commissariat du Plan.

Commission of the European Communities[CEC] (1975) A Study of the Evolution of Concentration in the United Kingdom Textile Industry. Brussells: European Economic Community.

Confédération Général du Travail [CGT] (1979) Structures et Evolutions de l'Emploi et du Chômage Depuis, 1968. Paris: CGT, Centre Confédéral d'Etudes Economiques.

_____ (1978) L'Industrie Française depuis 1985 un Bilan Accusateur. Paris: CGT.

Conseil Economique et Social [CES] (1979) Journal Officiel, No. 11: 536-543.

_____ (1978a) L'Avenir des industries françaises et la nouvelle répartition internationale de la production industrielle. M. Peillon, rapporteur. Paris: CES.

_____ (1978b) Liste des Conseillers Economiques et Sociaux et des Membres de Section. Paris: CES.

_____ (1967) Problèmes posés par la concentration des entreprises. M. Francois Lagandre, rapporteur. Paris: CES.

DAFSA (1978) Les Industries de Filature. Paris: DAFSA, Collection Analyses de Secteurs.

_____ (1974) L'Industrie Cottonnière en Europe. Paris: DAFSA, Collection Analyses de Secteurs.

DeBRANDT, J. (1978) Long Term Perspectives of the World Textile Industries. PARIS: IREP.

DELANOE, G. (1975) Etude sur l'évolution de la concentration dans l'industrie du textile en France. Brussels: Commission de Communautés Européenes.

La Documentation Française (1979) Huitieme Plan: Options. Paris: La Documentation Française.

Dollfus-Mieg and Cie. [DMC] (various years) Annual Report.

EHRMANN, H. W. (1957) Organized Business in France. Princeton, NJ: Princeton University Press.

France. (1975, 1976, 1977) Project de Loi Portant Réglement Définitif du Budget de 1975, Annexe, . . . du Budget de 1976, . . . du Budget de 1977, . . . Rapport au Parlement sur les fonds publics attribués à Titre d'aides aux entreprises industrielles. Paris: Imprimerie Nationale.

FRIEDBERG, E. (1976) L'Etat et l'Industrie en France, Rapport d'enquête. Paris: CNRS, Centre de Sociologies des Organisations.

FRÖBEL, F., J. HEINRICHS, and O. KREYE (1978) "The world market for labour and the world market for industrial sites." Journal of Economic Issues 12, 4: 843-858.

GUIBERT, B. et al. (1975) La Mutation Industrielle de la France du Traité de Rome à la crise Pétrolière, Tome I and II. Les Collections de l'INSEE, No. 31-32E.

HAY, F. (1976) Les Transferts des Entreprises Françaises en Afrique Noire Francophone. Paris: CNRS.

Institute de Développment Industriel [IDI] (various years) Rapport annuel d'activités.

International Labor Organization [ILO] (various years) Yearbook of Labor Statistics.

INSEE (various years) Annuaire Statistiques/Yearbook.

_____ (1978) Economie et Statistiques. Paris: INSEE.

JENNY, F. and A. P. WEBER (1976) "Profit rates and structural variables in French manufacturing industries." European Economic Review 7: 187-206.

_____ (1975) Concentration et Politique des Structures Industrielles. Paris: La Documentation Français.

JENSON, J. (1979) "The domestication of the European election: the left in France." Presented at a Workshop on the Smaller European Democracies and European-Canadian Comparison, EPG, CPSA, University of Western Ontario.

Journal Official (1971) Le VIe Plan de Développement Economique et Social (1971-1975). Rapport General: les objectifs généraux et les actions prioritaires du VIe Plan. Paris: Imprimerie Nationale.

_____ (1965) "Le Ve plan (1965-1970)" 1,1278. Paris: Imprimerie Nationale.

MANDEL, E. (1978) La Crise 1974-1978. Paris: Flammarion.

MAURUS, V. (1979) "S.O.S. canards boiteux." Le Monde (March 22, 23, 24).

MATHIEU, G. (1980) La crise, an VII." Le Monde (May 15-19).

―――― (1979) "La politique Française et le bilan de trois années de 'plan barre.'" Le Monde, pp. 1, 6-7.

Ministère de l'Industrie (1980) Enquête Annuelle d'Entreprise 1976 Industrie Textile. Paris: STISI, Publication No. 12-07.

―――― (1979) La Concentration des Entreprises Industrielles de 1972 à 1976. Paris: STISI, Publication No. 13.

Ministère de l'Industrie et Recherche (various years) Les Structures Industrielles Françaises. Paris: Textile et Bonnetaire.

MERLOZ, G. et al. (1976) "Les CES en France sous la 5e Republique." Droit Social, No. 11: 413-456.

MORIN, F. (1974) La structure financière du capitalism français. Paris: Calmann-Levy.

MORVAN, Y. (1972) La Concentration de l'Industrie en France. Paris: Arman Colin.

MYTELKA, L. (1981) "Direct foreign investment and technological choice in the ivorian textile and wood industry," pp. 61-80 in Dieter Ernst (ed.) Vierteljahresberichte der Entwicklungs-Landerforschung, No. 83. Bonn: Friedrick-Ebert-Stiftung, March.

―――― and M. DOLAN (1980) "The political economy of EC-ACP rleations in a changing international division of labour," pp. 237-260 in D. Seres and C. Vaitos (eds.) European Integration and Unequal Development. London: Macmillan.

Organization for Economic Cooperation and Development [OECD/OCDE] (1978) L'Industrie Textile dans le Pays de l'OCDE Textile Industry in OECD Countries. Paris: OECD.

―――― (1970-1976) Trade by Commodities. Market Summaries, Series C.

―――― (1975) La Politique Industrielle de la France. Paris: OECD.

―――― (1974) La Politique Industrielle de la France. Paris: OECD.

PRECHEUR, J. (1965) "La situation de l'industrie textile française." Paris: Council Economique et Social.

REYNAUD, J.-D. (1966) Les Syndicats en France. Paris: Armand Colin.

SEIBEL, C. (1975) "Planning in France," pp. 153-184 in M. Bornstein (ed.) Economic Planning, East and West. Cambridge, MA: Ballinger.

Sénat (1978) Première Session Ordinaire de 1978, Rapport General sur le Project de Loi de Finances pour 1979, No. 74, Tome III, Annexe No. 15, Industrie.

SGICF (1977) L'Industrie Cotonnière francaise en 1976. (Paris: SGICF).

―――― (1969) "L'Industrie cotonnière française de 1964 a 1968." Report presented to the Assemblée Général, April 16, by M. Guy de Frondeville.

―――― (1956) La Reconversion dans l'industrie cottonnière française. Paris: Société Général de l'Industrie cotonnière française.

SHEAHAN, J. (1963) Promotion and Control of Industry in Postwar France. Cambridge, MA: Harvard University Press.

SHONFIELD, A. (1965) Modern Capitalism. London: Oxford University Press.

SULEIMAN, E. (1975) "Industrial Policy Formulation in France, pp. 23-42 in S. Warnecke and E. Suleiman (eds.) Industrial Policies in Western Europe. New York: Praeger.

Syndicat Patronal Textile de Roubaix-Tourcoing (1978a) "Recapitulation générale Roubaix-Tourcoing-Valée de la lys, effectif du personel au 31 decembre 1977." (mimeo)

―――― (1978b) "Résultats de l'ênquete sur l'emploi dans les entreprises adhérentes au 31-12-1977." (mimeo)

Union des Industries Textile [UIT] (various years) Statistique Générale de l'Industrie Textile Française. Paris: UIT.

United Nations (1963) The Growth of World Industry, 1938-1969. New York: United Nations.

ZYSMAN, J. (1977) "The French state in the international economy." International Organization 31, 4: 839-877.

PART IV

Changes in the Global Political Economy and Third World States

Just as change in the global political economy will have serious implications for states that are already industrialized, it will also have serious implications for those that are in the process of industrialization. Indeed, the less developed countries have been the most vocal group in expressing their desire to change the character of their economies and the nature of their economic relationships with other countries, especially the western industrialized states. The now generally accepted goal of improving the standard of living of the inhabitants of LDCs is one of the principal forces for change in the contemporary global political economy.

The means of attaining this goal, however, are hardly agreed upon, and there is even disagreement about the precise meaning to be attached to the general goal. The chapters in this part of the book explore some of these issues. They deal primarily with international economic issues involving LDCs rather than with issues concerning their domestic economies.

In the years since the end of World War II there have already been major and significant changes in the economies of less developed countries. Production has increased on an absolute and a per capita basis, and the relative share of industry and manufacturing in total production has grown substantially. The processes of change that have already been set in motion are certain to continue. There is a dynamic force at work with its own inertia that is virtually irreversible. What is at stake is the pace of change, and external factors will play major roles in determining how easily and rapidly further change will occur.

From the perspective of change in the global political economy, the situation of the less developed countries is considerably different from that of the western industrialized countries. Given the overwhelming role of the western industrialized countries in the global political economy, the state of their domestic economies will have a profound impact on the rest of the world. The west is the primary source of concessional and nonconcessional capital transfers to the less developed countries; how much western states will provide will depend to a considerable extent on the condition of their economies. The West is also the primary market for the exports of LDCs; how much western states will be willing to import will depend on how healthy their economies are and what happens to domestic industries that produce goods that are competitive with the imports. In contrast, change in the economies of the less developed countries will be powerfully shaped by the amount of external capital that they can obtain, the amount that they can earn from their exports, and the amount that they will have to pay for their imports.

Many of the broad issues in the relationship between the less developed countries and the western industrialized countries, such as the general level and character of capital transfers and market opportunities for LDC exports, are explored elsewhere in this book. The two chapters in this part focus on narrower problems that affect specific—though large—groups of LDCs.

Chapter 7, by Kuniko Y. Inoguchi, deals with the short-term external responses of oil-importing developing countries to the 1973 decision of the members of the Organization of Petroleum Exporting Countries (OPEC) to increase sharply the price of their petroleum exports. This action sharply increased the revenues that they earned from their exports and enormously expanded their opportunities for improving the standard of living of their inhabitants. It was a dramatic and significant action that radically changed the position in the global political economy of a group of hitherto relatively poor countries. The price of OPEC's petroleum exports was increased, however, for all importing countries, not just for the western industrialized countries. After 1973, oil-importing LDCs also had to pay sharply increased prices for the petroleum that they imported, and this had serious consequences for their economies and also posed a dilemma for them. OPEC was the most powerful leverage that the LDCs had in their efforts to induce the western industrialized countries to change the international economic order, yet the use of this leverage had serious negative effects on some LDCs. Professor Inoguchi develops five possible responses that LDCs might adopt when faced with this dilemma and then, using regression analysis, develops mathematical models that predict the choices they would make. The models that she develops have remarkable explanatory power, far greater than is normally the case in the social sciences. Although her analysis deals with a limited time period, her conclusions have a more general validity and the techniques of analysis that she utilizes have much broader applicability. LDC responses to other external events could be analyzed in a similar manner.

In chapter 8, Abdul Aziz Jalloh probes the meaning of development and crafts a multifaceted definition that would be widely accepted by Third World leaders. The definition is helpful because it lays bare the roots of the pressure for a new international economic order. Accelerating the growth in the economies of LDCs is one issue, but as Professor Jalloh makes clear, there are several other issues that LDC leaders feel are at least as important. Basing his analysis on the definition of development that he has set forth, Professor Jalloh then analyzes the special constraints on sub-Saharan African states (other than South Africa) achieving this goal. He argues that because of these constraints these states deserve special, favorable treatment by the world community.

Since harmony between oil-exporting and oil-importing LDCs is crucial to maintaining the unity of the Group of 77 and since African states comprise the most numerous group of LDCs, the issues posed in these two chapters are terribly important for determining how much pressure will continue to be exerted on behalf of the creation of a new international economic order and thus on the interaction between international institutions where the Group of 77 voice their demands and change in the global political economy. This interaction will be explored in the final part of the book.

CHAPTER 7

THIRD WORLD RESPONSES TO OPEC
The External Dimension

K U N I K O   Y .   I N O G U C H I

The OPEC offensive that began in October 1973 posed a major threat to the dominance of the North in the international economic order, which had long been unchallenged by the Third World. For the first time, industrialized nations saw that their prosperity rested upon the deep-rooted dependence on those outside their "club," and at the same time, Third World countries came to realize that raw materials could be transformed from a reservoir of industrial supply to a forceful power base for their holders. Thus the impact of the OPEC strike is manifold. While the economic impact of the drastic price increase of petroleum hit all nations, rich and poor alike, according to the degree of their oil imports, the oil crisis had differential psychopolitical effects. To put it in a crude dichotomy, for those at the core of the international system, it meant the shrinking of their bargaining power and the decline of their self-confidence. For those at the periphery, it stood as a source of aspiration and a spectacular example of endeavor in search of an alternative North-South economic order.

The oil crisis added about 10 billion dollars to non-oil-exporting LDCs' 1974 oil import bill of 7 billion. The percentage share of their imports from

AUTHOR'S NOTE: An earlier version of this chapter was presented at the Spring Convention of the Japan Association of International Relations, Tokyo, May 19-20, 1979 and at the Eleventh World Congress of the International Political Science Association, Moscow, August 12-18, 1979. I have benefited greatly from helpful comments made by Takashi Inoguchi (University of Tokyo), Harold K. Jacobson (University of Michigan), Gregory Kasza (Yale University), Bruce M. Russett (Yale University), Bradford H. Westerfield (Yale University), Mitsuru Yamamoto (Hosei University), Yoshinobu Yamamoto (Saitama University), and anonymous referees. I would like to thank all of them.

the OPEC countries doubled within a year from 9.4 percent in 1973 to 17 percent in 1974, severely cutting their nonoil imports from the rest of the world. The oil-induced decline in aggregate demand and the aggravated inflationary processes in industrialized countries also had pernicious consequences for their economies.

Yet despite such economically crippling effects of the oil crisis, most Third World countries applauded OPEC for launching the single most forceful manifestation of the united Third World power against the North. "We are gratified by the victories chalked by OPEC. . . . We believe this to be a precious achievement, an example, and a source of hope. Even if it leads to a temporal upset of our economies, we are still happy," avowed a representative from a little non-oil-exporting LDC at the United Nations General Assembly a few months after the oil crisis. Numerous other Third World countries, though they may have been the most severely hit "victims" of the higher oil prices, publicly expressed similar views, and joined in praising OPEC as their role model and its success as a symbol of their aspirations. Even if we take into account their expectation for OPEC aid, their support for OPEC was striking. This suggests that Third World countries were sensitive to much more than just the economic repercussions of the oil crisis.

Thus the impacts of the OPEC action can not be grasped comprehensively by merely analyzing disturbances in macroeconomic statistics, however essential a first step this may be. Economists have examined adjustment policies taken by oil-importing LDCs, such as the development of indigenous energy sources, energy conservation, external borrowing, demand restraint, import restriction, and export expansion (OECD, 1975; Tims, 1975; Dunn, 1974), though this topic has not received nearly the attention given to adjustment policies in the industrialized countries. If these strategies were crucial to the determination of development potential and domestic policy priorities, no less vital in many cases were measures aimed at reshaping North-South relations, such as the moves toward a New International Economic Order (NIEO), which came in response to the psychopolitical stimuli of the OPEC strike. Both were integral to OPEC-induced behavior in the Third World.

This chapter analyzes the major patterns of behavior taken by non-oil-exporting developing countries in response to economic and psychopolitical impacts of the OPEC action. By "response behavior" we mean both the actions they have taken in order to overcome the economic consequences of higher oil prices, and/or the ways in which they have joined the OPEC's initiative to seek an alternative international economic order. First, a comprehensive framework for identifying their response patterns is presented. Then, narrowing down our scope to selected forms of responses that are basically external-oriented, we build explanatory models to specify the common factors behind their response behavior.

Inward-Oriented and Outward-Oriented Responses

When nations face an external challenge such as the OPEC strike, there are basically two complementary ways in which they can respond. First, they can take what we call inward-oriented responses which are confined to the domestic arena and focus on new ways of exploiting, mobilizing, and allocating domestic resources. Second, they can resort to outward-oriented responses involving a reallocation of external resources and/or mobilization of other actors in the international system. For example, among common adjustment measures cited above, the development of indigenous energy sources, energy conservation, demand restraint, and import restriction fall into the category of inward-oriented responses, while external borrowing is an outward-oriented response. Export expansion might belong to either category. If it were achieved primarily by breaking into foreign markets that were traditionally exclusive, it can be considered as a kind of outward-oriented response. On the other hand, if it were achieved by increasing international competitiveness, it would constitute inward-oriented response behavior, since the major thrust of the policy would be aimed at improvements in the domestic export sector. Most export-expansion strategies launched after the oil crisis seem to have taken the latter path. (Note that the terms "inward-oriented" and "outward-oriented" are not used here as they are in conventional economics to indicate whether production is aimed at the domestic or international market.)

It should be stressed that this analysis will focus on relatively short-term response patterns (1974-1976) for two reasons. First, at the time when the research was carried out (1977-1979), most data beyond 1976 were unavailable for the majority of the developing countries. Second, it becomes increasingly difficult to isolate the effects of the oil crisis as time passes. It is very likely that actions initially triggered by the oil crisis later developed their own dynamics and can no longer simply be attributed to the original impetus. Thus our focus is on the initial response behavior of non-oil-exporting LDCs (Figure 7.1).

As a student of international relations, my interest lies mainly in the outward-oriented responses that seem to have had a significant influence upon the evolution of post-OPEC North-South relations. For this reason, and because a thorough examination of both types of response patterns is beyond the scope of a single chapter, the present work is limited to an analysis of the outward-oriented responses of non-oil-exporting LDCs.

However, before the outward-oriented responses are taken up for an elaborate examination, here is a brief note on various forms of inward-oriented responses to place our argument in a broader context.

There are two major subdivisions of inward-oriented responses: first, the vulnerability-minimizing option, whereby nations strive to reduce their vul-

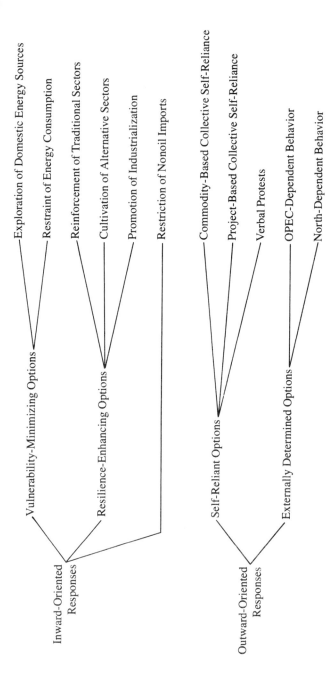

FIGURE 7.1 A Typological Framework of Response Patterns

NOTE: This set of major response patterns is derived from interviews at the UNCTAD secretariat (Geneva), reports and statistics put out by international organizations, *Quarterly Economic Reviews* (Economist Intelligence Unit) of about forty non-oil-exporting LDCs, and weekly magazines from several countries.

nerability to the international petroleum market by decreasing their dependence on foreign oil; and second, the resilience-enhancing option, whereby nations try to increase the resilience of their domestic economy to external shocks and uncertainties by fortifying their national economic strength in general.

As for the former, there are basically two ways by which oil-importing countries can reduce their vulnerability to the external energy supply: first, by exploiting domestic energy resources; and second, by restraining their energy consumption. Before the oil crisis, low-cost discoveries in the Middle East discouraged many oil-importing LDCs from developing their domestic energy resources to the fullest. However, with the drastic rise of oil prices, many of them launched vigorous oil exploration projects aiming at self-sufficiency in energy supply (IBRD, 1978: 1). Those with little or no prospects for domestic production of petroleum turned to alternative sources of energy. Among others, Costa-Rica, Nicaragua, Kenya, the Ivory Coast, and Uruguay started new, large-scale hydroelectric projects and/or expanded the capacity of existing facilities. Turkey and Colombia increased their coal production, and others such as Ghana, South Korea, India, and Chile sought nuclear energy (EIU-QER: OECD, 1975). Virtually all developing countries acted to reduce their dependence on foreign oil by promoting energy conservation measures in industries and the household.

As for the resilience-enhancing option, among the most often observed strategies were: (1) reinforcement of traditional sectors, whereby nations strengthen the export sector in which they traditionally enjoyed a comparative advantage; (2) cultivation of alternative sectors, which is to explore new sources of export revenue and/or to strive for self-sufficiency in the traditionally import-dependent sectors; and (3) the promotion of industrialization.

Various policy alternatives ranging from fiscal and monetary measures to tax incentives, production subsidies, market controls, and project-based programs were employed to achieve the reinforcement and restructuring of the domestic economy. The Gambian government's firm commitment to subsidize groundnut production, the enlargement of the "Green Belt Operation" to encourage food production in Cameroon, Burma's increased investment in its forestry sector, and Kenya's fiscal and monetary measures to stimulate investment in agriculture are prime examples of reinforcement of traditional sectors. Efforts such as these combined with the high prices prevailing in some commodity markets resulted in an increase of export earnings for a number of oil-importing LDCs. Examples of cultivating alternative sectors are Ghana switching from "Operation Feed Yourself" to "Operation Feed Your Industry" to expand and diversify agricultural production, Malaysia launching its "Green Book" scheme to attain self-sufficiency in most food products, and many nations heavily increasing their investment in the tourism sector. To give one example of the promotion of industrialization, Brazil established a full range of incentives for the export of manufactures by a decree in late 1973. Mexico, South Korea, Malaysia, and Taiwan also followed fiscal, monetary, price, and exchange policies to increase the international competitiveness of their manufactures (OECD, 1975: 43). Although resilience-enhancing measures were not designed as an instant panacea for oil-induced economic stagnation, their aim was in the long-run to increase export earnings and/or substitute domestic production for imports to correct a sharply deteriorated trade balance. The oil crisis alerted the developing countries, as no other events could have, to the need for increasing their economic resilience against the vicissitudes of the international economy.

Along with such active inward-oriented responses to adjust to the era of higher oil prices, many oil-importing LDCs were quick to adopt measures restricting nonpetroleum imports as a temporary remedy for their increased oil import bill. Brazil raised import duties on a vast number of "nonessential" goods, Kenya banned imports of all luxury consumer goods, Zambia revoked licences for nonessential imports, and Jamaica, under the slogan of "survival of the nation," also imposed an import ban on a number of luxury goods, to give but a few examples.

While the inward-oriented responses involve a reallocation of domestic resources, outward-oriented responses are based on the Third World's search for a redistribution of wealth between the North and South and within the South. Thus outward-oriented responses reflect not only the need for greater income in the South to offset the economic impacts of the oil crisis, but also the Third World's responsiveness to and sympathy for OPEC's defiance of northern domination of international economic affairs. This clearly distinguishes outward-oriented responses from inward-oriented responses.

Based on empirical evidence, we have identified the following major types of outward-oriented response patterns: (1) commodity-based collective self-reliance; (2) project-based collective self-reliance; (3) Verbal protests; (4) OPEC-dependent behavior; and (5) North-dependent behavior.

COMMODITY-BASED COLLECTIVE SELF-RELIANCE

Commodity-based collective self-reliance is an attempt to emulate OPEC formula for reallocating wealth between the North and the South. It aims at utilizing the commodity power so unduly underrated in western development models, by means of breaking the long-standing taboo against the Third World's unilateral price-and-supply control of primary commodities. By resorting to OPEC-like behavior, they were responding simultaneously to the urgent imperative of coping with the OPEC-induced economic crisis and the morale boost ignited by OPEC's success in challenging northern economic hegemony.

As for the economic motives, the launching of miniature OPEC-like associations to improve terms of trade was a quick solution to the problem of increasing export earnings to finance a skyrocketing oil import bill (Bergsten, 1977: 214, 1975: 292; Morton and Tulloch, 1977: 105). Admittedly, these associations were not expected to raise income on the scale of OPEC, but for some nations, most notably for Jamaica and Morocco, the new strategy served as a major instrument for correcting the deterioration in their balance of payments.

At the same time, emulative behavior was the most straightforward response to OPEC's call for Third World solidarity to seek a "fairer" distribution of global wealth by means of attacking northern economic hegemony. For many commodity exporters, OPEC became at least "a referent point if not indeed a target" (Connelly and Perlman, 1975: 68) in reassessing and mobilizing their commodity power. They saw in OPEC a new model that might help them arrest the primary commodity syndrome that had plagued their trade and development for decades.

Whether non-oil-exporting primary commodity producers would have the skill to follow the OPEC offensive was a popular topic of debate in the early post-oil-crisis years (Krasner, 1974; Bergsten, 1975; Mikesell, 1974; Mikdashi, 1974). The answer to the question: "Is OPEC unique?" is both yes and no. The OPEC strike was indeed unique in terms of its financial and social impact upon industrialized countries, but as a strategy to increase national revenues of southern commodity producers it was not unique. As the forerunner in utilizing a commodity to achieve a breakthrough in the development process, OPEC saw not a few emulators.

The most often cited case is the International Bauxite Association (IBA), established five months after the oil crisis under the leadership of Jamaica (Bergsten, 1976; Pindyck, 1977; Mikdashi, 1976; Edwards, 1975). For a long time the bauxite market had remained a "closed" market dominated by vertically integrated large multinational firms that controlled all stages of production from bauxite mining to aluminum product manufacturing (Girvan, 1976; UNCTAD, 1978a). The horizontally organized network of the multinationals deterred producing governments from taking radical action against firms in fear of revenge in the form of their transferring operations abroad. Political/military intervention by the United States was also considered probable by Jamaicans if they made a move on bauxite (Bergsten, 1976: 13). However, seeing that northern consuming states did not retaliate against even OPEC's drastic challenge, and being inspired by OPEC's striking success in activating commodity power, seven major bauxite exporting countries met in Conakry, Guinea in March 1974 to establish an intergovernmental bauxite association. The international economic climate was favorable for producers of industrial raw materials, and the political timing was ideal on the eve of the monumental declaration of a program for a New International Economic Order.

With successful expansion of its membership, IBA producers accounted for practically all bauxite exports from market economies by 1975, and the total value of IBA bauxite shipments rose from .5 billion dollars in early 1974 to 1.2 billion dollars in 1976 (Pindyck, 1977: 344). If the success of bauxite producers was far from matching that of OPEC in terms of its economic impacts on northern industrialized countries, its significance as a success in effectuating commodity power to sharply increase the national revenue of non-fuel-producing nations should not be undervalued.

Acting less formally than the bauxite countries, phosphate producers also resorted to unilateral market interventions to increase their national revenue. Although no formal association was set up until 1977, Third World phosphate producers acted with a tacit agreement to support Morocco's dramatic price increase immediately following the OPEC strike. Morocco's lead was followed by a concerted price increase administered by Tunisia, Senegal, Algeria, and several other small producers. As an example of a small country taking unprecedented drastic action in its export sector, the Togolese government declared a full takeover of the country's major phosphate rock mining (U.S.) firm.

In the iron market, the Association of Iron Ore Exporting Countries (AIOEC) was set up in October 1975 by ten exporting nations with the aim of ensuring orderly growth in iron ore exports and favorable returns to the producers. Yet the effectiveness of the AIOEC differs markedly from the bauxite and phosphate cases since it is endowed with no price-fixing power. The Association of Tungsten Producing Countries was established in 1975. The International Association of Mercury Producers came into existence in 1974, but has not functioned successfully.

Attempts at OPEC-like market interventions were initiated among some agricultural producers as well. For various reasons, however, exporters of agricultural products were generally less successful than mineral/metal producers, as seen in the examples of the UPEB (Unión de Productores y Exportadores de Banano) and Café Mondial.

Some producers initiated joint policies to activate previously established associations. Faced with the deterioration of market conditions and encouraged by the success of the oil-exporting countries, CIPEC, the Intergovernmental Council of Copper Exporting Countries, which had been established in 1967 but remained dysfunctional, agreed in late 1974 to launch joint market intervention by cutting exports (Mingst, 1976).

PROJECT-BASED COLLECTIVE SELF-RELIANCE

Although the OPEC success was a success in commodity-based collective self-reliance, its spectacular performance stimulated not only the emulation of other commodity exporters, but also boosted enthusiasm for cooperative efforts among the poor in general. This is due to the fact that the OPEC strike was a concerted action among a group of less developed countries and provided an indisputable demonstration of the enormous power and potential of unity in the South. At the same time, one can hardly overlook the role of petrodollars recycled from the new center of affluence to southern have-nots as a financial booster to help convert the spirit of solidarity into tangible cooperative programs.

The major outlets for cooperative endeavors can be found in trade among developing countries and joint ventures in production and infrastructure (UNCTAD, 1976). Total South-South trade increased from 23 billion dollars in 1973 to 55 billion in 1978, while trade among non-OPEC developing countries increased from 12 billion dollars to 22 billion during the same period. However, despite the impressive numbers, given the rampant inflation during the period, in real terms the growth was not as large as expected. Since trade flows are subject to market forces and ad hoc speculations that are beyond policymakers' ready control, and since a considerable portion of trade may be predetermined by long-term agreements and contracts, it was not always possible to realize instant gains in the direction of trade from Third World solidarity.

On the other hand, joint planning and investment among developing countries mushroomed behind militant calls for the cohesion of the South. By 1975, the UNCTAD Secretariat observed:

> At present, a number of initiatives are beginning to give concrete shape to the new trend toward collective self-reliance. Significant among them are a number of bilateral ventures among developing countries, particularly in the productive sectors [UNCTAD, 1975: 439].

> The number of projects and proposals for joint ventures in many developing countries has substantially increased in recent years covering a wide variety of activities [UNCTAD, 1975: 451].

Such joint projects include those along regional integration lines such as cooperation among the Andean countries or the interlinking of the Egyptian and Sudanese economies, as well as those transcending "regional boundaries," such as Petrobras, the Brazilian state oil company, assisting Morocco's offshore oil prospecting activities.

The general impression that joint projects among developing countries increased sharply with the drive for a NIEO is backed up by a good deal of empirical evidence. In the absence of systematic data on the number of South-South joint ventures, events data were compiled by the author for all joint ventures in which one or more of our sample nations was a partner and that were reported in the *Quarterly Economic Reviews of the Economist Intelligence Unit*. The *Quarterly Economic Reviews* for the forty countries under study have been examined for the 1970-1977 period (32 *Reviews* for each country, 1280 *Reviews* in all).

The results are clear: There was a startling leap in the number of South-South joint projects after the OPEC strike. The 1974-1977 period saw a fourfold increase in joint ventures among developing countries compared to the same time span before the OPEC action in late 1973.

This phenomenon should not be understood as the Third World simply dancing to the fashionable tune of collective self-reliance, or in our terminology, responding to the psychopolitical impact of the OPEC success. The economic causes were also powerful. First, cooperation among nations with fewer differences in productivity, technology, and real wages is thought to foster a more equal partnership than commercial links between North and South, where it is feared that the North will dictate exploitative deals (Díaz-Alejandro, 1978: 115). Cooperation among developing countries is also believed to serve their real needs directly in their own socioeconomic milieu, instead of satisfying their interests only as a by-product of the primary task of meeting northern needs. Second, and more importantly, some joint ventures served as a pipeline for recycling petrodollars from the OPEC countries which were to some extent compelled to cooperate in the grand cause of collective self-reliance among southern countries. By starting joint projects with the OPEC countries themselves, or by persuading them to invest in other South-South cooperative endeavors, non-oil-exporting developing countries could keep some portion of petrodollars from being absorbed by northern banks and investment firms (Wriggins, 1978: 57). Third World joint ventures, rooted in the principle of collective self-reliance, offered a legitimate basis upon which to press for a distribution of the new wealth in the South.

VERBAL PROTESTS

Along with efforts at substantive measures as discussed above, rhetoric calling for northern concessions and urging on exploratory efforts by developing countries surged as the verbal counterpart of experiments in alternative external economic relations. Taking advantage of the politics of numbers in one nation/one vote international forums and supported by OPEC's oil weapon against the North, the South succeeded in registering its request for a NIEO and placing the reduction of the North-South gap on the top of the global agenda.

Although the concept of a NIEO emerged prior to OPEC's move in October 1973, it was OPEC's success that elevated the issue to the forefront of world politics. In September 1973, the Fourth Conference of the Non-aligned Movement took place under an Algerian leadership which actively sought to mobilize the entire nonaligned political apparatus to combat North-South economic inequality. At this meeting, the rough outlines of a NIEO were drawn, incorporating themes already articulated by the UN-CTAD Secretariat and by some Third World activists (Wriggins, 1978: 68). However, the leap from forming a Third World "lobby" and acting as a "pressure group" to winning an undeniable position as the "opposition party" in international politics took place when the OPEC countries struck the single most forceful blow against the conventional North-South economic order. As the whole world watched OPEC's success in dramatically changing the global flow of wealth, the rest of the Third World felt its plea for North-South adjustments pass from a "priority item on the agenda of the Non-Aligned Countries to a priority item on the agenda of the international community" (Sauvant, 1977: 9). Two months after the initial OPEC strike, the General Assembly of the United Nations voted to consider "new concepts and options" for the solution of the economic problems facing developing countries (Bahattacharga, 1976: 3), and in January 1974, as Chairman of the Nonaligned Coordinating Council, President Boumedienne of Algeria requested a special session of the United Nations General Assembly to consider the Third World's development problems, particularly in conjunction with raw materials, including nonfuel minerals and agricultural commodities. Despite the North's persistent attempts to contain the OPEC problem within the domain of the energy crisis, and keep it from being fused to general North-South conflicts, the nonaligned countries perceived OPEC's power as a symbol of the South's wrath against the conventional North-South order and strove to "transform the oil crisis into a means for pursuing the goals they had elaborated at Algiers prior to the oil crisis" (Wriggins, 1978: 69).

After a short but intensive period of preparation, the United Nations Sixth Special Session on Raw Materials and Development took place, drawing the world's attention to the South's development problems and adjustments in the North-South economic order. The time was ripe, with the multiple effects of the OPEC strike being felt by the entire world and other commodity producers lining up in similar fronts. The sense on the side of the North that the "threat is real" (Bergsten, 1974) kept the session from degenerating into a southern monodrama. The South's verbal counterstrike was at last on the stage of global politics.

At various subsequent conferences in and out of the United Nations, the provisions enunciated at the Sixth Special Session were further elaborated to enhance their legitimization and encourage their implementation. In short, the Sixth Special Session served as the pacesetter for the Third World's revolt in search of an alternative paradigm for the international economic order.

The tough tone was somewhat mitigated as the process shifted from apparent confrontations to more substantive North-South negotiations. The Seventh Special Session of the General Assembly, held in September 1975, is generally thought to mark the shift from confrontation to conciliation (Gwin, 1977). By UNCTAD 4 (Nairobi) in the spring of 1976, the debate focused on the detailed mechanisms to implement some provisions on a NIEO. Methods of "indexation" of prices, the assessment of proposals for an Integrated Program for Commodities, and other substantive and operational matters dominated the conference rooms. Rhetoric and cliché had completed their roles, opening up a channel for negotiations that would not have occurred at this point in time without the radical outcries triggered and supported by a "real threat."

OPEC-DEPENDENT BEHAVIOR

OPEC-dependent behavior is an outward-oriented response whereby non-oil-exporting LDCs try to alleviate the economic difficulties caused by the OPEC-triggered confusion in the international economy by securing aid from the OPEC countries and their multinational institutions. With the quintupling of their trade surpluses and the nearly fifteenfold increase of their aggregate current account surpluses, the OPEC countries suddenly emerged as a promising source of aid. Although the OPEC countries consistently repudiated requests for discriminatory pricing of oil in favor of developing countries, they were eager to offer foreign aid to win political support from the Third World and to justify their market intervention as a step toward global redistribution of wealth. Knowing that OPEC needs to play the "Robin Hood role" (Williams, 1976: 308) of taking from the rich and providing for the poor in weathering the blasts of blame from the North, the non-oil-exporting developing countries launched a strenuous campaign to attract aid from the OPEC countries. This statement by the Zambian representative at the UN General Assembly provides an example of their often repeated claims:

> There should be an agreement in principle by the oil-producing countries that they would provide substantial relief to the oil-consuming countries of the Third World to finance their oil import bill . . . the oil-producing countries should set aside a certain proportion of their oil resources on funds to promote the economic development of the Third World [United Nations, General Assembly, 1974, 2211th Plenary Meeting].

Although the degree of success of their plea depended rather heavily on the "Islam factor," as is explained later, disbursements of OPEC concessional flows to other developing countries more than trippled compared to the pre-oil crisis level. Disbursements of OPEC concessional flows to developing countries and multilateral institutions increased from 1.1 billion dollars in 1973 to 3.5 billion dollars in 1974, and to nearly 5 billion dollars in 1975 (UNCTAD, 1977: Table 1, 1978: Table 5.8A). Commitments expanded equally sharply, to more than 7 billion dollars in 1974 from 2 billion in 1973 (UNCTAD, 1977: Table 1). Although we primarily focus on concessional flows, which is still the dominant form of their financial dependence on the OPEC countries, we cannot overlook the fact that many developing countries began to rely heavily on nonconcessional flows from OPEC as well. OPEC nonconcessional flows to developing regions increased even more sharply than concessional flows, from 499 million dollars in 1973 to nearly 3.6 billion in 1974.

Besides increasing the national revenue of some developing countries, the OPEC-dependent behavior had at least two important political and psychological implications. First, the emergence of the southern donors meant that the Third World countries had finally found alternative sources of aid, which were independent from and unaffected by the traditional aid sources. Their range of aid options has broadened. The northern donors/southern recipients encapsulation is no longer their "only" choice. The fact that OPEC sources are independent of preferences of traditional donors makes their emergence more significant than the proliferation of donors within the North.

Second, the creation of a financial center within the South "has given developing countries the chance to begin putting into effect the principle of collective self-reliance enunciated in the programme of action on the Establishment of a New International Economic Order" (UNCTAD,1977: 1). Such common political causes as Third World self-reliance and the reduction of global inequality brought Third World countries together to seek an alternative North-South order. The new financial center can play the role of a "locomotive" in their endeavor to attain revolutionary goals in international relations.

NORTH-DEPENDENT BEHAVIOR

North-dependent behavior is an outward-oriented response whereby developing countries try to cope with the financial burden imposed by the oil crisis and subsequent recession by relying heavily on aid from industrialized countries. Confronted with unusual economic difficulties, this is perhaps the most "traditional" option for developing countries. For weak states in the international system, to depend on the strong when in trouble is a foreign policy strategy of a long-standing tradition. Thus, as opposed to other outward-oriented responses, North-dependent behavior is not peculiar to the oil crisis, for it simply aims at mitigating economic difficulties by making the best use of the conventional strategy.

Nevertheless, the changing international political-economic climate has added a somewhat different nuance to this traditional external policy. Asking for aid used to be an act of begging, which succeeded only if the well-being of the poor nations proved to be essential in the context of political, strategic, and economic considerations of the rich states. The humanitarian rationale has also played a role in the allocation of foreign aid, but basically, aid has for long remained a foreign policy "instrument" of powerful states (Griffin and Enos, 1970: 315). Yet with the growing consciousness about international inequality, the Third World countries have come to press for reconceptualization of aid by declaring the *right* of the poor to receive aid and the *duty* of the rich to guarantee foreign aid as an institutionalized channel for reducing the global inequality. The Article 22 of the Charter of Economic Rights and Duties of States adopted by the United Nations General Assembly at the Twenty-Ninth Session includes the following passage:

> All states should respond to the generally recognized or mutually agreed development needs and objectives of developing countries by promoting increased net flows of real resources to the developing countries from all sources, taking into account any obligation and commitments undertaken by States concerned, in order to reinforce the efforts of developing countries to accelerate their economic and social development. In this context, consistent with the aims and objectives mentioned above and taking into account any obligations and commitments undertaken in this regard, it should be their endeavour to increase the net amount of financial flows from official sources to developing countries and to improve the terms and conditions thereof.

The decade preceding the oil crisis saw a secular decline in both the real value of Offical Development Assistance (ODA) as well as the ratio to GNP of net ODA from OECD's Development Assistance Committee (DAC) countries (Brookings Institution, 1975: 30). However, the declining trend was clearly reversed after the oil crisis: the ODA/GNP ratio of DAC countries recovered to .35 percent by 1975 from a low of .30 percent in 1973 (UNCTAD, 1978: Table 5.4B), the real value of ODA by DAC countries increased by 20 percent by 1975 compared to the 1973 level, and the actual dollar volume nearly doubled by 1976.

EXTERNALLY DETERMINED AND SELF-RELIANT RESPONSES

Note that from the viewpoint of non-oil exporting LDCs, there is an important difference between the first three and the latter two patterns of outward-oriented responses. Their own decisions and initiatives were cru-cial to the rise of commodity-based collective self-reliance, project-based collective self-reliance, and verbal protests, whereas external actors held decisive power over OPEC-dependent and North-dependent behavior. Namely, the OPEC members and the DAC countries determined the latter sets of response behavior by controlling the availability of these options. Although campaigns for aid by developing countries may have influenced the donors' decisions to some extent, the donor's own preferences and calcu-lations are considered to have been overwhelmingly important in determin-ing whether or not a country could resort to these response options. Hence OPEC-dependent and North-dependent behavior are "externally deter-mined" outward-oriented responses.

On the other hand, commodity-based collective self-reliance, project-based collective self-reliance, and verbal protests are initiated and pursued as decisions of the non-oil-exporting LDCs themselves. The act of resorting to these response options is determined by factors internal to each country, and obviously not by powerful external actors, who have done their utmost to deter the rise of OPEC-triggered Third World militancy. Thus while OPEC-dependent and North-dependent behavior are grouped as "externally determined," commodity-based collective self-reliance, project-based col-lective self-reliance, and verbal protests are characterized as "self-reliant outward-oriented responses" (see Figure 7.1). The word "self-reliant" also implies that these actions are expected to promote individual and collective self-reliance in non-oil-exporting LDCs, most of which have been severely trapped in dependency.

Theorizing about Inward-Oriented and Outward-Oriented Response Patterns

We have described the major patterns of outward-oriented responses of non-oil-exporting LDCs to the OPEC action, citing some illustrative cases to support our argument. However, we hope to develop more general state-ments as to which nations resorted to each of five patterns of response behavior. Thus we will specify explanatory multiple regression models for each response behavior and estimate them with data collected for forty non-oil-exporting LDCs. The OLS (Ordinary Least Squares) method will be used to estimate the models.

The data set used for estimating the models includes aggregate data from international organizations and various other sources, events data for forty non-oil-exporting LDCs for the period of 1970-1977 compiled by the author from the *Quarterly Economic Reviews of the Economist Intelligence Unit,* and content analysis data compiled from the Sixth Special Session of the United Nations General Assembly.

The criteria for the inclusion of nations into the sample for the present study were as follows:

(a) They had to be developing countries with per capita GNPs of 1000 dollars or less in 1970.

(b) They had to be non-oil-exporting countries (i.e., their exports of petroleum and petroleum products, SITC 33, had to be 20 percent or less than their total exports in 1972).

(c) They had to be located outside the European continent.

(d) There had to be no major internal crisis in the country around 1973-1974.

(e) Sufficient data for the country had to be available.

COMMODITY-BASED COLLECTIVE SELF-RELIANCE

What are the factors that account for the behavior of the OPEC emulators? To start with, for each country we compute the net sum of the magnitude of its efforts at commodity-based collective self-reliance in different international commodity markets. This index does not comprise an accurate interval scale, but it at least provides an ordinal-scale measurement of the OPEC-emulating behavior of the Third World countries in the immediate post-OPEC years. This variable will be labeled as Y_1, the dependent variable of the commodity-based collective self-reliance model (Inoguchi, forthcoming). Sources for data for Y_1 are the information given in *Quarterly Economic Reviews of the Economist Intelligence Unit* for each country, *Political Handbook of the World, 1978* (Banks, 1978), *International Politics of Natural Resources* (Mikdashi, 1976), and *Trade and Developing Countries* (Morton and Tulloch, 1977).

The model that explains the variance in this dependent variable is specified as follows:

$$Y_1 = a_1 - b_{11} X_1 + b_{12} X_2 / X_3 + e_1$$

where Y_1 = efforts at commodity-based collective self-reliance

X_1 = disadvantages in the conventional trade regime

X_2 = degree of unexpected growth of petroleum imports

X_3 = vulnerability to northern retaliatory sanctions

The OPEC strike came after decades in which there was an unfavorable trade climate for primary commodity exporters. The demonstration of the possibilities of exerting power on trade on the basis of commodity control inspired those who had tolerated the inherent disadvantages of primary commodities in the world transaction formula. Hence we hypothesized that the greater the disadvantages that countries experienced in the conventional trade regime, the stronger their incentive to pursue radical commodity power in response to the psychopolitical stimulus of the OPEC success. One of the most comprehensive and representative indicators of the Third World's "disadvantages" in trade is terms of trade. The decline in terms of trade for Third World countries has often been one of the major sources of their frustration with the international economy. The use of OPEC-like commodity power primarily aims at a quick and dazzling reversal in the secular trend of their terms of trade. Thus the first part of the model says that the greater the deterioration in one's terms of trade, the greater the chance that one would resort to commodity power. The data are obtained from UNCTAD *Handbook of International Trade and Development Statistics Supplement 1977* (Inoguchi, forthcoming).

The second term on the explanatory side of the model is expected to verify the statement made earlier that OPEC-emulating behavior was partly a response to the need for greater export earnings to finance a skyrocketing oil import bill. Since the success of OPEC-like producers' associations would instantly provide members with an amount in dollars unlikely to be made available by any other quick measure, it is reasonable to assume that those confronted with unexpected large oil expenditures would exercise commodity power to overcome their financial plight. Thus the greater the degree of unexpected growth in the cost of petroleum imports, the stronger the incentive to resort to the radical use of commodity power. This variable, the degree of unexpected growth in the cost of petroleum imports, is represented by the ratio between actual value of oil imports in the post-oil-crisis years and the value of the oil imports we might have expected if there had not been an oil crisis, based on an extrapolation of the 1970-1972 trend.

X_2 enters the model not by itself, but as a multiplicative term deflated by X_3, which represents one's vulnerability to northern retaliations. Of all outward-oriented response patterns, the resort to OPEC-like commodity power is the most extreme alternative, comprising a major attack on the North-centered conventional economic regime. Therefore, in pursuing this strategy, one would certainly consider the possibilities of northern retaliatory sanctions. Those highly vulnerable to northern counterattacks are less likely to turn to this strategy and would probably prefer some more moderate means to weather the economic crisis. Hence we hypothesize that the attractiveness of the commodity power option in alleviating the oil burden is curbed according to the degree of one's vulnerability to northern retaliatory sanctions.

What are the likely northern countermeasures? One of the most common means of maintaining the northern grip over developing countries is the allocation of loans and grants. Whereas other retaliatory measures may result in overpublicizing northern intent, cessation of aid is probably the most "handy" option, its threat to the South being by no means insignificant. We can hypothesize that the greater the weight of foreign aid in one's economy, the greater the vulnerability to retaliatory sanctions. The variable X_3 is represented by an index of gross loans and grants as a percentage of imported goods and services for the year 1973. Since this variable enters the model only as a deflator of X_2, it is standardized before it is entered into the equation.

The result of the estimation is given below:

$$Y_1' = 6.053 - .551X_1 + .427X_2/X_3 \text{ (standard error}$$
$$(.149) \quad (.022) \quad \text{beta weight)}$$
$$-.522** \quad .273*$$

$R^2 = .61$
$N = 35$
** = significant at .01 level
* = significant at .05 level

All signs of the independent variables are correct, and the coefficients for both terms are statistically significant. This gives strong support to the hypothesis presented above that: (1) the greater the disadvantages of developing countries in the conventional trade regime, defined in terms of deterioration of their terms of trade, the greater the probability that they would resort to radical commodity power; and (2) the greater the unexpected growth in the cost of petroleum imports, the greater the incentive to emulate OPEC to meet the urgent need for additional income, provided that the vulnerability of one's economy to northern retaliatory measures defined as the cessation or decrease of aid is relatively small.

The joint linear explanatory power of the model amounts to more than 60 percent, which is very substantial given the soft nature of the model.

The estimation result of this model is interesting particularly in respect to the following two points. First, the performance of the model suggests that what is seen by some, especially in the North, as OPEC-triggered "chaotic" behavior in the South, in fact stands on a solid foundation of political-economic calculations and expectations. The model shows that Third World countries were not trying to imitate OPEC in a blind or random manner, in which case no model could "explain" their behavior. On the contrary, our analysis of their efforts to pursue commodity power has identified explicit political-economic reasons that account for the behavior of new aspirants to commodity power. Thus the very fact that we have successfully articulated the model substantiates the thesis that the external economic behavior of these countries in the immediate post-OPEC years was based on definite calculations of their interests and needs.

Second, the regression reveals that the rise of producer power can best be conceptualized as a political and political-economic rather than a purely economic phenomenon. Variable X_1, disadvantages in the conventional trade regime defined as deterioration of the terms of trade, is by itself an "economic" concept, but as employed in the present model, it constitutes a genuine political concept. The assumption that if one suffers from external "injustice" in the form of unfavorable terms of trade, one would resort to "power"—commodity power—to arrest the cause of one's suffering, involves a highly political perspective. Thus the terms of trade variable in this model is a hybrid of political and economic concepts.

The concept behind X_2 is more economic since it represents the assumption that if one is faced with a sharp rise in import costs, one is likely to turn to strategies that may increase one's revenue instantly and by a large margin. But if this variable enters the model all by itself, the coefficient will have the right sign but will not be statistically significant (Inoguchi, forthcoming). It is when this variable is deflated by the index of "vulnerability to northern retaliatory sanctions" that the coefficient becomes stable enough to verify the hypothesis. The assumption is that where aid might significantly deflect the rising cost of imports, there will be strong political-economic motivations for avoiding policies that would sour relations with the North. Again, this deflator is, by itself, an economic indicator, but when aid dependence is incorporated into the model to represent the concept of the actor's vulnerability to donors' retaliation, it becomes a legitimate political concept.

With the increasing politicization of foreign economic relations, the Third World's search for commodity power cannot be explained without paying due attention to the political forces and constraints behind economic behavior.

PROJECT-BASED COLLECTIVE SELF-RELIANCE

To add depth to the generalization that Third World efforts at project-based collective self-reliance increased following OPEC's demonstration of southern solidarity and with the recirculation of petrodollars, here we investigate which nations deserve most of the credit for this change. Not all non-oil-exporting developing countries were equally involved in South-South projects. Our aim is to explain the variance in the change in their efforts to pursue project-based collective self-reliance after the oil crisis.

Thus the dependent variable is the change in the magnitude of efforts at project-based collective self-reliance after the OPEC stimuli. This is Y_2. The operational indicator for this concept is obtained by computing the ratio of difference in the number of South-South joint projects between 1970-

1973 and 1974-1977 for each country of our sample. The computation of the index is based on the events data.

The model hypothesized to account for the variance in this dependent variable is as follows:

$$Y_2 = a_2 + b_{21}X_4/X_5 + b_{22}X_6 \cdot X_7 + e_2$$

> where Y_2 = change in the magnitude of efforts at project-based collective self-reliance
>
> X_4 = past experience in South-South project cooperation
>
> X_5 = domestic political instability
>
> X_6 = degree of governmental influence in economy
>
> X_7 = political support for cooperation among developing countries

The first term in the explanatory construct is the "past experience in South-South project cooperation" deflated by an index of "domestic political instability."

Ties among nations do not change overnight. It is not so likely that new channels of cooperation emerge suddenly in response to some external stimulus. However, timely external stimuli may be able to spur the expansion of forms of cooperation already in motion. Given some basis for and confidence in cooperative ventures with other developing countries, the demonstration effect of the OPEC strike and the subsequent financial benefits therefrom can be hypothesized to invigorate efforts in pursuit of southern solidarity along the lines already explored. Thus past involvement in South-South joint projects is considered to be one of the major variables determining the growth of efforts at project-based collective self-reliance in the OPEC-led drive for a NIEO. Hence, the greater the past experience in South-South projects, the greater the likelihood of investing more heavily in such projects following OPEC's demonstration of the power of the unified South. This variable, X_4, is represented by the frequency of joint projects in which each of our sample nations was engaged with other developing countries during 1970-1973.

A multiplicative term is made by deflating this variable by a standardized index representing the degree of domestic political instability. This is X_5. In other words, domestic political instability is assumed to curb the positive relationship between Y_2, the growth of efforts at project-based collective self-reliance, and X_4, past experience in South-South project cooperation. Very often, cross-national projects tend to be large in scale and ambitious in goals. The government is in a better position to take the initiative in such projects when it is in firm command of its civil society. Exploring new possibilities in one's foreign economic relations requires a considerable concentration of power, skill, and resources; it is a luxury enjoyed only by regimes with a minimum of internal political instability. An unstable political setting will discourage the private sector from seeking dynamic interaction with external economies as well. As for the possibility of being invited in as a partner in cross-national projects, politically instable economies ranking high in the "country risk" list will scare away not only northerners but southerners as well.

The proxy for X_5 is based on a "z score for rebellion" compiled by the Yale Dependency Project.

The second term is the "degree of governmental influence in the economy" (X_6) inflated by "political support for the Third World solidarity" (X_7).

The "degree of governmental influence in the economy" is a political-economic concept. A considerable number of South-South projects are either sponsored or backed in some way by the government, and hence the greater the governmental involvement in the domestic economy, the greater the chance that it can implement the political principle of southern solidarity in the form of cross-national economic ventures. Also the greater the governmental influence in economic affairs, the greater the possibility that the government can encourage or guide the private sector to take timely cooperative moves consistent with political objectives. Hence the larger the values for X_6, the greater the readiness and flexibility of the economy in increasing its efforts at project-based South-South cooperation if political conditions are ripe. The index for this variable is rather difficult to construct, but one of the proxies is the share of public investment in gross fixed capital formation. This indicates the extent of governmental control over the capital-generating capacity of the economy.

However, no matter how large the flexibility of the economy in complying with political goals, if the state is neither supportive nor enthusiastic about mutual cooperation among developing countries, South-South ventures will not necessarily increase. Thus it is important that variable X_6 interact with a variable that represents political support for cooperation among developing countries. This is variable X_7. By having X_6 interact with X_7, our hypothesis is modified as follows: The larger the governmental influence in the economy, the more likely that the nation's commitments to the South-South joint projects will increase, given the state's intent to seek cooperation among developing countries. The index of political support for collective self-reliance was compiled by carrying out a content analysis of the speeches made on agenda item 7 (Study of the Problems of Raw Materials and Development) at the Sixth Special Session of the United Nations General Assembly.

This is the estimation result:

$$Y_2' = .0877 + .141X_4/X_5 + .019X_6 \cdot X_7 \text{ (standard error beta weight)}$$
$$ (.067) (.007)$$
$$ .415** .588**$$

$R^2 = .73$
$N = 15$
** = significant at .01 level

First of all, the model has succeeded in explaining 73 percent of the variance in the dependent variable, the growth of joint ventures among developing countries. This is indeed an exceptional performance for a model with highly political hypotheses.

Coefficients for both explanatory terms are significant at the .01 level, which guarantees their statistical stability. Our only regret is that the sample has become rather small, mostly due to missing values for the "domestic political stability" variable. Nevertheless, the high statistical significance of the coefficients, despite the size of the sample, attests to strong support for the hypotheses discussed above. It seems safe to conclude that (1) the greater the past experience in South-South joint ventures, the greater the intensification of efforts at project-based collective self-reliance following the OPEC strike, given that domestic political instability is relatively low; and (2) the greater the governmental influence in the economy, the greater the likelihood of increasing investment in cross-national projects in the South, if the government supports cooperation among developing countries.

The importance of the political variables is again worth noting. If we omit X_5 and X_7, the "domestic political instability" and the "political support for cooperation among developing countries" variables, the explanatory power of the model drops by nearly 25 percent.

Politics has a significant impact upon external economic behavior in the South-South context as well.

VERBAL PROTESTS

Compared to the two patterns of behavior examined above, it tends to be more difficult and somewhat less interesting to explain a nation's verbal behavior, since the latter is more likely to reflect random elements such as the mood and personal preferences of draft writers and speech makers. On the other hand, the importance of verbal behavior must be acknowledged, particularly in the context of the NIEO debate where the rise of an alternative concept has exerted significant influence upon the evolution of an existing system.

If verbal behavior is important, it will be interesting to see whether it is explicable in terms of rational motivations. If one speaks out more harshly than others because one has a reason to, and not because of some ad hoc superficialities, then we should be able to specify a model.

Not all countries maintained the tone set at the Sixth Special Session. In subsequent conferences, some modified while others escalated their verbal militancy. But since our focus is on the early response of the developing countries to the OPEC's initiative, the speeches made at the Sixth Special Session are the best proxy for the dependent variable Y_3, the verbal protests.

Content analysis was carried out for speeches made under agenda item 7 (Study of the Problems of Raw Materials and Development). The author coded paragraphs containing "complaints" concerning at least one of the following items, and/or "demands" to correct them: (1) inequitable distribution of wealth, (2) inequalities and disadvantages for exporters of primary commodities, (3) deterioration of the prices of Third World export commodities, and (4) other general aspects of the conventional world economic order. The index for Y_3 was computed on the basis of the frequency of such paragraphs in each speech.

We specify the model for Y_3 with simple but powerful explanatory variables. Since the main purpose is to explain statements, and not actions, a complex construct is misleading, as it tries to explain residual variance, which after all may be ascribed to random factors. Thus the model is not intended to account for as much variance in Y_3 as possible, but rather aimed at identifying a few principal factors that were integral to the Third World's militant verbal confrontations.

Hence the model for Y_3 is specified simply by two independent variables:

$$Y_3 = a_3 + b_{31}X_1 + b_{32}X_8 + e_3$$

where Y_3 = verbal protests
X_1 = disadvantages in the conventional trade regime
X_8 = political support for OPEC

The first simple hypothesis is that one would speak out more militantly if one has endured more disadvantages in the conventional international economic order. In other words, the first independent variable tests whether one's contentious verbal behavior is based on undue difficulties in trade, the most salient aspect of international economic transactions. This is the same concept as the first independent variable in the model specified for commodity-based collective self-reliance. OPEC-emulating behavior and verbal protests are somewhat isomorphic in that both are "revolts" against the North. Although the means employed to rebel are different—commodities in one case, concepts in the other—they seem to share a common origin—dissatisfaction and frustration with the conventional international economic regime.

The latter part of the model is based on the observation that the series of verbal protests launched by the developing countries was a supportive response to OPEC's assault upon the traditional formula of North-South transactions. Although the Third World as a whole continued to support OPEC verbally at least for a few years following the oil crisis, in reality some developing countries, embittered by the sudden upturn in their oil import bills, were far from expressing positive support for the oil cartel. Despite the tacit agreement to provide OPEC with the political support of the entire Third World, some openly blamed OPEC for the colossal oil burden. Some who would not go so far as to blame OPEC in public nonetheless refrained from expressing positive support. Thus, just as the magnitude of the economic impacts of the oil crisis differed from country to country, the significance of OPEC's lead in revolutionizing North-South relations was not evaluated uniformly by the rest of the Third World. Our hypothesis is that those more strongly inspired by OPEC's initiative and hence more supportive of OPEC would be more likely to demonstrate militancy in protesting against the conventional international economic regimes. In other words, the greater the political support for OPEC, the stronger the tendency to become more critical of the conventional order against which OPEC took its stand.

The Sixth Special Session provided the first worldwide occasion for countries to take a stance in respect to OPEC and its consequences. Also, at this forum, OPEC was in dire need of the Third World's support to counter criticism from the North. Thus the speeches made at the Sixth Special Session were analyzed to establish a measure for variable X_8, political support for OPEC.

The result of the estimation of this simple model is as follows:

$$Y_3' = 18.925 - .132X_1 + 1.742X_8 \text{ (standard error}$$
$$ (.057) \quad (.606) \quad \text{beta weight)}$$
$$ -.370** \quad .460**$$

$R_2 = .63$
$N = 27$
** = significant at .01 level.

The coefficients for both independent variables are significant at .01 level. The joint linear explanatory power of the model amounts to 63 percent. Since the verbal behavior of a nation is likely to involve random factors, as stated at the outset, there is a chance that the independent variables are in fact correlating with some random elements in the dependent variable by coincidence. However, this concern is tempered by the extremely stable coefficients demonstrated in this estimation result. Thus, it is fair to conclude that (1) the greater the disadvantages of developing countries in the conventional trade regime, defined in terms of deterioration of their terms of trade, the greater the probability that they would manifest militant verbal protests against the conventional North-South economic order, and (2) the greater the political support for OPEC, the more likely a nation would be critical of the conventional North-South economic order, which OPEC defined.

Hence, to a considerable extent, we were able to explain the Third World's militancy in verbal protests. What seemed to be OPEC-led "hysteria" at international forums was not the random and erratic phenomenon it was claimed to be in some quarters. In particular, note the startling significance of X_1, the disadvantages felt by developing countries in the conventional international economic order. If the more deprived are speaking out more violently, their pleas are worth serious assessments by the North.

OPEC-DEPENDENT BEHAVIOR

In modeling OPEC-dependent and North-dependent behavior, one must respect the critical difference between self-reliant and externally determined outward-oriented responses, as pointed out earlier. Although the militant campaign for aid launched by a number of developing countries may have had some effect upon donors, the latter's own preferences and calculations are usually decisive in determining the ultimate flow of aid. Hence the models must be constructed taking into account the preferences of the donors. The models will aim at identifying the variables that distinguished aid recipients among non-oil-exporting LDCs, most of which were not in a financial position to decline aid options if these were made available.

The dependent variable of the OPEC-dependent behavior model is Y_4 and is expressed in terms of the increase in total concessional receipts from the OPEC countries and multinational agencies funded mainly by the OPEC countries.

UNCTAD offers a reasonably reliable data set on concessional flows from the OPEC countries (UNCTAD, 1978b). In the presence of some extreme outlyers, the natural logarithm of Y_4 enters the left side of the equation.

Logged Y_4 is explained by the following model:

$$\log Y_4 = a_4 + b_{41}\log X_9 + b_{42}\log (X_{10} \cdot X_{11}) + e_4$$

where Y_4 = OPEC-dependent behavior
X_9 = common cultural identity
$X_{10} \cdot X_{11}$ = economic tie
X_{10} = trade tie
X_{11} = project tie

The first part of the model claims that the closer the cultural similarities with major OPEC countries, the greater will be the magnitude of OPEC-dependent behavior. It seems evident that the OPEC donors manifest a conscious bias in favor of Islamic countries. They make no apologies for doing so, since Islamic solidarity is justified as a legitimate counterforce to the predominant political-economic hegemony of the West. Also, the Islamic world supplied strong political support for OPEC's petroleum policy, and it reinforced Arabic solidarity against Israel (Hallwood and Stuart, 1981: 94). It comes as no surprise, then that the Muslim non-oil-exporting LDCs flocked around OPEC with liberal requests for aid. The index for this variable X_9 is the percentage share of Muslims in the total population.

The latter part of the model captures the opportunity given to countries that have strong economic ties with the oil exporters, whether Islamic or not. The assumption is that along with the Islamic preference, OPEC donors would also exhibit the common propensity among aid donors, to favor nations that are closer economically. Thus we hypothesize that the closer the economic ties with the OPEC members, the greater the magnitude of OPEC-dependent behavior.

The concept of economic ties is broken down into two subconcepts, trade ties and project ties. As an indicator of trade ties, we use total exports to the OPEC members rather than total trade between the OPEC members and the nation concerned. Importation of oil, which occupies a predominant portion of imports from the OPEC members, is a very weak measure of economic intimacy between them, since it is mostly determined by the level of industrialization of the importing countries. Hence to measure the intimacy in trade relations, we simply take total exports to OPEC. The degree of project ties is measured by the frequency of joint projects with OPEC members in the 1971-1973 period. We hypothesize that the trade and project variables interact with each other in accounting for the variance in Y_4, rather than each explaining some portion of its variance. Thus X_{10}, trade ties, and X_{11}, project ties, enter the model as a multiplicative term.

This term as well as X_9 are logged in accordance with the left side of the equation. The result of the estimation of the model for OPEC-dependent behavior is given below.

$$\log Y_4' = -3.483 + .356 \log X_9 + 2.590 \log (X_{10} \cdot X_{11}) \text{ (standard error}$$
$$(.123) \qquad (.464) \qquad \text{beta weight)}$$
$$.317** \qquad .611**$$

$R^2 = .80$
$N = 40$
** = significant at .01 level

The model was estimated with the full sample set. The strong explanatory power and the outstanding stability of the parameters speak well for the model. The estimation result confirms the claim that (1) the greater the common cultural identity with the Arabs, the greater the chance for the OPEC-dependent behavior; and (2) the greater the economic ties with the OPEC members as expressed in terms of trade flows and frequency of joint projects, the greater the likelihood of having access to OPEC aid. It should be added that the problem of multicollinearity, which we feared could undermine the relevance of this model, did not turn out to be serious (Inoguchi, forthcoming).

We have verified the statistical significance of the variables that are generally believed to have affected the allocation of OPEC aid. At the same time, we can show that the moralistic expectation that OPEC aid would reach the most troubled first remained far from reality. Let us assume a model with an alternative second independent term: Namely, we replace the "economic ties" variable by a variable that represents the degree of "damage" caused by the oil crisis and subsequent worldwide economic abnormality. The degree of "damage" is represented by an indicator compiled from the MSAs (most seriously affected countries) list announced by the United Nations. The earlier the appearance on the MSA list, the larger the weight, and obviously those that did not appear on the list were given the lowest value. Here is the estimation result:

$$\log Y_4' = -.0758 + .630 \log X_9 + .092 \log X \text{ (damage)} \quad \text{(standard error}$$
$$(.170) \qquad (.549) \qquad \qquad \text{beta weight)}$$
$$.562** \qquad .025$$

$R^2 = .57$
$N = 40$
** = significant a t .01 level.

The statistical insignificance of the coefficient of the "damage" variable is evident.

NORTH-DEPENDENT BEHAVIOR

Like OPEC-dependent behavior, North-dependent behavior is basically an externally determined adjustment behavior, and hence the model will explore the factors that seem to have been decisive in formulating the donors' judgment as to who ought to be able to resort to this privileged option.

The dependent variable of the North-dependent behavior is Y_5, and is expressed as a ratio of net concessional receipts from DAC countries and multilateral agencies in 1974-1975 to the amount received in pre-oil-crisis years. Namely, it is an index that shows the growth of aid receipts following the oil crisis. The data come from OECD.

One factor that can be hypothesized to serve as a criterion of OECD's aid allocation is the degree of neediness on the side of recipients. This is represented by a compound index of the severeness of the damage resulting from the oil crisis and other related economic vicissitudes of the early 1970s, and the general poverty level of the country. The indicator for the former, X_{12}, is compiled from the MSAs (most seriously affected countries) list announced by the United Nations, as discussed earlier. The higher the value for X_{12}, the greater the aid receipts. At the same time, we hypothesize that general level of poverty, X_{13}, is also significant in determining the "neediness" of aid. For example, the poorer the country, the more aid it tends to win, given the same level of the "severeness of the impact" of the oil crisis. Thus X_{13} interacts with X_{12} in explaining the variance in Y_5. The general level of poverty is simply indicated by the average GDP per capita for the years 1971-1972. Both variables are standardized, and the term is hypothesized to have a positive relationship with Y_5.

Let us first of all see whether this hypothesis holds, and if so to what extent this term can account for the variance in Y_5. Here is a tentative model and its estimation:

$$Y_5 = a_5 + b_{51}X_{12}/X_{13} + e_5$$

where Y_5 = North-dependent behavior
X_{12}/X_{13} = neediness of on the side of recipients
X_{12} = severeness of damage
X_{13} = general level of poverty

$Y_5' = 1.252 + .460 X_{12}/X_{13}$ (standard error
          (.152)   beta weight)
          .447**

$R^2 = .45$
$N = 39$
** = significant at .01 level.

The "neediness" term shows the hypothesized relationship with the dependent variable, and the coefficient is highly stable. The term alone accounts for nearly half of the variance in Y_5.

This finding is in accordance with the observation that to some, if limited, extent, the degree of the neediness on the side of the recipient is taken into account when aid decisions are made, and that this tendency has become increasingly more established in recent years. But meanwhile, it is often considered that aid also functions as an instrument of the donor's foreign policy. The incompleteness of the performance of the model above in terms of its explanatory power might be improved with the introduction of some political variable.

On the basis of the accumulated literature on aid allocation and in the light of emerging features of the contemporary North-South relations, we can discern several ways by which aid might have been used as an instrument of foreign policy in post-oil-crisis years. But, to state the conclusion in advance, the analysis reveals that none of such "political" variables add much to the "neediness" variable in terms of the explanatory power of the model.

First, foreign assistance is said to be intended to achieve greater national security for donors. This may have been particularly true with respect to U.S. assistance during the Cold War years when massive aid was dispatched to stabilize the regimes such as Taiwan, Iran, and Turkey bordering communist states (Frank and Baird, 1975: 140-141). "[The] successive shifts in emphasis from South Asia, to Southeast Asia, to Latin America, the Middle East, and back to Southeast Asia during the 1950s and 1960s reflect the changes in U.S. strategic and political interests more than changing evaluations of economic need" (Todaro, 1977: 337) admits an economist.

But in the wake of the economic turmoil in the 1970s, did those cooperating for the achievement of greater national security for donor states see a more rapid growth of aid compared to others? Not necessarily, as shown below:

$$Y_5' = 1.486 + .431\, X_{12}/X_{13} - .335 \times \text{(strategic tie)} \quad \text{(standard error}$$
$$ (.156) \phantom{X_{12}/X_{13}} (.322) \phantom{\times \text{(strategic tie)}} \text{beta weight)}$$
$$ .418** \phantom{X_{12}/X_{13}} -.157$$

$$R^2 = .47$$
$$N = 38$$
$$** = \text{significant at .01 level}$$

Strategic ties are represented by a dummy for those countries that maintain bilateral defense treaties with the United States and/or France and/or the United Kingdom. This variable fails to show the hypothesized (positive) relationship with the dependent variable, but in any case, since the coefficient is statistically insignificant and highly unstable, the sign of the coefficient does not provide us with any substantial implication. Strategic ties simply turned out to be an irrelevant factor in explaining the incremental flow of aid to weak nations in economic crisis. This finding may not be surprising if we assume that unless the economic crisis is perceived to harm the foundations of the strategic ties, by destabilizing the political basis of the existing regime, for example, the donor finds no strong reason to be sensitive to the economic difficulties of the alliance partner.

Second, those that are procapitalist and more open to foreign investment can be assumed to become a more promising candidate for aid (Blake and Walters, 1976: 133), particularly in time of economic crisis. The greater the investment interests, the greater the incentive to protect that economy and to preserve the general economic milieu in which the donor's investment activities take place. But again the result turned out to be disappointing:

$$Y_5' = 1.353 + .423\,X_{12}/X_{13} - .001 \times \text{(investment tie)}\quad \text{(standard error}$$
$$(.163)\qquad\qquad (.002)\qquad\qquad\qquad \text{beta weight)}$$
$$.410** \qquad\qquad - .114$$

$R^2 = .56$
$N = 38$
** = significant at .01 level

Data on direct investment is compiled by the Yale Dependency Project.

Other variables conventionally believed to have determined the aid flows such as colonial ties were also not powerful enough to explain the residual variance in Y_5.

Let us look now into another North-South connection that has become particularly salient with OPEC's use of the oil weapon, namely the leverage of the mineral-exporting countries and the vulnerability of the North to their sudden resort to raw material power. If aid can be used to appease the would-be OPEC emulators and deter their militancy in search of resource power, we speculate that the advanced industrialized countries would be inclined to allocate some portion of their aid for this purpose. Thus we hypothesize that the degree of importance as mineral resource suppliers would explain the residual variance in Northern aid receipts.

For each country, we take the sum of its percentage share in the world exports of major minerals and metals. This indicates the degree of importance of each mineral exporter in the total world supply.

$$Y_5' = 1.205 + .476\,X_{12}/X_{13} + .005 \times \text{(leverage of raw}\quad \text{(standard error}$$
$$(.163)\qquad\qquad (.017)\qquad \text{material suppliers)}\ \text{beta weight)}$$
$$.462**\qquad\qquad .046$$

$R^2 = .45$
$N = 39$
** = significant at .01 level

This raw material supplier shows the hypothesized (positive) relationship with Y_5. Compared to strategic ties, investment ties, and other political factors that are generally believed to affect aid flows, this resource variable turned out to be more relevant. Nevertheless, the coefficient is statistically insignificant, and the explanatory power of the model does not improve with the introduction of this variable. Thus we cannot claim that our hypothesis has been verified.

If we were to look into individual specific cases, we should be able to find matching empirical counterparts for each of the "political" hypotheses examined above. But in aggregate terms, we could not determine any political factor that serves as a major determinant of aid flows. The fact that we could only confirm the "neediness" factor to be the single most powerful and stable explanatory variable of northern aid flows in post-OPEC years seems to suggest that aid has become more of an instrument for modifying global wealth inequality rather than an instrument of a donor's foreign policy.

Concluding Remarks

Our perspective has been to look at and examine the efforts of non-oil-exporting LDCs to respond to the economic as well as the political and the psychological impact of the OPEC strike in 1973. After having conceptualized the inward-oriented and outward-oriented response patterns, we have focused on the latter, because the latter reveals not only their efforts to cope with the financial hardships of the oil crisis, but also their attempts to ride on the OPEC-triggered "campaign" to restructure their foreign economic relations and establish a new international economic order.

In examining response behavior, we went beyond the conceptualization of behavior and the presentation of illustrative cases. For each response, a formal model was built to test the hypotheses concerning the causal elements behind the behavior. For the most part, the models have been successfully specified. The high explanatory power of the models verifies that what has been seen as random and erratic behaviors manifested by southern countries in the immediate post-oil-crisis years, in fact, have solid foundations in their political-economic calculus and expectations.

Nevertheless, while their efforts marked some phenomenal accomplishments in their foreign economic relations, at the same time, new problems rose to challenge the long-term significance of their crisis-led breakthrough. We shall round off our discussion by illustrating some of the problems that those countries would have to surmount if their initiatives were to develop into an authentic force in creating and maintaining a new international economic order.

COMMODITY-BASED COLLECTIVE SELF-RELIANCE

The attractiveness of this strategy lies in the thrill of dramatic success, the instant rise of revenues, and the profound sense of acquiring tangible power in foreign economic relations. But this is only possible if and only if most of the major suppliers of the commodity are united by a common price and supply policy, making it impossible for the market forces to operate. It can easily fall to pieces unless each member is firmly committed to a producers' association endowed with credible power to offset various challenges from consuming countries, and unless the supply outside the association is very limited. Thus in most cases, this initiative tends to aim at the immediate success rather than long-term impacts. Consequently, from the global point of view, it may successfully alert the world to the long-neglected "frustration" of the southerners in commodity trade, but it is unlikely to develop sufficiently to become a lasting counterveiling power against the conventional trade regime (e.g., bauxite). Also, excessive use of commodity power may result in the reduction of its effectiveness in the long run due to demand restraint by importers, either simply by curbing consumption or by investing heavily in synthetics and substitutes. Given the present level of technological development, urgent and massive research efforts in search of alternatives by consuming nations can hardly be overlooked as an ultimate threat to commodity power. To stop producers' power from being caught in such difficulties and also to seek less radical, but more predictable and lasting ways of protecting commodity power, UNCTAD has devoted considerable efforts to establishing an Integrated Program for Commodities, the most comprehensive and far-reaching commodity policy scheme ever negotiated in an international forum. Whether there emerges a new alternative to commodity power à la OPEC is yet to be seen.

PROJECT-BASED COLLECTIVE SELF-RELIANCE

The Third World's collective self-reliance via joint projects and cooperative ventures tends to be less dramatic, but it is probably more durable than rallying for price and supply control of commodities. Nevertheless, there are a number of obstacles that hinder the steady growth of project-based collective self-reliance. First, although southerners may be well aware of the charm of an equal partnership with those at the similar stage of development, the affluent capital, managerial expertise, and technological superiority of northern partners are often too attractive to be resisted, and the general sense of security assured by economic giants tends to hold aspirations for alternative partnerships at bay. Second, countless plans of joint projects are never realized due to disagreements on the distribution of costs and benefits of the project; where the project should be located; who should contribute what, when, and how; and who gets what portion of the profit in what form. The more equal the power relationship among the participants, the greater the probability that profit allocation will become a contested issue; profit allocation in ventures between northern and southern countries has more often been dictated by the former than disputed by the two. If cooperative plans among the "equal" are thwarted by a self-defeating struggle for a better deal among themselves due to the absence of a dominant player, a possible way out of this problem may ironically be found in dependency between the "strong South" and the "weak South" whereby, just as in many North-South partnerships, the former dictates the terms. One may argue that this is still an "improvement" for the "weak South" since the degree of inequality is smaller for weak countries if they are coupled with the "strong South" than with the North. But this is a pseudocollective self-reliance that relegates the "weak South" from the periphery to the ultraperiphery in the global system. In fact, the direct threat to the cause of collective self-reliance may be found in pseudocollective self-reliance that stratifies, rather than unifies, developing countries, and increases, rather than reduces, their disparities.

VERBAL PROTESTS

The Third World's speak-out behavior bore highly significant political consequences in two respects: It helped North-South economic issues win primacy in global politics, and second, it elevated the political-economic connotations of the oil crisis from a critical juncture in North-OPEC relations to a new threshold in North-South relations. But speak-out behavior is only a verbal action that by itself does not signify a reallocation of resources. There inevitably arises the challenge of transforming verbal contestations into actual changes in the North-South relations. First of all, the political cohesion achieved through symbolic commitments and grandiose resolutions may not be strong enough to sustain down-to-earth negotiations that involve adjustments of specific national interests, as already revealed at some negotiation tables for a NIEO. Second, the temptation of grabbing immediate benefits resulting from the North-appeasement strategy may ultimately lead the South not to the exit from dependency, but to enter a more "comfortable dependency" (Inoguchi, 1981). Third, many developing countries lack sufficient technical and administrative capacity to take genuine initiatives at implementing verbally claimed ambitious principles. And finally, there is an inherent vulnerability in speak-out behavior in a world basically subject to the dynamics of power politics. There is not much incentive for the strong to listen to "public contestations" in international politics unless there is a "real threat" to their supremacy, and hence the weak in the international community cannot expect to achieve major tangible gains via internationally led "public contestation" unless equipped with due leverage. In the seventies, OPEC's oil weapon provided leverage to the entire Third World. How long this will last is a question that worries many Third World activists today.

OPEC-DEPENDENT BEHAVIOR

The rise of OPEC as a financial engine for the development of some Third World countries has been one of the most positive and enduring aftermaths of the oil crisis. Along with it, the "political map" of the Third World is going through a delicate transition. A new subglobal order is emerging between the new rich and their beneficiaries, and the stratification of states among southern countries is gradually taking place along the network of petrodollar channels. Thus although OPEC aid provides the Third World with the possibility of exiting from North-South aid-bound relations, it inevitably forces them to enter a new pecking order, and the eventual erosion of autonomy of the OPEC aid beneficiaries may remain as stubborn a problem as it has in the case of North-South aid relations. On the other hand, while such problems exist for countries lucky enough to have access to OPEC aid, the problem for the bulk of oil-importing LDCs is that the resort to the OPEC-dependent behavior remains a nonoption.

NORTH-DEPENDENT BEHAVIOR

The problems associated with aid-led intervention of northern states in the domestic affairs of southerners have a long-standing tradition in North-South relations. At least for the time being, however, the economics of foreign aid have turned out to be much more burdensome and problematic than the politics of foreign aid. Namely, the problem here is the debt burden. UNCTAD estimates that for a sample of 55 non-oil-exporting LDCs, debt service payments in 1974 corresponded to over 40 percent of the increase in their combined current account deficit (UNCTAD, 1976b). The external public and publicly guaranteed debt owed by the non-oil-exporting LDCs bulged from 60 billion dollars at the end of 1972 to more than 114 billion at the end of 1976 (Smith, 1977: ix) and accordingly, debt service doubled between 1973 and 1977 (Watson, 1978: 17). Debt relief became one of the most important items for the South in North-South negotiations and at UNCTAD V in 1979, the developing countries pressed for an international debtor-creditor conference to rationalize debt relief measures, only to find out that debt relief is more difficult than aid to win. It is high time for developing countries to reassess the ultimate efficacy of aid in correcting the North-South disparity in wealth.

Thus, quite apparently, the South's new initiative gave rise to new problems and concerns. But this fact does not undermine the significance of the weak states mobilizing unprecedented efforts in search of a new international economic order in which their interests are better represented. Their behavior unfailingly contributes to the dialectical evolutionary process of our international system.

REFERENCES

BAHATTACHARGA, A. K. (1976) Foreign Trade and International Development. Lexington, MA: D. C. Heath.

BANKS, A. (1978) Political Handbook of the World: 1978. New York: McGraw-Hill.

BLAKE, D. H. and R. S. WALTERS (1976) The Politics of Global Economic Relations. Englewood Cliffs, NJ: Prentice-Hall.

BERGSTEN, C. F. (1977) "Access to supplies and the New International Economic Order," pp. 199-218 in J. N. Bhagwati (ed.) The New International Economic Order: The North-South Debate. Cambridge, MA: MIT Press.

———— (1976) "A new OPEC in bauxite." Challenge 19 (July/Aug.): 12-20.

———— (1975) "The new era in world commodity markets," pp. 287-302 in C. F. Bergsten, Toward a New International Economic Order: Selected Papers of C. Fred Bergsten, 1972-74: Lexington, MA: D.C. Heath.

———— (1974) "The threat is real." Foreign Policy 14 (Spring): 86-90.

The Brookings Institution (1975) The World Economy in Transition: A Tripartite Report. Washington DC: Brookings.

CONNELLY, T. and R. PERLMAN (1975) The Politics of Scarcity. London: Oxford University Press.

DIAZ-ALEJANDRO, C. F. (1978) "Delinking North and South: unshackled or unhinged?" pp. 87-162 in A. Fishlow et al., Rich and Poor Nations in the World Economy. New York: McGraw-Hill.

DUNN, Jr., R. M. (1974) "The less developed countries," pp. 163-181 in J. A. YAGER and E. B. STEINBERG (eds.) Energy and U.S. Foreign Policy. Cambridge, MA: Allinger.

Economist Intelligence Unit (various years) Quarterly Economic Reviews.

EDWARDS, A. (1975) The Potential for New Commodity Cartels: Copying OPEC, or Improved International Agreement? London: Economist Intelligence Unit.

FRANK, Jr., C. R. and M. BAIRD (1975) "Foreign aid: its speckled past and future prospects," pp. 133-167 in C. F. Bergsten and L. B. Krause (eds.) World Politics and International Economics, Washington, DC: Brookings.

GRIFFIN, K. B. and J. L. Enos (1970) "Foreign assistance: objectives and consequences." Economic Development and Cultural Change 18, 3: 313-327.

GIRVAN, N. (1976) Corporate Imperialism: Conflict and Expropriation. White Plains, NY: M. E. Sharpe.

GWIN, C. B. (1977) "The Seventh Special Session: toward a new phase of relations between the developed and the developing states?" pp. 97-117 in K. P. Sauvant and H. Hasenpflug (eds.) The New International Economic Order: Confrontation or Cooperation between North and South. Boulder, CO: Westview Press.

HALLWOOD, P. and S. STUART (1981) Oil, Debt and Development: OPEC in the Third World. London: George Allen & Unwin.

International Bank for Reconstruction and Development [IBRD] (1978) Petroleum and Gas in Non-OPEC Developing Countries: 1976-85. World Bank Staff Working Paper 289. Washington, DC: World Bank.

INOGUCHI, K. J. (forthcoming) "The political economy of the non-oil-exporting LDCs: the oil crisis as the threshold of exploratory change." Ph.D. dissertation, Yale University.

———— (1981) "Exit and voice: the Third World response to dependency since OPEC's initiative," pp. 255-276 in C. W. Kegley, Jr. and P. McGowan (eds.) The Political Economy of Foreign Policy Behavior. Beverly Hills, CA: Sage.

KRASNER, S. D. (1974) "Oil is the exception." Foreign Policy 14 (Spring): 68-83.

MIKDASHI, Z. (1976) The International Politics of Natural Resources. Ithaca, NY: Cornell University Press.

―――― (1974) "Collusion could work." Foreign Policy 14 (Spring): 57-68.

MIKESELL, R. F. (1974) "More Third World cartels ahead?" Challenge 17 (Nov./Dec.): 24-31.

MINGST, K. A. (1976) "Cooperation or illusion: an examination of the Intergovernmental Council of Copper Exporting Countries." International Organization 30, 2: 263-288.

MORTON, K. and P. TULLOCH (1977) Trade and Developing Countries. London: Croom Helm.

Organization for Economic Cooperation and Development [OECD] (1975) Development Co-operation: 1975 Review. Paris: OECD.

PINDYCK, R. S. (1977) "Cartel pricing and the structure of the world bauxite market." Bell Journal of Economics 8, 2:343-360.

SAUVANT, K. P. (1977) "Toward the New International Economic Order," pp. 3-19 in K. P. Sauvant and H. Hasenpflug (eds.) The New International Economic Order: Confrontation or Cooperation between North and South. Boulder, CO: Westview Press.

SMITH, G. W. (1977) The External Debt Prospects of the Non-Oil-Exporting Developing Countries: An Econometric Analysis. Washington, DC: Overseas Development Council.

TIMS, W. (1975) "Developing countries," pp. 169-195 in E. R. Fried and C. L. Schltze (eds.) Higher Oil Prices and the World Economy: The Adjustment Problem. Washington, DC: Brookings.

TODARO, M. P. (1977) Economic Development in the Third World. London: Longman.

United Nations Conference on Trade and Development [UNCTAD] (1978a) Consideration of International Measures on Bauxite (TD/B/IPC/BAUXITE/2). New York: United Nations.

―――― (1978b) Handbook of International Trade and Development Statistics: Supplement (TD/STAT.7). New York: United Nations.

―――― (1977) Financial Solidarity for Development: Efforts and Institutions of the Members of OPEC (TD/B/627). New York: United Nations.

―――― (1976a) "The elements of the New International Economic Order," pp. 8-33 in UN-CTAD, Trade and Development Issues in the Context of a New International Economic Order (UNCTAD/OSG/104/Rev.1). Geneva: UNCTAD.

―――― (1976b) International Financial Co-operation for Development (TD/188/Supp.1.). New York: United Nations.

―――― (1975) "Economic cooperation among developing countries: report by the UNCTAD Secretariat (TD/192)," pp. 437-456 in K. P. Sauvant and H. Hasenpflug (eds.) The New International Economic Order: Confrontation or Cooperation between North and South (1977). Boulder, CO: Westview Press.

WATSON, P. M. (1978) Debt and the Developing Countries: New Problems and New Actors. Washington, DC: Overseas Development Council.

WILLIAMS, M. (1976) "The aid program of the OPEC countries." Foreign Affairs 54 2: 308-324.

WRIGGINS, W. H. (1978) "Third World strategies for change: the political context of North-South interdependence," pp. 21-117 in W. H. Wriggins and G. Adler-Karlsson (eds.) Reducing Global Inequalities. New York: McGraw-Hill.

CHAPTER 8

EXTERNAL CONSTRAINTS ON AFRICAN DEVELOPMENT

A B D U L   A Z I Z   J A L L O H

It is now approximately twenty years since the vast majority of African countries achieved political independence. Disenchantment with the economic gains from colonial rule was a major factor in the struggle for independence and the belief was widely held that independence by itself would almost automatically transform a situation of poverty to one of economic plenty for all concerned.

At the beginning of the 1980s, the optimism of the early 1960s has been replaced by a profound pessimism. For the fact is that in general, the economic progress of African countries in the 1960s and 1970s was minimal and less than the economic progress made by Asian and Latin American countries in general. What is worse is that as the Organization of African Unity (OAU) heads of state noted in the preamble to the Lagos Plan of Action for the Economic Development of Africa: 1980-2000, which they adopted in Lagos in April 1980, "If the world economic forecast for the next decade is to be believed, the over-all poor performance of the African economy over the past 20 years may be a golden age compared with future growth rates" (OAU, 1981: 7-8).

This chapter seeks to shed some light on the problem of why the economic performance of African countries in general has fallen far below expectations, why they have not done as well as other Third World countries in Asia and in Latin America in general, and why a few African countries have done much better than most of the others.

Roughly speaking, there are two strands of thought which seek to explain the persistence of economic underdevelopment in Third World countries in general. The first draws attention to factors internal to these countries which inhibit growth and development, while the second holds that the integration of Third World countries into the international capitalist system is the main cause of underdevelopment. Neither body of thought, in our view, holds that either internal or external factors are wholly responsible for underdevelopment. The difference between the two schools is essentially in the degree to which they emphasize internal or external factors, and this same difference exists among writers belonging to the same school.

Our concern in this chapter is essentially with the impact of external factors on the economic development of African countries. One reason for this restriction in the scope of our enquiry is that we share the view that while internal factors are certainly important (see Jalloh, 1981 for an analysis of these factors in the African context), external factors are more decisive. We will not try to prove this point of view here, and it is not necessary for us to do so since our concern is with the impact of external factors on African development and not with the relative weight of external and internal factors on this development. The second reason for our limitation is the direct bearing of these external factors on efforts at creating a New International Economic Order. We hope this chapter will be of use to African policymakers in deciding on what policies to adopt on the North-South dialogue.

The analysis will proceed in four stages. We will first examine the various definitions of development and how they have evolved. It is our view that confusion over what development is or should mean was partly responsible for many development efforts going astray and failing to produce the desired results. Thus the importance of clarity in defining what is meant by development. Next, we look at the economic development of African countries. The emphasis will be on the relative performance of African countries compared with Asian and Latin American countries. We will also identify those countries in Africa which have done better than others. Third, focusing only on external factors, we will seek to explain why African countries in general have not done as well as those in Asia and in Latin America, and why some African countries have done better than others. We will conclude with some thoughts on what our analysis means for the development of Africa during the next decade, and for the position African countries should adopt in the North-South dialogue.

The Meaning of Development

It is doubtful that disagreements and confusion as to what development means can be resolved in the foreseeable future. The definition of a concept such as development is bound to be heavily influenced by interests and values. And yet how one defines the concept is crucial in that it determines what will be sought after, and what will be achieved. An unacceptable definition is therefore unlikely to lead to the desired results. The way out, in our view, is to accept the inevitability of a certain degree of subjectivity in any definition of development while making sure that the definition meets the following criteria: (a) it captures the fundamental differences between developed and underdeveloped countries, and (b) it embodies the essence of the changes people generally have in mind when they talk of promoting the economic development of Third World countries. The result will not be the "true" definition of development, but it will certainly be a more useful one.

From the above perspective, traditional and more recent efforts at defining development are inadequate in many respects. The inadequacies of these definitions are certainly responsible to some degree for the disappointing results of the last two decades of developmental efforts. We will examine a few of the more widely known definitions of development to bring out their inadequacies.

The standard view until recently was that development was synonymous with growth, meaning the increase in the quantity of goods and services produced within a country (Lewis, 1955). But the limitation in this definition was quickly recognized, for if one adopts this definition it will mean that the oil-rich countries in an area such as the Middle East will rank higher on the development scale than most developed market economies. This would run counter to what is generally understood by development.

The size of the per capita income does differentiate to some extent developed from underdeveloped countries, but it is not sufficiently discriminating and is therefore not enough. Development cannot therefore be equated with growth. The distinction between the two is made by Kindleberger who notes that "economic growth means more output, and economic development implies both more output and changes in the technical and institutional arrangements by which it is produced" (1965: 3). This laudable effort is unfortunately immediately abandoned when the author decides on the same page to use national income as a measure of development on the grounds that growth and development go together up to a point and that in the early stages, an economy that grows is also likely to develop, and vice versa. But the exact relationship between growth and development is a complex one, and there are several cases of countries that have experienced growth and not development. It therefore seems that the more sensible approach is to maintain the distinction between growth and development.

Recent efforts at defining development have for the most part maintained the distinction between growth and development, with development being regarded as much broader than growth. One such effort is that of Samir Amin, who sees underdevelopment as characterized by "sectorial inequality of productivities, disarticulation, and domination" (1976: 381). In contrast therefore, development means a balance in sectoral productivity, high linkage among the sectors, and autonomy of the economy.

We see two limitations in the above definition. One is that it abandons the merit that was contained in the view that development was the same as growth. For it is possible to imagine a premodern economy with low levels of production and productivity, which meets the above three conditions of development. The Amin definition therefore fails to differentiate between developed and underdeveloped countries and to capture fully what people usually have in mind when they talk of development. A second and related limitation is that while focusing on economic aggregates as measures of development, the definition completely leaves out the humanistic element that is invariably behind the concern with development.

It is our view, which is certainly in part normative, that development is generally understood to mean that more and more people live "better" lives. This normative preoccupation must be reflected in any definition of development.

The development trends in Third World countries during the last two decades have brought these normative concerns to the center of attempts at defining development. Multilateral aid agencies, especially, the World Bank, now see development as largely concerned with reducing and eliminating absolute poverty. According to this view, "Development goals should be expressed in terms of the progressive reduction and eventual elimination of malnutrition, disease, illiteracy, squalor, unemployment and inequalities" (Haq, 1976: 43). It is this view of development that is embodied in the basic needs approach.

The danger in this approach is in its one-sidedness. Concern with growth disappears or is at least minimized and so is the structural transformation of the economy. For it is again possible for an oil-rich country to completely abolish poverty and raise living standards for most of its citizens to levels as high as those prevailing in the developed market economies while remaining underdeveloped in terms of its structure of output. Finally, when the element of growth is brought in, the question immediately emerges as to the necessary trade-off between growth and the eradication of poverty.

One approach which maintains the concern with the reduction of poverty and still links it with growth is that which focuses on redistribution. According to this approach, development must be concerned "with the level and growth of income in lower-income groups. Distributional objectives therefore cannot be viewed independently of growth objectives. Instead they should be expressed dynamically in terms of desired rates of growth of income of different groups" (Ahluwalia and Chenery, 1979: 38). Defining development as "growth with redistribution" therefore means it is a process in which per capita income increases, poverty is progressively eliminated, and inequality is reduced, with the central feature being a relatively greater growth in the income of the poor and therefore a reduction in the degree of their poverty.

Ahluwalia addresses the problem of the relationship between growth and inequality and concludes that higher growth rates do not inevitably generate greater inequality. He notes however that "the predicted share (of income) of the lowest 40 percent decline sharply up to per capita income levels of $400 and then flattens out rising steadily after per capita GNP crosses $1,200" (1974: 17). Further on, Ahluwalia notes that "the most important finding is that income shares are related not only to structural factors such as per capita income levels but also to variables which can be influenced by policy" (1974: 17-18). In sum, given the balance in the range of political power and interests among domestic groups, growth and redistribution leading to a reduction in poverty are compatible.

It may be asked in a continent such as Africa, in which most countries have low income levels, whether the problems of inequality and redistribution are relevant. Our answer to this is in the affirmative. It has been estimated that in 1973, 83.5 percent of the African population had incomes of less than $300, 69 percent of them were living in conditions of extreme poverty, 39 percent of them were destitute, and the number of Africans living in extreme poverty increased by 10.8 percent between 1963 and 1972 (Doo Kingué, 1979: 95). Certainly, one way out of this situation is increased growth. But as trends in the 1960s and 1970s have shown, high growth rates by themselves have not reduced poverty. What is therefore needed is for development policies that attempt to promote redistribution in order to reduce the worst forms of poverty, without neglecting growth. In essence then, while redistribution is in some ways a goal in itself, it is also one of the ways of reducing poverty in a context such as Africa.

However, it must be admitted that the exact trade-off between growth on the one hand and redistribution and the reduction of poverty on the other has not been indicated. The fact is that there is no general response to this problem. The exact trade-off that is desirable and/or feasible will depend on among other things the income level and its growth rate, the degree of poverty, and the degree of inequality. Countries may well have to make different trade-offs at different times, and countries will certainly differ in what they decide to opt for and to forgo. What is critical in our view is that decisions on trade-offs be made explicitly and self-consciously, based on the long-term desire of maximizing growth, equality, and prosperity within the limits of what is possible. This formulation is bound to be unsatisfactory, but aiming at a greater degree of precision is bound to be futile and irrelevant in most cases.

Does this then mean that the definition of development as "growth with redistribution" is fully acceptable? Our view is that while this definition is a step forward compared with definitions that equate development with growth, structural change, or the elimination of poverty alone, it still lacks some important elements. These are the capacity of an economy to produce a wide range of goods and services that its citizens demand or need and the ability of the society to enjoy a certain degree of autonomy from outside forces. Both are clearly related.

A striking contrast between developed and underdeveloped countries is the ability of the former to provide a wide range of goods and services for their citizens and the failure of the latter to do the same. This ability is conditioned in part by the response base of a society. Far more important is the level of technological development of a society—which can go a long way in mitigating the adverse effects of limited resources. In African and many other Third World countries, the problem is not the absence of resources but technological underdevelopment. Thus their inability to supply a broad range of goods and services to their citizens. For these countries, therefore, a central element of development is to correct this inadequacy.

It is possible for a society to satisfy the demands for goods and services of its citizens without having to produce these goods and services itself. This is the case, for example, of the oil-rich countries that can use their wealth to purchase from others those goods and services that they do not produce. While such countries are undoubtedly wealthy, they are far from developed. In the final analysis, they are dependent on others for their well-being.

There are, of course, varying forms and degrees of dependence, with the dependence of oil- and other mineral-rich countries on the developed countries being only one of these types of dependence. Only a handful of African countries fall under this category, while most of the others lack even this ability to buy from others the goods and services their people need. The dependence of African countries on the developed countries is too well known to necessitate presenting pages of statistical data. Suffice it to say that it is most glaringly manifested in the discrepancy between what is produced and what is consumed. Thomas (1974: 123) notes that "These divergences (among domestic needs, production, and consumption) are rooted in such basic structural relationships as foreign ownership and control of domestic resources, export specialization for metropolitan markets, the pervasiveness of foreign decision-making over domestic economic processes," and so forth. He then defines development in the most basic and fundamental way, as the "initiation of economic processes which overcome this divergent pattern of needs, domestic production, and domestic consumption." Development therefore means a relative degree of autonomy.

Autonomy must be contrasted with interdependence. For us, interdependence refers to a situation in which two or more actors engage in economic exchange not because of an inability to produce a wide range of the goods and services they need, but because they stand to gain from a certain degree of specialization. Thus while no society may be able to satisfy all its needs as a result of purely national efforts because of resource limitations, an interdependent society is one that has such a capacity for a wide range of its needs even though it has to pay a high price for it. This capacity clearly distinguishes developed from underdeveloped countries. It is also a capacity that most countries desire for its own sake, even if a certain economic price must be paid for it. African countries clearly lack this capacity at present even though the desire for it is by no means absent.

In sum then, we consider development as consisting of five elements: (1) high income levels resulting from high growth rates; (2) the absence of or a low level of poverty; (3) a relatively low degree of income inequality; (4) the capacity of the economy to produce a wide range of goods and services to satisfy domestic consumption; and (5) a certain degree of autonomy. These features are certainly not present in equal degrees in developed economies, but by and large, they are to be found more often in the developed than in the underdeveloped countries. Moreover, they strike us as the most significant elements of developed economies and embody the crucial features that most people have in mind when they talk of development.

Different individuals will certainly put the stress on different aspects of this definition, but we doubt that many will reject any of them as having nothing to do with development. Finally, the definition is not free from a normative bias but as we said earlier, this is unavoidable. Thus while our definition will not put an end to controversy, we hope it supplies a broader perspective that highlights the most important goods and aspirations that surround development. It is this definition of development that will serve as the basis for our evaluation of development experiences in Africa during the last two decades.

African Development Trends in the Sixties and Seventies

Our task in this section is essentially descriptive. We intend to describe the development trends in Africa during the 1960s and 1970s in order to determine how positive this trend has been in general. Comparisons will be made to ascertain whether trends in Africa were more positive or negative than the trends in Asia and Latin America. And finally, African countries will be compared to determine which did relatively better or worse. (Figures in this section are taken or computed from the International Bank for Reconstruction and Development/World Bank, 1980 unless otherwise indicated.) The task of explaining the trends identified in this section will be undertaken in the next section of this essay.

Per Capita GNP. What is immediately striking about Africa is the degree of widespread poverty. With a population of about 401 million, Africa accounts for only 2.7 percent of the world's GNP. Of the 33 countries that had an annual per capita GNP of $300[1] or less in 1978, 21 were in Africa. Of the 38 African countries not including South Africa for which figures are available, 27 were classified under the low-income category in 1978 by the World Bank, meaning they had an annual per capita income of $360 or less.

In 1980, the GNP per capita in sub-Saharan Africa excluding South Africa and Nigeria was $282, while it was $633 for East Asia excluding the planned economies, $1398 for Latin America excluding Cuba, and $1847 for the Middle East and North Africa excluding Afghanistan, Israel, and Turkey. The only region with a lower per capita GNP than Africa in 1980 was South Asia with a per capita GNP of $164 dollars.

Worse yet is the fact that not only is per capita income in Africa lower than in most other areas of the Third World, but growth rates have been significantly lower in Africa since the 1960s, and this situation is expected to persist during the 1980s. Low-income sub-Saharan countries had average annual percentage growth rates in their per capita GNPs of 1.7 in 1960-1970 and 0.2 in 1970-1980, and they are expected to experience growth rates of 0.1 in 1980-1985 and 1.1 in 1985-1990. The comparable figures for low-income countries in Asia are 1.8, 2.0, 2.4, and 2.7, respectively. As far as middle-income countries are concerned, the average annual percentage growth rates in per capita GNPs are as follows: sub-Saharan Africa, 2.3 in 1960-1970; 1.6 in 1970-1980; 1.7 in 1980-1985; and 1.4 in 1985-1990. For the Middle East and North Africa they are: 1.1 in 1960-1970; 3.8 in 1970-1980; 2.4 in 1980-1985; and 2.7 in 1985-1990. For Latin America and the Caribbean they are: 2.9 in 1960-1970; 3.2 in 1970-1980; 2.9 in 1980-1985; and 3.8 in 1985-1990. For East Asia and the Pacific they are: 4.9 in 1960-1970; 5.7 in 1970-1980; 4.8 in 1980-1985; and 5.2 in 1985-1990. Given the significantly lower projected per capita income growth rates in Africa compared with other areas of the Third World, Africa will fall even further behind by the year 1990.

A look at other features of development reveals an equally gloomy picture of the economic situation and trends in Africa. In the first section of this chapter, we presented figures showing that a greater percentage of the African people live in conditions of extreme poverty and are destitute compared to Asians and Latin Americans. In 1975, it is estimated that 60 million Africans, or 30 percent of the labor force, were unemployed or underemployed, and this figure is projected to jump to 70 million, or 39 percent of the labor force, by the year 2000 (Adedeji, 1979: 68-69).

Life Expectancy. Life expectancy in Africa was below 50 years in 1978, with the exception of Tanzania, Lesotho, Uganda, Kenya, Zimbabwe, and the North African countries. Similarly, the adult literacy rate in 1975 in sub-Saharan Africa was 25 percent or less except in Somalia, Tanzania, Lesotho,

Madagascar, Kenya, Ghana, Liberia, Zambia, and the People's Republic of the Congo. On both measures, Africa ranked far lower than other Third World regions. Given the projected growth trends we described earlier, it is not surprising that the World Bank concludes that absolute poverty is likely to increase during the present decade (1980: 10-11), nor should one be taken aback to read that "Africa is equally familiar with the sombre reality of death—massive infant mortality, violent deaths in all its forms. The prospects of impending disaster are not just a figment of the imagination" (Tevoedjre, 1980: 13).

Income Inequalities. With respect to income inequalities, World Bank figures published in 1971 show that of seventeen African countries including South Africa, the bottom 40 percent of the population had less than 12 percent of the national income while in six other countries, the bottom 40 percent of the population had between 12 percent and 17 percent of the national income. In only five countries—Chad, Benin, Ivory Coast, Niger, and Tanzania—did more than 17 percent of the national income go to the poorest 40 percent of the population. Data for twenty-three other Third World countries show that income inequalities in Africa were comparatively higher than in the rest of the Third World (see Fritsch, 1976: 105-106).

Manufacturing. With respect to the capacity of an economy to provide a wide range of the goods and services that its people consume and demand, this can be captured by the size and growth of the manufacturing sector since evidence does suggest that this is an important indicator of the stage a country has reached in the process of structural transformation. In 1960, Africa's share of world manufacturing value added was only 0.7 percent while the figure was 4.1 percent for Latin America, 1.9 percent for South and East Asia, and 0.3 percent for West Asia. In 1975, Africa's share was still only 0.8 percent while the figure for Latin America was 4.8 percent; for South and East Asia, 2.5 percent; and 0.5 percent for West Asia. Between 1960 and 1975, the growth rate in manufacturing output was 7.3 percent in South and East Asia, and a remarkable 9.2 percent in West Asia (United Nations Industrial Development Organization, 1979: 37-38). Once again, we find another case in which Africa started near the bottom of the ladder compared with other Third World countries and is also making comparatively slower progress than its Third World counterparts.

Autonomy. On the question of autonomy or dependence, Zartman (1976: 339-340) argues that at both the bilateral and multilateral levels, the "European presence as a base for influence in Africa is being diminished and diluted" and that "Africa is moving at a steady pace, without abrupt shocks, to gain complete control of its own affairs and to improve the terms of its relations with European states." But studies of relations between Europe and Africa, specifically in the multilateral context of the Lomé Convention, arrive at conclusions different from those of Zartman (Green, 1976; Galtung, 1976). Also, a study of the relationship between France and French-speaking West Africa demonstrates continued dependence on France (Tunteng, 1976). And another study concludes that "political independence in Africa has not brought economic independence or development to the continent; rather, it has intensified the inheritance of economic dependence" (Shaw and Grieve, 1978: 11).

What conclusion can one draw about the autonomy of African countries in the face of these findings? It seems to us that the question of the autonomy of African countries must be viewed in a much broader perspective than that of the relationship between African and EEC countries either at bilateral or multilateral levels. For, even though it still remains high, there is a clear tendency for a reduction in the degree of dependence of individual African countries on their former European colonial rulers. This is usually compensated for by increased ties with other Western European countries and with other capitalist countries (see Amaning, 1977; Nkobena, 1977). Thus while bilateral dependence decreases, dependence on the world capitalist system as a whole remains unaffected. The resulting situation is what Caporaso (1978) calls dependency as distinguished from dependence, with dependency entailing the incorporation of less developed and less homogeneous societies into the global division of labor. Seen in this light, there is little doubt that African dependency on the global system remains high.

Thus far we have been looking at development trends in Africa during the last two decades and comparing them with similar trends in Asia and Latin America. The conclusion we draw from these trends is that Africa remains one of the least developed regions of the world and that its performance during this period has been comparatively poorer than in the other developed regions. This comparison clearly hides variations in performance among African countries. We must now therefore look at comparative development trends among African countries themselves.

CROSS-AFRICAN TRENDS

Per Capita Income. Per capita GNP data for 38 African countries excluding South Africa show that in 1978, the range varied from a low of $120 (Ethiopia and Mali), to the extreme figure of $6,910 in the case of Libya. If Libya is excluded, Algeria, with a per capita income of $2382, had the highest per capita income in 1978, followed by Tunisia with a per capita income of $950. In 1978, 20 African countries had per capita incomes of less than $300, and five had per capita incomes between $300 and $340 (Angola, $300; Sudan, $320; Togo, $320; Kenya, $330; and Senegal, $340). While Egypt and all four North African states fell under the World Bank's middle-income category—countries with per capita incomes of $390 or above—

only eight countries in sub-Saharan Africa fell into this category in 1978 (Ghana, $390; Cameroon, $460; Liberia, $460; Zambia, $480; Zimbabwe, $480; People's Republic of the Congo, $540; Nigeria, $560; and Ivory Coast, $840).

There is clearly a significant variation among African countries as far as per capita GNP is concerned, even if the extreme cases of Algeria and Libya are excluded. Two-thirds of the remaining 36 African countries fall under the low-income group; the median income in 1978 was $270. In sum, one is forced to conclude that especially in sub-Saharan Africa, the picture is one of unrelieved poverty except for the eight middle-income countries identified in the preceding paragraph.

More important than the present per capita GNP as one measure of development is the growth rate in per capita income during the last two decades. While all 38 low-income countries had average annual growth rates of 1.6 percent in per capita GNP between 1970 and 1978, 5 of the 25 African countries in this group had negative growth rates (Somalia, -0.5; Chad, -1.0; Niger, -1.4; Madagascar, -0.3; and Senegal, -0.4) and only 7 had growth rates of 1.5 percent or above in national income during 1970-1978 (Ethiopia, 1.5; Burundi, 2.2; Malawi, 2.9; Tanzania, 2.7; Lesotho, 5.9; Togo, 5.0; and Kenya, 2.2). Of the eight middle-income countries in sub-Saharan Africa, Ghana had a negative growth rate of 0.5 percent and four others had growth rates of 2.0 percent or above (Cameroon, 2.9; Liberia, 2.0; Nigeria, 3.6; Ivory Coast, 2.5). However, for Egypt and the North African states, the growth rates in per capita income in percentages were 3.3 for Egypt, 2.5 for Morocco, 4.5 for Tunisia, 2.3 for Algeria, and 9.7 for Libya, while the growth rate for all middle-income countries was 3.7. These growth rates must be compared with the percentage growth rates achieved by the following countries during the same period: Republic of Korea, 6.9; Taiwan, 6.6; Brazil, 4.9; Yugoslavia, 5.4; Hong Kong, 6.5; and Singapore, 7.4.

It is clear from the above that while significant differences exist among African countries, only tiny countries such as Lesotho (population and per capita income in 1978 of 1.3 million and $280, respectively) and Togo (1978 population and per capita income of 2.4 million and $320, respectively) have achieved anything close to the very high growth rates achieved by some other Third World countries if Libya and Nigeria are excluded. The other low-income countries that experienced growth rates of 1.5 percent or more and the middle-income countries that experienced growth rates of 2.0 percent or higher, which were mentioned in the above paragraph, only look better because of the merger growth rates that have prevailed on the continent since 1960.

Birth and Literacy Rates. Variations in the level of poverty can be measured in part by changes in life expectancy at birth and increases in adult literacy rates. Between 1960 and 1978, the average life expectancy in low-income countries increased by eight years from forty-two to fifty years. In five low-income African countries, life expectancy during this period increased by eight years while it increased by nine years in ten other countries. In two other countries, the increase was seven years, and in two other cases (Zaire and Kenya) it was six years. In six other countries, life expectancy at birth increased by five years or less (Ethiopia, 3; Mali, 5; Upper Volta, 5; Niger, 5; Mauritania, 5; and Senegal, 5). Thus except for Ethiopia and Kenya, all the other low-income African countries with growth rates in per capita income of 1.5 percent or more had increases in life expectancy at or above the average increase for low-income countries. All thirteen middle-income African countries had increases in life expectancy of eight or nine years, while the average for all low-income groups was seven years. Of the four middle-income sub-Saharan African countries with per capita income growth rates of 2.0 percent or more during 1960-1978, in all but Liberia, life expectancy increased by 9 years.

Still, it must be recalled that as of 1978, life expectancy in relation to income per person was below the worldwide norm in twenty-five sub-Saharan countries and was above the norm in only six countries—Kenya, Tanzania, Lesotho, Rwanda, Mozambique, and Burundi (World Bank, 1980: 87). Nor should it be forgotten that life expectancy is lowest in Africa. Thus while a majority of African countries, especially the middle-income ones, are keeping up with or making slightly greater progress than other countries in their income group, none are making remarkable progress.

Data on changes in adult literacy rates between 1960 and 1975 point to Somalia and Tanzania as the outstanding cases of success among a group of fourteen low-income African countries. In the case of Somalia, the adult literacy rate jumped from 2 percent in 1960 to 60 percent in 1975, while for Tanzania the figures were 10 percent and 66 percent, respectively. The country with the next highest increase was Kenya with a jump from 20 to 40 percent. Among four middle-income sub-Saharan African countries, the People's Republic of the Congo had the highest increase (from 16 percent to 50 percent) followed by Liberia with an increase from 9 percent to 30 percent. Ivory Coast also performed relatively well with an increase from 5 percent to 20 percent. In 1975, only Somalia, Tanzania, Lesotho, and Kenya had adult literacy rates above the average figure for low-income countries (33 percent). And not even Tunisia, which had the highest adult literacy rate in middle-income Africa in 1975 (55 percent), came close to the average for middle-income countries which was 71 percent.

The achievements of many African countries in the area of reducing poverty should not be minimized. But given the high degree of poverty that prevails in the continent, the achievements of the 1960s and 1970s must be judged as insufficient in the case of most African countries. In the bleak landscape, Somalia, Tanzania, Lesotho, and Kenya among low-income countries, and the People's Republic of the Condo, Liberia, and the Ivory Coast among middle-income sub-Saharan African countries stand out as those that have made relatively significant progress in reducing absolute poverty.

Inequality. Figures on the evolution of inequality in Africa are almost impossible to come by. What little data there is show that during the 1967-1970 period, six African countries were classified as having high inequality meaning that the lowest 40 percent of the population had less than 12 percent of the national income. They were Kenya, 10 percent; Sierra Leone, 9.6 percent; Ivory Coast, 10.8 percent; Zimbabwe, 8.2 percent; Tunisia, 11.4 percent; and Gabon, 8.8 percent. Inequality was moderate in Tanzania, the lowest 40 percent of the population having 13 percent of the national income in 1967. And Uganda was the only African country with a low inequality rating during the late 1960s, with the lowest 40 percent of its population having 17 percent of the national income (Ahluwalia, 1974: 8).

Compared with these figures, the lowest 40 percent of the population in India had 17.2 percent of the national income in 1964-1965; 19.2 percent in Sri Lanka in 1969-1970; 16.9 percent in the Republic of Korea in 1976; 21.9 percent in Taiwan in 1971; 14.1 percent in Argentina in 1970; and 18.4 percent in Yugoslavia in 1973. The only other Third World countries with high inequality ratings during the same period were Honduras, 7.3 percent; Peru, 7.0 percent; the Philippines, 11.9 percent; Malaysia, 10.6 percent; Mexico, 9.9 percent; Brazil, 7.4 percent; and Venezuela, 10.3 percent. Out of eighteen industrialized market economies, none was ranked in the high inequality category and only Italy (16.6 percent), France (14.1 percent), Canada (16.8 percent), the Federal Republic of Germany (16.8 percent), and the United States (15.2 percent) fell under the moderate inequality category (World Bank, 1980: 156-157).

It would certainly be better to have more data on the trends in inequality in more African countries, especially during the 1970s. We can nonetheless conclude that few African countries had made much progress in reducing inequality by the late 1960s compared with the Third World countries cited above with impressive records in this domain or with developed market economies. Uganda and Tanzania stand out in this respect, and Tunisia, Ivory Coast, and perhaps Kenya are borderline cases.

Manufacturing. We will again look at the growth in the manufacturing sector to determine the increase in the capacity of African states to produce a wide range of goods and services. Figures exist for only eight African countries during the 1960-1970 period. They show that all low- and middle-income African countries experienced average annual growth rates higher than the average for the group in which they belonged, except for Senegal, which had an average annual growth rate of 6.2 percent while the average for all low-income countries was 6.6 percent. Impressive gains were registered by Mauritania (18.0 percent), Somalia (14.3 percent), and Ivory Coast (11.6 percent). However, during the 1970-1978 period, the manufacturing sector grew by an average annual rate of only 2.9 percent in Mauritania and 7.5 percent in Ivory Coast (data unavailable for Somalia).

During the 1970-1978 period, figures for seventeen low-income countries show that eight of them had average annual growth rates in manufacturing above the group average of 4.2 percent. The highest growth rate was recorded by Kenya with 11.7 percent, followed by Guinea with 9.4 percent, Lesotho with 8.7 percent, and Malawi with 6.7 percent. Three out of seven middle-income African countries had growth rates greater than the average for their group, with Nigeria registering an average annual growth rate in manufacturing of 13.4 percent; Liberia, 8.7 percent; and Ivory Coast, 7.5 percent.

Six African countries had negative average annual growth rates in manufacturing during the 1970-1978 period. They were Angola, −12.8 percent; Mozambique, −6.1 percent; Ghana, −6.0 percent; Uganda, −5.0 percent, Zaire, −0.6 percent; and Madagascar, −0.4 percent. There were five other countries with minimal growth rates. Ethiopia, 1.3 percent; Upper Volta, 1.6 percent; Mauritania, 2.9 percent; Zambia, 0.6 percent; and Congo, 2.3 percent.

If we focus on the more recent figures for the 1970-1978 period, Guinea, Lesotho, Kenya, Liberia, Nigeria, and Ivory Coast are the sub-Saharan African countries that registered the most impressive gains. However, during the same period, the average annual growth rate in manufacturing was 12.3 percent in Malaysia, 18.3 percent in the Republic of Korea, 13.2 percent in Taiwan, and 9.2 percent in Singapore. Thus, as impressive as the performance of these African countries in the African context might be, they dim when compared with the remarkable performance of the most successful newly industrializing countries in Asia.

Autonomy. Dependency or autonomy of an economy can be measured by the degree of commodity concentration (the three leading commodity exports as a percentage of total exports) and by the degree of partner concentration (the percentage of exports going to the three most important trading partners). In 1961, commodity concentration ranged from a high of 96 percent in the case of Zaire to a low of 37 percent in the case of Nigeria. By 1975 however, the range was from 97 percent for Nigeria to 33 percent for Kenya. In 1961, only Nigeria, Togo, Cameroon, Botswana, Kenya, Tanzania, and Madagascar had commodity concentrations of less than 60 percent, and in 1975, countries with commodity concentrations of less than 60 percent were Ivory Coast, Mali, Niger, Cameroon, Kenya, Madagascar, and Tanzania. The Ivory Coast in particular made remarkable strides in this area, reducing its commodity concentration from 82 percent in 1961 to 57 percent in 1975 (Langdon and Mytelka, 1979: 154-158).

Ten African countries reduced the percentage of their exports going to their three most important trading partners by 20 percentage points or more between 1961 and 1975. These countries and the reductions in their partner concentration are Zambia, 21 percent; Ghana, 28 percent; Ivory Coast, 26 percent; Liberia, 25 percent; Senegal, 24 percent; Upper Volta, 45 percent; Chad, 55 percent; Gabon, 34 percent; Zaire, 24 percent; and Ethiopia, 22 percent (Langdon and Mytelka, 1979: 154-158).

The above measures of dependence are inadequate and incomplete. Ideally one must also look at the concentration in the flow of aid and investments. They suggest nonetheless that some though by no means a majority of African countries have been making some progress in reducing some aspects of their dependence.

SUMMARY

We can now summarize our findings with respect to development trends in Africa during the 1960s and 1970s. One not very surprising discovery is that important variations exist among African countries, some doing rather poorly and others doing remarkably well within the African context. However, compared to the most successful developing countries in Asia such as Taiwan, Hong Kong, Singapore, Malaysia, and the Republic of Korea, the most successful African country comes out second best on virtually all of our measures of development. Finally, only the Ivory Coast ranked high in all measures of development. Kenya ranks high in all except in the case of increases in the life expectancy rates, Liberia ranks high in all but degree of income inequality, and Tanzania ranks high in all but average annual rate of growth in manufacturing. The diversity among countries is immediately striking.

In the rest of this chapter, we will seek to explain the above findings. To repeat, we will try to explain why African countries in general, even the most successful African countries, did not perform as well as other Third World countries, especially the most successful Asian countries. Next, we will focus on why some African countries have done better than others. Here, we will focus especially on Kenya and Ivory Coast since these are generally regarded as the most successful cases in Africa.

External Factors and African Development

Marxists and dependency theorists explain the perpetuation of underdevelopment in Third World countries in general by reference to imperialism and the domination of Third World countries by the industrialized capitalist countries (see Brown, 1974; Amin, 1972). A recent study of Africa asserts that "the structural change and capital accumulation taking place in [Africa's] interrelationship with these strong external links [with the capitalist world economy] have led and are leading to increasing segmentation and inequality in many African countries, to growing employment problems, and to ongoing poverty for most Africans" (Langdon and Mytelka, 1979: 127). The main culprit in the domination and exploitation of Third World countries according to this thesis is the multinational corporation.

A counter thesis to the above argues that imperialism brought many progressive changes to Third World countries (Semmel, 1968) and that multinational corporations bring in modern skills, technologies, capital, revenues to governments, and access to world markets for domestic products (Vernon, 1971). In support of this view, a study of Africa during the mid-1960s concludes that "despite every effort in working with these data, the general conclusion reached in this *exploratory* study is that the proposition that economic dependence is associated with underdevelopment, and hence with poor economic performance, is simply not supported by the evidence" (McGowan, 1976: 35, emphasis in original).

The debate between the above two contending positions has been intense, and strong arguments have been presented on both sides even though, in our view, the data base has been inadequate. In all likelihood, the debate is also likely to be persistent and inconclusive. The problem is not only one of improving the data base; it is also one of determining who gains and who loses, who gains more and who gains less and why, and how important external factors of domination and exploitation are compared with internal factors in the economic achievements of Third World countries. Not only are such questions difficult to answer, but the political implications of the answers presented are very likely to color the responses with a certain degree of subjectivity.

It is not necessary, for our purposes, for us to enter into the above debate. For what it is worth, let us state that we find the domination/exploitation explanation more persuasive than its opposite. Nevertheless, we agree with critics of this thesis that it tends to be too coarse. It does not address itself to the question of the uneven performance of Third World countries which the preceding section of this chapter shows exists among African countries and between Africa and other Third World regions. Whatever the degree of truth or falsity in the domination/exploitation thesis, these variations need to be explained. And it is not sufficiently convincing to suggest that the differences are more apparent than real.

No doubt, variations among Third World countries are due in part to internal factors such as resource endowment and political effectiveness. But this is certainly not the whole story. Resource rich-countries are not necessarily those with more impressive development records. Further, many of the resources usually pointed to, for example, skilled labor, entrepreneurial ability, and even political effectiveness, are themselves features of development. Treating them as cases of development only makes the argument circular and tautological.

While we certainly and most emphatically do not hold that internal factors have no bearing on the variations in performance among Third World countries, we believe that external factors do also in part explain this variation. In what follows, we will suggest some of the external factors that might explain the variations between African and other Third World countries and among African countries themselves. We will limit ourselves to the external historical and political factors since external economic factors are more widely known and analyzed.

A first fact to note is that African countries entered the international scene as independent political actors and launched their development efforts at a time when the field was already crowded. Latin American countries achieved independence between 1808 and 1825, while in Asia independence was a phenomenon of the immediate post-World War II period. Libya, Morocco, Sudan, and Tunisia attained independence between 1951 and 1956, while the vast majority of African countries had to wait until the 1960s to achieve their independence.

All these countries, starting with those in Latin America in the nineteenth century, saw independence not only as an end in itself, but also as an opportunity for the achievement of prosperity and economic development. Given what they perceived as centuries of exploitation and poverty, they made economic development a key goal. Most if not all of them counted on external help to further their development. Already at the Bretton Woods and the San Francisco conferences, the Latin American and the few Asian states that were represented insisted that the World Bank be concerned not only with the reconstruction of Europe, but also with the development of the Third World and that the United Nations should give more emphasis to problems of development. Within the United Nations itself, Third World countries were urging even before 1960 the creation of a United Nations Capital Development Fund that would make capital investments in their respective countries.

Thus when African countries arrived on the scene in the 1960s, they found many other actors already present and demanding the resources they were also demanding. In 1961, the underdeveloped countries were estimated to have a population of 1509 million people. Nearly 18 percent of these people (270 million) were in Africa excluding South Africa. Even without the entry of over a quarter billion Africans into the race for access to scarce international development resources, it is doubtful that the international system had the resources or political will to satisfy the demands of those who were on the scene first. The significant increase in the number of those seeking help that resulted from Africa's entry onto the scene meant that the available resources had to be spread more thinly. True, the resources made available for development did increase (for evidence of this in the United Nations, see Kay, 1970: 101). But the continued push by Third World countries for more international development assistance shows that they did not consider this increase to be enough.

Not only did African countries enter a crowded and highly competitive field comparatively later than others, but precisely because of this in part, they were at a comparative disadvantage. Latin American countries had over a century and Asian countries around a decade and a half headstart in the development competition compared with African countries. Thus, around 1960, they were generally more developed than African countries and so had a competitive edge. Figures provided by the U.S. Agency for International Development (1963) show that in 1961, for example, Latin America had a per capita GNP of $265; the Near East, $205; and Africa excluding South Africa, only $100. The Far East excluding Japan had a per capita GNP of $95 and South Asia was at the bottom with a per capita GNP of $80. For adult literacy, however, the same source shows that the rate was 65 percent in the Far East excluding Japan, 55 percent in Latin America, 30 percent for the Near East, 25 percent in South Asia, and only 15 percent for Africa excluding South Africa.

One result of the earlier entry and comparative advantage in level of development of other Third World areas compared with Africa is that they have been more successful in attracting external resources for development. One example of this is the flow of foreign direct investments. In 1967, ten developing countries had 36.5 percent of the total stock of foreign direct investments in developing countries. They were Brazil, Mexico, India, Malaysia, Argentina, Singapore, Peru, Hong Kong, the Philippines, and Trinidad and Tobago. Venezuela alone had 10.6 percent of these investments while all OPEC countries had 27.7 percent out of which Nigeria had 3.3 percent. The tax havens of the Bahamas, Barbados, Bermuda, Cayman Islands, Antilles, and Panama accounted for another 7.0 percent of these investments. The remainder of the developing countries had to share among themselves the remaining 28.8 percent. The clear tendency for multinational corporations to invest in the wealthier countries is revealed by the fact that in 1967, 43.4 percent of their investments went to countries with per capita incomes of $1000 or more; 23 percent to countries with per capita incomes of between $500 and $999; 16.4 percent to countries with per capita incomes of between $200 and $499; and only 16.8 percent to countries with per capita incomes of less than $200 (United Nations, 1978: 254). And since most

African countries fell under the last category in 1967, they got very little of the available direct foreign investments.

To compound the above situation, the United Nations notes that "the countries that most attract the transnational corporations are also those that have borrowed most on the international capital markets. Just two countries—Brazil and Mexico—together accounted for almost one-third of all the developing countries borrowing in 1976" (United Nations, 1978: 58). In 1975, all developing countries had private borrowings amounting to $88,462 million. But African countries had borrowings of only $9088 million or 10.26 percent of the total. Brazil, Mexico, the Republic of Korea, Argentina, Peru, and the Philippines had 44.22 percent of this total, while the share of the Middle East was 10.34 percent (United Nations, 1978: 255). Clearly, given its comparatively greater needs, Africa has not been getting a fair share of private loans to developing countries.

Finally, Africa is also comparatively disadvantaged with respect to the distribution of official development assistance. In 1969, the members of the Development Assistance Committee of the Organization for European Cooperation and Development and multilateral aid agencies gave net concessional assistance that amounted to $6452.7 million globally. Out of this amount, Asia received $3047.1 million or 47.2 percent; Africa, $1582.9 million or 24.5 percent; and Latin America, $1094.1 million or approximately 17.0 percent (Organization For Economic Cooperation and Development, 1977: 2-3).

The population of Africa around 1969 was estimated to be 360 million, while that of Latin America was 260 million and that of Asia excluding China 640 million. Thus the above aid distribution seems to follow roughly the population distribution in these three regions. However, when the comparatively greater degree of absolute poverty in Africa is taken into account, coupled with the fact that Africa receives significantly less private foreign direct investments and foreign private loans, the distribution of official development assistance has not been comparatively favorable to Africa.

Thus far, we have explained the comparatively poor performance of African States in relation to Asian and Latin American countries on the grounds that African countries arrived later in a crowded field and that the comparatively competitive edge of Latin American and Asian countries meant that they received substantially more private foreign direct investments and private loans while Africa received no compensation in the area of official foreign assistance. But there is more to it than this. The greater success of Asian and Latin American countries in attracting foreign resources is not only due to their relatively higher degree of development, but also to political considerations.

The fact is that on the world diplomatic and strategic scene, Asia and

Latin America have been for more important than Africa. The United States is a Pacific power and one of the most important economic and political partners of the United States, Japan, is to be found in Asia. In addition, until recently China, which is in Asia, was one of the United States' arch-enemies. The two major wars the United States has been engaged in since World War II, the Korean and Vietnam wars, have both been in Asia. And the second most populous country and the largest democracy in the world is India, which is also in Asia. Asia has, therefore, been of major strategic and political importance to the United States, which is the most powerful member of the western alliance.

Latin America has also been of prime importance to the United States. After all, Latin America is in the backyard of the United States and the Castro revolution and the Cuban missile crisis of 1962 underlined the strategic threat of the United States of the USSR gaining a foothold in this area. Thus the U.S. military interventions in Latin America in the 1960s and the Alliance for Progress.

As far as Africa is concerned, it remained peripheral to the main focus of U.S. interests and was not regarded as an area offering great opportunities. True, votes had to be counted in the UN General Assembly and left-wing tendencies in Africa were not particularly welcome developments. But beyond a narrow circle of specialists and interested people, there was not much interest in Africa even among the elite in the United States (Foltz, 1979). France was still burdened with the Algerian war in the early sixties and Britain was still engaged in the retreat from empire. And the Federal Republic of Germany had not yet started showing much interest in Africa. In any event, these countries were no substitute for the United States in terms of the potential resources they could make available for development.

It is plausible to suggest that the comparatively greater flow of resources to Asia and Latin America were the result of the greater importance of these countries to the United States. True, some of these resources came from the private sector. But the government clearly has the ability to influence in part the perceptions and behavior of private investors and bank officials. Nor are these individuals insensitive to the importance of Asia and Latin America to the political and therefore corporate interests of the United States, thereby influencing them to do what they could to facilitate the development and thus the stability and membership in the western camp of these countries. It is our guess that both factors were at work. The result was a greater flow of resources to Asia and Latin America.

In sum then, our explanation of the comparatively better performance of Asian and Latin American countries is that they had the advantage over African countries of having arrived at the scene earlier and with comparatively higher levels of development. They were also more important strategically and politically for the United States, the leader of the western alliance.

As a result, they have been able to attract greater resources to fuel their development. It now remains for us to explain the differences in the performances of African countries.

As noted earlier, the two African countries whose relatively better economic performances we will try to explain are Kenya and the Ivory Coast. Differences in the endowment in natural resources might conceivably play a role, although these two countries are not endowed with much in the form of mineral resources. Differences with respect to the colonial legacy, especially in the case of Kenya, must also be taken into account, but this is not especially so in the case of the Ivory Coast. The colonial legacies of countries such as Senegal, Uganda, and Ghana were not significantly different from those of Kenya and the Ivory Coast. It is our view that external political factors comparable to those which explain variations in performance between African and other Third World countries also help to explain the comparatively better performance of these two countries.

In Africa, Kenya and the Ivory Coast enjoyed especially privileged positions as far as the West was concerned. Kenya had gone through a bitter racial and colonial war in the 1950s, but went through a peaceful decolonization process in the early 1960s which sharply limited the feared exodus of the whites. The Kenyatta government pursued moderate policies and was strikingly pro-West and pro-free-enterprise. It was important for the West to ensure the success of the Kenyan model. Such a success would preserve the already significant western interests in Kenya, prove to countries such as the then Rhodesia where racial tensions were significantly greater that multiracialism does work and that whites need not fear majority rule, and persuade other African countries that a pro-western and a pro-capitalist orientation was more likely to result in greater economic progress.

The Ivory Coast enjoyed a similar status in French West and Central Africa. After an initial phase of radicalism and communist leaning, Houphouet-Boigny was by the late 1940s a staunch supporter of maintaining Franco-African ties. He strongly supported the break-up of the Federation of French West Africa which France pushed in the mid-1950s and opposed the creation of political federations by independent French West African states. Houphouet-Boigny actively collaborated with France in pressuring Upper Volta and Niger not to join the Mali Federation with Senegal and the then French Sudan. Further, in the 1958 referendum on independence or continued membership in the French Community, Houphouet-Boigny used his considerable influence to ensure that the other colonies stayed in the French Community. In sum, Houphouet-Boigny actively supported and promoted the French policy of dampening African nationalism and African unity.

Like Kenya, the Ivory Coast pursued a pro-capitalist and a pro-western policy with a striking bias toward France. Houphouet-Boigny was one of the main architects in the creation of the Union Africaine et Malgache which later became the Organization Commune Africaine et Malgache. These organizations served essentially to maintain close ties among French-speaking African states and to keep them within the French orbit. Finally, Houphouet-Boigny led the fight against leaders such as Nkrumah who were pushing for African countries to adopt socialism and radical pan-Africanism. In all these ways, Houphouet-Boigny demonstrated that he was an important and faithful ally of France. This allegiance had to be rewarded in order to promote pro-capitalist and pro-French tendencies in French-speaking Africa.

Because of the political considerations mentioned above, Kenya and the Ivory Coast had to be rewarded with a greater flow of resources. Thus between 1969 and 1971, Kenya received a total of $71.25 million in aid from bilateral and multilateral sources while the aid received by the Ivory Coast was $55.49 million. On the other hand, during these years, Tanzania, with a larger population and a lower per capita income, received only $53.16 million and Ghana, with about twice the population as the Ivory Coast but with more or less the same per capita income, got $61.26 million. Per capita aid was thus $6.54 million for Kenya, $4.23 million for Tanzania, $11.23 million for the Ivory Coast, and $7.34 million for Ghana (OECD, 1972: 284).

Kenya and the Ivory Coast benefited from an additional and related factor. Because of their ability to attract external resources in part, and also because of the external encouragement and support for the retention of regional economic groupings such as the East African Community and the West African Economic Community, these countries came to dominate the exports within the regional groupings to which they belonged and emerged as what is known as "sub-imperialist" states (Shaw and Grieve, 1978). Kenya, for example, accounted for 63.6 percent of the intraregional exports in 1964, 61.1 percent in 1967, and 61.8 percent in 1970 (East African Community, 1973). The Ivory Coast also controls a substantial share of regional exports within the West African Economic Community (see Research Center for Cooperation with Developing Countries, 1978) and in 1974, 22 percent of Ivorian experts went to these countries. In 1970, 1973, and 1975, the Ivory Coast had a healthy balance of trade surplus with these countries (World Bank, 1978: 101-102). The serious economic difficulties Kenya has been experiencing since the recent break-up of the East African Community, though certainly due to other factors, merely serve to underscore the importance of access to regional markets for countries like Kenya and the Ivory Coast.

In sum then, our contention is that because of political considerations, Kenya and the Ivory Coast enjoyed comparatively more favorable treatment from external actors. They also gained from their ability to play leading roles in the regional groupings to which they belonged. These two factors partly account for their comparatively better economic performances.

Conclusion

At this stage, we must first address an apparent contradiction in our reasoning. Earlier, we stated our inclination to accept the validity of the domination/exploitation explanation of underdevelopment. Yet our explanation of variations in performances between African and other Third World countries and among African countries holds that the greater the inflow of external resources, the better the economic performance. And yet the inflow of resources is one main element in the domination/exploitation syndrome.

Our response to this apparent contradiction is to stress that we have not analyzed the *distribution of benefits* between the donors and recipients of resources. And this is a key element in the domination/exploitation thesis. Second, it should be recalled that on our measures of the reduction of poverty, these countries did not score better than others. Kenya, for example, was not among those who registered significant gains in the increase in adult life expectancy, and many other countries made more significant progress than Kenya or the Ivory Coast in increasing adult literacy. Figures on the reduction in inequality are too limited for meaningful comparison. Finally, it may be that the growth in the manufacturing sector is not a good measure of the ability of an economy to meet the consumption demands of its people and tells us more about growth than development.

In sum, while these two countries did well with respect to growth, it is not that certain that they did well with respect to reducing poverty, eliminating inequality, and becoming more autonomous. In any event, our purpose in this chapter has not been to try to prove or disprove the domination/exploitation thesis. We have been concerned only with noting and explaining variations in economic performance between African and other Third World countries and among African countries themselves. The essence of our explanation is that a high level of political importance for external actors leads to a greater inflow of economic resources and to greater economic growth if not to development. Access to regional export markets also helps.

Our findings suggest that with the recent increase in U.S. and western interest in halting Soviet penetration of Africa and in protecting western access to African resources, more external resources are likely to flow to Africa. This though is likely to benefit mostly the mineral-rich countries like Zimbabwe, Zaire, and Nigeria. For the fact is, not many African countries are rich in minerals. Whether the political tensions that will result from this are an acceptable price to pay remains to be seen. In any event, it is extremely unlikely that Africa will relace Asia and Latin America in terms of political importance to the United States.

A second implication of our study is that the creation of a New International Economic Order is not likely to benefit Africa as much as the newly industrializing nations of Asia and Latin America because of the comparative advantage these regions enjoy compared with Africa. While working for changes in the present international order, African countries must make sure that their Third World allies accept the principle of special concessions for African countries. Otherwise, the creation of a New International Economic Order will raise unfounded hopes which will most likely be disappointed.

NOTE

1. All per capita income and GNP figures in U.S. dollars unless otherwise noted.

REFERENCES

ADEDEJI, A. C. (1979) "Perspectives of development and economic growth in Africa up to the year 2000," pp. 53-88 in Organisation of African Unity, What Kind of Africa by the Year 2000? Addis Ababa: Organisation of African Unity.

AHLUWALIA, M. S. (1974) "Income inequality: some dimensions of the problem," pp. 3-37 in H. Chenery, M. S. Ahluwalia, C. L. G. Bell, J. H. Duloy, and R. Jolly (eds.) Redistribution With Growth. New York: Oxford University Press.

AHLUWALIA, M. S. and H. CHERNEY (1974) "The economic framework," pp. 38-51 in H. Cherney (ed.) Redistribution With Growth. New York: Oxford University Press.

AMANING, K. O. (1977) "Ghana's relations with Great Britain, 1957 to 1977: a study of the evolution of dependent ties." Master's thesis, International Relations Institute of Cameroon, Yaounde.

Amin, S. (1976) Unequal Development. New York: Monthly Review Press.

BARNET, R. J. and R. E. Miller (1974) Global Reach: The Power of the Multinational Corporations. New York: Simon & Schuster.

BROWN, M. B. (1974) The Economics of Imperialism. London: Cox & Wyman.

CAPORASO, J. A. (1978) "Dependence, dependency, and power in the global system: a structural and behavioral analysis." International Organization 32 (Winter): 13-43.

DOO KINGUE, M. (1979) "What kind of development does Africa need," pp. 89-109 in Organisation of African Unity, What Kind of Africa by the Year 2000? Addis Ababa: Organisation of African Unity.

East African Community (1973) Review of Economic Integration Activities Within the East African Community. Arusha, Tanzania: East African Community.

FOLTZ, W. (1979) Elite Opinion on United States Policy Toward Africa. New York: Council on Foreign Relations.

FRITSCH, B. (1976) Growth Limitation and Political Power. Cambridge, MA: Ballinger.

GALTUNG, J. (1976) "The Lomé Convention and neo-capitalism." Africa Review 6, 1: 33-42.

GREEN, R. H. (1976) "The Lomé Convention: updated dependence or departure toward collective self-reliance?" African Review 6, 1: 43-54.

HAQ, M. U. (1976) The Poverty Curtain. New York: Columbia University Press.

JALLOH, A. A. (1981) "The state in Africa: creating the New International Economic Order and Development strategies." Presented at the University of Addis Ababa/United Nations University Symposium on African Perspectives on the New International Economic Order, Addis Ababa, May 3.

KAY, D. A. (1970) The New Nations in The United Nations, 1960-67. New York: Columbia University Press.

KINDLEBERGER, C. P. (1965) Economic Development. New York: McGraw-Hill.

LANGDON, S. and L. K. MYTELKA (1979) "Africa in the changing world economy," pp. 132-211 in C. Legum, I. W. Zartman, S. Langdon, and L. Mytelka (eds.) Africa in the 1980's: A Continent in Crisis. New York: McGraw-Hill.

LEWIS, W. A. (1955) The Theory of Economic Growth. Homewood, IL: Irwin.

NKOBE, B. F. (1977) "Cameroun-EEC relations: a comparative study of the liberal and dependency theories of international economic relations." Masters thesis, International Relations Institute of Cameroon, Yaounde.

Organization of African Unity [OAU] (1981) Lagos Plan of Action for the Economic Development of Africa: 1980-2000. Geneva: International Institute for Labour Studies.

Organization for Economic Cooperation and Development (1977) Geographical Distribution of Financial Flows to Developing Countries. Paris: Organization for Economic Cooperation and Development.

Organisation de Coopération et de Développement Economique (1972) Coopération Pour le Développement: Efforts et Politiques Poursuivis Par les Membres du Comité d'Aide au Développement. Paris: Organisation de Coopération et de Développement Économique.

Research Center for Co-operation With Developing Countries (1978) Trade Among Developing Countries, 1964-1976: A Statistical Handbook. Ljubljanja: Research Center for Co-operation with Developing Countries.

SEMMEL, B. (1968) Imperialism and Social Reform: English Social-Imperial Thought 1895-1914. New York: Anchor.

SHAW, T. M. and M. J. GRIEVE (1978) "Africa's future in the global environment." Journal of Modern African Studies 16 (March): 1-32.

TEVOEDJRE (1979) "Final report of the symposium on the future development prospects of Africa towards the year 2000," pp. 9-31 in Organisation of African Unity. What Kind of Africa by the Year 2000? Addis Ababa: Organisation of African Unity.

THOMAS, C. Y. (1974) Dependence and Transformation: The Economic of the Transition to Socialism. New York: Monthly Review Press.

TUNTENG, P. K. (1976) "External influences and subimperialism in francophone West Africa," pp. 212-231 in P. C. W. Gutrind and I. Wallerstein (eds.) The Political Economy of Contemporary Africa. Beverly Hills, CA: Sage.

United Nations (1978) Transnational Corporation in World Development: A Reexamination. New York: United Nations.

United Nations Industrial Development Organization (1979) World Industry Since 1960: Progress and Prospects. New York: United Nations.

United States Agency for International Development (1963) Selected Economic Data for the Less Developed Countries. Washington DC: Government Printing Office.

VERNON, R. (1971) Sovereignty at Bay: The Multinational Spread of U.S. Enterprises. Harmondsworth: Penguin Books.

World Bank (1978) Ivory Coast: The Challenge of Success. Washington, DC: World Bank.

World Bank (1980) World Development Report. Washington, DC: World Bank.

ZARTMAN, I. W. (1976) "Europe and Africa: decolonization or dependency?" Foreign Affairs 54, 2: 325-343.

PART V

Changes in International Institutions and Regimes

Changes in the global political economy imply changes in the international institutions and regimes that constitute the international economic order as well as changes within the political economies of the states that constitute the global system. Indeed, the concept of a New International Economic Order has largely been defined in terms of changes at this level. This part of the book deals with the changes that have been made during the latter half of the 1970s in international institutions and regimes and with the prospects for further changes.

The international economic order is the superstructure of the global political system. In the relations among states the debate about change in the global political economy has largely been expressed in terms of changes in international institutions and regimes even though a New International Economic Order could only be achieved as a consequence of changes within the political economies of states, and the ultimate goal of NIEO would be to bring about changes that would improve the lives of individuals.

The relationship between the political economies of states and the international economic order is complex. It merits a brief comment before we turn to the chapters that constitute this part of the book. Because the international economic order structures economic relationships among states, it creates both opportunities and constraints for states. The international economic order can facilitate or hinder international trade, and it can do more to promote certain types of trade, or trade among certain states, rather than others. By affecting possibilities for international trade, international institutions and regimes inescapably affect the domestic political economies of states. In the contemporary period no state can do without international trade. For only a few large states such as the People's Republic of China, the Soviet Union, and the United States, is international trade a relatively minor issue; for other states it is quite important and generally, the smaller the state, the more important trade is for it. In shaping their domestic political economies, states must therefore in varying degrees take into account the possibilities open to them for international trade. International institutions and regimes can also pursue redistributive policies through transfer payments of one type or another from some states to others.

In the contemporary global system, states have sovereignty, and international institutions and regimes must be accepted voluntarily by the participating states. For this reason, the international economic order reflects what states, and especially the most powerful and important among them, will accept. Given their voluntary character, international institutions and regimes cannot order states to accept and implement changes. What institutions and regimes can do is to alter the understanding of issues so that governments of states become willing to envisage and adopt changes. For this to occur the governments of states must become convinced that there is a humanitarian duty for them to embrace the proposed changes or—and this is more likely to be effective—that it is in their states' self-interest, at least in the long run.

Given the nature of the interaction between the political economies of states and the international economic order, it should not be surprising that changes in the international institutions and regimes that constitute the order generally occur relatively slowly. This must be kept in mind in evaluating what has been achieved in the latter half of the 1970s.

Chapter 9 by Ural Ayberk analyzes the progress that has been made toward achieving the several elements of the Program of Action on the Establishment of a New International Economic Order that was adopted at the Sixth Special Session of the UN General Assembly in 1974. Much of the program of action involved changes in international regimes, and Dr. Ayberk focuses on these proposed changes. The balance sheet that he develops presents a picture of mixed accomplishments; more progress has been made in some areas such as trade in commodities and debt relief than in others such as transport. He then examines the reasons for this mixed record of accomplishments.

In the final chapter, John P. Renninger assesses the progress that has been made in restructuring international institutions. Again, the results have been mixed. Dr. Renninger shows how different groups of states have different interests and perspectives with respect to restructuring international institutions. It is only when areas of common or overlapping interest can be found that progress can be made. Dr. Renninger also shows how the bureaucracies of international institutions have become an independent force in the restructuring exercise.

Both chapters show that immediate short-term interests are an important but not the only factor responsible for the disagreements among groups of states concerning the creation of a New International Economic Order. The industrialized states, both western and socialist, can naturally be expected to resist the adoption of programs that would result in their transferring significant sums of money to less developed countries. The dispute about the NIEO, however, also has philosophical elements. The changes favored by the Group of 77 involve much greater governmental and intergovernmental intervention in the global political economy than several major western states consider desirable. Thus the issues in the debate about the evolution of the international economic order, how much redistribution, and how much governmental intervention in market forces there should be, are not generically dissimilar from those in the debates about the evolution of domestic economic order, though the context and details are certainly different. But it is not unreasonable to view the demand for the creation of a New International Economic Order as a reformist attempt to recast the international economic order more in the image of the welfare states so prevalent in the West.

CHAPTER 9

OU EN EST L'INSTAURATION DU NOEI?

URAL AYBERK

La déclaration et le programme d'action concernant l'instauration d'un Nouvel Ordre Economique International (NOEI), depuis leur adoption par l'Assemblée Générale des Nations Unies, suscitent un large débat, sans précédent, tant dans les milieux économiques, politiques, financiers nationaux ou internationaux qu'au sein des milieux universitaires. Les publications, les réunions qui traitent cette question semblent souvent oublier ou négliger les travaux menés au sein des divers organismes des Nations Unies (NU) depuis 1974. Le NOEI est devenu un sujet de réflexion, de spéculation si vaste et si complexe qu'on s'y perd assez facilement. Les uns voient dans le NOEI une stratégie du changement des relations économiques internationales et les autres pensent que ce slogan plein d'attraction va permettre le maintien du système économique actuel sous une forme nouvelle.

L'objet de cette recherche est d'explorer les travaux de la Conférence des Nations Unies pour le Commerce et le Développement (CNUCED) sur le NOEI et de dresser un bilan schématique des résultats obtenus. Les travaux menés par la CNUCED sur les différents chapitres du NOEI sont extrêmement vastes et trop techniques. Leur examen détaillé dépasse de loin les limites et l'objectif de cette recherche. C'est pourquoi en poursuivant une double démarche analytique, l'une sur le contenu du NOEI et l'autre sur les résultats obtenus jusqu'à présent, l'élaboration d'un bilan schématique et provisoire des travaux accomplis devient-elle peut-être possible.

Dans la premièr partie nous dégagerons différents éléments du NOEI d'après les travaux de la CNUCED et dans la seconde nous essaierons de dresser un bilan des progrès accomplis jusqu'à présent. Le tableau composé à la fin de cette recherche (Annexe 9) permettra de récapituler et de systématiser les résultats obtenus. Ce tableau schématise les travaux effectués depuis 1974 dans le cadre des organismes des NU sur le NOEI.

Contenu du NOEI

La VIe session extraordinaire de l'Assemblée Générale des NU convoquée pour la première fois pour étudier les problèmes des matières premières et du développement, a adopté une déclaration et un programme d'action concernant l'instauration du NOEI. "Les projets de ces deux documents ont été élaborés par le groupe des 77, qui ont été repris par la suite par le comité spécial de la VIe session spécial créé par l'Assemblée en debut de session" (Touscoz, 1977: 544). Ces résolutions sont adoptées sans vote.

Le NOEI devrait être fondé sur vingt principes d'ordre politique, économique et social (NU, 1974; 3). Le premier principe sur lequel le NOEI se base est composé de plusieurs élements: respect de l'égalité souveraine, autodétermination, inadmissibilité de l'acquisition des territoires par la force, intégrité territoriale et noningérence dans les affaires intérieures d'autres états. Un autre principe important demande une participation pleine et réelle de tous les pays, sur une base d'égalité, au règlement des problèmes économiques mondiaux dans l'intérêt commun de tous les pays. Chaque pays a le droit d'adopter le système économique et social qu'il juge le mieux adapté à son propre développement. La souveraineté permanente intégrale de chaque état sur toutes ses activitiés économiques et sur ses ressources naturelles lui donne le droit d'exercer un contrôle, de nationaliser ou de transférer la propriété à ses ressortissants.

Une série de principes plus spécifiques qui concerne particulièrement les pays en voie de développement (PVD) vise à orienter les aides économiques, financières, et techniques en vue d'assurer leur développement économique. L'Organisation des Nations Unies (ONU) doit traiter les problèmes de la coopération économique internationale dans une optique d'ensemble et jouer un rôle plus grand dans l'établissement de ce NOEI. Ces principes sont très généraux, assez souvent vagues et surtout peu structurés. En outre, il n'y a pas un ordre de priorité pour leur réalisation. Le programme d'action concernant l'instauration d'un NOEI apporte quelques éclaircissements bien qu'insuffisants sur le contenu de cette déclaration, qui est considérée comme "une des bases les plus importantes sur lesquelles reposeront les relations économiques entre tous les peuples et toutes les nations."

PROGRAMME D'ACTION CONCERNANT L'INSTAURATION D'UN NOEI

Le programme d'action vise, dans ses dix parties complémentaires, à corriger le grave déséquilibre économique entre les pays développés et les PVD. Ces dix parties sont les suivantes:

(1) Problèmes fondamentaux posés par les matières premières et les produits primaires dans le cadre du commerce et du développement.

(2) Système monétaire international et financement du développement des PVD.

(3) Industrialisation.

(4) Transfert de la technologie.

(5) Réglementation et controle des activities des Societes Transnationales (STN).

(6) Charte des droits et devoirs économiques des États.

(7) Promotion de la coopération entre pays en voie de developpement.

(8) Aide à l'exercice de la souveraineté permanente des États sur les ressources naturelles.

(9) Renforcement du rôle des organismes des NU dans le domaine de la coopération économique internationale.

(10) Programme spécial.

Une aide urgente et des mesures efficaces sont nécessaires en faveur des PVD moins avancés, des PVD sans littoral et insulaires, des PVD les plus gravement touchés par les crises et catastrophes naturelles.

QUELQUES REMARQUES SUR LE NOEI

Les principes et le programme d'action concernant l'instauration d'un NOEI méritent quelques eclaircissements.

Le NOEI a comme cadre l'ONU et comme acteur principal les États. La participation des autres forces politiques et les agents économiques qui sont directement ou indirectement concernés par le NOEI n'a pas été officiellement prévue (Ayberk, 1980). On n'a pas créé un nouveau cadre institutionnel capable de réaliser les réformes envisagées. *On fait donc confiance aux prises de décision de l'ONU.* Ce sont essentiellement les organisations, institutions spécialisées et les organes subsidiaires des NU qui sont chargés d'élaborer les décisions nécessaires en vue d'instaurer le NOEI. Le Conseil Economique et Social (ECOSOC), plus particulièrement, a la tâche de définir les concepts et coordonner les travaux de divers organismes des NU. La CNUCED constitue la cheville ouvrière du NOEI. C'est elle qui offre le cadre de négociation et le cadre opérationnel; ensuite c'est l'ECOSOC qui prend la relève et en dernière instance, c'est l'Assemblée Générale des NU, qui est saisie de la question. Le cadre à élaborer, les acteurs concernés par le NOEI pour son instauration restent dans la tradition classique bien connue des relations économiques internationales. Ce sont l'ONU et les États qui vont prendre les mesures nécessaires. La stratégie envisagée par le NOEI est pourtant relativement originale. Elle marque un changement et une évolution lente sur le plan conceptuel du développement économique. La stratégie pour les années 70 visait essentiellement à résoudre le problème du développement au moyen d'une série de mesures connexes dans le domaine commercial, financier et technologique destinees à assurer aux PVD une réception plus large des avantages tirés de l'expansion économique des pays développés, à l'interieur du cadre institutionnel existant (CNUCED, 1977). Cette approche a montré ses insuffisances à l'occasion de la crise économique et du ralentissement de l'expansion économique des pays développés. L'approche du NOEI procède de la volonté de réformer le cadre institutionnel lui-même pour que le système économique international puisse, dans son fonctionnement, favoriser beaucoup plus les efforts de développement des PVD qu'il ne le peut actuellement. Cette nouvelle stratégie s'attaque timidement à la structure existante: la structure des marchés mondiaux des produits de base dans le cadre institutionnel régissant le système monétaire et financier international, les opérations des societes transnationales (STN), l'implantation internationale des industries, l'accès à des technologies modernes et la composition des échanges.

La question principale est de savoir si ces changements peuvent être efficacement opérés ou non dans le cadre du système actuel de l'ONU. La deuxième partie de notre étude tente de répondre à cette question.

Bilan des Resultats Obtenus dans l'Instauration du NOEI

Sans prétendre à une evaluation complète il s'agit de dresser un bilan schématique des progrès réalisés depuis 1974 en matière de l'instauration du NOEI.

PROBLÈMES FONDAMENTAUX POSÉS PAR LES MATIERES PREMIÈRES ET LES PRODUITS PRIMAIRES

Matières premières

Dans ce domaine un progrès sensible est réalisé depuis la IVe session de la CNUCED qui a adopté le principe du programme intégré pour les produits de base en 1976. Cette question a également été discutée dans la conférence sur la coopération économique international (CCEI) mais sans succès (Ayberk, 1978). Dans le cadre de la CNUCED, après des négociations laborieuses qui ont duré presque quatre ans, on a enregistré quelques progrès réels dans ce domaine.

Le programme intégré adopté lors de la IVe session de la CNUCED en 1976 visait une série de produits (la banane, la bauxite, les bois tropicaux, le cacao, le caoutchouc, le coton et les filés de coton, le cuivre, l'étain, les fibres dures et les produits de ces fibres, les huiles végétales, le jute et les produits de jute, le manganèse, le minerai de fer, le sucre, le thé, et la viande) qui présentent un intérêt pour les PVD.

Le programme intégré comportait:

—institution d'un dispositif international de stockage de produits de base;
—harmonisation des politiques de stockage et constitution de stocks nationaux coordonnés;
—institution d'arrangements en matière de prix;
—adoption, à l'échelon international, de mesures de régulation de l'offre; et
—amélioration et extension des facilités de financement compensatoire en vue de stabiliser, dans le sens d'un accroissement, les recettes d'exportation des PVD (CNUCED, 1975).

La mise en application de ce programme nécessitait la création d'un fonds commun et la constitution de stocks internationaux. Sur le premier point les négociations ayant commencé en mars 1977, c'est en juin 1980 qu'un accord a pu être réalisé entre les États.

L'acte constitutif prévoit un fonds commun de 750 millions de dollars, composé de deux comptes dont le premier est doté de 400 millions de dollars provenant de contributions obligatoires et destiné à financer les stocks régulateurs prévus par les accords de produits de base existants ou à venir; le second qui compte 350 millions de dollars dont 280 en contributions volontaires, doit financer toute autre mesure que les stockages, telle que la diversification des structures de production, la commercialisation ou la recherche. Le système de vote est assez complexe, on peut le résumer schématiquement comme suit: les PVD ont 47 pourcent; les pays développés 42 pourcent; les pays de l'Est 8 pourcent, et la Chine 3 pourcent. Le fonds commun entrera en vigueur après la ratification de 90 pays (CNUCED, 1979a).

En ce qui concerne les autres aspects du programme intégré les observations suivantes s'imposent: En matière de politique de fixation des prix, ce programme prévoit l'institution d'arrangements notamment d'échelles de prix négociés, qui seraient examinés périodiquement et révisés de façon appropriée, compte tenu des fluctuations des prix des articles manufacturés importés, des taux de change, des coûts de production ainsi que de l'inflation mondiale et du volume de la production et la consommation. Toute forme d'indexation automatique des prix des produits de base sur l'inflation mondiale, ainsi que le principe du maintien du pouvoir d'achat des exportations des PVD n'entrent pas en ligne de compte du programme intégré. Aucune autre initiative n'a encore été prise dans le cadre du programme intégré concernant l'amélioration et l'extension des facilities de financement compensatoire afin de les stabiliser. Cette question est à l'étude au secrétariat de la CNUCED en consultation avec le Fonds Monétaire International (FMI). Un seul accord international a pu être conclu sur la stabilisation des prix du caoutchouc naturel dans le cadre de ce programme en octobre 1979 après deux ans et demi de négociation. Les négociations pour un nouvel accord international sur le jute ont commencé des le janvier 1981. L'accord sur le cacao a été renouvelé en novembre 1980, mais un pays exportateur important (Côte d'Ivoire) et un pays importateur important (Etats-Unis) n'ont toutefois pas accepté la résolution finale de la conférence portant conclusion de l'accord. L'accord international sur le caoutchouc est entré en vigueur à titre provisoire.

La convocation d'une conférence de négociation sur l'examen périodique des prix, la création d'un cadre de coopération internationale pour améliorer les structures des marchés des produits de base (transformation, commercialisation, distribution) sont à l'étude.

Alimentation

Les céréales vivrières ne font pas partie des produits visés par le programme intégré. La constitution et le maintien des réserves mondiales suffisantes de céréales vivrières se poursuivent sur deux plans:

(1) Plusieurs pays ont souscrit à l'arrangement sur la sécurité alimentaire internationale patronné par l'Organisation pour l'agriculture et l'alimentation (FAO). Aucun stock de céréales vivrières n'a été prévu sous un contrôle international.

(2) La constitution de stocks nationaux, mais coordonnés a l'échelle internationale, de céréales vivrières d'un montant déterminé est envisagée dans le cadre de l'arrangement international destiné à remplacer l'accord international sur le blé de 1971. La conférence de négociation n'a pas pu se mettre d'accord sur le volume de ces stocks jusqu'à présent.

Commerce Général

Un premier problème important concerne le principe du statu quo, c'est-à-dire l'imposition de nouveaux obstacles aux importations en provenance des PVD devrait faire l'objet de consultation concernant la surveillance et l'indemnisation multilatérale d'après les critères et des procédures approuvés sur le plan international. Plusieurs violations de ces principes sous forme de mesures de sauvegarde, restrictions volontaires à l'exportation ou arrangements de commercialisation ordonnée ont permis aux pays d'imposer des restrictions à l'importation sans qu'une surveillance ou le versement d'une indemnité aient lieu. On les a remplacés par un système de consultation. La négociation de Tokyo n'a pas abouti à un code multilatéral de sauvegarde revisé. Le second problème important est le principe de la non-réciprocité et du traitement préférentiel en faveur des PVD dans les négociations commerciales multilatérales (NCM). La "clause d'habilitation" selon laquelle les membres de l'Accord général sur le tarifs douaniers et le commerce (GATT) sont autorisés à accorder un traitement différentiél et plus favorable aux PVD par dérogation à la clause de la nation la plus favorisée de l'accord général permet l'application d'une telle mesure aux domaines où était déjà accordé un traitement différencié et plus favorable en application du système des preférencé généralisées (SPG). Toute autre forme de traitement spécial et différencié tels les arrangements préférentiels de type non tarifaire conclu entre les PVD, doit être approuvée par les Parties Contractantes (PC) a l'Accord Général. Par ailleurs, les pays développés en introduisant "le principe de gradation" à l'application de la cause d'habilitation ont limité sa portée. Selon ce principe les PVD s'attendent à ce que leur capacité d'apporter des contributions ou d'accorder des concessions négociées s'améliore avec le développement progressif de leurs économies et l'amelioration de leur situation commerciale. Les PVD ont accepté avec réserve ces principes mais se sont montrés réticents à les traduire en mesures non tarifaires lors du *Tokyo round*. Leurs demandes concernant l'insertion de "clauses de progressivité" n'ont pas trouvé de solution dans le cadre des NCM. Enfin, l'Assemblée Générale a décidé qu'une conference des NU, sous les auspices de la CNUCED, élabore un ensemble de principes et de règles équitables régissant les pratiques commerciales restrictives préjudiciables au commerce international en particulier au commerce des PVD. Cette conférence s'est réunie en novembre 1979 et en avril 1980 et finalement un code de conduite a été élaboré adopté.

Transport et Assurance

En matière de transport, le NOEI n'a pas fait de progrès sensibles. Tout d'abord, le code de conduite élaboré par la conference maritime de 1974 n'est pas encore entré en vigueur car de nombreux pays tardent à devenir parties contractantes. Les travaux ont été poursuivis, sans résultats tangibles sur l'accès des PVD aux transports de vrac relatif à leur propre commerce et la suppression progressive du régime de libre immatriculation.

SYSTÈME MONÉTAIRE INTERNATIONAL ET FINANCEMENT DU DÉVELOPPEMENT DES PVD

Réforme du Système Monetaire International

L'élévation du droit des tirages speciaux (DTS) au rôle d'instrument central de réserve semble encore lointaine malgré le large consensus concernant sa nécessité. La création limités de DTS, qui ne représente que 3 pourcent du stock total des liquidités internationales, ne s'est accompagnée d'aucun contrôle international efficace des réserves monétaire. Pour accroître le rôle des DTS, il faudrait améliorer leurs avantages comme instruments de réserve ct aussi assouplir leurs mécanismes de création; mais jusqu'à présent, seules des actions limitées ont été entreprises dans ce sens. En outre, une réduction du rôle des réserves du dollar des Etats-Unis et d'autres monnaies sont à l'étude. Pour ce qui est de la réforme du système monétaire international, on peut remarquer que cette question a été étudiée par le Comité des 21 du FMI de 1972 à 1974 et par la suite par le Comité intérimaire, qui ont abouti aux accords de Jamaïque en 1976 sans apporter de solution à cette interrogation fondamentale. L'idée de créer un "compte de substitution" qui accepterait des dépôts en dollars de la part des détenteurs officiels en échange d'un montant équivalent de créances libellées en DTS, est à l'examen au Conseil des Gouverneurs du FMI depuis octobre 1979. En ce qui concerne les taux de change, le second amendement aux statuts du FMI entré en vigueur en avril 1978 prévoyait que le FMI exercerait une surveillance sur les politiques des taux de change des membres en vue de promouvoir à la fois un système stable de taux de change et une plus grande symétrie de processus d'ajustement. Il reste à voir quelle sera son efficacité. Aucune recommandation n'a été faite au sujet des mouvements des capitaux. Le lien à établir entre les DTS et les moyens supplémentaires de financement du développement est discuté à la CNUCED et au FMI sans grand succès depuis des années. De même aucun progrès n'a été réalisé pour une participation accrue et plus efficace des PVD à la prise de décision du FMI et dans les institutions internationales de financement du dévelopment.

Amélioration des Facilitiés de Financement

Les conditions de remboursement des crédits ont été légèrement assouplies en décembre 1979. Selon ces dispositions qui entrent dans la catégorie des conditions de remboursement au titre de la facilité élargie du Fonds, on peut fournir ainsi aux pays membres (à des conditions rigoureuses) une assistance pour l'exécution de programme d'ensemble destinés à corriger les déséquilibres structurels de la production, du commerce et des prix. La période maximale pour le remboursement est passés de huit à dix ans. Le remboursement des tirages dans les tranches de crédit ordinaires n'a pas subi de modification. Un progrès a été fait vers l'assouplissement des conditions des accords de confirmation en mars 1979. Ainsi la durée d'un accord de confirmation peut être prolongée au-delà de la durée normale d'un an maximum de trois ans, si le Fonds estime que cette prolongation est nécessaire pour permettre à ce pays d'appliquer avec succès son programme d'ajustement.

La facilité de financement compensatoire du FMI a été libéralisée d'abord en 1975 et une second fois en 1979 (c'est-à-dire possibilité de tirage jusqu'à 100 pourcent de la quote-part d'un membre; la suppression du plafond annuel précédemment appliqué aux tirages; la faculté pour les membres de tenir compte, moyennant certaines conditions des recettes du tourisme et des envois de fonds des travailleurs lors du calcul des déficits; le calcul de la valeur tendancielle des recettes d'exportation de biens et de services en tant que moyenne géométrique, et non arithmétique comme précédemment). Ces progrès ne sont pas suffisants pour répondre aux besoins des PVD. Le Comité de développement du FMI et de la Banque Mondiale réexaminent la question de la stabilisation des recettes d'exportation depuis 1980. De même, peu de choses ont été faites pour améliorer les moyens offerts par le Fonds en matière de stocks régulateurs: en vertu du deuxième amendement aux statuts, un pays peut désormais effectuer des tirages au titre de la facilité de Fonds pour le financement des stocks régulateurs sans perdre ses droits de tirage dans la tranche de réserve comme c'etait le cas précédemment. Quant à la création d'une nouvelle facilité pour le financement des importations de produits alimentaires, la proposition faite au Conseil mondial de l'alimentation est au stade des échanges de vue préliminaires avec le FMI.

Atténuation de la Charge de la Dette des PVD

En cette matière d'une série de progrès était enregistrée depuis la décision du Conseil de la CNUCED de 1978. Les pays développés donateurs s'engageaient sur un plan général à améliorer rétrospectivement les conditions de remboursement de la dette liée à l'aide publique au développement (APD) en faveur des pays en développement les plus pauvres. Les mesures prises à la suite de cette decision ont abouti à l'annulation ou au refinancement à des conditions très favorables de la dette d'APD d'une valeur supérieure à 5 milliards de dollars.[1] L'examen au niveau international du problème de la dette d'un pays en développement, entrepris à la demande de ce pays, devrait se dérouler dans un cadre multilatéral.

Garantie des Apports Financiers à des Conditions de Faveur

De même, peu de progrès ont été réalisés en matière de transfert de ressources réelles aux PVD dans des conditions prévisibles, sûres et continues.

INDUSTRIALISATION

Dans le cadre de l'Organisation des NU pour le développement industriel (ONUDI) et d'autres organismes internationaux appropriés, un système de consultation a été prévu entre les pays développés et les PVD et entre les PVD eux-mêmes pour réaliser le plan d'action de Lima: l'industrialisation et le redéploiement de certaines capacités de production existant dans les pays développés. Ce système de consultations sectorielles fonctionne uniquement pour l'industrialisation des PVD, mais n'englobe pas encore le redéploiement des capacités industrielles des pays développés.

TRANSFERT DES TECHNIQUES

La négociation d'un code international de conduite pour le transfert de technologie est en cours à la CNUCED. Un concensus s'est dégagé sur la question de réglementation nationale et sur les fonctions du mécanisme institutionnel et sa nature, mais quelques difficultés subsistent encore à propos des objectifs et leur champ d'application (CNUCED, 1979b). L'organisation Mondiale de la Propriété Intellectuelle (OMPI) essaye de procéder à la révision du système de la propriété industrielle, depuis plusieurs années. Mais des divergeances persistent entre les pays industrialisés et les PVD. Enfin, la question soulevée par le transfert inverse (exode des cerveaux) de technologie est à l'étude à la CNUCED.

REGLEMENTATION ET CONTROLE DES ACTIVITES DES STN

Par sa résolution 1721 (LIII) adoptée à l'unanimité le 28 juillet 1972, l'ECOSOC a prié le secrétaire général des NU de désigner un groupe de pesonnalités éminentes "pour étudier le rôle et les effets des STN dans le procéssus de développement en particulier des PVD." Les rapports publiés ont montré l'importance de la question. L'Assemblée Générale a créé un centre d'information et de recherche sur les STN et une commission des STN par les résolution 1908 (LVII) et 1913 (LVII). Le groupe des 77 réuni à Lima en mars 1976 a précisé en 21 points leurs préoccupations à l'égard des STN. Enfin un groupe de travail intergouvernemental qui relève de la commission sur les STN de l'ECOSOC travaille depuis 1977 a élaborer un code de conduite pour les STN. Un premier projet va être présenté à cette commission pour sa 6e session. Certaines divergences semblent diviser encore les pays industrialises et les PVD sur les objectifs et le contenu de ce code de conduite.

CHARTE DES DROITS ET DEVOIRS ECONOMIQUES DES ETATS

L'Assemblée Générale avait créé par sa résolution du 19 décembre 1972, 3037 (XXVII) un groupe de travail composé des représentants des gouvernements pour élaborer un projet de charte des droits et devoirs économiques des États. En 1974 l'Assemblée Générale a adopté cette Charte qui comporte quatre chapitres et trente-quatre articles et constitue un instrument de base pour l'instauration du NOEI. Le consensus sur les principes et sur douze articles sur trente-quatre acceptés à la majorité indique qu'un desaccord significatif subsistait entre les pays industrialisés et les PVD (Virally, 1974: 58). D'où les difficultés à traduire ces normes dans les faits lors de la création du NOEI.

PROMOTION DE LA COOPERATION ENTRE LES PVD

L'automie collective a été précisée depuis la réunion du groupe des 77 à Mexico en 1976, et un programme étendu a été adopté en vue de promouvoir cette coopération à l'echelle sous-régionale, régionale et mondiale. Les arrangements recommandés sont de deux types: le premier est un mécanisme approprié par lequel les PVD défendraient les prix de leurs produits d'exportation et amélioreraient leur accès aux marchés et la stabilité de ces marchés, le second est l'octroi d'un traitement préférentiel entre les PVD pour leurs importations mutuelles. Le secrétariat de la CNUCED est chargé de faire une étude sur les divers aspects de ce système projété et sur les divers types de coopération. La coopération a été egalement envisagée dans les domaines suivants: commerce, production, infrastructure, services, monnaie, finances, sciences, technologie, et coopération technique.

Une grande commission de la coopération entre les PVD a été créé pour fournir aide et soutien aux PVD afin qu'ils puissent renforcer leur coopération mutuelle à tous les niveaux. Le programme de travail établi par cette commission donne priorité: (a) à la mise en route d'études concernant: un système mondial de préferénces commerciales entre les PVD; la coopération entre organismes de commerce d'État; la création d'entreprises multinationales de commercialisation; (b) à l'intensification des travaux et activités en cours concernant: le renforcement de la coopération économique et de l'intégration aux niveaux sous-régional, régional et interrégional; l'instauration de système sous-régionaux, régionaux et inter-régionaux de crédit à l'exportation et de garantie du crédit à l'exportation; la coopération dans le transfert et la mise au point de technologies; les problèmes de transit et de transport des PVD sans littoral et insulaires; les arrangements régionaux et sous-régionaux d'assurance et de réassurance entre PVD; la promotion et la facilitation des courants de capitaux entre PVD; la création d'entreprises multinationales de production.

Le programme d'Arusha pour l'autonomie collective comprend un premier plan d'action à court et à moyen terme concernant les priorités globales en matière de coopération économique entre pays en développement (CEPED) (CNUCED, 1979c). Pour la mise en marche du système complet de CEPED, une session extraordinaire de la commission de la coopération a eu lieu en 1980 en vue d'examiner les études du secrétariat sur les questions prioritaires. Par la suite, la réunion de Caracas sur le dialogue Sud-Sud des 77 qui a eu lieu en mai 1981, marque un tournant décisif: le dialogue Nord-Sud étant dans l'impasse, il faut accélérer le dialogue Sud-Sud. Dès lors, le groupe des 77 accepte l'idée de la création d'un secrétariat permanent des 77. En effet, ce changement, cette prise de conscience est la suite logique de l'evaluation du groupe des 77. Depuis 1977, nous assistons à une coordination plus efficace de l'activité du groupe des 77. Les grandes orientations du groupe ont été généralement décidées lors de la réunion ministérielle qui se tient régulièrement à la veille des sessions de la CNUCED ou de l'ONUDI. Depuis 1977, les ministres des affaires étrangères des pays membre ont pris l'habitude de se réunir à New York, à l'occasion de l'Assemblée Générale des NU. Le président élu a la charge de coordonner des travaux pour une durée variable. Le groupe qui cherchait à ses débuts à obtenir des réformes principalement dans le domaine des relations commerciales, a étendu progressivement son action au point de toucher pratiquement tour le spectre des relations économiques internationales entre les pays industrialisés et les PVD. La création d'un secrétariat permanent facilitera l'organisation des travaux et des recherches ainsi que l'action du groupe des 77 en vue d'accroître leur capacité de négociation.

Par ailleurs, le groupe des 77 a proposé des mécanismes susceptibles d'assurer un "suivi" efficace à la CEPED. Des comités d'action du type de ceux qui fonctionnent dans le cadre du Système Economique Latino-américain (SELA) pourraient servir de modèles. L'idée de base de cette structure souple qui se veut efficace est qu'il suffit à trois pays membres de se mettre d'accord sur un projet quelconque pour créer un comité d'action chargé de la coordination et de la réalisation des projets communs dans ce cadre général. Enfin, la démarche du groups des 77 va dans le sens d'une redistribution de la production industrielle mondiale en faveur du tiers-monde (CNUCED, 1979d; *Le Monde*, 1981).

RENFORCEMENT DU RÔLE DES ORGANISMES DES NU DANS LE DOMAINE DE LA COOPÉRATION ECONOMIQUE INTERNATIONALE

Sur cette question vitale, le programme d'action et les résolutions concernant le NOEI ont maintenu la structure institutionnelle existante. Une définition des tâches et une meilleure coordination entre les organismes des NU ont été prévues. La CNUCED est l'organisme pivot pour l'ensemble des questions concernant le NOEI. Les travaux effectues par la CNUCED ont été examinés par l'ECOSOC et en dernier lieu par l'Assemblée Générale. Sur le plan pratique, aucune décision importante n'a été prise pour renforcer le rôle des organismes des NU dans le domaine de la coopération économique internationale. L'ONUDI est devenue une institution spécialisée des NU en 1978.

PROGRAMME SPÉCIAL

Le fonds d'urgence des NU dont la création a été décidée lors de la VIe session extraordinaire de l'Assemblée Générale a pour objectif d'aider les PVD les plus touchés par la crise économique. Cette action qui comportait une contribution d'environ 3 milliards de dollars a touché 42 pays qui, grâce à cette aide ont pu importer des biens et services essentiels (produits alimentaires, engrais, biens d'equipement). L'action spéciale décidée à la Conférence sur la coopération économique internationale a prévu un montant total d'aide d'un milliard de dollars. C'est l'Association Internationale du Développement (AID) qui gère ce fonds. Ces prêts sont utilisés pour financer des projets et programmes de développement urgents dans les PVD.

Conclusion

Le tableau ci-après (Annexe 9) reproduit clairement les résultats obtenus jusqu'à présent qui peuvent etre regroupés en trois catégories:

Premièrement, des résultats relativement satisfaisants ont été enregistrés au titre du programme intégré pour les produits de base de l'elaboration de la Charte des droits et devoirs économiques des Etats et du programme spécial. Il faut signaler néanmoins que le fonds créé par ce programme reste bien en deçà des projets initiaux: la dotation prévue est de 750 millions de dollars alors que le groupe des 77 souhaitait un fonds de 6 milliards de dollars (Sardais et Milien, 1981: 10). Quel sera l'impact réel de ce fonds sur la régulation du marche (Nusbaumer, 1981: 238).

Deuxièmement, les domaines où aucun progrès n'a été enregistré: secteur alimentaire, transport, réforme du système monétaire, garanties des apports financiers.

Troisièmement, les secteurs où l'on a pu réaliser quelques progrès: amélioration des facilités de financement, dette des PVD et promotion de la coopération entre les PVD.

Sur certaines questions, comme le code de conduite pour le transfert des techniques, le code de conduite sur la règlementation et le contrôle des activités des STN, les travaux sont avancés, mais les divergences existant entre les pays industrialisés et les PVD sur l'objectif et le contenu de ces codes tellement grandes qu'on se demande, quels codes verront le jour, quels seront leur efficacite et leur utilité. Puisque les PVD n'ont pas pris "fermement position en faveur des droits de propriété des entreprises étrangères qui investissent chex eux" (Nusbaumer, 1981: 240), ils n'ont pas accepté non plus que les dispositions contraignantes ne figurent pas sur le code de conduite relatif aux activités des STN. Cet examen des travaux de la CNUCED sur le NOEI ainsi que le bilan synthétique dressé montrent que plusieurs obstacles persistent quant à la réforme du système économique qui avaite ete mis sur pied par l'Accord de Bretton Woods et par l'Accord général sur les tarifs douaniers et le commerce. Ces intruments élaborés à la fin de la seconde guerre mondiale par les pays industrialisés à économie de marché n'ont associé ni les pays à économie planifiée, ni les PVD qui étaient absents de la scène internationale à cette époque.

Nous constatons à présent que les principes et les règles qui régissent les relations économiques internationales se sont révélés inadéquats, non seulement pour résoudre les problèmes du développement et les difficultés des pays du tiers-mond mais aussi pour libéraliser les échanges commerciaux entre les pays industrialisés. Sur ce second point, la pratique des limitations "volontaires" des exportations et les "arrangements de commercialisation ordonnée" qui semblent échapper au champ d'application des règles du GATT necessitent, à notre avis, une réforme des structures institutionnelles. Une des principales questions à prendre en considération est de savoir si ces réformes peuvent être réalisés ou non dans le cadre du système actuel de l'ONU. En nous basant sur les travaux de la CNUCED et des divers organismes spécialisés des NU, nous pouvons constater que des obstacles de tailles demeurent encore. Tout d'abord, la réforme du systeme monétaire international, ainsi que la réforme des règles du commerce international ne peuvent être réalisées qu'au sein du FMI et du GATT où les PVD ont peu ou pas d'influence. Les réformes en question ne peuvent être réalises sans un large accord des pays industrialisés, accord qui par ailleurs apparait nécessaire à la mise en oeuvre de toute réforme impliquant la participation et la contribution des pays industrialisés. Ensuite, les résolutions de l'Assemblée Générale sur le NOEI sont assez hétérogènes, mal structurées; les priorités et les calendriers ne sont pas fixés. Par ailleurs, la répartition des tâches entre les différentes instances n'est pas clairement précisée. Un grand décalage existe entre les objectifs ambitieux du NOEI et les moyens disponibles fort limites. En effet, les résolutions de l'Assemblée Générale sur le NOEI n'ont pas de force obligatoire; mais constituent de simples recommandations ou invitations.

Enfin, ces travaux sont menés sans aucun ordre de priorité au sein des divers organismes des NU où les rapports de force entre les pays industrialisés et les PVD sont inégaux. C'est pourquoi les résultats obtenus, ou ceux qui le seront, sont souvent en-dessous des objectifs fixés et difficilement comparables d'un domaine à l'autre. Un NOEI visant à une réforme du système économique international global ne peut pas naître au sein du système de négociation des NU. Face à ces divers obstacles à l'instauration du NOEI, les PVD d'une part, et les pays industrialisés d'autre part, essaient de mettre au point de nouveaux instruments tout en poursuivant leurs stratégies initiales.

Les PVD ont une approche globale et dirigiste. Le tiers-monde répresenté par le group des 77 est très hétérogène: il se compose des pays exportateurs de pétrole, des pays nouvellement industrialisés, des pays à economie liberale ou planifié; mais présente une grande cohésion dans son comportement, malgré ces différences, il parvient à constituer un front commun face aux pays industrialisés.Ce groupe souhaite une négociation globale, universelle pour une nouvelle convention économique internationale à l'instar de l'accord de Bretton Woods. En revanche, les pays industrialisés sont plus homogènes quant à leur niveau économique et défendent dans leur majorité le système économique libéral. Le principe du libre échange qui a assuré leur prosperité depuis la fin de la seconde guerre mondiale, influe considérablement sur leur comportement. L'administration Reagan par exemple n'est pas prête pour le moment à accepter une réforme substantielle du système économique international. "L'un des meilleurs moyens d'améliorer la situation des PVD était de relancer l'économie américaine et de s'appuyer sur le commence et les investissements privés plutôt que sur l'aide [trade but not aid] (*Le Monde,* 1981)." Cette position est en partie partagée par d'autres pays industrialises. En d'autres termes, certains pays industrialisés ne souhaitent pas une négociation globale (les Etats-Unis, le Royaume-Uni, la République fédérale allemande) et préfèrent une approche ponctuelle. Dans cette strategie, la situation des pays les moins avances (PMA) apparaît comme un test révélateur. La conférence de Paris de septembre 1981 était la première de cette envergure consacrée à un groupe spécifique de pays. De par son importance et son urgence, la question des PMA est au centre des problèmes du développement (OECD, 1981: 3; *Le Monde,* 1981). Cette approche a été également confirmée dans la reprise du dialogue Nord-Sud à Cancun les 22 et 23 octobre 1981. Les Etats-Unis souhaitent une discussion informelle, sans ordre du jour et sans communiqué (*Le Monde,* 1981; CEE, 1981a). A ce propos la 11e session extraordinaire de l'Assemblée Générale des NU consacrée au développement et à la coopération économique internationale, qui s'était tenue à New York du 25 aoûtau 15 septembre 1980, a fait apparaître une fois de plus la divergence entre les PVD et les pays industrialisés. Quant aux négociations globales, et malgré l'intensité des travaux préparatoires et des efforts déployés, les discussions se sont limitées aux modalités sans qu'un accord ait pu être trouvé. Une grande difficulté résidait dans la définition des rôles à confier, d'une part à la conférence elle-même (que le groupe des 77 entend investir de pouvoirs de négociation réels, ainsi que de pouvoirs de renégociation pouvant porter sur les accords intervenus dans les institutions spécialisées des NU, le PMI par exemple et d'autre part, aux institutions spécialisées dont les compétences devraient être scrupuleusement respectées notamment aux yeux des pays industrialisés (CEE, 1981b). Tous les États membres des NU ont convenu d'organiser une nouvelle série de négociations globales (Forum du développement, 1981: 12) car selon l'avis général, l'ordre international actuel a réellement besoin de réformes et même d'une restructuration. Mais des divergences subsistent quant à la nature et l'ampleur de ces réformes.

Les PVD considèrent le NOEI, les négociations globales et le dialogue Nord-Sud comme des instruments permettant de réorganiser et redistribuer des pouvoirs économiques, financiers et techniques au sein de la communauté internationale. En revanche, la plupart des pays développés semblent seulement accepter le principe de certaines réformes limitées et ne remettent pas en cause le fonctionnement libéral du système actuel. Ainsi, à l'heure actuelle, quels que soient les termes utilisés, le NOEI ou le dialogue Nord-Sud ou les négociations globales, le dialogue se poursuit, mais les stragégies des pays en présence ne semblent pas se modifier.

ANNEXE 9: BILAN DES TRAVAUX CONCERNANT L'INSTAURATION OU NOEI

NOEI	ORGANISMES COMPETENTS — *Assemblée Générale des Nations Unies —ECOSOC*	TRAVAUX ENTREPRIS	COMMENCEMENT DES TRAVAUX	RESULTATS OBTENUS
(1) Problèmes Fondamentaux posés par les matières premières et les produits primaires dans le cadre du commerce et du développement	CNUCED			
(A) Matières premières	CNUCED	Programme intégré pour les produits de base	1976	
		—Fonds commun		Accord en juin 80 un accord est conclu
		—Accords internationaux		
		—Mesures sur les prix	1979	Travaux en cours
		—Amélioration des structures	1979	
(B) Alimentation	FAO—Conférence mondiale de l'alimentation	—Sécurité alimentaire internationale	1978	Engagement inter.
		—Stocks nationaux	1978	Tentative de coordonner les stocks alimentaires nationaux

(L'annexe se continue à la prochaine page)

ANNEXE 9: (continuée)

NOEI	ORGANISMES COMPETENTS Assemblée Générale des Nations Unies—ECOSOC	TRAVAUX ENTREPRIS	COMMENCEMENT DES TRAVAUX	RESULTATS OBTENUS
(C) Commerce général	CNUCED—GATT—CIC—CNUDCI	—SPG	1968	Application en 1971 (Amélioration)
		—NCM	1973	Accord en 1979
		Principe du statu quo	1973	Pas de résultat
		Principe de la non-reciprocité	1973	Accord partiel
		Clause de progressivité	1973	Pas d'accord
		Practiques commerciales restrictives	1973	Code de conduite adopté avril 80
(D) Transport et assurance	CNUCED—OMCI		1974	Code de conduite des conférences maritimes—Pas d'adhesion suffisante pour son entrée en vigueur
(2) Système monétaire international et financement du développement des PVD	FMI—Banque mondiale—CNUCED	—Réforme du système monétaire	1976	Pas de progrès réel
		—Amélioration des facilites de financement	1976-1979	Quelques progrès
		—Atténuation du problème de la dette des PVD	1978-1980	Quelques progrès
		—Garantie des apports financiers		Aucun progrès réel
(3) Industrialisation	CNUCED—ONUDI—BIRD—PNUD		1976	Système de consultations

	Organisme	Objet	Date	État d'avancement
(4) Transfert de la technologie	CNUCED		1977	Code international de conduite pour le transfert de la technologie en élaboration
	OMPI	—Révision du systèm de propriété industrielle	1975	Travaux en cours
(5) Reglementation et controle des activités des STN	ECOSOC—OCDE		1977	Code de conduite en élaboration
(6) Charte des droits et devoirs des états	Assemblée Générale des Nations Unies		1972	La charte est acceptée en 1974
(7) Promotion de la coopération entre pays en voie de développement	CNUCED		1976	Travaux en cours
		—Autonomie collective	1976-1979	Travaux en cours
		—Préférences commerciales entre les PVD	1979	Travaux en cours
		—Coopération entre les PVD	1979	Travaux en cours
(8) Aide à l'exercice de la souveraineté permanenta des Etats sur les ressources naturelles	Système des Nations Unies CNUCED			A l'étude
(9) Renforcement du rôle des organismes des NU dans le domaine de la coopération economique internationale	Système des Nations Unies CNUCED			A l'étude
(10) Programme special	CCEI—CNUCED—ONUDI—AID		1974	Programme continu depuis 1976

NOTE

1. Les dettes publiques de ces pays ont été evaluees a environ 23 milliards de dollar en 1976-dette publique bilaterale-TD/B/757, p. 13. Pour les statistiques, voir TD/B/C.3/148.

RÉFÉRENCES

AYBERK, U. (1980) "Le Nouvel Ordre Economique International et le syndicalisme international." Il Politico, No. 4: 685-697.

———— (1978) "Le mécanisme de la prise des décision communautaires en matiere de relations internationales." Bruxelles: Ed. Bruylant.

CEE (1981a) Lettre d'information, No. 8.

CEE (1981b) Quatorzième rapport general sur l'activité des Communautés europèennes en 1980, p. 262 et s.

CNUCED (1975). IVe session de la CNUCED, Actes de la CNUCED. Vol. 1, pt. 6 et s.

CNUCED (1977) TD/B/642.

CNUCED (1979a) TD/IPC/CF/Conf/19, TD/IP/CF/Conf/14 (part 1 et 11), TD/B/757.

CNUCED (1979b) TD/CODE TOT/147.

CNUCED (1979c) TD/235.

CNUCED (1979d) TD/244.

Forum du développement (1981) Juin, p. 12.

Le Monde (1981) 16 et 19 mai.

Le Monde (1981) 19 et 20 juillet.

Le Monde (1981) 2 Sept.

N.U. (1974) Résolution 3201 (SVI) p. 3 et suiv.

NUSBAUMER, J. (1981) "L'enjeu du dialogue Nord-Sud." Paris: Ed. Economica, p. 238, 240.

OECD (1981) L'observateur de l'OCDE, No. 112 (Sept.): 3.

SARDAIS, L. et S. MILIEN (1981). "La fin des accords de produits?" Le Monde Diplomatique (janvier): 10.

TOUSCOZ, J. (1977) "La coopération internationale et les matières premieres exportées par les pays du Tiers Monde." Revue du Tiers Monde, No. 66: 544.

VIRALLY, M. (1974). "La charte des droits et devoirs économiques des États." Annuaire Francais de Droit International (AFDI), p. 58.

CHAPTER 10

RESTRUCTURING THE UN SYSTEM

JOHN P. RENNINGER

The New International Economic Order has been a major concern of most UN bodies in recent years. Discussion and debate, in what has come to be known as the North-South dialogue, has focused on substantive issues concerning trade, commodities, aid, finance, and related areas. The quest for a new order also has a quite significant institutional dimension. The basic institutional design of the UN system is one that was forged in 1945 when the maintenance of international peace and security was the dominant preoccupation. Beginning in the 1960s, the United Nations began to respond to the challenge of development and a plethora of new units and organizations were added to the system. This process of expansion has been described in the following terms (Development Forum, 1978: 12):

> This growth explosion was unblessed by master-plans, overall organization charts, or even an inter-agency chair of command. As new units were created, they negotiated the details of their relationship to the centre and the whole. The result is a crazy-quilt of different interlocking patterns.

The growth and accompanying fragmentation of the system have created different types of problems which have not unexpectedly led to various attempts to deal with the consequences of institutional proliferation.[1] The perceived inadequacy of these efforts to deal with problems created by rapid growth provided the rationale and impetus for the present restructuring exercise.

AUTHOR'S NOTE: The views expressed in this chapter are those of the author and do not necessarily reflect the official position of the United Nations Institute for Training and Research.

As this chapter will relate, restructuring, or the reform and rationalization of UN structures in the economic and social sectors, has been a major issue before the United Nations in recent years. Restructuring has been the subject of innumerable resolutions and reports and more importantly, it has led to a variety of institutional changes. Yet serious questions remain concerning the significance and impact of restructuring. Both the process and outcome of restructuring can only be fully understood within the context of the North-South dialogue. Restructuring has been and continues to be intimately related to attempts to create the New International Economic Order. The positions of various groups of countries on restructuring are definitely linked to their positions on the substantive issues involved in the North-South dialogue. The lack of significant progress in the North-South dialogue explains in part the difficulties associated with implementing restructuring. More entrenched institutional attributes are also salient. The restructuring exercise demonstrates that institutional issues cannot be considered in isolation from substantive outcomes related to the New International Economic Order.

The Process of Restructuring

The recent institutional and other structural changes that have occurred in the UN system and which are attributed to the restructuring effort are the result of the deliberations of the Ad Hoc Committee on the Restructuring of the Economic and Social Sectors of the United Nations System. This committee was created by the General Assembly in 1975 and given the mandate of:

> initiating the process of restructuring the United Nations system so as to make it more fully capable of dealing with problems of international economic co-operation and development in a comprehensive and effective manner . . . and to make it more responsive to the requirements of the provisions of the Declaration and Programme of Action on the Establishment of a New International Economic Order as well as those of the Charter of Economic Rights and Duties of States [UN General Assembly, 1975].

Membership was open to all member states of the United Nations. At its first session, Ambassador Kenneth K. S. Dadzie of Ghana was elected chairman.

In the long and sometimes tortuous negotiations which ensued, the Ad Hoc Committee was strongly influenced by the report of the Group of Experts on the Structure of the United Nations Systems (United Nations, 1975). This expert group had been appointed by the secretary-general and completed its work prior to the opening of the Seventh Special Session of the General Assembly in 1975. For example, the Ad Hoc Committee decided, at an early stage to concentrate its deliberations on eight problem areas which were the same as those given most attention by the Group of Experts. These were the General Assembly; the Economic and Social Council; other UN forums for negotiation; structures for regional and interregional cooperation; operational activities of the UN system; planning, programming, budgeting, and evaluation; interagency coordination; and secretariat support services.

At the Ad Hoc Committee's third session, three position papers were submitted to facilitate discussion (UN General Assembly, 1976). These papers were prepared by the United States, the EEC countries, and the Group of 77. They are of interest because of the differences in approaches to restructuring that they reveal. If one compares, for instance, the paper prepared by the United States with that of the Group of 77, differences along various dimensions become apparent. The U.S. paper referred more frequently to the Group of Experts report and, while not totally endorsing the recommendations, was definitely sympathetic toward them. The Group of 77, on the other hand, did not make as many references to the Group of Experts. But perhaps the more crucial difference between the two papers was one of intent, which of course can only be discerned by "reading between the lines."

It seems clear that the Group of 77 had two primary goals. One was to make the UN system responsive to the concerns of the majority of developing countries and the other was to increase the flow of resources generated by the system. In order to make the system more responsive, the Group of 77 sought to strengthen those forums and institutions that were amenable to their interests. There was thus great emphasis placed on making the General Assembly the main policy-making and negotiating forum of the system. There were also repeated references to making other organs of the system, such as the IMF and the World Bank, more responsive to the directives of the General Assembly. The Group of 77 paper also sought to increase the influence of developing countries in bodies where it is felt to be lacking. Accordingly, there was a proposal to increase the membership of the Advisory Committee on Administrative and Budgetary Questions (ACABQ) by adding three members from developing countries. The Group of 77 paper also sought to ensure that those UN institutions firmly under their control would be granted greater authority. For example, several suggestions were put forth with regard to UNCTAD. The Group of 77 paper states:

> The vital function of UNCTAD as a generator of new ideas and new policy approaches should be retained and strengthened in order to increase its effectiveness as an international organ for improving the condition of international trade and accelerating the economic development of the developing countries [UN General Assembly, 1976: 53].

In a similar vein, proposals were made for centering more operational activities in the regional economic commissions. The Group of 77 was also favorably disposed to creating the post of Director-General for Development and International Economic Cooperation.

The second major emphasis in the Group of 77 paper was on adding to the resources dispensed by the UN system. Thus under the topic of "Operational Activities of the United Nations System" there is no reference to the consolidation of funds and programs as had been recommended by the Group of Experts. Many developing countries are of the opinion that the consolidation of funds would result in a net decrease of resources available to them. Therefore, the Group of 77 paper states (UN General Assembly, 1976: 55) that the restructuring of operational activities should be undertaken to ensure "an increased flow of resources."

The U.S. paper had a different tone as well as substance. A U.S. Department of State publication has stated (Department of State, 1978) U.S. goals with regard to restructuring in these terms:

> In the operation of the economic and social activities in the UN system, the US is pursuing improved leadership and management; more efficient planning, programming, budgeting and evaluation capabilities; better policy analysis and research; and improved co-ordination and effectiveness of technical assistance.

These goals are reflected in the U.S. paper which on the whole called for fewer changes than the Group of 77 paper. The emphasis was on efficiency and making the structures of the system conform to accepted administrative models. There was no mention of strengthening the role of the General Assembly in policy making or negotiations. Instead, the U.S. paper limited its comments on the General Assembly to some suggestions for changing the operations of the committee system. Neither were there any suggestions for making other parts of the system more responsive to the wishes of the General Assembly. There was obviously no desire to limit the autonomy of the IMF, the World Bank, or GATT, institutions over which developed countries exercise the effective control. In contrast to the Group of 77, which endorsed an enhanced role for the regional economic commissions, the U.S. paper called for a study of how the commissions might best relate to the rest of the system. There was also a clause (UN General Assembly, 1976: 44) which suggested that the regional commissions "ensure the full participation of both member donor nations and member recipient nations in the formulation and monitoring of development assistance programmes and projects." This was an effort to maintain developed country influence when more operational activities are assigned to the regional commissions. The U.S. paper, with certain qualifications, endorsed the recommendations of the

Group of Experts with regard to the consolidation of development funds and programs. It also favored a reduction of the subsidiary machinery of ECO-SOC and in other ways sought to rationalize structures. The U.S. paper finally placed great emphasis on increased efficiency which was to be achieved through a variety of administrative, budgetary, and personnel reforms. Great importance was attached to program evaluation, a long-standing U.S. favorite.

In general, if not in specifics, the EEC position paper was quite similar to that of the United States. Among the developed countries, the Nordic group did develop a position somewhat distinct from those of United States and the EEC. The Nordic countries were somewhat more sympathetic to the Group of 77 position and because of this, they played a pivotal role in the negotiations.

Debates on the New International Economic Order and on restructuring which have taken place in UN forums have generally involved three main sets of actors. Two of these sets of actors, the developing countries and the western developed countries, have been mentioned above. The third set of actors are the developed socialist countries of Eastern Europe. The socialist states did not submit a position paper to the Ad Hoc Committee, but they did have a point of view which was vigorously put forward in the negotiations. As major contributors to the UN budget, socialist states placed a high priority on economy and efficiency and thus found themselves aligned with the developed western countries on certain issues. For example, along with some western countries, the socialist bloc countries were unenthusiastic about establishing the new post of Director-General for Development and International Economic Cooperation. They were also opposed to any changes which would involve revision of the UN Charter. On the other hand, by repeatedly referring to the Charter of Economic Rights and Duties of States and by strongly supporting the developing countries on other issues, socialist countries were more closely aligned with the Group of 77 position.

The differences among the three sets of actors should not however obscure certain important areas of agreement. There was a widespread belief that the UN development system had become so unwieldly as to be incapable of responding to the wishes of the international community. There was a general concensus that a certain amount of reform and rationalization was desirable, indeed even essential. But as the position papers referred to above make clear, different groups of countries were interested in structural reform and rationalization for quite different reasons.

Developed nations, including the socialist states, were largely interested in a rationalization of structures and institutions because they provide the largest portions of the budgets of UN organizations. Consequently, they wanted the UN system to be as efficient and economical as is possible. Developing countries were primarily interested in rationalization because they wanted the UN system to be the primary vehicle for the creation of the New International Economic Order. While they had an interest in efficiency, their primary concern was to make the system effective in achieving its objectives. Developing countries also viewed restructuring as an opportunity to expand their influence in international organizations.

The debates in the Ad Hoc Committee then to some extent mirrored the debates in other North-South forums. The developing countries saw all of these debates as opportunities to reshape the international order in ways more congenial to their interests. Most western developed countries in the substantive negotiations over the New International Economic Order and in negotiations over restructuring, were trying to preserve their privileged and entrenched positions in the existing international system. The socialist countries, of course, had a quite different perspective from the West with regard to the substantive issues in the North-South debate.

The fact that the main actors in the restructuring debate had "hidden agendas" made it extremely difficult to reach agreement. It is not surprising then that the Ad Hoc Committee took over a year longer than had originally been expected to finish its work.

The committee's final report (UN General Assembly, 1978b) completed in December of 1977, is in itself an indication of the intense bargaining and negotiation between the interested parties. The final report was adopted without a vote, but several countries found it necessary to put their reservations and special interpretations on the record (U.N. General Assembly, 1978b: 20-31). The reservations were required because the language in some of the sections is vague and subject to differing interpretations.

Vagueness in language often results when compromises must be made. The final report is very much that of a document of compromise. As such, it satisfies no one completely. The developing countries, working through the Group of 77, had a large majority in the committee but were anxious to avoid a bitter and divisive confrontation with the developed countries. The final report on the whole, however, reflects the Group of 77 position to a great extent. The committee's final recommendations are divided into the eight "problem areas" that had been identified earlier. The final report was adopted by the General Assembly with only minor changes.

With regard to the General Assembly, the report (UN General Assembly, 1978a) called for a general strengthening of its role as "the principal forum for policy-making" in international economic, social and related problems. It was suggested that the General Assembly rationalize its methods of work.

ECOSOC would operate as the main arm of the General Assembly in devising solutions to international economic and social problems and would monitor progress in solving these problems. In order to carry out its functions, ECOSOC was to schedule its work on a biennial basis and meet regularly during the year in subject-oriented sessions. This should allow many of the subsidiary bodies of ECOSOC to be eliminated. The report (UN General Assembly, 1978a: 14) also stated that consideration should be given to making ECOSOC "fully representative."

With regard to other forums for negotiation, the report reaffirmed the overall supervisory role of the General Assembly and identified UNCTAD as the appropriate forum for detailed international economic negotiations.

The section on structures for regional and interregional cooperation (UN General Assembly, 1978a: 15) singled out the regional commissions "as the main general economic and social development centers within the United Nations system." The organizations of the UN system were also called upon (UN General Assembly, 1978a: 16) to "take early steps to achieve a common definition of regions and subregions and the identical location of regional and subregional offices."

Regarding operational activities for development, the two major reforms called for (UN General Assembly, 1978a: 18) were the holding of a single annual UN pledging conference for all operational activities for development and the establishment of a "single governing body responsible for the management and control, at the international level, of United Nations operational activities for development."

The sixth area of emphasis concerned planning, programming, budgeting, and evaluation. Here it was recommended that the Committee for Program and Coordination be given increased responsibilities in this area. It was also suggested that the size of the ACABQ be increased to sixteen and that there be close cooperation between the Committee for Program and Coordination and the ACABQ.

The major innovation called for with regard to interagency coordination was a new and enhanced role for the Administrative Committee on Coordination and the elimination of other coordination bodies such as the Environment Coordination Board, the Inter-Agency Consultative Board, and the Advisory Committee of UNIDO.

Some of the potentially most important reforms relate to the final problem area, secretariat support services. Here it was recommended that (UN General Assembly, 1978a: 22) that the UN Secretariat "should be restructured so as to effectively meet the requirements and the policy directives" of the General Assembly and of ECOSOC. Specific guidance was given for this restructuring effort. This section of the report (UN General Assembly, 1978a: 26) also invited the secretary-general to appoint a Director-General for Development and International Economic Cooperation. This person would be in charge of:

(1) ensuring the provision of effective leadership to the various components of the UN system in the field of development and international economic cooperation and in exercising overall coordination within the system in order to

ensure a multidisciplinary approach to the problems of development on a system-wide basis; and

(2) ensuring, within the United Nations, the coherence, coordination, and efficient management of all activities in the economic and social fields financed by the regular budget or by extrabudgetary resources.

The Implementation of Restructuring: Progress to Date

In accepting the committee's report in December 1977, the General Assembly (UN General Assembly, 1977) characterized it as "a valuable initial contribution." The manner in which restructuring is implemented is therefore crucial. It can definitely be said that the restructuring issue has not receded in importance. It has been debated in a variety of forums including recent sessions of the General Assembly and of ECOSOC. The UN Secretariat, including the secretary-general and bodies such as the ACC, has also devoted considerable attention to the implementation of restructuring. Here we will briefly highlight some of the most important actions thus far taken.

With regard to both the General Assembly and ECOSOC, progress has been somewhat limited. The restructuring resolution recommended an enhanced role for the General Assembly in international policy making. There is no evidence that this recommendation has of yet had a significant impact but perhaps it is unrealistic to expect that it would have had any in so short a time. The enhancement of the role of the General Assembly obviously depends upon the willingness of member states to allow the General Assembly to play such a role. The experience of the Committee of the Whole and the failure of the Eleventh Special Session of the General Assembly to reach agreement on the procedures to be followed in global negotiations indicates that certain member states are still not prepared to see the General Assembly play an enhanced role. Resolution 32/197 also called upon the General Assembly to "rationalize its methods of work" and suggested specific measures with regard to the operations of the Second and Third Committees. A variety of measures have been adopted and others are under active consideration. It is generally agreed that the operations of the Second Committee, in particular, have been improved.

ECOSOC has had less success in implementing the restructuring recommendations. It is doubtful if ECOSOC can fulfill the role assigned to it under the Charter unless it changes its mode of operation significantly. The restructuring resolution made specific recommendations to accomplish this. ECOSOC was asked to streamline its subsidiary machinery, organize its work on a biennial basis, and provide for shorter but more frequent subject-oriented sessions spread throughout the year. Little progress has been made in implementing these recommendations. ECOSOC has proven completely incapable of streamlining its subsidiary machinery and has in fact created some additional machinery. Neither has ECOSOC succeeded in arranging for shorter, subject-oriented sessions although a biennial work program has been produced. The Thirty-Third General Assembly (UN General Assembly, 1978c) reviewed the restructuring process and called upon ECOSOC to "intensify" its efforts to implement the restructuring recommendations. ECOSOC grappled with the problem again in 1979 but had to report (UN Economic and Social Council, 1979b) to the General Assembly that it was not able to reach agreement. An effort was made at the Thirty-Fourth Session of the General Assembly to break the impasse. Argentina and Jamaica presented a draft resolution which proposed to abolish most of the ECOSOC subsidiary machinery and accomplish certain other reforms while at the same time revising the Charter to expand the membership of ECOSOC to include all members of the United Nations. Despite considerable support for such an approach, the General Assembly decided (UN General Assembly, 1979a) that consideration of the proposal be postponed until the Thirty-Fifth General Assembly.

This scenario was essentially repeated at that session when a similar resolution was introduced. It was eventually agreed (UN General Assembly, 1980c) to postpone consideration of the resolution until the Thirty-Sixth Session of the General Assembly in the Fall of 1981.

Progress in implementing the recommendations concerning other forums for negotiations has also been quite limited but for entirely understandable reasons. The main thrust of these recommendations, contained in paragraphs 16 and 18 of resolution 32/197, was first to make other parts of the UN system more responsive to the directives of the General Assembly and ECOSOC and second to enable UNCTAD to play a major role in the deliberation, negotiation, review, and implementation of policies relating to international trade and international economic cooperation. With regard to the first set of recommendations various other parts of the UN system have expressed their willingness to collaborate more fully with the General Assembly and ECOSOC, but at the same time they have unequivocally stated (UN Economic and Social Council, 1978a) that for such collaboration to be fruitful, the General Assembly and ECOSOC must be willing to alter some of their past practices which hindered collaboration. As has been previously mentioned, neither the General Assembly nor ECOSOC has had much success in changing their established methods of operation.

With regard to the second set of recommendations, it cannot be said that UNCTAD has as of yet been able to play a more prominent role in the deliberation and negotiation of international economic issues, although the success of UNCTAD in negotiating the Common Fund should not be underestimated. However, this is another area in which the cooperation of member states is essential. At the Eleventh Special Session of the General Assembly, developed western countries strongly resisted efforts to restrict the autonomy of GATT, the IMF, and the World Bank. They will undoubtedly continue to favor these institutions to UNCTAD.

Somewhat more action has been generated by the recommendations regarding structures for regional and interregional cooperation. The restructuring resolution called for considerable decentralization in the UN system with the regional economic commissions playing greatly expanded roles in carrying out the developmental activities of the UN system. Plans are being made (UN General Assembly, 1980e) to deploy certain staff and other resources from headquarters to the commissions, for shifting control to the commissions of certain projects now being carried out at headquarters, for designating the commissions as executing agencies, and for ensuring that inputs from the commissions are fully utilized by various UN forums and bodies. Only with regard to the common definition of regions and subregions has there been no movement whatsoever. It must also be stated that decentralization has been an issue before the United Nations for a considerable period of time. There have been other efforts at decentralization that somehow always seem to get sidetracked.[2] It is still too early to tell whether this particular decentralization effort will likewise conform to this pattern. There are indications that there continues to be considerable resistance to genuine decentralization.

In the deliberations of the Ad Hoc Committee much attention was given to operational activities of the UN system. The primary goal of the recommendations made by the Committee in this area was to achieve a measure of integration in UN field-level activities. Thus there were recommendations concerning uniformity of administrative and financial procedures and for the creation of a single governing body responsible for management and control, at the intergovernmental level, of UN operational activities for development.

Some progress has been made in implementing these recommendations. The first single pledging conference was held in November 1978 and it is generally agreed that this innovation is a quite useful one. Ways of achieving greater financial and administrative uniformity are under active consideration, even if it is not clear that there will be positive, concrete results. With regard to coordination at the country level, the United Nations Development Program (UNDP) is seeking to develop a more effective and efficient relationship with executing agencies by drawing them more fully into the UNDP country programming process (UN Development Program, 1979). It has been agreed that normally the UNDP resident representative would be the single official empowered to oversee UN development activities in each country. This official would be designated by the secretary-general and be given the title of resident coordinator. This recommendation has been ratified by the Thirty-Fourth Session of the General Assembly (UN General Assembly, 1979a) and the first resident coordinators have now been appointed. No definitive action has been taken with regard to recommendations concerning a single governing body for the management and control of operational activities.[3]

The sixth area of recommendations of the Ad Hoc Committee concerned planning, programming, budgeting, and evaluation. Here, at least some of the recommendations were already under active consideration and review. The recommendations of the Ad Hoc Committee have of course given added impetus to these types of measures.

Interagency coordination was another area in which the Ad Hoc Committee made recommendations. Here there have been quite significant changes. The Ad Hoc Committee recommended the streamlining of the subsidiary machinery of ACC and a host of other reforms. Most of these have now been effected and it has generally been agreed that this reorganization of the ACC has been most successful although further changes should not be precluded. Other aspects of recommendations such as those that called for the review by ECOSOC of relationship agreements between the United Nations and the specialized agencies and the exercise by the General Assembly of the powers under Article 17, paragraph 3, of the Charter have yet to be acted upon.[4]

We come finally to the recommendations with regard to the restructuring of headquarters secretariat services in the economic and social sectors. Here significant changes have now been made. An extensive reorganization of the UN secretariat has been completed. Several new departments and offices have been created, and attendant redeployment of staff and resources has been made. Among the important new entities are the Department of Technical Cooperation for Development which brings together staff components dealing with technical cooperation activities. These components had previously been found in various other departments. The Department of International Economic and Social Affairs will concentrate on two clusters of functions—those relating to interdisciplinary research and analysis and those relating to program planning and coordination. The new Office of Secretariat Services for Economic and Social Matters brings together all technical secretariat support services for such bodies as the General Assembly, ECOSOC, and CPC and ad hoc conferences in the economic and social areas.

But probably the potentially most important change at the secretariat level relates to the establishment of the post of the Director-General for Development and International Economic Cooperation. The idea of establishing this new post caused great debate in the Ad Hoc Committee. The developing countries generally supported the concept while both western and socialist developed countries were somewhat skeptical. Nevertheless, agreement was finally reached on this issue and the recommendation for the creation of this post was contained in the committee's final report.

The secretary-general subsequently appointed K. K. S. Dadzie to fill the post. He has now been succeeded by Jean Ripert. The Ad Hoc Committee had described the duties of the director-general in rather general terms. The tasks of the director-general have since been defined in considerably more detail.[5] The responsibilities of the post relate to the provision of effective leadership and overall coordination within the UN system; ensuring within the United Nations the coherence, coordination, and efficient management of all activities in the economic and social fields; and other tasks related to the ensemble of economic and social activities. An example is the leadership exercised by the director-general in formulating the development strategy for the Third United Nations Development Decade.

The developing countries insist that the post of director-general must be more than a figurehead. A resolution (UN General Assembly, 1978c) on restructuring passed by the Thirty-Third General Assembly sought to increase the authority of the post by declaring that the director-general "should have fully and effectively authority over all services and organs within the United Nations at the level of the secretariats in the economic and social sectors, without prejudice to their respective spheres of competence or the terms of reference as contained in their relevant legislative mandates." The resolution also urged "the specialized agencies . . . to offer their full and effective co-operation and assistance to the Director-General" in discharging certain of his functions. Another resolution (UN General Assembly, 1980a) passed at the Thirty-Fifth Session of the General Assembly again reaffirmed the leadership role of the director-general.

The director-general has been active on a variety of fronts and has already had a considerable impact on UN activities. But it must be pointed out that the tasks assigned to the director-general are awesome. Unless he is given adequate resources, and more importantly, the requisite cooperation of other components of the system, he will not be able to have the kind of impact envisioned in the recommendations of the Ad Hoc Committee. Recent resolutions of the General Assembly (UN General Assembly, 1980a) and reports on restructuring (UN General Assembly, 1980d) indicate that there is still some resistance to having the director-general perform the type of role envisaged for him by the Ad Hoc Committee and the General Assembly.

Conclusions: The Significance of Restructuring

Restructuring has been characterized (Development Forum, 1978: 1) as providing the UN system with a "new internal structure of command which

. . . would make United Nations bodies more efficient, flexible, coherent and responsive to the membership's wishes." Elsewhere it has been described (Meltzer, 1978: 1017) as representing "a basic structural trend towards a more centralized and integrated United Nations system, after more than a decade of rapid organizational growth and uncoordinated institutional pluralism." At the present time such statements represent more the aspirations of restructuring than the reality.

Restructuring is indeed in the eyes of many observers a disappointing failure. Certainly if one compares the progress to date in implementing restructuring with the expectations generated by the reports of the Group of Experts and the Ad Hoc Committee there are more than enough reasons to be disappointed. The Group of Experts produced a comprehensive blueprint for a new framework for UN activities in the economic and social sectors. As was to be expected, the Ad Hoc Committee, being a political body as opposed to an expert one, diluted many of the recommendations of the Group of Experts and substituted vague statements of intent for concrete specific recommendations for action. The Ad Hoc Committee, it should be noted, did not fulfill its mandate, which was to formulate "detailed action proposals" for restructuring. Instead it provided, for the most part, ambiguous and broad guidelines. The difficult decisions were to be made by other bodies as the implementation process unfolded. To some extent this has happened, but all too often other bodies find it just as difficult as the Ad Hoc Committee to make the hard and complicated decisions that would give meaning to restructuring. The inability of ECOSOC to make any significant progress whatsoever is but one example. It is indeed significant that progress on the implementation of restructuring has been most rapid in those areas where action by the secretary-general was required.

The situation is indeed bleaker than as is presented in the official reports on the implementation of restructuring. Many of the areas in which it is claimed progress has been made, such as the rationalization of procedures in the General Assembly, would most probably have occurred anyway. A careful reading of the documents (UN Economic and Social Council, 1979a: part B) also indicates that even in such noncontroversial areas as planning, programming, budgeting, and evaluation, very little has been accomplished. The insistence of the specialized agencies and other programs on maintaining their independence makes it likely that not much of real significance will be achieved in this area, at least in the short run.

Beyond this, one can see total disregard for the intent of restructuring in numerous other actions taken in various parts of the system. Prominent examples would be the decisions to establish yet more funds for specific purposes, such as those called for by the UNCSTD and UNIDO III meetings, and the reluctance of specialized agencies and parts of the UN Secretariat itself to recognize the role of the Director-General for Development and International Economic Cooperation.

It is fully to be expected that none of the main sets of actors are satisfied with the results of linking restructuring to the creation of a New International Economic Order and restructuring in its present form can be directly traced to the Sixth and Seventh Special Sessions of the General Assembly which gave content to demands for the New International Economic Order. The developing countries saw restructuring as an opportunity to increase their influence over the machinery for international economic cooperation and development as well as to facilitate the achievement of the substantive goals of a new order. The assertion of control by the General Assembly and the enlargement of other bodies to make them "more representative" is thus one of the main themes of the restructuring recommendations. Other "endogenization" measures, designed to increase the control of developing countries over UN development activities, such as the enhancing of the role of the regional commissions, are aspects of this same theme.

There can be little doubt that restructuring has contributed to the endogenization of the United Nations and has created opportunities for the developing countries to increase their control over UN machinery for economic and social development, although to a limited extent. While this is an important goal, the link between restructuring and the creation of a New International Economic Order is far from direct. While restructuring may lead to increased control by developing countries over UN machinery, it must be asked for what purpose. The answer presumably would be to create a new and more equitable international order. But the creation of such an order depends very largely upon the willingness of certain, mostly western developed countries to make changes in their international economic and other policies. Control of international institutions, restructured or otherwise, does not guarantee progress on substantive issues. The experiences of organizations such as UNCTAD and UNIDO confirm this proposition.

The realization that restructuring has contributed almost nothing to the creation of a New International Economic Order has led to a certain amount of frustration among the developing countries. This frustration has given way on the one hand to repeated calls for rapid implementation to the restructuring recommendations. This was the intent of the numerous resolutions of recent sessions of the General Assembly concerning restructuring.[6] There is at the same time considerable disillusionment with the limited scope of restructuring exercise. For example, Mohammed Bedjaoui (1979: 204), the Algerian ambassador to the United Nations, has asserted:

> It is certainly true that restructuring and internal improvements in the functioning of the United Nations system can help make this system more capable of meeting the requirements of the new international economic order. But

these measures are not sufficient in themselves. More fundamental changes are necessary. First of all, it has become clearly necessary to take a new look at the constitutions of international organizations, in particular the Charter of the United Nations. In addition, thought is being given to the creation, with a view to their ultimate merger, of specialized institutions with a specific responsibility for economic problems.

In view of the limited impact of restructuring, developing countries are increasingly emphasizing Charter reform. The attempt of Argentina and Jamaica to break the ECOSOC deadlock is merely the first of what will undoubtedly be other attempts. In a quite unintended way, then, restructuring has contributed to the impetus for more radical restructuring measures, including Charter reform.

If developing countries are frustrated with the paucity of results, developed countries of both camps are also disappointed with restructuring. The disappointment for the western developed countries is not as great, however, since one of their unstated goals has been to maintain the status quo which is congenial to their interests. In the restructuring exercise, the developed countries stressed the goal of making the U.N. system more cost effective through the introduction of managerial and other reform. Behind the code words of "effectiveness" and "efficiency" is, of course, a strong desire on the part of major donors to make the system less expensive and to maintain their entrenched positions in the secretariats of various UN organizations. Socialist countries have the same interest in controlling the growth of expenditures, and they have consistently resisted measures necessitating growth of budgets. Certainly, the innovations with regard to programming, planning, budgeting, and evaluation; the single annual pledging conferences; the streamlining of the subsidiary machinery of certain bodies; the increase in coherence in activities at the field level; and similar measures must be considered as positive first steps from the perspective of developed countries. Yet the changes which might have had a truly significant impact on efficiency and levels of expenditures were either discarded during the deliberations of the Ad Hoc Committee, or have yet to be acted upon. Such changes would include the concept of a single governing body for operational activities related to development, the confining of technical assistance activities to voluntary programs, the complete rationalization of procedures of UN legislative bodies, the elimination of ineffective subsidiary bodies (such as those of ECOSOC), the common definition of regions and subregions within the system, the integration of UN programs and funds, and so forth. Because so little progress has been made in these areas, developed countries are not satisfied with the results of restructuring.

One of the most interesting questions is the explanation of why the restructuring exercise failed to achieve its major goals. Certainly, in retrospect the restructuring recommendations adopted by consensus by the Ad Hoc Committee do not seem unrealistic or overly ambitious. Yet despite nearly four years of effort, they have proven to be largely unattainable.

One prominent explanation is that structural reform and rationalization are an integral part of the effort to create a new international economic order. As such, it cannot be unaffected by the general malaise in the North-South dialogue. Negotiations over the New International Economic Order are now stalled and little substantive progress has been made in realizing the objectives proclaimed at the Seventh Special Session of the General Assembly. Despite the persistent effort of many western developed countries to confine restructuring to discussions of increased efficiency and economy, restructuring cannot be isolated from the substantive goals of the NIEO. As the secretary-general (UN Secretary-General, 1979) recently stated, "The expectations generated by the restructuring exercise will only be realized if there is appropriate action by governments as part of a collective effort." The restructuring exercise in fact proceeded on the premise that there would be progress in achieving these substantive goals. With no significant results on the substantive side, developing countries understandly have little enthusiasm for continuing with restructuring. Restructuring, if implemented, could lead to a more efficient and economical use of resources and to more coherent policies in general, but these are not recognized by developing countries as legitimate goals in and of themselves. Structural and institutional reforms are desirable only if they can contribute to the achievement of a new international economic order.

This line of argument is persuasive, and without question it goes a long way toward accounting for the present failure of the restructuring exercise. However, it would be a mistake to conclude that the present stalemate in the NIEO negotiations by itself can explain the lack of results. We will therefore conclude with a brief consideration of some of the more obvious obstacles that confront any effort at reform and rationalization of UN structures.

If the UN system has faced immense difficulties in attempting to coordinate its activities to achieve an integrated approach to development, it is partly because of the attitudes and actions of governments. As the Group of Experts (United Nations, 1975: 2) commented in their report, "We would also emphasize that most of the structural deficiencies of the United Nations system are the result of actions by its Member States, and the correction of these deficiencies will require action by the same states." Every new fund, organization, or body that has been established over the years has fulfilled the perceived needs of certain groups of states. And a very good case could be made that at least some of these funds and organizations succeeded in mobilizing resources that otherwise could not have been raised. But once established, such funds and organizations develop constituencies and appeal to vested interests. This makes their consolidation or alteration in any manner an extremely difficult undertaking. Martin Hill has chronicled what happened to one effort to rationalize the system in the past. According to Mr. Hill (1974: 43):

> In 1968, its newly-elected Director-General [of FAO], Mr. Boerma, supported by the Secretary-General of the United Nations, was anxious to bring about closer integration between regional policies and programmes of FAO and the United Nations regional economic commissions in matters relating to agriculture. Mr. Boerma proposed as a first step, to appoint the Executive Secretary of ECA as FAO Regional Director of Africa and to transfer the FAO regional office from Accra to the seat of ECA at Addis Ababa. The proposal was decisively rejected at the Kampala session of the African Regional Conference of FAO, consisting, of course, mainly of representatives of African ministries of agriculture, who inveighed against the danger of FAO losing its independence. In view of this reception, the whole initiative was dropped and other means had to be explored for improving co-ordination in regional agricultural work of the United Nations system.

Even though the new arrangement would have perhaps been more "rational" and "efficient" from an administrative point of view, it would have denied African ministers of agriculture an important "pressure point."

Governments are also often themselves not organized in such a way as to facilitate coordination and coherence of the activities of international organizations. For member states to derive maximum benefit from the activities of international organizations, there must be internal governmental coordination. The government must be organized in such a way as to be able to benefit from the resources made available through international cooperation. It would also be helpful if governments followed consistent external policies. At the present time, the same government often follows contradictory policies in various UN forums. This can result in considerable confusion and has impeded the present, as well as past, restructuring efforts.

Efforts to improve coordination by restructuring are also complicated by the phenomenon of bureaucratic politics. Although we have stressed the necessity of analyzing the restructuring exercise within the context of the North-South dialogue, bureaucratic actors also influenced the outcome. It is well known that over time, bureaucracies acquire identities and distinct interests of their own. In national governments there is a constant competition for power and resources between various departments. Such competition also exists among international organizations. The disagreements which arose over what roles would be played by various units in Sahelian relief operations in 1974 is just one example. One reason coordination is difficult is that it often involves agreement as to who will play major roles and who will play minor ones. Naturally, every agency wants to play the major role since that usually means an increase in prestige, power, and resources. Progress in decentralizing activities has been painfully slow for somewhat the same reason. Those at headquarters are reluctant to yield power and authority that they have perhaps spent years accumulating.

Certainly in the restructuring exercise bureaucratic actors played an important role in influencing the outcome. The goals of such actors in the restructuring exercise were to enhance their own positions, both in a personal and organizational sense. These goals could be achieved through a variety of means. Among them would be the creation of new posts, the increase of organizational resources, the discarding of threatening new concepts, and so forth. The interests of bureaucratic actors were definitely reflected in some of the restructuring decisions and the pervasive role of bureaucratic actors is an important factor which cannot be ignored.

Another complicating factor is that the UN system, despite certain ambitions, is not a world government. All too often recommendations for structural reform of the UN system are based on models derived from national experience. But since the UN system does not possess some of the vital characteristics of a government, such models are really not appropriate. As Secretary-General Waldheim (UN General Assembly, 1979c: 17) recently stated, "We have to accept that a perfectly logical and functional institutional system is not within our reach." On the national level, it is feasible and indeed desirable to have governmental units with clearly defined responsibilities. In this way, uniform and coherent national policies can be formulated. But the world community is too complex and varied for this approach to be workable. A pluralistic approach in which a diverse set of organizaitons, servicing different clienteles, attempt to deal with complex and multifaceted problems is perhaps a better one.[7] Moreover, the confusion that results from two or more organizations attempting to deal with the same set of problems can be counterbalanced by the gains that result from the competition injected into the system.

These factors constitute inherent and permanent obstacles to reform efforts. In conjunction with the absence of movement in the negotiations over the New International Economic Order, they provide an explanation for the limited impact of the restructuring exercise. However, in conclusion it should be stressed that although the term "failure" has been used repeatedly in this chapter in conjunction with restructuring, the restructuring endeavor has had some positive results.

Restructuring has definitely facilitated the more complete integration of developing countries into the UN system. There is a cynical view, given the number of new high-level posts created by restructuring, that the exercise has advanced many careers but little else. But it is significant that most of the new posts have gone to Third World nationals. Since the previously existing high-level posts were considered the reserve of one or the other developed countries, this phenomenon must be evaluated as being beneficial to the UN system. Other restructuring measures are in similar ways part of the endogenization process mentioned earlier.

Equally important, a great deal has been learned through restructuring concerning the parameters of structural and institutional change in the United Nations. Given the pluralistic nature of the system, the formulation of grandiose master plans may not be the most efficacious way of bringing about desired changes. The restructuring exercise has likewise highlighted two other pitfalls. One is that reform, rationalization, coordination, efficiency, economy, and similar goals are not ends in themselves and cannot be pursued in isolation from the substantive goals established by the United Nations. Second, restructuring has shown that in certain areas at least, genuine change cannot be achieved without Charter reform, although it must be pointed out that these areas are quite few.

NOTES

1. The most important of these was the 1970 Consensus which assigned to UNDP the role "first among equals" among the agencies involved in development activities. The Consensus can be traced to the "Jackson Report," a study (United Nations, 1970) prepared by Sir Robert Jackson for the United Nations Development Program in 1970. For further background on the general problem see Hill (1978).

2. For background on decentralization in the UN system see United Nations (1974).

3. The Thirty-Fourth session of the General Assembly (UN General Assembly, 1979a) did request ECOSOC to further study this question.

4. Article 17, paragraph 3 refers to the power of the General Assembly to review the budgets of the specialized agencies.

5. For the most recent report on the Office of the Director-General, see United Nations General Assembly (1980d).

6. It should also be noted that there has been a great deal of discussion of restructuring in bodies such as the CPC and the ACC. In 1980, the CPC recommended that the General Assembly should carry out an analysis of the impact of restructuring on the UN Secretariat. This recommendation was endorsed by ECOSOC and the General Assembly. It was requested specifically that the Joint Inspection Unit participate in this exercise. See UN General Assembly (1980b).

7. For an elaboration of this viewpoint see White (1976) and de Seynes (1976).

REFERENCES

BEDJAOUI, M. (1979) Towards a New International Economic Order. New York: UNESCO/ Holmes & Meier.
Development Forum (1978) "General Assembly picks up the cards." 6 (Jan.-Feb.): 1, 12.

HILL, M. (1978) The United Nations System: Co-ordinating its Economic and Social Work. London: Cambridge University Press.

―――― (1974) Towards Greater Order, Coherence and Co-ordination in the United Nations System. New York: UNITAR.

MELTZER, R. (1978) "Restructuring the United Nations system: institutional reform efforts in the context of North-South relations." International Organization 32 (Autumn): 993-1018.

de Seynes, P. (1976) "Broadening the scope of international co-operation." Presented at a meeting of the Experts on the Study of the Role of the International Organizations in the Contemporary World, Geneva, March 15-19, 1976 (UNESCO doc. SHC. 76/CONF. 623/10, Paris).

United Nations (1975) A New United Nations Structure for Global Economic Co-operation (Sales No. E.75.II.A.7), United Nations, New York.

―――― (1974) Report on the Decentralization of United Nations Economic, Social and Related Activities and the Strengthening of the Regional Economic Commissions by S. Illie, C. S. Jha, and A. F. Sokirkin, Joint Inspection Unit (JIU/REP/74/5), United Nations, New York.

―――― (1970) A Study of the Capacity of the United Nations Development System (Sales No. E.70.I.10), United Nations, New York.

UN Development Program (1979). "Restructuring of the economic and social sectors of the United Nations system." Document DP/408, United Nations, New York.

U.N. Economic and Social Council (1979a). "First progress report by the secretary-general for 1979." Document E/1979/81, United Nations, New York.

―――― (1979b). "Restructuring of the economic and social sectors of the United Nations system." Decision 1979/57, United Nations, New York.

―――― (1978a) "Progress report by the administrative committee on co-ordination pursuant to paragraph 7 of General Assembly resolution 32/197." Document E/1978/107, United Nations, New York.

―――― (1978b) "Implementation of the conclusions and recommendations annexed to General Assembly resolution 32/197." Document E/1978/118, United Nations, New York.

UN General Assembly (1980a) "Implementation of section VIII of the annex to General Assembly resolution 32/197 on the restructuring of the economic and social sectors of the United Nations system." Resolution 35/203, United Nations, New York.

―――― (1980b) "Implementation of section VIII of the annex to General Assembly resolution 32/197 on the restructuring of economic and social sectors of the United Nations system." Resolution 35/223, United Nations, New York.

―――― (1980c) "Implementation of section II of the annex to General Assembly resolution 32/197 on the restructuring of the economic and social sectors of the United Nations system." Decision 35/439, United Nations, New York.

―――― (1980d) "Restructuring of the economic and social sectors of the United Nations system: implementation of section VIII of the annex to General Assembly resolution 32/197 and section IV of Assembly resolution 33/202." Document A/35/527, United Nations, New York.

―――― (1980e) "Implications of General Assembly resolutions 32/197 and 33/202 for the regional commissions." Document A/35/546, United Nations, New York.

―――― (1979a) "Implementation of section V of the annex to General Assembly resolution 32/197 on the restructuring of the economic and social sectors of the United Nations system." Resolution 34/213, United Nations, New York.

―――― (1979b) "Implementation of section II of the annex to General Assembly resolution 32/197 on the restructuring of the economic and social sectors of the United Nations system." Decision 34/453, United Nations, New York.

―――― (1979c) Report of the Secretary-General on the Work of the Organization (Official Records of the General Assembly, Thirty-Fourth Session, Supplement 1 (A/34/1), United Nations, New York.

_____ (1978a) Report of the Ad Hoc Committee on the Restructuring of the Economic and Social Sectors of the United Nations System. Official Records of the General Assembly, Thirty-Second Session, Supplement 34 (A/32/34), United Nations, New York.

_____ (1978b) Addendum to the Report of the Ad Hoc Committee on the Restructuring of the Economic and Social Sectors of the United Nations System. Official Records of the General Assembly, Thirty-Second Session, Supplement 34A (A/32/34/Add.1.), United Nations, New York.

_____ (1978c) "Restructuring of the economic and social sectors of the United Nations system." Resolution 33/202, United Nations, New York.

_____ (1977) "Restructuring of the economic and social sectors of the United Nations system." Resolution A/RES/32/197, United Nations, New York.

_____ (1976) Report of the Ad Hoc Committee on the Restructuring of the Economic and Social Sectors of the United Nations System. Official Records of the General Assembly, Thirty-First Session, Supplement 34 (A/31/34), United Nations, New York.

_____ (1975) "Development and international economic co-operation." Resolution 3362 (S-VII), United Nations, New York.

UN Secretary-General (1979) "Text of statement by secretary-general in General Assembly on restructuring of economic and social sectors of UN system." U.N. Press Release SG/SM/2670, United Nations, New York.

U.S. Department of State, Bureau of Public Affairs (1978) Gist. (November).

WHITE, J. (1976) "International agencies: the case for proliferation," in G. K. Helleiner (ed.) A World Divided: The Less Developed Countries in the International Economy. Cambridge: Cambridge Univ. Press.

ABSTRACTS/RESUMES

1

L'évolution de l'économie internationale

Harold K. Jacobson
Dusan Sidjanski

Depuis la fin de la deuxième guerre mondiale et jusqu'au début des années 1970, l'économie mondiale a connu un taux de croissance sans précédent. Cette croissance était due notamment à la reconstruction des économies nationales, à l'application des nouvelles technologies ainsi qu'à l'action des institutions et politiques économiques nationales et internationales. A partir des années 1970 l'ordre économique international a été soumis à des contraintes et a connu des crises qui ont amené les responsables politiques à réexaminer sa structure et ses politiques dans l'intention de procéder à des ajustements. Le présent ouvrage a pour objet l'économie globale. Il porte sur divers aspects des institutions nationales et internationales ainsi que sur des exemples de leurs politiques qui contribuent à modeler cette économie globale. A ce titre les contributions analysent les forces et les contraintes qui influent sur les changements et qui imposent des ajustements. En se concentrant sur le passé récent, cet ouvrage collectif se propose de dégager et d'éclairer les directions, la nature et les dimensions du changement qui s'opère dans l'ordre économique international.

LA STRUCTURE DE L'ÉCONOMIE GLOBALE

Les états qui participent à la communauté internationale ont des systèmes politiques et économiques différents et des niveaux de développement économiques largement divergents. En effet, aux côtés des pays hautement industrialisés qui font partie du Comité d'aide au développement figurent les pays à économie planifiée ainsi que les pays en développement. Ces derniers, dont les 122 membres du Groupe des 77, se subdivisent en plusieurs catégories: les pays les moins avancés côtoient des pays à revenu moyen ainsi que les nouveaux pays industrialisés. Ces caractéristiques structurelles engendrent des pressions en vue de la rénovation de l'ordre économique international tout en dessinant ses limites.

Le premier groupe de pays industrialisés représente moins de 20 pourcent de la population mondiale, bénéficie de 60 pourcent du produit mondial et totalise plus de 60 pourcent des exportations mondiales. La moyenne des PNB par tête d'habitant se situe au-dessus de $7000 par an. Les pays à économie planifiée, qui constituent le deuxième groupe, représentent 32 pourcent de la population mondiale et 19 pourcent du produit mondial. Leur PNB moyen par habitant est de $1200, la République Populaire de Chine qui a le PNB le plus bas se situant à $230 et les autres pays au-dessus de $700.

La troisième catégorie comprend les pays en développement du Tiers Monde qui représentent plus de 50 pourcent de la population mondiale et seulement 18 pourcent du produit mondial. A l'intérieur de ce groupe le PNB par habitant varie de moins de $100 par an à plus de $3000. Ce groupe comprend également les pays exportateurs de pétrole et parmi eux l'Arabie saoudite dont le PNB est comparable ou supérieur à celui des pays occidentaux. Les pays à économie planifiée totalisent environ 10 pourcent des exportations mondiales, et les pays en développement en représentent moins de 30 pourcent. Le commerce mondial se trouve par surcroît concentré principalement autour des pays occidentaux qui procèdent à des échanges intenses entre eux et avec les autres pays. Ils occupent de ce fait une position dominante dans l'économie mondiale. Dans ces conditions tout effort visant à promouvoir le développement des pays du Tiers Monde ne peut se passer de la contribution des pays occidentaux, d'autant que le commerce entre pays en développement demeure marginal de même que celui qu'ils pratiquent avec les états à économie planifiée.

L'ORDRE ÉCONOMIQUE INTERNATIONAL D'APRÈS-GUERRE

Cet ordre est constitué par les structures de base mais aussi par un ensemble d'institutions et de politiques qui modèlent les relations entre acteurs économiques: systèmes commercial, monétaire, de transport maritime, etc. qui rendent les relations plus prévisibles.

Les événements des années 1970 ont lancé un sérieux défi à l'ordre économique international d'après-guerre. L'échec des institutions et des politiques mises en oeuvre, combiné avec le ralentissement de la croissance et l'explosion des prix du pétrole ont provoqué une remise en question de cet ordre néo-libéral mis en place par les puissances occidentales. L'objectif premier en était la suppression des obstacles au commerce et la coordination, du moins dans une certaine mesure, des politiques économiques. Cette finalité transparaît dans la plupart des institutions internationales économiques dont le Fonds monétaire international (FMI) et l'Accord général sur les tarifs douaniers et le commerce (GATT). Clairement affirmée à l'origine par l'OECE, elle continue à inspirer l'oeuvre de son successeur l'OCDE qui, en regroupant les Etats occidentaux, vise à maintenir la santé économique des ses membres, à lutter contre l'inflation et à harmoniser les concours apportés aux pays en développement. Cet ordre international néo-libéral a permis une expansion florissante du commerce international dont la valeur a été multipliée par six entre 1948 et 1973 (NU, 1976: I, 96). Cette expansion du commerce a été, malgré une part prépondérante des pays occidentaux et de leurs sociétés transnationales, un stimulus puissant de la croissance économique mondiale. Il est significatif qu'au cours de la même période les investissements directs en provenance des pays occidentaux ont enregistré un taux d'expansion plus rapide que celui de leurs exportations.

Cette prospérité générale a été partagée de manière inégale entre pays occidentaux, le Japon et les six membres fondateurs de la Communauté économique européene—Allemagne, Belgique, France, Italie, Luxembourg et Pays-Bas—ayant connu un taux de croissance tant de leur PNB que de leur commerce plus élevé que ceux des Etats-Unis et des autres pays occidentaux. Cette différence de rythme peut être attribuée à la capacité de reconstruction du Japon et des Six ainsi qu'au soutien que les Etats-Unis leur ont apporté sous la forme du Plan Marshall et de leur contribution à la création de la CEE, malgré certains effets négatifs qui pouvaient en résulter notamment pour leurs exportations de produits agricoles à destination des Six. Quant aux pays en développement, leur participation aux échanges ainsi régis n'était que le reflet de leurs liens avec les pays occidentaux qui absorbaient dans l'immédiat après-guerre plus de 70 pourcent de leurs exportations. De la sorte, les PVD ont été amenés à adhérer en nombre croissant aux principales institutions piliers de cet ordre économique: en 1979, le FMI compte 138 membres, la Banque mondiale 135 et même le GATT en réunit 84.

Par contraste, les pays à économie planifiée ne jouent qu'un rôle marginal en raison de leur faible participation au commerce avec les PVD et du volume modique de leur aide publique. Sur un total de 82 milliards de dollars de l'apport des ressources aux pays en développement en 1980y compris l'aide publique au développement (APD), les dons privés et les apports aux conditions du marché—les pays membres du Comité d'aide au développement (CAD) de l'OCDE ont fourni 73,2 milliards (89,3 pourcent)—dont 35,5 milliards au titre de l'APD, 44,2 milliards en apports aux conditions du marché et 2,3 milliards en dons d'organismes privés bénévoles des pays du CAD; les pays membres de l'OPEP ont apporté 7 milliards soit 8,5 pourcent alors que les pays membres du Conseil pour l'assistance économique mutuelle (CAEM: Bulgarie, Hongrie, Pologne, RDA, Roumanie, Tchécoslovaquie, et URSS) n'ont contribué que pour un montant estimé à 1,8 milliards de dollars, soit 2,2 pourcent. Cette répartition selon les chiffres publiés par l'OCDE ne prend pas en considération les apports aux conditions du marché des pays de l'OPEP et du CAEM qui ne sont pas disponibles. Si on limite la comparaison à l'APD, la répartition est la suivante: sur 35,5 milliards de dollars en 1980, les pays membres du CAD ont fourni 26,7 milliards soit 75,2 pourcent, les pays de l'OPEP ont contribué pour 19,7 pourcent avec 7 milliards alors que les pays du CAEM se sont contentés d'un apport de 5,1 pourcent à l'aide publique globale.

Malgré cette contribution et l'action dynamique du Groupe des 77 qui compte à présent 122 membres au sein de la CNUCED, l'écart entre les PVD et les pays industrialisés n'a cessé de croître en raison en particulier de l'explosion démographique du Tiers Monde et de la concentration de la puissance économique et technologique dans les pays industrialisés. De surcroît, les pays occidentaux exerçaient une influence prépondérante dans les organisations internationales économiques en contrôlant une part substantielle des ressources et des échanges économiques mondiaux. De leur côté, les pays socialistes formaient un sous-ensemble: l'URSS et, jusqu'en 1980 la Chine, ne faisaient pas partie des principales institutions de cet ordre néo-libéral. En revanche, grâce à leur poids numérique les PVD avaient la capacité de dominer les procédures du système de l'ONU et d'exprimer de cette façon leur opposition à l'égard de la structure existante de l'ordre économique international.

LA CRISE DE L'ORDRE ÉCONOMIQUE INTERNATIONAL NÉO-LIBÉRAL

Dans les années 1970, le défi lancé à cet ordre économique par les PVD joint à d'autres facteurs, a conduit à une remise en question du système. Parmi ces divers facteurs, le changement essentiel concerne le rôle des Etats-Unis qui supportaient une charge considérable en tant que puissance dominante dans l'économie mondiale et qui formaient le plus grand marché avant l'achèvement de l'union douanière de la CEE en 1968. Leur prépondérance était d'autant plus marquée que leur PNB représentait plus d'un tiers du PNB mondial et que le système monétaire mondial avait pour base le dollar. De ce fait, les Etats-Unis tout en accusant de forts déficits de leur balance des paiements n'étaient pas obligés de recourir à des crédits extérieurs et de se soumettre à des disciplines fiscales et au contrôle du FMI. Lorsque vers 1970, leur PNB est réduit à un quart du produit mondial, leur rôle apparaît moins acceptable et parallèlement, les Etats-Unis deviennent moins disposés et moins capables de supporter les charges qu'impose ce système mondial.

Au cours des années 1970, l'économie mondiale a été confrontée à de multiples défis: réadaptation des Etats-Unis à un rôle plus modeste mais plus conforme à leur capacité économique; ajustement des structures des pays occidentaux à la concurrence croissante des PVD sur leurs propres marchés; neutralisation des effects négatifs des sociétés transnationales et maximalisation de leurs apports bénéfiques; ajustements rendus indispensables par l'émergence d'un nouveau pouvoir économique des pays exportateurs de pétrole mais aussi par la pression des besoins en biens de première nécessité et des aspirations des PVD ainsi que par les intéractions accrues entre les États à économie planifiée et les autres membres de la communauté internationale. Ces ajustements impliquent des changements dans la structure de l'ordre économique international: divers chocs et crises ont précipité les négociations visant à instituer un NOEI. A la suite de l'abandon par les Etats-Unis de la partité dollars-or, les pays non alignés ont lancé en 1973 à Alger un appel en faveur du NOEI, appel qui a été repris par l'Assemblée générale de l'ONU lors de sa 6e session extraordinaire en avril 1974 sous la forme d'une Déclaration et d'un Programme d'action. Cet appel a par ailleurs coïncidé avec l'augmentation brutale des prix du pétrole et son utilisation en tant qu'arme politique à l'égard des pays occidentaux qui ont soutenu Israël dans le conflit avec les pays arabes.

Ainsi, la contestation de l'ordre économique existant prend une forme active au moment même où l'économie mondiale entre en crise et où les théories empreintes de "catastrophisme" redeviennent à la mode. La disparité s'accentue entre d'une part la situation réelle caractérisée par les taux de change flexibles, par des fortes pressions inflationnistes et par un accroissement inquiétant du chômage et du niveau de sous-emploi, et d'autre part les aspirations vers un ordre économique plus équitable. Les difficultés économiques des pays nantis coïncident avec des besoins et des exigences accrus des pays du Tiers Monde. Face à cette situation, les sept pays économiquement les plus importants du monde occidental—Canada, Etats-Unis, France, Italie, Japon, République Fédérale d'Allemagne, Royaume-Uni—décident de tenir dès 1974 des sommets annuels afin de coordonner leurs politiques économiques. Par ailleurs, la négociation de Tokio qui aboutit en 1979 à un accord supprimant diverses barrières non tarifaires se poursuit en parallèle avec les efforts concertés des pays occidentaux visant à accroître les mesures d'aide et de soutien aux pays en voie de développement. C'est ainsi que les pays industrialisés ont adopté le système des préférences généralisées en faveur des importations en provenance des pays en voie de développement et que certains ont même annulé les dettes des pays les moins avancés. A titre d'exemple, les états membres de la CEE ont conclu la Convention de Lomé associant une soixantaine de pays d'Afrique, des Caraïbes et du Pacifique (ACP) à la CEE et instituant le système "Stabex" de stabilisation des recettes de 36 produits de base. En 1980-1981, des conférences sont organisées en vue d'apporter une aide particulière aux 31 pays les moins avancés du monde. Il n'en reste pas moins que plus d'un pays en voie de développement qui échappe à cette catégorie du fait de son PNB par habitant plus élevé, comprend de nombreuses régions faisant partie des sphères les moins développées de l'humanité. S'agissant principalement des masses de populations rurales privées des biens de première nécessité, un des problèmes auquel se heurte toute aide extérieure est de savoir comment s'assurer que les contributions parviennent directement à leurs destinataires. D'où la position centrale qu'occupent l'alimentation et le développement rural dans cette stratégie d'aide qui commence à se faire jour. En octobre 1981, les représentants du Nord et du Sud réunis à Cancun formulent enfin la résolution d'entreprendre une négociation globale, conscients de l'insuffisance des mesures prises jusqu'à présent, mesures qui n'ont pas altéré profondément la nature néo-libérale de l'ordre international économique ni amèlioré substantiellement la situation des pays en voie de développement. Pour l'heure néanmoins, il s'agit d'un cheminement tortueux à travers toutes sortes d'obstacles et de difficultés, de pressions et d'exigences contradictoires.

Deux tendances divergentes se profilent sur le tableau de bord du NOEI notamment: une tendance au retour vers le protectionnisme des pays industrialisés au premier chef; et une tendance à l'insatisfaction croissante des pays en voie de développement à l'égard de la situation actuelle, toutes deux tendances qui menacent l'acquis de l'ordre économique néo-libéral. Le présent ouvrage traite de ces deux pressions qui constituent les défis immédiats à l'ordre néo-libéral. Les résponses à ces défis auront une part significative dans la construction et dans l'avenir du NOEI.

2

Production et hegémonie: vers une économie politique de l'ordre mondial

Robert W. Cox

Les économies-mondes (terme employé par F. Braudel) peuvent être décrites comme structures de pouvoir. Trois formes de pouvoir sont comprises dans de telles structures: la direction du processus de production, le pouvoir social ou les rapports entre classes, et le pouvoir politique ou la domination à travers les États. La production comme relation de pouvoir est prise comme point de départ pour une étude de l'ordre mondial (le niveau d'analyse des économies-mondes), tout en tenant compte de ses rapports avec les deux autres formes de pouvoir mentionnées. L'hégémonie existe dans l'ordre mondial quand la domination d'un état ou d'un groupe d'États et de la classe sociale dominante dans toute son extension internationale est exprimée à travers des règles et des institutions à portée universelles qui s'accommodent des intérêts subordonnés sans entraver les intérêts dominants. La dynamique profonde de l'hégémonie fondée par les Etats-Unis dans l'après-guerre se trouve dans l'internationalisation de la production. Les mécanismes et les conséquences de cette hégémonie sont examinés aux niveaux des forces sociales à l'echelon mondial, des formations sociales centrales et des formations sociales périphériques.

Production and Hegemony: Toward a Political Economy of World Order

World economies are structures of power relations. Three forms of power are distinguished: control over the production process, social power or the relationship among classes, and political power or control over the state. Production is taken as the starting point for the study of world order, though this form of power should be understood in relation to the other two. Hegemony in world order expresses the dominant position of a founding state and the social class which has created that state, but does so in terms of universal rules and institutions which accommodate subordinate interests without undermining those of the dominant group. The internationalizing of production is the dynamic process underlying the post-World War II hegemony founded by the United States. The chapter considers the mechanisms and consequences of this hegemony at the levels of global forces, core social formations and peripheral social formations.

3

Pourquoi un NOEI? Le point de vue du Tiers Monde

Robert S. Jordan

Le NOEI a été a l'origine de nombreuses discussions et préoccupations dans les milieux internationaux. Certains gouvernements perçoivent le NOEI comme l'incarnation de la justice économique alors que d'autres tranchent cette question en considérant qu'il s'agit d'une demande de "tous biens présentée par ceux qui n'ont rien." L'object de ce chapitre est d'explorer et d'analyser la nature de ce NOEI en particulier sous l'angle du Tiers Monde. Quatre thèmes de base ont été abordés: (1) pourquoi les pays en voie de développement ont-ils proposé la création d'un NOEI; (2) comment ces pays ont-ils formulé leurs demandes; (3) le contenu et la nature de leurs demandes; et (4) les réactions du monde occidental industrialisé à ces demandes? Il apparaît à présent que tant les pays industrialisés que les pays en voie de développement semblent déçus, momentanément du moins, par le rôle des Nations Unies dans la conduite des négociations Nord/Sud. La préférence pour l'assistance bilatérale et l'utilisation de forums en dehors des Nations Unies est probablement une réaction à la demande des pays en voie de développement en faveur de leur plus grande participation au sein des institutions des Nations Unies, du Fonds monétaire international, du GATT et de la Banque mondiale. Il est compréhensible que les pays industrialisés et, en particulier, les Etats-Unis, la Grande-Bretagne, et l'Allemagne fédérale, ne désirent pas voir s'amenuiser leur influence dans ces institutions et cependant un système économique équitable requiert une meilleure distribution du pouvoir de décision à l'intérieur des organisations internationales économiques et financières. Il se pourrait bien néanmoins que la recherche d'une formule de négociation ou d'un forum ou d'une institution appropriée devienne caduque du fait même que le rythme de changement dans le monde sera plus rapide que celui des decisions des hommes.

Why a NIEO? The View From The Third World

The New International Economic Order (NIEO) has been a source of considerable international discussion and not a small bit of concern. Some governments view the NIEO as the embodiment of economic justice, while others dismiss it as "demands for everything from those who have nothing." The purpose of this chapter is to explore and to analyze the nature of the NIEO, particularly as it is viewed by the Third World. Four basic themes are discussed: (1) why the developing states called for the creation of NIEO; (2) how the developing states have pressed their demands; (3) the nature of their demands; and (4) the reaction of the western industrial states to these demands. It appears that, at present, both industrial and developing states seem to have, at least temporarily, become disenchanted with using the United Nations to carry on the North-South NIEO negotiations. The current interest in bilateral assistance and the use of forums outside the United Nations is probably a reaction to the developing states' demand for greater participation in such UN institutions as the IMF, GATT, and the World Bank. Understandably, the industrial states, particularly the United States, Britain, and West Germany, do not want to relinquish their influence in these institutions; yet, an equitable global economic system requires a greater distribution of decision-making authority over multilateral economic and financial agencies. It may well be, however, that efforts to find a formula for negotiation, or to agree upon an appropriate forum or institution, will become beside the point because the rate of change going on all over the world simply will not await human events.

4

Cohesion and Dispersion at the Center of the New International Economic Order

Alice Hougassian-Rudovich

Although the achievements of coalitions of developing countries—the Group of 77, the nonaligned countries, and the ACP states in the Lomé Convention—are quite unequal, these coalitions seek to achieve the same goal: to maintain the solidarity and the unity of Third World. The crucial question is how to maintain solidarity and unity in the face of the great diversity of the developing countries. Answers given to this question have been quite different from case to case. The ACP states have institutionalized their group since its creation in 1973. The ACP states, however, are caught in a contradiction. They claim their solidarity with the Third World but they are unwilling to contemplate giving up their special relations with Europe. Facing Europe, on the other hand, they belong without any doubt to the Third World. The Group of 77 has no institutional structure. In spite of growing demands for improving the operational capacity of the group, its structure still remains informal. On the other side, developing countries coalitions must be considered as channels through which Third World demands are pressed. In this context, the Group of 77 and the ACP states are quite similar. They defend the same interests and several themes are common to both movements. Institutionalization does not seem to assure Third World unity. Moreover, developing countries cannot go beyond a certain threshold in their activities, for if they do, cleavages which divide developing countries may threaten these coalitions.

Cohésion et Dispersion au sein du NOEI

Les regroupements de PVD—groupe des 77, mouvement des non-alignés, groupe des États ACP dans le cadre de la convention de Lomé ou OPEP—connaissent des succès divers mais tous recherchent le même objectif: assurer la solidarité et l'unité du Tiers Monde. Une question se pose: comment cette solidarité et cette unité peuvent résister à l'extrême diversité des PVD? Les réponses ont été diverses. Les ACP ont institutionnalisé le groupe dès sa création, en 1973. Mais, les ACP vivent une contradiction. Ils s'affirment solidaires du Tier Monde sans pour autant songer à abandonner leurs relations privilégiées avec l'Europe. Et, face à l'Europe, les ACP appartiennent bien au Tiers Monde. Le groupe des 77, quant à lui, est dépourvu de cadre institutionnel et, malgré des demandes de plus en plus précises visant à augmenter la capacité opérationnelle du groupe, sa structure reste informelle. D'autre côté, on doit concevoir les regroupements des PVD comme autant de relais par lesquels passent les revendications du Tiers Monde. Sur ce plan, ACP et groupe des 77 défendent les mêmes intérêts et plusieurs thèmes sont communs aux deux groupes. Si l'institutionnalisation ne semble pas un critère déterminant pour assurer l'unité du Tiers Monde, ceux-ci ont toutefois conscience qu'ils ne peuvent dépasser un certain seuil au-delà duquel les clivages qui divisent profondément les PVD risqueraient de menacer l'existence de ces coalitions.

5

L'industrie de l'acier aux Etats-Unis: politiques nationales et commerce international

Robert S. Walters

Le respect de la part des Etats-Unis des règles libérales du commerce international dépendra dans les années qui viennent de leur capacité à s'adapter aux changements fondamentaux des conditions de concurrence internationale dans un large éventail de secteurs industriels importants dans lesquels la compétitivité américaine a été traditionnellement élevée. Les efforts de l'industrie et du gouvernement pour faire face à la crise de l'acier depuis 1977 sont examinés en détail afin d'évaluer la capacité des Etats-Unis à affronter les changements structuraux dans la production et dans le commerce international. L'exemple de l'acier indique que les forces politiques et la capacité institutionnelle aux Etats-Unis limitent la possibilité d'envisager une politique d'ajustement industriel. Les économistes appartenant aux milieux industriels et gouvernementaux préfèrent en réalité les mesures protectionnistes face aux importations malgré leur engagement à l'égard d'une politique commerciale libérale et en raison du fait que cette solution réduire au minimum l'intervention gouvernementale dans l'industrie.

The U.S. Steel Industry: National Policies and International Trade

The U.S. commitment to a liberal trade order in the years immediately ahead will depend upon the country's rapid domestic adaptation to basic changes in international competitiveness for a wide array of important industrial sectors within which U.S. competitiveness has traditionally been very strong. Industry and government efforts to deal with the steel crisis since 1977 are examined in detail to assess the U.S. capacity to deal with structural shifts in international production and trade. The steel experience indicates that political forces and institutional capabilities in the United States inhibit public policy focus on industrial adjustment. Industry and government economists prefer import protection despite philosophical commitment to liberal trade policy, because this "solution" keeps government at the industry's edge.

6

L'industrie textile française: crisis et ajustement

Lynn Krieger Mytelka

L'objet de cette étude est d'explorer la dynamique sociale qui soutend le processus des ajuste-ments industriels en France en analysant l'évolution de l'industrie textile. Ebranlée par trois crises, marquée par l'insuffisance de compétivité, par le chômage manifeste ou déguisé et par des faillites, l'industrie textile a cherché à se réadapter au cours de chacune des trois décades d'après-guerre. Cette analyse éclaire l'èmergence et l'affirmation du grand capital dans l'économie française, le rôle de l'État dans la promotion de la concentration industrielle et dans la mise en place en accord avec le grand capital des mécanismes chargés des ajustements industriels; elle met l'accent en outre sur la marginalisation des organisations syndicales en regard de la planification industrielle qui relève principalement de l'industrie et de l'état. Dans ce contexte général, la politique textile a été en grande partie une résultante de ces changements structurels et socio-politiques dans l'économie française ainsi que dans ses rapports avec les pays industrialisés et les pays en voie de développement. Ce cas illustre bien la relation qui existe entre les processus internes et les contraintes du NOEI en voie de formation.

The French Textile Industry: Crisis and Adjustment

This paper explores the social dynamics underlying the process of industrial adjustment in France, focusing in particular upon the textile industry as it moved through three successive crises—marked by noncompetitiveness, manifest or disguised unemployment, and bankruptcies—in each of the three postwar decades. The analysis highlights the rise and consolidation of big capital in the French political economy, the role of the state in promoting industrial concentration and in collaborating with big capital in the elaboration of industrial adjustment mechanisms, and the marginalization of organized labor from the process of indus-trial planning by industry and the state. Textile policy was very much a function of these broader structural and political changes.

7

Les réponses du Tiers Monde à l'OPEP: la dimension extérieure

Kuniko Y. Inoguchi

L'objet de ce chapitre est d'examiner les efforts entrepris par les pays moins avancés non producteurs de pétrole afin de faire face aux effets économiques aussi bien que politiques et psychologiques de la décision de l'OPEP d'augmenter les prix en 1973. Après avoir conceptualisé les différents types de réponse fondés sur une approche de politique intérieure ou orientés vers l'extérieur, l'auteur se concentre sur cette dernière approche. En effet, celle-ci révèle non seulement leur effort visant à maîtriser les contrecoups financiers de la crise du pétrole, mais aussi leur tentative de tirer profit de la campagne lancée par l'OPEP en vue de la restructuration des relations économiques extérieures et de l'établissement du NOEI. Pour chaque type de comportement et de réponse un modèle formel a été défini afin de tester les hypothèses concernant les éléments sousjacents au comportement des pays les moins avancés.

Third World Responses to OPEC: The External Dimension

The purpose of this chapter is to examine the efforts of non-oil-exporting LDCs to respond to the economic as well as political and psychological impact of the OPEC strike in 1973. After having conceptualized the inward-oriented and outward-oriented response patterns, we have focused on the latter, because the latter reveal not only the LDCs' efforts to cope with the financial hardships of the oil crisis, but also their attempts to ride on the OPEC-triggered "campaign" to restructure their foreign economic relations and establish a New International Economic Order. For each pattern of response behavior, a formal model was specified to test the hypotheses concerning causal elements behind the behavior.

8

Les contraintes extérieures sur le développement des pays africains

Abdul Aziz Jalloh

Les définitions du développement sont en général unilatérales et incomplètes. Une définition plus ample et plus utile contient des éléments suivants: croissance, capacité d'équilibrer la consommation et la production nationales, réduction de la pauvreté et de l'inégalité, autonomie accrue. Dans cette optique, les pays africains ont enregistré moins de progrès que les pays asiatiques et latino-américains. Même les pays africains qui ont eu les meilleurs résultats ne peuvent être comparée avec les pays tels que Taiwan, Hong-Kong et Corée du Sud. Ce résultat relativement modeste des pays africains s'explique par le fait que leurs efforts de développement ont été amorcés plus tardivement que ceux entrepris par les pays asiatiques et latino-américains. D'où résultent des désavantages comparatifs. Par surcroît, l'Afrique a joué un rôle moins important sur la scène politique mondiale, bénéficiant des transferts moins substantiels de ressources en provenance de l'extérieur. Parallèlement, les pays africains qui ont connu les plus grands succès notamment la Côte d'Ivoire et le Kenya sont aussi ceux qui ont le plus d'importance politique pour l'Ouest et qui dominent les groupements économiques sous-régionaux. Tel qu'il est conçu maintenant et tel qu'il est en formation, le nouvel ordre économique international profitera davantage à d'autres régions qu'à l'Afrique elle-même et à l'intérieur de l'Afrique surtout aux pays comparativement les mieux nantis.

External Constraints on African Development

Definitions of development tend to be one-sided and incomplete. A broader and more useful definition of development includes elements of growth, the ability to balance domestic consumption and production, reduction in poverty, less inequality, and greater autonomy. Viewed from this perspective, African countries in general have progressed less than the countries of Asia and Latin America. Even the most successful African countries did not do as well as countries such as Taiwan, Hong Kong, and South Korea. The relatively poor record of African countries in general is a result of the fact that they started their development efforts later than Asian and Latin American countries and thus suffered from a comparative disadvantage. Africa has also been less important on the world political scene and therefore received less transfer of resources from outside. Similarly, African countries that have done comparably better, notably the Ivory Coast and Kenya, are those that are politically important to the West and dominate subregional economic groupings. Creation of a New International Economic Order, as presently conceived, will benefit other regions of the Third World more than Africa, and within Africa itself, it will benefit only the comparatively well off countries.

9

How Much of the NIEO Has Been Established?

Ural Ayberk

This chapter, which complements and extends the essay by Robert Jordan, attempts to strike as systematically as possible, an initial balance, of the work of UNCTAD concerning the establishment of a New International Economic Order. The first part stresses the reformist character of NIEO by specifying the reforms that have been achieved within the framework of the United Nations and by its member states. The second section describes some of the results that have been obtained concerning the integrated program for commodities, the charter of economic rights and duties of states, and the work in progress concerning the international monetary system, the transfer of technology, the regulation and control of the activities of transnational corporations, and the promotion of economic cooperation among developing countries. The conclusion reclassifies in three categories the results that have been achieved and the work in progress: first, the areas where certain satisfactory results have been obtained; then the areas concerning which work is in progress; and finally, the areas in which no progress has been registered. The research concludes by an analysis of the strategies of the less developed countries and the industrialized countries concerning NIEO.

Ou en est l'instauration du NOEI?

Cette recherche qui constitue un prolongement de la contribution de R. Jordan essaye de dresser un premier bilan, aussi systématique que possible, des travaux de la CNUCED sur l'instauration du NOEI. La première partie met l'accent sur l'objectif réformateur du NOEI en précisant que ces réformes se réaliseront dans le cadre des Nations Unies et par les États membres. La deuxième partie décrit en revanche d'une part les résultats obtenus par le programme intégré, par la charte des droits et devoirs économiques des États et d'autre part les travaux en cours sur le système monétaire international, sur le transfert de la technologie, sur la réglementation et contrôle des activités des STN, sur la promotion de la coopération entre les PVD etc. La conclusion regroupe les résultats obtenus ou les travaux en cours en trois parties: d'abord les domaines où certains résultats satisfaisant ont été obtenus, ensuite les domaines dans lesquels les travaux sont en cours et enfin les domaines dans lesquels aucuns progrès n'ont été enregistrés. La recherche prend fin par un examen des stratégies des PVD et des pays industrialisés sur le NOEI.

10

La restructuration du système des Nations Unies

John P. Renninger

Ce chapitre fournit une description et une analyse de divers essais de restructuration qui ont constitué une des préoccupations majeures des Nations Unies au cours de ces dernières années. La restructuration qui a été amorcée en 1970 par le rapport du Comité ad hoc sur la réorganisation des activités économiques et sociales du système des Nations Unies a abouti à divers changements institutionnels. Des difficultés sérieuses ont été rencontrées dans les efforts visant à mettre à exécution les recommandations du Comité ad hoc et des doutes ont été exprimés quant à la portée et la signification des changements entrepris. Dans ce chapitres les problèmes de restructuration sont reliés au dialogue Nord/Sud. En conclusion il ressort que les problèmes institutionnels ne peuvent être envisagés indépendamment de l'effort des pays en voie de développement d'utiliser les institutions des Nations Unies afin de promouvoir un NOEI.

Restructuring the UN System

This chapter provides a description and analysis of the restructuring exercise which has been a major concern of the United Nations in recent years. Restructuring, which was initiated by the 1977 report of the Ad Hoc Committee on the Restructuring of the Economic and Social Sectors of the United Nations system, has resulted in a wide variety of institutional changes in the UN system. Serious difficulties have been encountered in attempting to implement some of the recommendations of the Ad Hoc Committee and the significance of some of the changes has been questioned. The chapter relates restructuring issues to the North-South dialogue and concludes that institutional issues cannot be considered in isolation from the effort of developing countries to utilize UN machinery to bring about a New International Economic Order.

ABOUT THE CONTRIBUTORS

URAL AYBERK is Assistant Professor in the Department of Political Science and the Graduate Institute for European Studies, University of Geneva. His publications include: *Mécanisme de la prise des décisions communautaires en matière de relations internationales* (Brussels: Bruyland, 1978) and "Le Nouvel Ordre Economic International et le syndicalisme international" (*Il Politico* 45).

ROBERT W. COX is a Professor of Political Science at York University, Toronto, Canada. He was Professor of International Organization at Columbia University, New York City, from 1972 to 1977 and prior to that was a senior official in the International Labor Organization and director of the International Institute for Labor Studies. He collaborated with Harold K. Jacobson in writing *The Anatomy of Influence: Decision Making in International Organization* and has published numerous articles on international organization, labor and production relations, and international political economy.

ALICE HOUGASSIAN-RUDOVICH is a teaching assistant in the Department of Political Science at the University of Geneva. Her current research topic is "Community Aid Policy for Regional Cooperation: An Example of North-South Cooperation" (Ph.D. thesis).

KUNIKO Y. INOGUCHI is Assistant Professor of Political Science at the Department of International Legal Studies, Faculty of Law, Sophia University (Tokyo). She received her BA in 1975 from Sophia University, and her MA and M.Phil. from the Department of Political Science, Yale University, where she is completing her Ph.D. dissertation entitled *The Political Economy of Non-Oil-Exporting LDCs: The Oil Crisis as the Threshold of Exploratory Change*. Recently, she contributed a chapter on North-South relations to *The Political Economy of Foreign Policy Behavior* edited by Charles W. Kegley, Jr. and Pat McGowan.

HAROLD K. JACOBSON is Professor of Political Science and a Program Director in the Center for Political Studies of the Institute for Social Research at the University of Michigan. His publications include *Networks of Interdependence: International Organizations and the Global Political System* and *The Anatomy of Influence: Decision Making in International Organization,* which he wrote in collaboration with Robert W. Cox and others.

ABDUL AZIZ JALLOH is presently serving as Director of the Multinational Programming and Operational Center of the subregional office at Niamey, Niger of the United Nations Economic Commission for Africa. He was Professor and Director of Studies at the International Relations Institute of Cameroon, Yaoundé. His writings include *Regional Integration in French-Speaking Africa* (Berkeley: International Relations Institute, University of California, 1973).

ROBERT S. JORDAN is Professor of Political Science and Dean of the Graduate School at the University of New Orleans. While serving as Dag Hammarskjold Visiting Professor of International Relations at the University of South Carolina in 1979-1980, he edited the forthcoming book, *Dag Hammarskjold Revisited: The UN Secretary-General as a Force in World Politics.* He has also served as Director of Research at the United Nations Institute for Training and Research.

LYNN KRIEGER MYTELKA is Associate Professor at Carleton University. She is the author of *Regional Development in a Global Economy: The Multinational Corporation, Technology and Andean Integration* (Yale University Press, 1979), *Africa in the 1980's* with C. Legum, I.W. Zartman, and S. Langdon (McGraw-Hill, 1979), and numerous articles on technology and industrial change in France and French-speaking Africa, on multinational corporations, and on the changing international division of labor.

JOHN P. RENNINGER is a Research Officer at the United Nations Institute for Training and Research. He is the author of *Multinational Cooperation for Development in West Africa* (Pergamon, 1979). His reviews and articles on African development issues and on international organizations have appeared in numerous scholarly journals.

DUSAN SIDJANSKI is Professor in the Department of Political Science and in the Graduate Institute of European Studies at the University of Geneva. His books and articles cover aspects of regional integration and comparative politics and include: *Dimensiones institucionales de la integracion latinoamericana* (Buenos Aires, 1967); *Les groupes de pression dans la Communauté européenne,* with J. Meynaud (Brussels, 1971); *The Role of Institutions in Regional Integration Among Developing Countries* (UNCTAD, 1974); and *De la Démocratie Européenne* (Paris, 1979).

ROBERT S. WALTERS is Professor of Political Science at the University of Pittsburgh. His principal publications include *The Politics of Global Economic Relations* (with David Blake) and *American and Soviet Aid.* This article is part of a larger study being conducted on U.S. industrial and trade policy.